THE
CHASTENING

▲

INSIDE THE CRISIS THAT ROCKED

THE GLOBAL FINANCIAL SYSTEM

AND HUMBLED THE IMF

PAUL BLUSTEIN

PublicAffairs *New York*

Book design and composition by Mark McGarry, Texas Type & Book Works
Set in Meridien

Library of Congress Cataloging-in-Publication data

Blustein, Paul.
The chastening: the crisis that rocked the global financial system and
humbled the IMF / Paul Blustein.
p. cm.
Includes bibliographical references and index.
ISBN 1-58648-181-9 (pbk.)
1. Financial crises—Asia. 2. International finance. 3. International
Monetary Fund—Economic Assistance—Asia. I. Title.

HB3808 .B58 2001
322'.042'095—dc2001

2001041678

10 9 8 7 6 5 4 3 2

To Yoshie, Nina, Nathan, and Dan
And in case I never get a chance to write another book,
To my mother, too
And to the memory of my father

CONTENTS

AUTHOR'S NOTE AND ACKNOWLEDGMENTS

In all my years as an economics journalist, I have never covered a story as dramatic as the global financial crisis of the late 1990s. And I have never covered an institution more sorely in need of thorough journalistic dissection than the International Monetary Fund. As I was writing for *The Washington Post* about the crisis and the IMF's often vain efforts to quell it, I realized I had the makings of a good yarn about economic phenomena of great significance. In spring 1999, once the crisis had abated, I began arranging the time and resources to research and write this book, which entailed a leave from the *Post* lasting from mid-September 1999 to mid-January 2001.

My research consisted mainly of interviews with approximately 180 people, many of whom were interviewed a number of times in person, on the phone, and by e-mail. They included more than fifty current and former IMF officials, staffers, and board members. Other important interviewees included top officials at the U.S. Treasury, the Federal Reserve Board, the Federal Reserve Bank of New York, the White House National Economic Council, the National Security Council, and the State Department; senior economic policymakers and staffers in the Group of Seven major industrial nations, the World Bank, and the five major crisis-countries that had IMF programs (Thailand, Indonesia, South Korea, Russia, and Brazil); and bankers, hedge-fund managers, and bond traders as well as academic economists. The majority of the interviews took place in Washington, D.C., but I also traveled to Bangkok, Jakarta, Seoul, Tokyo, Moscow, London, Paris, Frankfurt, and New York. The only major crisis country I did not visit was Brazil, because I was able to interview most of the key players in the Brazilian government during their visits to the United States.

I am grateful to everyone who took time to speak with me, particularly those whom I contacted for repeated follow-up interviews. Several people underwent at least ten bouts of questioning at various times, and I greatly appreciate the good humor with which they endured my endless queries.

The vast majority of my interviews were conducted on a deep-background basis, which meant I could use the information but could not quote interviewees or cite them as sources unless granted permission to do so. Much of the information conveyed was obviously of a sensitive nature, especially at the time the interviews were conducted and during the period the book was being written; the Clinton administration was still in office then, and many of the key players were still in their jobs. (In quite a few cases, this remains true in early 2003.) So although I have tried as much as possible to attribute quotes by name, I must ask readers' indulgence and understanding that obtaining permission for attribution often proved impossible; I can only offer assurances that unattributed material in the book has been carefully researched and checked. In cases of conversations or meetings where a number of people were present, I tried as much as possible to confirm the information with multiple participants. In numerous important instances, sources checked their notes or produced contemporaneous documents that helped illuminate the events in question.

A list of interviewees appears in the notes section. It includes those who spoke on the record, plus those who were interviewed on deep background and later granted permission to be named as sources for the book. It thus excludes a substantial number of people who chose to remain entirely anonymous. In many cases, the source of unattributed information may be fairly obvious, but in a number of instances, appearances will be deceiving. This is particularly true in episodes where I identify one policymaker or another as having correctly analyzed a problem or situation before others did. I obviously had to be wary of policymakers eager to revise history about themselves, but in quite a few cases, people would inform me of the positions taken during the crisis by certain of their colleagues who, in retrospect, had "gotten it right," or at least more right than others—Mike Mussa, the IMF's chief economist, is one example; another is Joshua Felman, a senior staffer on the Fund's mission to Indonesia in late 1997. When further investigation showed these tips to be accurate and noteworthy, I wrote about them, and although it may look as if certain policymakers or staffers were tooting their own horns, the facts are otherwise.

Some people refused to grant interviews. I don't want to be too specific about who did and who didn't, but I feel obliged to mention that Michel Camdessus, the managing director of the IMF during the crisis, was among those who declined my request even after he had retired from the Fund. With that exception, I generally found IMF officials to be extraordinarily accommodating and helpful. My hat is off to Thomas Dawson and the rest of the IMF's able External Relations Department for having given free rein to Fund staffers to accept my interview requests and meet me privately to the extent they felt comfortable doing so. A few years ago, the Fund would not have been nearly so open to this sort of inquiry. My thanks also go to the Treasury's public affairs office, and particularly Michelle Smith, who was assistant secretary for public affairs, for having arranged meetings with the department's busy policymakers.

Aside from those who provided information, a large cast of characters and institutions supported me in the process of transforming this book from a gleam in my eye to a finished volume.

My first call went to Peter Osnos, the publisher of PublicAffairs, whom I knew to be an enthusiastic and nurturing supporter of many book projects by friends and colleagues in journalism. Peter's warm reaction and sound counsel confirmed that I had made a wise choice. A book concerning the IMF and financial crises, he told me, wouldn't command a large advance from him or any other publisher, but I could obtain supplementary financing from foundations. This proved to be sagacious advice, and although Peter urged me to shop my book around to other publishers if I wanted to, I have never regretted sticking with him and PublicAffairs. (On a personal note, I was gratified to be writing for a publisher who had inherited the name and legacy of Public Affairs Press, which was founded by the late Morris Schnapper, a dear friend of my family.)

My next move was to seek permission from my editors at *The Washington Post* for a leave from my reporting duties. Jill Dutt, the assistant managing editor for business news, not only consented to my request but also went to bat for me with Leonard Downie and Steve Coll, the *Post's* executive editor and managing editor respectively; Len not only approved but granted me a partially paid sabbatical as well under the terms of a provision in the *Post's* union contract. I am deeply grateful to Jill, Len, and Steve in particular, and to the *Post* in general, for this opportunity and generous support. I owe profound thanks also to several of my *Post* colleagues who made sure that my beat, international economics, was covered during my absence. John Burgess performed so ably in the job that he was soon promoted to an editing job on the foreign desk; he was followed by Steve Pearlstein, whose reporting preferences lay elsewhere but who covered the beat in the only way he knows how—with tenaciousness and a passion for making sense of difficult subject matter. All this was made possible because of the skill and cheer with which Nell Henderson, the *Post's* economics editor and my immediate supervisor, juggled story assignments and elicited the best from her charges. To top all this off, Jill and Nell acceded to my request in autumn 2000 for an additional four months of leave beyond the year that I was originally granted. To Jill, Nell, and Steve, I am in everlasting debt.

The Institute for International Economics offered me an office to work from, as well as a fancy title—Visiting Fellow. But I got much more than that from Fred Bergsten, IIE's director, and his colleagues. I had wanted to do my research at a place where I could pick brains, and IIE has the best pickings around, certainly in my field of interest. The institute's fellows held a luncheon session early in my leave to discuss my outline, and later they convened for two other sessions to discuss drafts of my manuscript. (Names of sources were excised from the drafts that were distributed in advance of those sessions.) The comments I received, both in verbal form during the sessions and in written form afterward, helped me enormously both in conceptualizing the book and in avoiding the sort of doltish errors we journalists are all too prone to make. I am particularly obliged to John Williamson and Morris Goldstein for their extensive and wise counsel; others to whom special thanks are owed include Catherine Mann, Gary Hufbauer, Marcus Noland, Adam Posen, Randall Henning, Choi Inbom, Marcus Miller, Kim In Joon, Cho Hyun Koo—and, of course, Fred Bergsten and his deputy, Todd Stewart. By the time my leave was over, I had come to appreciate that IIE's fellows and staff are not only tops at what they do but a very pleasant bunch of people as well.

Financial support came first as the result of a call to the Pew Charitable Trusts, whose Venture Fund director, Donald Kimelman, kindly put me in touch with John Schidlovsky, director of the Pew Fellowships in International Journalism. In an inspired act of entrepreneurship for which I am immensely thankful, John arranged for me to become the first "Journalist in Residence" at the program, which is based at the Paul H. Nitze School of Advanced International Studies of The Johns Hopkins University. In exchange for a stipend, John and his deputy, Louise Lief, asked that I conduct two seminars about the IMF for the Pew fellows—a task that proved more pleasurable than burdensome. As the "guinea pig" for this position, I was gratified to learn in early 2001 that Pew had decided to institutionalize it.

I still needed funding to cover my expenses—especially for travel—and I had the good fortune to obtain a generous grant from the Smith Richardson Foundation. I would like to express my gratitude to Smith Richardson and especially to Marin Strmecki, vice president and director of programs, and Allan Song, one of the foundation's program officers, for their help and encouragement.

When I realized that I would need more than a year to finish the book, financial salvation came from the United States–Japan Foundation, which provided me with another grant that enabled me to take four extra months of leave at the end of 2000. My deep thanks go to James Schoff, a program officer for the foundation, for helping me convey to the foundation's management that my project, although not specifically focused on U.S.–Japan relations, would shed light on issues that had caused sharp divisions between Washington and Tokyo. I also thank George Packard, the foundation's president, for perceiving the potential value of my book to informing the policy dialogue across the Pacific.

I would be remiss in omitting several colleagues and friends who assisted me both at home and abroad with advice and contacts. They include David Hoffman, the *Post*'s former Moscow bureau chief (and now the paper's foreign editor), whose book *The Oligarchs* was published in February 2002, by PublicAffairs; John M. Berry, the *Post*'s famous Fed-watcher; Paulo Sotero, Washington correspondent for *O Estado de São Paulo*; Thanong Khanthong of *The Nation* newspaper in Bangkok; Atika Shubert, a *Post* stringer in Jakarta; Cho Joohee, a *Post* stringer in Seoul; Manley Johnson and David Smick of Johnson Smick International; and Richard Medley and Nicholas Checa of Medley Global Advisors in New York.

When it came time to edit the manuscript, Paul Golob managed to engineer massive and sensible organizational revisions without inflicting damage on my ego. The book is immeasurably better thanks to Paul's many interventions. Ida May B. Norton, who copy-edited the book, also improved the manuscript in numerous ways. I owe an appreciative nod also to others at PublicAffairs, including Managing Editor Robert Kimzey, his assistant Melanie Peirson Johnstone, and Assistant Editor David Patterson, for ably handling many production and administrative tasks.

I would have loved to send copies of the manuscript—or even individual chapters—to my sources to obtain their comments and suggestions. But the press of time made that impossible, especially since I returned to the *Post* in January 2001, before the book was finished. The one exception was Stan Fischer, the IMF's first deputy managing director, who asked me in August 2000 to send him what I had written to help him prepare for a series of lectures he was giving. With considerable trepidation, I sent Stan a draft of the material that would later become Chapters 1 through 8 (again, with source names excised). As I had hoped, I was eventually repaid with extraordinarily thoughtful feedback, much of which I incorporated into the man-uscript—although in the case of the Indonesian crisis, I'm afraid Stan and I continue to see the story rather differently. I hasten to add the usual caveats that he bears no responsibility for errors or omissions that remain in the text (nor do the scholars at IIE who read the man-uscript); blame for all goofs and shortcomings rests entirely with me.

My children Nina and Nathan enjoyed teasing me about writing a book on such an arcane subject, yet they helped sustain me by con-ceding that it would be cool to have a published author as a dad. I thank them for accepting the demands the book put on my time, for ignoring the files piled in the living room, and for enduring such unspeakable inconveniences as being forced to log off of the Internet so that I could send urgent e-mails and conduct research. I also thank my son Dan, whose entry into the world six weeks prematurely in May 2001 added a dash of, um, excitement to the final, frantic couple of months of quote-clearing, fact-checking, and footnote-writing. His good health—and that of his sister and brother—helped me keep my perspective about what is truly important in my life.

Finally, I could never have survived this undertaking without the love and support of my wife Yoshie, who despite her own heavy work responsibilities made many sacrifices for the sake of my com-fort at home during long, mentally draining days of writing. Yoshie heroically kept our newborn son from waking me on nights when I had to get a decent rest so that I could plow through the final ver-sions of the manuscript the next morning. Most important, she let me know she is with me all the way.

A note on Asian names: In keeping with common usage and local custom, Southeast Asian names will appear in this book with the first (given) name used in second reference; Chinese and Korean names, in which the family name cus-tomarily appears first, will likewise appear with the first name on second refer-ence; and Japanese names are rendered in the Western style, with given name first and family name second, with the family name used on second reference.

THE COMMITTEE TO
SAVE THE WORLD

Hubert Neiss spent most of his career as an economic disciplinarian for troubled countries, and with his flattop haircut and sober demeanor, he looked every bit the part. A native of Austria, Neiss was a veteran of three decades at the International Monetary Fund, which he had joined in 1967 after finishing his Ph.D. in economics at the Hochschule für Welthandel in Vienna. He was short but remarkably barrel-chested, the result of an enthusiasm for fitness that evoked both admiration and amusement among colleagues and friends. He often limited himself to eating, say, a banana at midday so he could spend lunchtime at a gym lifting weights.

Among Neiss's strengths was an ability to remain serene and businesslike amid turbulent circumstances. His steeliness had helped him rise through the IMF's ranks, culminating in his appointment in early 1997 at age sixty-one to one of the institution's highest staff positions, director of the Asia and Pacific Department. But nothing in Neiss's career prepared him for the series of events that began the morning of Wednesday, November 26, 1997, when he landed in Seoul, the capital of South Korea, following a sixteen-and-a-half-hour plane trip from Washington.

After a brief stop at his hotel, Neiss and a couple of other IMF staffers were driven past glass and granite skyscrapers and the open-air Nam Dae Mun market, where digital watches and handheld computer games are on sale alongside dried squid, boars' heads, and vats of *kimchi*. The car passed through the iron gate of the Renaissance-style headquarters of the Bank of Korea, the nation's central bank, and Neiss was ushered into its international department for a briefing on Korea's latest financial data. He expected the news to be grim; he didn't know the meeting would thrust him into a frenzy of activity aimed at staving off global economic disaster.

Neiss had come to Seoul to launch a process at which he was well practiced—negotiating an IMF "program." In simple quid pro quo terms, the Fund would make a loan to the South Korean government in exchange for Seoul's agreement to undertake a specific list of steps to put the nation's economy on a sound footing. Normally, IMF programs take two or three months to negotiate. But the Korean situation was shaping up as unusually urgent.

Korea's financial markets were undergoing a bout of turmoil similar to the crisis that had devastated another of Asia's dynamos, Thailand, about five months earlier, during summer 1997. In late October, the Hong Kong stock market had crashed, followed by a 554-point drop in the Dow Jones industrial average on October 27, and once-thriving Indonesia had turned to the IMF for help in shoring up the value of its currency. Now many big international investors and lenders were betting that Korea would be the next domino to fall; the Korean currency, the won, had fallen 17 percent against the dollar in the past four weeks. The "Electronic Herd" (a term popularized by journalist Thomas Friedman), whose ranks included mutual funds, pension funds, commercial banks, insurance companies, and other professional money managers, was spooked by revelations about Korea's financial problems, such as the increasing amount of unrecoverable loans held by Korean banks.

Korean government officials had taken the humiliating step of seeking IMF assistance only after considerable anguish and debate. They were enormously proud of having guided their nation from the ruins of war in the 1950s to the status of an export powerhouse that boasted the eleventh-largest gross domestic product in the world. But the country's financial position was becoming increasingly precarious. The Herd's actions were depleting the Bank of Korea's reserves of hard currency—the U.S. dollar and the handful of other major currencies that are essential for nearly all transactions across international borders. Foreign banks were calling in short-term loans to Korean banks, and foreign investors were dumping the Korean won for dollars as they unloaded their holdings of Korean stocks and bonds. If this drain continued, the central bank's reserves would run so low that the bank would be unable to provide dollars to people who needed them. The ultimate nightmare was default, meaning that the government, the nation's banks, and virtually all the major corporate names in Korea Inc., such as Hyundai, Daewoo, and Samsung, would not be able to obtain enough dollars to make payments due to foreign creditors and suppliers.

Neiss's mission was to negotiate a plan that would calm the markets and banish the nightmare. The IMF, as well as top U.S. government officials who exercised major influence over the Fund, feared that a default by Korea could cause the country to suffer a prolonged, crippling cutoff of loans and investments from abroad; further, as the creditworthiness of neighboring countries came into question, they might follow Korea into default, sending the entire Asian region into a decade of stagnation and depression like the one that afflicted Latin America during most of the 1980s. Conceivably, the nerves of investors and lenders the world over would be so shattered that the financial conflagration would leap across the Pacific, lay waste to the U.S. economy, and engender global recession.

So when he arrived at the Bank of Korea that cool November day, Neiss thought he understood how dire the circumstances were—until he started examining the figures furnished by the central bank's international staff. To his horror, Neiss realized that Korea was far closer to default than anyone in the IMF had understood. The readily available reserves of dollars were so paltry that the country was almost certain to run out within days—perhaps as soon as a week.

Only a couple of weeks before, in conversations with IMF officials, the Koreans had put their reserves at $24 billion, which was low for an economy Korea's size but did not pose an emergency. Now Bank of Korea staffers were citing figures suggesting that "usable" reserves were about $9 billion and declining at a rate of roughly $1 billion a day. This was mainly because foreign banks, which had previously made short-term dollar loans to Korean banks and routinely extended them month after month, were suddenly demanding repayment as the loans came due. The situation was even worse because the bulk of the central bank's reserves couldn't be used in a crisis like this. The funds had been deposited in the overseas branches of Korean commercial banks, which had been using the money to pay obligations; withdrawing the funds would make it impossible for the banks themselves to avoid default, and that in turn would bring down the nation's entire financial system.

Seated at a small conference table across from Bank of Korea officials, IMF staffers heard increasingly bad news as they pressed for details about the country's international indebtedness. A couple of months earlier, an IMF mission conducting a routine annual review of the economy had been told that the short-term debts owed by Korean firms to foreigners totaled around $70 billion. Now it seemed clear that the previous mission had failed to ask sufficiently probing questions: The debts of Korean firms' overseas operations hadn't been included in the previous estimate; with those debts included, the figure was closer to $120 billion. Worse, Bank of Korea officials acknowledged that much of the debt would fall due in the next few weeks—so the need for dollars was particularly acute.

The more the IMF team queried the Koreans, the more desperate the situation looked. Neiss recalled that two things went through his mind: One, what to do? And two, how to inform IMF management quickly? Despite his relatively senior position, Neiss had no authority to cut a deal with Seoul on his own.

Back in Washington, the long Thanksgiving weekend was just starting, and the IMF, which prides itself on its rapid-response capacity in financial emergencies, was almost comically unprepared for the impending bankruptcy of a major economy. The managing director, Michel Camdessus, was in his native France. Stanley Fischer, the first deputy managing director, was attending a seminar in Egypt. Jack Boorman, the director of the Fund's Policy Development and Review Department and the man generally viewed as the Fund's third most powerful official, was at his vacation home in Rehoboth Beach, Delaware, where twenty-four guests were about to arrive for turkey dinner.

Neiss handwrote a fax to IMF headquarters explaining the depth of the problem he faced and listing a couple of options for dealing with it. First, a wealthy country such as Japan could extend a short-term emergency loan to Korea (though he knew the Koreans had already tried unsuccessfully to get such a loan). Second, Korean banks could obtain emergency permission to pay their foreign obligations with bonds instead of cash (though that would constitute a virtual default as far as many foreign creditors were concerned).

Another option would be to throw together an IMF rescue program before Korea ran out of reserves—an undertaking that Neiss described as "barely feasible" and "not credible." After all, one purpose of the rescue was to stem the market panic by showing banks and investors that plenty of dollars would be available for those who needed them, and this would require marshaling a loan package for the Korean government of unprecedented size, larger even than the $50 billion Mexico had received in 1995. Another purpose was to draw up plans for a thorough overhaul of Korea's economic policies to show the markets that the country was eliminating its most glaring weaknesses. A few days did not seem sufficient for devising a full economic program of this magnitude.

Yet this was the option Neiss was ordered to pursue, following a series of meetings and conference calls involving top officials of the U.S. Treasury, Federal Reserve, State Department, and National

Security Council and their counterparts in other governments belonging to the Group of Seven major industrial countries (the G-7). Proceeding with that option was an incredible ordeal, both mentally and physically, for almost everyone involved.

Starting on Friday, November 28, Neiss began conducting nearly around-the-clock negotiations in the Seoul Hilton with officials of Korea's Ministry of Finance and Economy concerning the bailout's conditions—that is, the painful economic changes and reforms that Seoul would have to pledge in exchange for an international loan. For three full days and nights, Neiss got no sleep; Wanda Tseng, a Chinese-born economist who was cochief of the IMF mission, went even longer without so much as a catnap—four days and nights. For nutritional sustenance, IMF team members resorted mainly to snacking on chicken wings and other hors d'oeuvres served on the hotel's executive floor. Taking the time to dine in a restaurant, or even to eat a proper meal ordered from room service, seemed out of the question given the mountain of work required to cobble together an IMF program that stood a chance of calming the markets before Korea's reserves ran completely dry.

Other distractions and inconveniences abounded—not to mention the fact that the Korean negotiators were strenuously resisting many of the reforms sought by the IMF. Most of the talks were held in the Kuk Hwa banquet rooms, located in the hotel's lower level a mere thirty paces from the entrance to Pharaoh's, a hotel disco with ancient Egyptian decor, which continued to operate and emanate a thumping beat. The main entrance to the negotiating room was quickly surrounded by hordes of Korean reporters and TV crews. Determined to avoid potentially market-rattling encounters with the media, IMF staffers had to take a circuitous route to a back entrance that involved going up and down flights of fire stairs and through the Hilton's vast kitchen. When they weren't talking directly with the Koreans, they were contacting their superiors and colleagues, by phone, fax, and e-mail, to discuss the complex details of the negotiations. They also had to contend with David Lipton, the U.S. Treasury undersecretary for international affairs, who had flown to Seoul and checked into the Hilton to convey the views of the U.S. government, a visible manifestation of the influence the United States wields over IMF policy.

Alas, all these heroic exertions were to produce an embarrassing flop.

On Wednesday, December 3, an agreement between the two sides was triumphantly announced by Michel Camdessus, who had flown to Seoul on the final day of talks to use his stature as managing director to close the deal. Under the accord, the Korean government would receive loans totaling $55 billion, more than any country had ever before received, including a record $21 billion from the IMF backed with additional loans and pledges of credit from the World Bank, the United States, Japan, and other countries. The program involved a staggeringly wide array of promises by Seoul: The budget would be cut; interest rates would be raised; ailing financial institutions would be closed for the first time in modern Korean history; government-directed bank loans for the nation's powerful conglomerates would be eliminated; foreign investors would be allowed greater freedom to buy stocks and bonds; and the economy would be liberalized in a host of other ways.

Camdessus pledged that the plan would be submitted within forty-eight hours to an emergency meeting of the IMF Executive Board, which represents the member countries. Following board approval, the IMF would immediately disburse $5.6 billion, and another disbursement would follow two weeks later—all of which, in accord with IMF custom, would be deposited in the nation's central bank. The "far-reaching" reforms that Korea had promised would enable the nation's economy to recover, Camdessus predicted, adding, "I am confident this program will also contribute to the needed return of stability and growth in the region."

But his optimism proved misplaced. The Electronic Herd showed little sign of being impressed by the Fund's rescue efforts, and within days, Korea was in even worse financial straits than before. During the week of December 8, trading in the Korean won was suspended every day because it had fallen against the dollar by the 10 percent limit set by the government—on some days, this occurred within three minutes after the start of trading. Foreign banks in New York, Tokyo, London, Frankfurt, and other financial capitals continued to cancel credit lines and demand immediate repayment on loans they had once routinely extended and reextended to Korean banks. The chaos in Korea sent markets tumbling anew in the United States, Europe, and Asia.

Shell-shocked members of the IMF mission in Seoul began an exercise they called the "drain watch." This involved sending a staffer or two to the Bank of Korea at around 9 P.M. until well after midnight, when markets were open in the United States and Europe, to monitor how the central bank was being forced to relinquish precious reserves to meet the demands of foreign banks for repayment on their loans. The long faces of the drain-watchers at breakfast the next day often betrayed the bad news that another $1 billion or so had been withdrawn from the country overnight in this manner.

By the week of Christmas, almost all of the $9 billion the IMF had disbursed had gone to pay off foreign banks that were calling in their loans to Korean borrowers. The Korean won was nearly 40 percent below its level at the time the IMF rescue was unveiled. And Seoul once again stood at the brink of default.

The failure of the IMF's rescue of Korea in early December 1997 was one of the scariest moments in the series of crises that rocked the world economy in the late 1990s. But it was far from the only such moment. Time and again, panics in financial markets proved impervious to the ministrations of the people responsible for global economic policymaking. IMF bailouts fell flat in one crisis-stricken country after another, with the announcements of enormous international loan packages followed by crashes in currencies and severe economic setbacks that the rescues were supposed to avert.

In August 1997 in Thailand, for example, the nation's currency, the baht, which had already fallen substantially in value, plunged further almost immediately after the approval of an IMF-led rescue totaling $17 billion. In Indonesia, a $33 billion package of loans marshaled by the IMF at the end of October 1997 generated only a brief rally in the Indonesian rupiah, which soon thereafter resumed its decline in currency markets. A "strengthened program" unveiled in January 1998 fizzled even more spectacularly, with the value of the rupiah shrinking to a sliver of its former level.

Likewise, Russia received a $22 billion IMF-led package in July 1998, followed about a month later by the announcement that Moscow was devaluing the ruble and effectively defaulting on its Treasury bills—a development that sent U.S. financial markets into a terrifying tailspin. In January 1999, the same script was followed in Brazil, where nine weeks after agreeing to a $41 billion IMF program, officials found themselves forced to abandon the fixed-rate policy for the Brazilian real, which promptly sank 40 percent against the dollar.

This book offers a retrospective of key events in the crisis and how they were handled by the global economy's "High Command," which includes not only the IMF but also powerful officials at the U.S. Treasury, the U.S. Federal Reserve, and other economic agencies among the G-7, who oversee IMF operations and steer international economic policy. (To some extent, the IMF's sister institution, the World Bank, is part of the High Command as well, though the bank took a distinctly subordinate role during the crisis.) I use the term "High Command" advisedly, and with a pinch of irony, for the tale recounted in this book suggests that this group's ability to safeguard the global economy from crises is neither high nor commanding.

The events of 1997–1999 cast disquieting doubt on the IMF's capacity to maintain financial stability at a time when titanic sums of money are traversing borders, continents, and oceans. The IMF is an institution designed to help countries correct problems in their economic fundamentals, and that was a manageable task when the flows of private capital moving around the world were much smaller than they are now. But the late 1990s brought crises of confidence in markets whose size, speed, and propensity for large-scale disruptions have vastly outstripped the Fund's resources and ability to keep up. The IMF's efforts to contain the crises were analogous to a team of well-trained orthopedic surgeons trying to cure a ward of patients experiencing emotional breakdowns, and the Fund has emerged from the experience with its credibility damaged. Thorough scrutiny of these developments lays bare how distressingly volatile the global economy has become in the new era of massive international capital flows. Unless steps are taken to make the system safer, future crises could be much more disastrous.

The IMF was itself at the vanguard of the movement that liberalized the flow of capital around the world in the 1990s, taking globalization to new heights. International trade in many goods—shoes, chemicals, microchips—was already substantially free. So was investment in overseas factories by multinational manufacturers. A new goal for the globalizers at the IMF—and their backers in major governments including the United States and Great Britain—was the elimination of national barriers to foreign funds, which was expected to help create a more efficient world economy, raising living standards in rich and poor countries alike. A further justification was that developing countries would reap enormous benefits by establishing modern stock and bond markets to finance their industries instead of relying heavily on traditional (and often corrupt) banking systems. The advocates of globalized capital were by no means unconcerned about the dangers of international crises, and they hedged their recommendations by urging countries to develop proper legal institutions and improve supervision of their banks before allowing the Electronic Herd to invest large amounts of money in their markets. But money poured into fast-growing emerging markets nonetheless, much of it "hot," meaning it could be sold or withdrawn quickly, often at the stroke of a computer key, by portfolio managers or commercial bankers or currency traders sitting in offices thousands of miles away.

The precipitous drop in the Mexican peso in late 1994 and early 1995 provided a jarring example of the potential for volatility that lurked within the system. But the Mexican crisis caused little contagion, and it ended triumphantly for the Clinton administration and the IMF in January 1997, when a recovering Mexico repaid—in advance—the $12 billion it had borrowed from the U.S. Treasury. If anything, the Mexican case gave the High Command an overblown sense of its power to manage such situations. Only after the much more widespread gyrations and perturbations of the late 1990s did the system's lack of governability begin to hit home.

The popular perception of the High Command was illustrated by an article published in *Time* in early 1999, titled "The Committee to Save the World." The magazine's cover displayed a photo of Robert Rubin, the secretary of the treasury, his deputy (and eventual successor) Lawrence Summers, and Alan Greenspan, chairman of the Federal Reserve Board, posing amid the marbled splendor of the Treasury with arms folded and faces cheerfully composed. As the photo and accompanying article suggested, these three men, working hand in glove with the IMF, were exercising extraordinary influence over the strategy for containing the crisis.

The soothing notion that the world was being "saved" by brilliant policymakers was understandable, for the crisis did have a more or less happy ending. In a couple of countries in particular, the IMF posted notable successes as well as failures. Following the Fund's abortive attempt to bail out Korea in early December 1997, a second rescue a few weeks later used a different approach to restore confidence in that country's financial system, averting what might have been a far wider crisis. A second IMF program for Brazil in March 1999 also worked, and even the earlier bailout, while failing in its avowed goal of preventing a Brazilian devaluation, at least staved off a collapse in the country's currency until global markets had recovered from other devastating shocks.

The global crisis was widely pronounced to be over in spring 1999, and that assessment by and large held up. Not only did world growth proceed apace in 1999 and 2000, but most of the hardest-hit countries bounced back. Korea was growing feverishly; the Brazilian economy was bounding along at a healthy clip; Thailand was on the mend; and Russia was posting positive growth, an achievement that eluded it for most of the 1990s. Even Indonesia, whose economy had been the most severely damaged, was growing, though its recovery was extremely fragile. Arguably, the crisis strengthened the long-term economic prospects of some of these countries; Korea, in particular, benefited from loosening the ties among its banks, conglomerates, and public officials.

Thus, despite all the hardships wreaked on people in places like Jakarta and St. Petersburg and Rio de Janeiro, the crisis might be viewed as a setback of little consequence for a world enjoying a spell of robust growth. Who cares that a handful of countries suffered a comeuppance for the crony capitalism, corruption, overborrowing, and other sins of which they were guilty—and since they didn't drag the rest of the world economy down with them, doesn't that reflect the resilience of the global financial system, the effectiveness of its safety nets, and the cleverness of its High Command?

On the contrary, such a blithe interpretation of the crisis ignores its implications, both for the stability of individual countries' economies and for that of the global economy as a whole. The affected nations, for all their flawed economic fundamentals, had been the darlings of financial markets not long before their crises struck, and once the Electronic Herd turned negative, the punishment it inflicted was grossly out of proportion to the countries' "crimes." Disregarding their fate is tantamount to shrugging off the crash of a new type of advanced aircraft on the grounds that the only passengers killed were a careless few who left their seatbelts unfastened—and concluding that since everyone else miraculously survived, worry about future flights is unwarranted.

The news accounts at the time of the crisis, as disturbing as they were, do not adequately convey how frightening, disorderly, and confounding it all was, most notably for the people in charge of quelling it. An extensive look inside the crisis-fighting effort illuminates the degree to which the policymaking wizards of Washington and other capitals found themselves overwhelmed and chastened by the forces unleashed in today's world of globalized finance.

The pace at which economies were felled by "contagion"—the spread of market turmoil from one country to another—caught top policymakers flat-footed. So rapid was the onset of Korea's crisis in November 1997 that it came less than a month after the IMF staff had drafted a confidential report assessing the Korean economy as essentially safe from the turbulence besetting Southeast Asia. Equally unsettling was the swiftness with which the markets often delivered their negative verdicts on the IMF's handiwork. Fund officials had just sat down to lunch in Jakarta on January 15, 1998, to celebrate the signing that morning of Indonesia's "strengthened" program when they heard the shocking news, from cellphone calls, that the rupiah was falling instead of surging as they had anticipated.

Most chilling of all was how perilously close the U.S. economy came to joining the global meltdown in September and October 1998, when U.S. financial markets, especially the bond market, ceased functioning normally as a provider of capital to business, and the near-collapse of a giant hedge fund threatened to paralyze the nation's financial system. Thanks to the benign outlook for inflation, the Federal Reserve felt free to cut interest rates sharply at that time—but had it not done so, the convulsions on Wall Street might well have engendered a worldwide slump.

Rubin, Summers, and Greenspan are brainy, all right—indeed, they rank among the smartest and most capable economic policymakers in recent memory—but the aura they attained as economic saviors conveys the false impression that the international economy was in the hands of masterminds coolly dispensing remedies carefully calibrated to tame the savage beast of global financial markets. The reality, as I describe in chapters to come, is that as markets were sinking and defaults looming, the guardians of global financial stability were often scrambling, floundering, improvising, and striking messy compromises.

The mad dash to rescue Korea in November 1997 was just one illustration of how the IMF and the rest of the High Command were knocked for loop after loop during the crisis. The second rescue of Korea, though successful, came harrowingly close to falling apart as the U.S. Treasury and the Fed, deeply uncertain about the viability of the plan, waited until the last minute to sign on. In Brazil, top Treasury and IMF officials backed a bailout, over the strenuous objections of European policymakers, aimed at propping up the Brazilian real—only to find when the real crashed that the Europeans' skepticism about the bailout's prospects was justified.

As the crisis progressed, fierce disputes erupted within the G–7 and between the World Bank and other players. The United States, which dominated G–7 decisions, was at loggerheads with Japan over the issue of the IMF's right to force crisis-stricken Asian countries to revamp their economic systems. U.S. officials also clashed repeatedly with their German counterparts, who criticized large IMF loan packages as bailouts for the rich that would foster reckless investor behavior in the future. By the time the Brazilian crisis rolled around in late 1998, British and Canadian officials were also taking sharp issue with the U.S. approach, urging that instead of resorting to large IMF loans, the international community should use its leverage to impose temporary halts on the withdrawal of money from countries in crisis by private lenders and investors.

These and other episodes afford a dramatic backdrop for understanding and scrutinizing the IMF, an institution that, even to well-informed laypeople, is a source of great perplexity—sinister to some, awe-inspiring to others. Demystifying the IMF has never been more important, not least because of its sudden notoriety as the target of antiglobalization protesters.

Fund officials may complain about how poorly the public understands their institution, but the IMF cultivates its mystique, seeking to appear all-knowing, scientific, and detached. To outsiders, it often comes across as a high priesthood with pretensions of divine powers and insight. Its public pronouncements and documents are loaded with economic jargon that seems almost deliberately designed to obfuscate or intimidate. Sometimes this practice descends into farce. Several years ago, for example, an IMF report described Vietnam's invasion of Cambodia as "a misallocation of resources due to involvement in a regional conflict."

The IMF has a tremendous stake in maintaining an image of omniscience as it dispenses loans and prescribes remedies for ailing economies, because it wants to convince everyone—especially financial markets and officials of the governments seeking its assistance—that it knows what it's doing. When a nation with an IMF program fails to regain stability, the Fund almost invariably blames the country's government for failing to meet the conditions and targets that were agreed to, or for failing to show convincing commitment to achieving them. IMF officials typically shake their heads in resignation over the difficulty the country's politicians are having in, say, slashing popular subsidies or maintaining painfully high interest rates. From their lofty positions, they enlist support from professional analysts and the press for their view that the fault surely does not belong with their prescriptions. "It's the only program that serious people can imagine putting together," a senior IMF official told me, with a touch of asperity, in mid-December 1997 as Korean markets were melting down after Seoul had just received the biggest IMF loan in history.

Peering behind the IMF's facade provides a less confidence-inspiring picture, even for those who broadly share the Fund's views about how to handle countries in economic difficulty. I have met current and former IMF staffers who, speaking candidly under a promise of anonymity, recall with anguish having been thrown into the midst of crises with bewildering origins and no obvious solutions. "Everyone was working on the assumption that all you need is an IMF program, but this was proved wrong over and over," lamented one such Fund economist. "We reached agreement with these countries just to see the currency go over and over again."

Often, IMF officials felt outgunned—and small wonder. While the Fund can marshal huge resources for the countries it aids and can demand far-reaching reforms from their governments, it has been dwarfed by the growth of global markets.

The Federal Reserve, one of the most potent crisis-fighting institutions around, provides an illuminating comparison. As the U.S. central bank, the Fed plays the role of America's "lender of last resort," standing ready during financial crises to use its power to create unlimited amounts of money. The classic scenario of Fed intervention involves a run on a bank caused by rumors that prompt depositors to withdraw their funds, which in turn causes runs on other banks that do a lot of business with the first bank. The Fed's duty is to lend as much cash as the banks need to cover their depositors' demands—and keep lending until the panic eases, because otherwise the whole system might crash.

The IMF plays a similar role on the international stage. As with Korea in 1997, countries sometimes run dangerously low on hard currency, so the IMF stands ready as a lender of last resort. But the IMF can't simply create more hard currency—be it dollars, Japanese yen, British pounds, euros, or any other such monetary units—the way a central bank like the Fed can. The IMF has a war chest of these currencies contributed by member countries, and the size of its loans is limited as a result. In absolute size, the war chest is gigantic, and it has grown—from $27 billion in 1980, to $60 billion in 1990, to $88 billion at the beginning of 1997, just before the advent of the crisis in Asia. (The figure in 2002 was $135 billion.) But during that same period, purchases and sales of bonds, stocks, and other securities across international borders by firms and individuals resident in the United States soared from $249 billion in 1980 to $5 *trillion* in 1990 and $17.5 trillion in 1997. (When similar figures are added for residents of other advanced countries such as Germany, Japan, and France, the sums are more than twice as big.) For emerging markets alone, the amount of private capital flowing into them from abroad rose from $188 billion in 1984–1990 to $1.043 trillion in 1991–1997.

Beyond the problem of the IMF's limited resources, though, is its sometimes inept deployment of them. It is no secret that the Fund made serious mistakes in its efforts to rescue countries from crises. Some of these involved the Fund's well-known penchant for over-prescribing austerity, an example being the excessive fiscal stringency it demanded of Thailand. Others reflected the Fund's lack of expertise in banking issues, an example being its decision to close sixteen banks in Indonesia without providing a proper safety net for the remainder of the country's banking system.

This weakness does not mean, as some suggest, that the IMF is a hopelessly misguided or malign institution that systematically imposes harmful economic blueprints on countries in distress. Universities and think tanks are full of people who believe that if only the Fund would follow their approach, crises like the ones in the late 1990s would never occur or would be much less severe. Whether these advocates are right is impossible to say with certainty, and the arguments continue to be the subject of much dispute. Some critics wage their attacks from diametrically opposite perspectives. Supply-side economists, for example, excoriate the IMF for being too quick in encouraging countries to devalue their currencies. By contrast, Jeffrey Sachs of Harvard University and his followers assert that the Fund errs grievously by forcing countries to stick too long with currencies that are overvalued. This book is not an economic treatise, however, and thus does not champion any particular ideology or school of thought about how the IMF should change its economic paradigm.

For anyone evaluating the IMF's performance, the question "compared with what?" must be constantly borne in mind. The fact that the Fund blundered does not mean that it failed to do a lot of good, or that it failed to keep outcomes from being even worse than they turned out to be. For example, the Korean economy, and quite possibly the global economy as a whole, might be far weaker today had Seoul not been prevented from defaulting in late 1997.

Even so, the crisis of the late 1990s exposed how woefully ill-equipped the IMF is to combat the new strain of investor panics plaguing recently liberalized markets. The Fund proved unable to prevent the countries victimized by crises, especially in Asia, from suffering much worse than they deserved. Its ineffectiveness at minimizing the punishment meted out by the Electronic Herd does not bode well for the future. Nor does its ineffectiveness at foreseeing and squelching contagion.

Subsequent events have reinforced these conclusions. A sizable IMF bailout for Turkey in late 2000 failed at keeping the Turkish lira from collapsing in value two months later. More tragic was the case of Argentina, whose economic performance had won acclaim from Washington and Wall Street during the late 1990s. Despite a $40 billion IMF-led package in December 2000 and another $8 billion program in August 2001, Buenos Aires was forced in early 2002 to default on its debts and abandon its pegged currency system; the result was an economic contraction that threw millions into poverty and obliterated the wealth of the country's middle class. Not long thereafter, financial paroxysms beset Brazil anew; in early 2003 it was unclear whether a $30 billion IMF program approved the previous summer would keep Brazil from following Argentina's course.

The global financial system showed its susceptibility to upheavals of intense destructive power in the late 1990s. We could leave the system more or less as it is and hope that when future crises strike, the Ph.D.s at the IMF, together with "the Committee to Save the World," rise to the occasion. But the account of how they struggled the last time around should chasten us all out of any sense of complacency.

ﾟ 2 ﾟ

OPENING THE SPIGOT

Every year the IMF extends positions to about 100 economists, many of them recent recipients of doctorates from the world's most prestigious graduate schools—Harvard, Stanford, MIT, Chicago, Oxford, Cambridge, the London School of Economics. The organization they are joining employs 2,600 people, including lawyers, computer technicians, and other support personnel, but the heart of its staff is the economists, who number more than 1,000.

Their new workplace stands on 19th Street in downtown Washington, three blocks west of the White House. It is a beige limestone building thirteen stories high with a curved driveway that is often the parking spot for one or two limousines bearing visiting dignitaries. In the lobby, which has a sunlit atrium and polished marble floor, a cosmopolitan atmosphere pervades, thanks to the patter of Spanish, French, Arabic, and other languages spoken by staffers (all of whom are required to be fluent in English) casually flicking their ID badges to pass through the electronic security apparatus. Although smartly tailored business clothing predominates, the occasional turban, head scarf, or dashiki adds a touch of color. Staffers hail from more than 120 nations; about a quarter are American.

The new recruits have been lured partly by the pay. In 2002, entry-level Ph.D.s at the IMF earned salaries between $69,000 and $103,500 a year—tax free. Another draw is their status as elite international civil servants, who fly business class (often, first class) and stay in deluxe hotels when on mission. But a major attraction for these newly minted Ph.D.s is the knowledge that, within months, they are likely to find themselves overseas sitting across the table from a finance minister or central bank governor, helping to design a country's economic policies.

Upon reporting for duty, the recruits head for the IMF Institute, located in an office building a couple of blocks north of the headquarters, where they undergo a two-week training program. In addition to lectures on technical economic issues, the students take a course called "Financial Programming," which teaches them how the IMF helps countries in trouble. The institute's director, Mohsin Khan, spent a couple of hours one wintry afternoon walking me through the course in a manner comprehensible to non-Ph.D.s. The result was an illuminating introduction to the IMF's modus operandi, and Khan, a cheerfully outspoken Pakistani, also treated me to some candid observations about deficiencies in the Fund's traditional approach.

We start the course [Khan told me] with a very simple analogy. Consider the case of an individual. He's faced with a negative net worth—that is, his liabilities, his debts, are greater than his assets—and his income is less than his expenditures. He's spending more than he's making.

How can he do this? Because he's got credit—he can borrow. But now he's maxed out on his credit cards. No one will give him credit anymore.

The bank says to him, "OK, we will bail you out. We will advance you some money. But now, everything you do has to be controlled by a financial planner. We can't allow you to keep spending the way you have, because you'll just run out of credit again. The financial planner is going to do two things: He's going to help you increase your income and help you control your spending. So that, in fact, you can only spend, beyond your income, to the extent we supply you with credit. We'll give you a loan of $10,000. The most you can overspend is that $10,000. And the financial planner is going to set targets for spending and help you earn more income, so you can pay the money back.

"Furthermore, you are going to be watched very carefully. You're not going to get the $10,000 all at once. It's going to be spread out over a year. If you're living up to your commitments, you'll get the money. If not, we'll have to talk again."

After being given this analogy, the students at the IMF Institute examine the case of a typical country that lives beyond its means and ends up coming hat in hand to the Fund. For simplicity's sake, I'll call this country Shangri-la, and its currency the rupee; in fact, these names are used in one of the Institute's textbooks.

Like most countries that seek the Fund's help, Shangri-la is running a large current account deficit—a term that is roughly equivalent to a trade deficit, though it's a little broader. Shangri-la's imports substantially exceed its exports, and the money the people of Shangri-la earn by providing services to foreigners—tourism, for example—still doesn't fill the gap.

Another way of looking at the situation is that Shangri-la is spending more than it is earning—measured in hard currency. These currencies, which include the U.S. dollar, the Japanese yen, the euro, the British pound, and a handful of others, are the only currencies commonly accepted in international transactions. Without a supply of hard currency, a country can barely function in the global economy. Unfair as it may seem, the people and companies who sell oil, wheat, computer chips, pharmaceuticals, and other products across national borders will almost always insist on being paid in dollars or yen or pounds or euros (the dollar being by far the most prevalent). The Ukrainian hryvnia, Vietnamese dong, and Haitian gourde may be essential for conducting business when both buyer

and seller are located within Ukraine, Vietnam, and Haiti respectively, but such currencies are usually refused as payment for goods
and services outside their borders. This is not just because richer
countries tend to be more stable than poorer ones; it is also because
hard currencies are easy and cheap to trade, invest, and hedge
against changes in their value. The world needs a stable medium of
exchange for commerce among nations, and hard currency is it.

So in a country like Shangri-la that is spending more than it is
earning, exporters are earning dollars, yen, and other hard currencies by selling their products to foreigners, and the tourist trade is
bringing in some more. But Shangri-la's importers are spending all
this and more on the goods they buy from abroad, and their demand
for hard currency is draining the central bank's reserves.

Just like the individual in Khan's analogy, Shangri-la can borrow
on credit when it is spending more hard currency than it is earning.
For example, its companies may obtain loans of dollars or yen from
international banks to buy foreign machinery. Sometimes running a
tab makes good economic sense—especially if, say, the foreign
machinery purchased on credit can be put to good use producing
high-quality products for export. In the nineteenth century, the
United States, Canada, and Australia pursued a similar economic
tack, running large trade deficits and borrowing heavily from abroad
to finance the development of railroads and other infrastructure.

But if Shangri-la runs too large of a tab, it may suddenly find
itself in the same situation as the individual who has maxed out on
his credit cards. Maybe there's an unexpected shock—a sudden
surge in the price of imported oil, for example, or a dip in the price
of a key export, such as coffee or computer chips. Whatever the reason, Shangri-la has developed what economists call a "balance-of-
payments problem." Sources of hard currency from abroad dry up,
because foreign lenders conclude that for the foreseeable future,
Shangri-la has little prospect of generating enough proceeds from its
exports to pay all its obligations to foreigners.

At this point, Shangri-la's finance minister and central bank governor are likely to be found stepping out of a limousine in that curved driveway in front of IMF headquarters. The Fund is the only place an overextended country like Shangri-la can obtain the hard currency it needs to obtain vital imports and keep its economy functioning. In fact, this is the Fund's main purpose—to serve as a sort of giant credit union, in which the members (the 183 nations belonging to the Fund) deposit hard currency into a kitty and borrow from it when they are strapped. Moreover, as Khan put it, "the Fund in a sense becomes the financial planner for this country, because it has to design a program that involves reductions in spending, and policies to increase income and production, so that the country is living within the constraints of what's available."

Now comes the creative part of the institute's course—where the students learn, in theory at least, how to design a rescue plan for a country that has landed in hot water. In graduate school, most have already studied the basic principles of economic policy. They have learned how to determine the proper levels for a government budget deficit and interest rates to help keep inflation and unemployment as low as possible. They have learned, too, that devaluing a country's currency has pros and cons. If, for example, Shangri-la devalues the rupee, its exports will presumably sell better, because they'll become cheaper relative to other countries' goods on world markets. At the same time, devaluing the rupee increases the cost of imports to Shangri-la's consumers, thereby lowering the country's living standards.

"What is completely new to the students is how you put all this together in designing and constructing an IMF program," Khan said. So, like medical students performing surgery on a cadaver, the IMF class considers a real case involving a real country that ran into a balance-of-payments problem in the not-too-distant past. The students are divided into teams of about ten each and told to produce a solution. The students' textbooks provide them with reams of data on the country's government budget, money supply, business investment, foreign indebtedness, and the like. They have learned, Khan said, to start with a fundamental question: "Suppose the country continues on its merry way, spending and producing as it has in the past. How much money [i.e., hard currency] would it need? So we project exports, imports, and so on, and then see what the gap is. If the country continues on its merry way, this is what it will need."

The students are provided with a figure showing how large a package of loans the country can expect to obtain, given its size and importance, from the IMF and other official sources, such as the World Bank. The loans help fill the gap between hard-currency "income" and hard-currency "outgo," but the country still needs to squeeze down its imports and increase its exports so that it can get itself on a sustainable path and earn enough hard currency to pay back the loans.

Thus the students must decide on a line of attack: Should the government slash its budget deficit by raising taxes and curbing government outlays? Should it raise interest rates and curtail the growth of the money supply? Almost certainly, their answer to both questions will be yes—the only real question is how much—because painful as those measures might be in terms of increasing unemployment, this is a country that needs to reduce its import bill, which entails a decline in overall spending. Should the currency be devalued? Again, the answer is likely to be yes. A lower value for the currency would also cause consumers to cut back on imports as foreign goods become more expensive, and by making exports more competitive, it would enable the country to sell more of its output overseas—the result being increased supplies of hard currency.

All this may sound as if the IMF trains its economists to prescribe little but torture for the countries it lends to. Indeed, as one of the institute's textbooks euphemistically puts it: "These policies often focus primarily on containing aggregate demand." That's because in many cases, imposing austerity makes sense; countries living beyond their means must face the consequences eventually, and are better off doing so with an international loan to ease the adjustment.

But there's a major omission from this line of reasoning—and once it comes into play, Khan said, "it's not clear our economic theory works." Here's the problem: In today's world, crises can erupt for reasons quite different from those at play in the traditional case of a country running a large current account deficit. With capital more globally mobile than ever, countries are proving susceptible to sudden withdrawals of foreign money for all sorts of reasons, often stemming from weaknesses that emerge in their banking systems, where considerable foreign funds may be invested. They can thus run out of hard currency even though they haven't been living beyond their means in the conventional sense.

To put it in the jargon of economics, such countries are suffering "capital account crises" rather than "current account crises." Before the 1990s, the IMF was largely confined to dealing with current account crises. Many nations, especially in the developing world, sharply limited the amount of money foreigners could invest in their stock markets or lend to their companies. To the extent they borrowed from abroad, the purpose was essentially to obtain the hard currency necessary to pay for imports or to finance government infrastructure projects. When they lived beyond their means and maxed out on their credit cards, the reason was almost invariably that the government had been overspending—running large budget deficits—and pumping up the economy, thereby importing foreign goods in abundance. The IMF's loans enabled them to avoid going cold turkey on imports, and its tried-and-true prescriptions of austerity helped them bring their national lifestyles within their productive capacities.

But the new types of crises—some IMF officials call them "twenty-first century crises"—may arise for entirely different reasons. Now that the Electronic Herd is much freer than before to send money zipping across borders, a country may suffer a precipitous loss of hard currency simply because many Herd members that have invested in that country come down with a severe case of the heebie-jeebies. The country's government may be running a tight ship with its budget, and its central bank may be keeping the money sup-

ply within prudent bounds. But those factors may count for little if
the Herd starts to worry that, say, the country's banks have been
making bad loans and may lack the hard currency to pay their foreign obligations.

In such cases, the IMF's traditional remedy of deep budget cuts
and the like isn't necessarily logical; it may even make matters
worse—and in Asia, Khan acknowledged, the Fund was slow to
shed its old mind-set: "To be very candid, in the countries we deal
with, we find ourselves making standard policy prescriptions. What
are the knee-jerk reactions? Well, very seldom would you go wrong
if you said 'raise interest rates and tighten fiscal policy.'...I thought
the teams in Asia were sort of conditioned by the framework they
had in mind. As you can imagine, our more recent courses have
stressed 'let's think these things through. Do we need to tighten fiscal policy? And why?'"

Worse, he added, most IMF staffers—with their heavy orienta-
tion in macroeconomics—lacked a good grasp of the complex banking issues that rose to the fore in Asia. In an acknowledgment of this
shortcoming, the IMF Institute, which offers training to seasoned
Fund economists as well as new recruits, hastily expanded its curriculum after the crisis erupted. "A lot [of the newer course material]
is related to financial sector issues, where the IMF staff did not have
necessary expertise at all," Khan said, adding that in 1996 the institute had "no course in that area" for the staff but planned to offer
ten one-week courses on banking-related topics in 2000.

"A very large majority of countries that come to the IMF are still
suffering to a large extent from current account crises," Khan
emphasized. "So we still focus largely on the current account [at the
institute]. Capital account crises only happen to countries that can
attract large amounts of private capital"—and among developing
countries, that is still a minority.

But it's those newfangled crises that are the most damaging, the
most dangerous to other countries, and the most difficult to halt.
"We don't know what underlying economic relationships will hold

in panic situations, and capital account crises are panic situations," Khan said. "People are trying to run as fast as they can. When a true panic hits, all bets are off. Some things may work, others may not. You just don't know how to respond."

While being taught the standard approach for saving a typical economy in distress, young IMF staffers soon learn that they are expected to function inside an extremely tight-knit, hierarchical organization.

A team of economists going on mission to a troubled country brings along a document, typically the product of weeks of debate within Fund departments, spelling out a negotiating position on a list of policies for the country to adopt. When negotiations commence with the country's officials, team members are expected to stick to this preagreed approach, with only modest leeway granted to a few trusted mission chiefs. Even when they find themselves sympathizing with the objections raised by the country's officials—as they often do—the whole issue has to be debated again, privately, with IMF headquarters before Fund negotiators make major concessions. Revealing internal differences of opinion to outsiders constitutes a serious breach of discipline, because of the Fund's need to convey (both to the country's authorities and to the markets) the impression that it knows what it is doing.

There are, to be sure, many internal disagreements. The departments with a regional focus, such as the Asia and Pacific Department, often tangle with departments that have global responsibilities, including the Research Department and, most particularly, the Policy Development and Review (PDR) Department. Known within the IMF as "the thought police," PDR is responsible for ensuring that a program in a particular country conforms to the institution's standards and is broadly consistent with programs in other countries, one reason being to minimize complaints about favoritism. Thus there is a natural tension between departments with specialized knowledge about conditions in individual countries and depart-

ments such as PDR that are immune to "clientitis." When economists in one department can't agree with their counterparts in
another, the department heads sometimes seek compromise; if they
can't agree, the managing director or deputy managing director
must resolve the dispute.

"I can tell you for sure there are heated arguments, but they are
resolved internally," said Michael Dooley, a former IMF staffer now
teaching economics at the University of California at Santa Cruz.
"Will it appear from the outside as if the Fund is a pretty uniform
place? Yes. If it were otherwise, there would be howls of complaint—like, 'How come you guys can't make up your minds?' You
don't want an institution like the Fund changing its mind every
week about how to do things. Financial markets are watching. While
you negotiate, Rome is burning."

Still, debate takes place within a highly structured pecking order
in which lower-level economists, having expressed an opinion, close
ranks behind a superior's decision even if they disagree with it.
"There is a very clear hierarchy," said Laura Papi, who left the Fund
in late 1997 to join a banking firm. "As a team member you discuss
things, but the head of the mission has the final say on what the mission's view is on Country X. Now, he is not the boss of the IMF
either; he will discuss his views with the Front Office—a group of
very senior people heading each department—and then Front Office
people have contacts with management [the managing director and
first deputy managing director]." Even when disagreements surface
within a mission team, "they will disappear," Papi continued,
"because the mission chief will say, 'I think X, even if you think Y.'
Then he goes to the Front Office and says, 'We believe X.'" A mission
team member, she added, "wouldn't dream of sending a memo to
management saying, 'By the way, I think the stance my mission
chief is taking on Country X is completely wrong.' That would be
unheard of."

Economists from the World Bank, who sometimes work in joint
missions with the IMF, express awe at the almost military manner in

which Fund staffers defer to their superiors. This protocol is in stark contrast to the code of conduct at the World Bank, an institution devoted to long-term development loans, whose economists or irrigation specialists or environmental experts might embark on a lively disagreement right in front of, say, a borrowing country's deputy finance minister. When an IMF mission enters a room to conduct a negotiation, it is often easy to tell who ranks where; one World Banker likens it to "a mother duck leading her baby ducks." The mission chief typically sits in the middle of the table and does most of the talking, allowing immediate subordinates to chime in on issues requiring their specialized expertise; lower-level staffers are likely to remain silent. Another World Banker recalled a stint in the Fund and how, on his first day there, one of his new colleagues explained the difference between the two institutions: "The Bank is the Stanford marching band," the IMF man told him, referring to the comically chaotic formations performed at Stanford University's football stadium. "The Fund is the Army."

Behind the hierarchy is a fairly rigid system of promotions that reserves high-ranking posts for people with considerable seniority. Unlike in many private-sector firms where talented people are promoted to management at relatively early ages, the economics Ph.D.s joining the IMF at the age of twenty-five to thirty can expect to wait at least until their late thirties to assume management responsibility—and then only if they are high flyers. The result is a staff headed mainly by people who have worked at the IMF for two decades or even longer, a feature critics often blame for making the Fund hidebound and sluggish at responding to the changing nature of the global economy. There are, to be sure, examples of senior officials joining the Fund from outside—Timothy Geithner, a former U.S. Treasury official who was named director of the Policy Development and Review Department in 2001, was one. But they are exceptions, not the rule.

At the very top, however, are two people who have been placed in their jobs by the world's most powerful governments—the managing director, who is traditionally a European choice, and the first deputy managing director, who is traditionally an American choice. The individuals who hold these positions often stamp their personalities on the institution they head.

Anyone inclined to view the IMF through the prism of conspiracy theories would find it difficult to square their suspicions with the personality of Stanley Fischer, the Fund's first deputy managing director from 1994 to 2001, whose pleasant, unpretentious manner and impish smile was as disarming as his intellect was formidable. A former professor at the Massachusetts Institute of Technology, Fischer commanded a reputation as one of the leading lights of modern-day economics, with a graciousness that set him apart from most of the temperamental prima donnas in the top rungs of the profession. "He's a very controlled person, and doesn't ever raise his voice," said Catherine Mann, a former student of Fischer's at MIT who recalled that he was in huge demand as a thesis adviser. "The power of his arguments just bore into you." Such was the admiration in which he was held that even the IMF's harshest critics, when blasting the Fund for one fault or another, often invoked the fact that Fischer had been struggling to correct it.

Although he occupied the number two spot at the IMF, Fischer became its most influential figure after joining it in 1994. This was partly because of the close ties he enjoyed with top officials at the U.S. Treasury, but it was also because the IMF staff almost universally viewed him as a superior economic mind to Managing Director Michel Camdessus, who wisely delegated to Fischer much of the authority that top management holds to render decisions and arbitrate differences among the staff.

A slender man with silver hair and oval glasses, Fischer was born in 1943 and grew up in Mazabuka, a small, isolated farming village in what is now Zambia but was then the British colony of Northern Rhodesia. His father, who had emigrated from Latvia in 1926 at the age of nineteen, owned a general store, and his mother, whose parents had immigrated to South Africa from Lithuania, did the accounting. At the time of his birth, the family lived behind the store in a house with no running water or electricity; later, they moved to a house that had a flush toilet and a small gasoline-powered generator that could power lights but not appliances. For most of Fischer's boyhood, his was the only Jewish family in the area, which was generally described as having 400 inhabitants—meaning 400 whites, since racism was taken for granted in a colony where 2 million blacks were kept subservient to a white population numbering one-fortieth as many. Although whites didn't socialize with blacks, Fischer would later conclude that his boyhood gave him a much greater understanding of the developing world than if he had grown up in a rich country.

Fischer's horizons began expanding in 1956 when his father sold his business in Mazabuka and moved the family 500 miles away to the larger town of Bulawayo, in what is now Zimbabwe, where Fischer met Rhoda Keet, his future wife. After finishing high school, he spent six months on an Israeli kibbutz to learn Hebrew. From there he went to England, obtaining bachelor's and master's degrees from the London School of Economics, and then to the United States, where, after earning his Ph.D. from MIT, he joined the MIT faculty in 1973 and became an American citizen in 1976.

His abiding interest in Israel lured Fischer from academic life to the world of public policy. The Israeli economy was suffering from runaway inflation and budget deficits in the early 1980s, and Fischer was asked by Secretary of State George Shultz to join economist Herb Stein in advising the Israeli government on what action to take.

The advice Fischer and Stein gave the Israelis worked—the Jewish state stabilized its economy in 1985—and when the World Bank offered Fischer the post of chief economist in 1988, Fischer jumped at it, having derived much satisfaction from the economy-fixing in Israel. "My first experience was highly successful, so I could easily get the wrong impression," he said wryly. He returned to MIT in the early 1990s but jumped again in 1994 at the Clinton administration's request that he assume the IMF's deputy managing directorship.

Michel Camdessus, the balding Frenchman to whom Fischer reported, also knew how to turn on the charm, which he occasionally punctuated with giggly bursts of Gallic exuberance. The father of six children, Camdessus had a penchant for optimistic pronouncements that agitated the U.S. Treasury, whose top policymakers feared that the managing director was eroding the IMF's credibility with his sunny rhetoric about troubled countries "turning the corner." Even Michael Mussa, the IMF's chief economist, once teased his boss at an Executive Board meeting about his tendency to adopt a cheerful outlook. "Michel not only sees the glass half full instead of half-empty," Mussa cracked, "he sees a half-full glass even when there isn't any glass!"

The IMF staff held Fischer in higher regard as an economist, but they knew Camdessus deserved his reputation as a consummate politician. It was not for lack of diplomatic skill, after all, that he was appointed an unprecedented three times—in 1987, 1991, and 1996—as managing director, a job that requires constant juggling of demands from the G-7 and other member countries. (As Fischer joked when Camdessus retired from the IMF in 2000, Camdessus managed to irritate "every bloc of the Fund's membership" but "never all at once.") A glad-hander who bestowed compliments and thank-you notes liberally, Camdessus was nonetheless extremely formal and often brusque toward the IMF staff. Besides Mussa, virtually no one on the staff called him by his first name; he was "Mr. Managing Director."

Camdessus, whose father was a journalist, joined the French Finance Ministry in 1960. He was a quintessential product of his country's elite civil service, having graduated from the prestigious Ecole Nationale d'Administration, with a taste for interventionist policies but a readiness to put practical politics above ideology. As a youth he belonged to the Catholic wing of the Socialist Party, and his career flourished after Socialist President François Mitterrand's

1981 election victory, which was followed in 1982 by Camdessus's promotion to the directorship of the Treasury, a post at the very pinnacle of the civil service. He helped design Mitterrand's ambitious program of heavy government spending, nationalization of industries, and increased benefits for workers. But when Mitterrand's policies engendered embarrassing devaluations of the franc, along with rising inflation and unemployment, Camdessus demonstrated the ideological dexterity for which he would later become noted among the IMF staff, helping to orchestrate the Socialist government's "great U-turn" in 1983 toward financially orthodox spending cuts, tax reductions, and deregulation. He left the ministry in late 1984 to become governor of France's central bank, where he presided over a tough anti-inflation stance and a loosening of controls over the financial markets. During his tenure at the IMF, his Socialist background was a source of derision among Republicans in the U.S. Congress, but Camdessus deflected the criticism good-humoredly, once telling reporters in Washington, "Your humble servant of course here is a French Socialist; while in France . . . I am an ultra neoliberal Anglo-Saxon."

But the role of the IMF staff and top management, important as they are, is only part of the story. As an international organization, after all, the IMF has political masters.

On the twelfth floor of the IMF's headquarters is its sanctum sanctorum, an oval-shaped room sixty feet long and two stories high with plush blue carpeting and suede-and-wood paneling, decorated only by six large portraits of past managing directors. In the center stands a horseshoe-shaped table with thirty gray swivel chairs around the periphery and microphones at each seat.

This is the meeting room for the IMF's twenty-four executive directors, who must pass judgment on every major Fund decision and, to do so, convene as often as three times a week, with the managing director or a deputy managing director chairing the session.

Each executive director represents a country or a group of countries, with voting power apportioned according to how much each country has contributed to the Fund. The voting power is adjusted periodically, but in 2002 the U.S. executive director held 17.10 percent of the votes. Japan's director was second with 6.14 percent, followed by Germany's with 6.00 percent. A director from Nigeria representing twenty-one African countries held 3.22 percent of the votes; another director, from Egypt, represented thirteen Arab countries and held 2.95 percent of the votes; still another, from Brazil, represented nine Latin American countries and held 2.46 percent of the votes; and so on. Many of the directors are well-trained international economists or high-level bureaucrats from their countries' finance ministries who engage in sharp repartee over fine points of economics. Others lack sufficient background to make much of a contribution to the debate.

Contested votes at the board are rare; most of the decisions are approved by consensus following informal negotiations. As a result, the Fund's critics often deride the board as a rubber stamp for the staff. But on the most critical issues, real power lies with the top economic policymakers of the G-7 countries, which control nearly half the votes. One select group, in particular, might be described without too much exaggeration as puppetmasters pulling strings behind a screen—the G-7 deputies, or G-7D for short.

The G-7D exercise extraordinary control over international economic policy while attracting little attention in the media. Some of the deputies are well known—Larry Summers, the U.S. representative to the group during his six years as deputy secretary and undersecretary of the Treasury, was a high-profile G-7 deputy, as was Eisuke Sakakibara, the former vice minister for international affairs at Japan's Finance Ministry who was dubbed "Mr. Yen." But the group's activities and discussions are kept out of the public spotlight as much as possible. The deputies hold unheralded gatherings, sometimes getting together in airport VIP lounges to ensure that the press stays in the dark. Although aides may accompany them to the meetings, they wait outside the meeting rooms while the deputies meet alone. The group remains in frequent contact by telephone conference call, even though at least some of them (almost always the Japanese) must stay up late at night to participate because of time-zone differences.

The spotlight instead shines on others: The deputies' immediate bosses, the finance ministers (in the U.S. case, the Treasury secretary), are the ones whose meetings every few months produce pronouncements and communiqués on currencies and other international monetary matters that draw scrutiny from hordes of financial reporters and analysts. Their ultimate bosses, the G-7 heads of state, are the ones whose annual summits attract worldwide attention in the mass media. But the deputies assume responsibility for reaching agreement on most economic issues—both in advance of their bosses' meetings and at other times as well.

Of course, the deputies are accountable to their superiors and may be overruled by them. But there are important practical reasons for their influence. "During crisis periods, there may be three or four conference calls a day. Ministers just can't do that," said Klaus Regling, who was Germany's representative to the G-7D in 1998. "Also, deputies can communicate in English; not all the ministers can. In any case, it's inappropriate for ministers to do technical work. They need their top bureaucrats to do that. These are pretty high-caliber people; many of them have been doing it for years, so they know each other, and they know they can rely on each other."

Arguments often rage within the G-7D, but countries on the losing side usually abide by the consensus and keep their criticisms as quiet as possible, to avoid roiling financial markets. The members "know they have to come to an agreement; otherwise there could really be a crisis in the world economy," Regling said. On occasion they are truly split, which forces ministers to get involved; in cases involving IMF issues, an unresolved rift within the group allows Fund management to decide the policy.

Given the superpower status of the United States, of course, the

G-7 is hardly a democratic organization, and the U.S. position usually prevails. Although Washington cannot dictate to the others and is obliged to try reaching consensus with them, it enjoys a unique ability to generate support, so the others tend to be content to play the role of checking and balancing. U.S. influence is particularly great in matters involving the IMF and dates to the days of the institution's founding.

On December 14, 1941, one week after the attack on Pearl Harbor, Secretary of the Treasury Henry Morgenthau Jr. directed his assistant for international affairs, Harry Dexter White, to prepare a memorandum on the establishment of a fund for the Allied powers that "should provide the basis for postwar international monetary arrangements." That memo began a process in which White would join with Britain's John Maynard Keynes, the twentieth century's most influential economist, to draft the plan for the creation of the IMF and the World Bank that was approved at a 1944 conference in Bretton Woods, New Hampshire. Although they shared a similar vision, White and Keynes would differ on some key points, and White's views would prevail, thanks to his country's preeminence in the global order.

Like most mainstream economists at the time, White abhorred the nationalistic economic policies adopted in the 1930s—in particular, the widespread practice of trade protectionism—that had led the world into depression and war. During that period, many countries erected high tariffs and imposed import quotas to protect struggling industries from foreign competition, and they deliberately devalued their currencies to reduce imports and provide their firms with competitive advantages. This endless cycle of beggar-thy-neighbor behavior provided some nations with short-term benefits, but it proved mutually destructive because it stifled international commerce and accelerated the downward spiral in the global economy.

Accordingly, White favored a system in which currency values would be fixed, with an international fund aimed at maintaining those exchange rates. For one thing, this would help foster a climate of international stability. For another, a system of fixed rates would help enable countries to reach mutually beneficial agreements to lower trade barriers. Each country would feel more assured that it could benefit from such accords if it didn't have to worry about other nations indulging in an orgy of currency devaluations.

White also favored controls on international capital, restricting investors and bankers from moving money across borders. Freely flowing capital, he believed, offered few benefits and threatened to reignite the monetary chaos that had preceded the war.

As he developed his plan, White began corresponding with Keynes, then an adviser to the British chancellor of the Exchequer, who drafted a proposal of his own. Keynes agreed with White's main points, but he favored the creation of an "International Clearing Union," a sort of global central bank, that would maintain control over the worldwide supply of credit. White opposed the idea as too ambitious—in part because he feared Congress would refuse to approve the large U.S. contribution that would be required, and in part because he wanted a system based on the primacy of the U.S. dollar.

Negotiations were stormy at times, but White and Keynes were able to find common ground, and their efforts culminated at Bretton Woods, in a nineteenth-century resort hotel nestled amid New Hampshire's White Mountains. There, three weeks after the invasion of Normandy, representatives of forty-five nations convened to draft and sign the articles of agreement of the IMF and World Bank. The design of the Fund and the new global monetary order was more in line with the White plan than the Keynes plan, for the "Bretton Woods system" had as its anchor the U.S. dollar, whose value was pegged to gold. The U.S. Treasury promised to exchange one ounce of gold for $35, and all other members of the IMF were required to set the values of their currency either in terms of gold or the dollar. If a country wanted to change its foreign exchange rate by more than 1 percent, it had to obtain the IMF's consent, and if it needed hard currency, it could draw from the Fund. Movement of private capital across national borders was highly restricted.

The system lasted for a little over a quarter century. Occasional crises flared, a prominent example being the turmoil that led to the devaluation of the British pound from $2.80 to $2.40 in 1967. But the fixed-rate regime worked more or less as envisioned until the early 1970s, when the United States fell victim to inflation, making the $35 gold price a bargain, which in turn put overwhelming demands on the Treasury's gold stocks and destroyed the dollar's anchoring role. After 1973, when the world's major currencies began moving freely against each other according to market forces, the IMF changed its rules to allow each member to determine whether to float or fix its currency or use some in-between method involving gradual adjustments, such as "adjustable pegs" or "bands" within which their currencies could fluctuate.

Still, the IMF retained its essential structure as a credit union for countries. Upon joining, each member deposited money, called a "quota," into the Fund, and 25 percent of this had to come in the form of gold or hard currency. A country that ran into a payments problem could immediately withdraw its 25 percent hard-currency deposit, and if it needed more, it could borrow up to three times its quota, provided it implemented an economic reform program approved by the Fund. In a real emergency, the Fund could approve loans exceeding that limit.

In a sense, the IMF lost its raison d'être with the death of the fixed-rate system. But it soon found new roles. During the oil shocks of the 1970s, it helped in "recycling" revenues from petroleum-producing countries to developing countries, and during the 1980s, it became heavily involved in resolving the Latin American debt crisis. In response to howls that it had become a self-perpetuating bureaucracy without a legitimate mandate for existence, the Fund cited its articles of agreement, in particular Article I (v), which declared that one of its purposes was "to give confidence to members by making the general resources of the Fund temporarily available to them under adequate safeguards, thus providing them with the opportunity to correct maladjustments in their balance of payments without resorting to measures destructive of national or international prosperity."

That was the justification for the IMF's involvement when trouble began looming in Asia in the mid-1990s. But by that time, the world financial system had undergone changes that far surpassed the end of the $35-an-ounce gold price.

The lights dimmed in Toronto's Roy Thompson Hall on July 18, 1996, at one of the largest shareholder meetings in the world. As 8,000 owners of Templeton mutual funds watched, some via closed-circuit TV in other cities, a bagpiper led Templeton's thirty-two global analysts, plus its managers and directors, into the hall.

Characteristically, Mark Mobius, head of the emerging-markets division for the Templeton funds, was on the road and had to be beamed into the meeting via satellite to make his presentation, in which he thanked investors for maintaining faith through some trying times in the funds he managed. A minor celebrity because of his distinctively shaved head and appearance in TV commercials, Mobius had cultivated an image as one of the most peripatetic people on earth, a sort of stateless financial adventurer whose private jet was the closest thing to home. Born on Long Island but a citizen of Germany, he prided himself on maintaining a 250-day-a-year travel schedule that entailed keeping residences in Singapore, Hong Kong, Shanghai, and Washington, D.C., and left no time for a family. That's what was required, after all, to get a close look at the hundreds of companies in the dozens of countries he visited annually in his relentless worldwide quest for promising investments. And it paid off: As Mobius loved to tell audiences and reporters, when his first emerging-markets fund had started in 1987, it managed just $87 million, and it could invest in only a handful of countries, including Hong Kong, Singapore, Mexico, and Brazil. Ten years later, the amount of money he managed in emerging markets had risen more than one-hundredfold, the number of countries targeted for investment had increased to over forty, and his funds boasted some of the best returns in the industry.

Mobius was not only a successful investment practitioner, but he also was an effective proselytizer for the view that investors in the world's wealthy countries ought to be placing their chips on the high-rolling arenas of Asia, Latin America, Eastern Europe, and the former Soviet Union. In a 1996 book, he spelled out the case: The value of all stocks in low- and middle-income countries, he noted, constituted only about 10 percent of the total value of the world's stock markets. But that ratio was increasing sharply, and the trend was bound to continue for the indefinite future, because economic growth in these emerging markets would far outstrip growth in the industrialized nations of the United States, Japan, Western Europe, and Canada.

For starters, the emerging markets had more people—4.6 billion, compared with 795 million in advanced industrial nations—and about three times as much land, too. "It's not hard to see what potential exists in mobilizing 85 percent of the world's population to work towards economic expansion, utilizing 77 percent of the world's land," Mobius wrote. Although he acknowledged that investing in developing countries carried obvious risks, he emphasized that a variety of factors were working to help the emerging markets close the wealth gap with the industrialized world. Many lower-income countries had embarked on a "virtuous cycle of development," in which a more well-to-do populace was becoming better educated and more literate; this in turn led to lower birthrates and higher job aspirations, which in turn generated more wealth, more literacy, and so on.

By spring 1995, enthusiasm for emerging markets had spread so widely that nearly 1,000 mutual funds were active in them, and the number of funds specializing in them had risen 38 percent over the previous year. Some offered middle-class investors the chance to take a flyer in particular regions of the world (the Vontobel Eastern

European Equity Fund, the Ivy South America Fund); others focused on individual countries (the Argentina Fund, the Pakistan Investment Fund). And mutual funds were only part of a broader rush to emerging markets in the first six years of the 1990s by financial institutions of all sorts, including banks, brokerage firms, pension funds, and insurance companies.

The chief draw was Asia, where the biggest providers of foreign capital weren't portfolio managers like Mobius but banks, which were lending primarily to private borrowers. The dominant players in Asia were Japanese banks such as Sumitomo, Sakura, Mitsubishi, Fuji, and the Bank of Tokyo. Carmen Reinhart, an economist formerly in the IMF's Capital Markets Division, traveled to Tokyo in early 1995 and offered this perspective:

> I visited a whole bunch of Japanese banks. The economy had been in a slump, and domestic demand for loans was nonexistent. So the banks were looking overseas, where you had all these vibrant markets. Between 1995 and 1997, their lending to the [East Asian] region just skyrocketed. It made a lot of sense— these economies were labeled as the miracle economies. This was right after the Mexican crisis, and of course the Mexican crisis was seen as something that could happen in Latin America—but could never happen *here*.

Not far behind the Japanese banks were the Europeans; American banks were less exposed in Asia, but they were a force as well.

In all the emerging markets combined—not just Asia—the net inflows of private capital, which totaled just $42 billion in 1990, soared to $329 billion by 1996. But the overall numbers tell only part of the story.

Long-term flows from multinational companies putting money directly into building factories, R&D facilities, warehouses, retail stores, and the like rose rapidly but steadily, year by year, reaching $92 billion in 1996. Much more fickle were portfolio investors— stock and bond buyers, in particular. Their flows to emerging markets, which totaled $32 billion in 1991, rocketed to $118 billion in

1993—a year of unbridled euphoria when the Hong Kong stock market gained 124 percent—but then collapsed to $53 billion in 1995 following the Mexican peso crisis, before rising again to nearly $112 billion in 1996. Fortunately, another variety of financial player, commercial banks, was fickle in a countervailing way: The banks were increasing their lending to emerging markets when the portfolio investors were retreating. The net result was that in 1996 and early 1997, optimism toward emerging markets prevailed among investors of all breeds.

The allure of the frontier was only part of the motivation driving the financial institutions and investment firms. Another major factor was the desire to "chase yield" overseas. In the early 1990s, interest rates were trending downward in the United States and Japan, in particular, and with yields on U.S. Treasury bonds dipping below 6 percent at some points, financial institutions couldn't resist the temptation to seek double-digit returns in places like Malaysia, Brazil, or Turkey.

It wasn't just that money managers in the West and Japan were prowling for higher yields abroad with the money they already had. Around 1992, many international commercial and investment banks began using a specialized technique of borrowing low-cost money in their home markets for the specific purpose of investing it for a short while in higher-yielding emerging-market securities. This was called the "carry trade," and it worked in a variety of ways. In one typical version, an international bank would borrow yen for three months in Japan, where the annualized rate for such borrowings by banks was a mere 0.5 percent in late 1996. By converting the proceeds into, say, Thai baht and putting the money in Thai bank time deposits or corporate promissory notes or government bills, the bank could earn annualized profits of 15 to 23 percent on its borrowed money during that period. To be sure, not every carry-trade transaction was nearly so lucrative, and not all international banks were comfortable borrowing yen for such transactions; a bank wanting to borrow dollars in New York for three months had to pay annualized interest of between 5 and 6 percent in 1996. But the carry trade became hugely popular in Asia, and it was especially appealing in countries like Thailand, which had fixed-rate currencies that made the deal seem almost risk-free.

Getting carried away is a hoary tradition in "emerging markets"—a term first coined in 1981 when Antoine Van Agtmael, a former World Bank official planning to start a "Third World Equity Fund," realized he needed a catchier name. In the early 1820s, excitement in Britain over the liberation of South America from Spanish colonial rule led to a fevered run-up in the bonds of countries such as Chile and Colombia, and South American gold mining shares enjoyed an even crazier surge, based partly on outlandish claims by their promoters. But by 1826, every South American state except Brazil defaulted, and gold mining shares crashed. One prominent booster, the future prime minister Benjamin Disraeli, was burdened with such crushing debts that he suffered a nervous breakdown.

Later in the nineteenth century, the United States became the favorite emerging market of financiers in London and on the European continent, who gobbled up the bonds of American states and railroads. Despite defaults that wiped out fortunes in the 1850s, 1870s, and 1890s, European investors also poured vast sums into Canada, Australia, and Russia. By the dawn of the twentieth century, the United States was providing more capital to the rest of the world than it was drawing in, and in the 1920s another emerging-market bubble arose, as "investment trusts" (precursors to emerging-markets funds) successfully lured thousands of ordinary Americans to pool their money for the purchase of Latin American bonds and other foreign securities.

It took the Great Depression to put a serious damper on such activity. When the Federal Reserve started raising U.S. interest rates in 1928, American money that had been previously invested abroad switched back to Treasury bills. Governments that had become dependent on American capital desperately scrambled for cash but were forced to suspend payment on their debts, led by Bolivia in 1931, followed soon thereafter by much of Latin America, countries in southern Europe, and finally in 1933 by Germany.

This catastrophe was one reason for White's and Keynes's determination to restrict international flows of private capital when they designed the Bretton Woods system of fixed currency rates. But with the breakdown of Bretton Woods in the early 1970s, rich countries began dismantling their controls on capital movements, and some developing nations followed a few years later, though others hung back.

The case for free movement of capital is based on a logical foundation. Poor countries need funds to develop, and rich countries tend to have a surfeit of savings; so why deprive the less fortunate of financial resources? Moreover, when investors are restricted from putting their capital into an investment overseas that offers more attractive returns than they can get at home, the world's overall resources are presumably being used less efficiently than they might.

But as the trend toward ending capital controls accelerated in the 1990s, some experts began to grow uneasy. Among their number was a small group of policymakers within the Clinton administration. Up to that point, U.S. policy had been to enthusiastically support the liberalization of the rules governing capital movements and to exhort the IMF to encourage the trend as well. But in the early years of the first Clinton term, economists at the Council of Economic Advisers (CEA) questioned whether the Treasury Department was committing a blunder by continuing the policy. "There was a considerable, though one-sided, debate," said Alan Blinder, a CEA member. "Treasury on one side, CEA on the other. You can see this wasn't a fair fight."

To Blinder and fellow CEA member Joseph Stiglitz, Treasury was acting as Wall Street's handmaiden and taking insufficient account of the risks involved in exposing developing countries to the ebbs and flows of global money markets. Blinder and Stiglitz did not object to direct investment by multinational corporations overseas; along with the overwhelming majority of economists across the political spectrum, they believed the building of factories and other business operations in low-wage developing countries was generally positive for living standards. Their problem lay with financial flows, especially short-term flows, which are susceptible to sudden reversals. In those days, Blinder recalled, "everything in the administration was about job creation," and Treasury wanted to prevent countries from maintaining barriers to one of the America's most competitive industries—banking and finance. Blinder and Stiglitz hotly disputed Treasury assertions that, besides providing benefits for U.S. firms, lowering obstacles to foreign financial institutions would confer benefits on emerging markets as well. "It was argued, correctly, that there were benefits from financial inflows into these countries. But there was also the danger of outflow," Blinder said, adding: "It was dangerous to put this fancy finance into these countries with underdeveloped financial systems."

The CEA's chief antagonist was Larry Summers, then Treasury undersecretary for international affairs. Though only in his late thirties, Summers was already emerging as a major force within the administration—partly because of the clout his agency possessed but also because of his raw brainpower.

Summers had grown up in a family notable for its distinctions in economics. Two of his uncles, Paul Samuelson and Kenneth Arrow, were Nobel prizewinners in the field, and both his parents were economists at the University of Pennsylvania. In the family's suburban Philadelphia home, control over the TV set was determined by an auction process that his father, Robert, devised to demonstrate how markets worked. Young Larry showed promise early at living up to the family tradition. At age eleven, he developed a mathematical formula aimed at determining how accurately a baseball team's standing on July 4 could predict its chances for winning the pennant. He entered MIT at sixteen, and in 1983, one year after getting his Ph.D. in economics from Harvard, the twenty-eight-year-old

Summers became one of the youngest individuals in the university's history to be awarded a full professorship. Ten years later, after having published over 100 articles in academic journals, many of them focused on unemployment and taxation issues, he won the John Bates Clark medal for the most talented economist under forty. But he found the policy arena too alluring to pass up, and in 1988 he served as an economic adviser to Democratic presidential candidate Michael Dukakis, battling the more left-leaning campaign officials who favored heavy taxes and interventionist industrial policy schemes. In a sign of the respect he enjoyed among conservatives, the Bush administration sanctioned his appointment in 1990 to become chief economist of the World Bank.

With his shirt often untucked, his schedule often a shambles, and his sharp wit often aimed at his own foibles, Summers could be endearing, and his Treasury colleagues fondly recounted "Larry stories" about his misplaced passports and missed planes. But his least lovable trait was his inability to conceal a high regard for his own intellect. Early on in his Treasury career, Summers became the target of numerous complaints about rolling his eyes and belittling the arguments of others during interagency meetings and even in negotiating sessions on Capitol Hill. His skill at interpersonal relations improved substantially in his later years at Treasury, but his contempt for what he viewed as substandard work sometimes boiled over in paper-flinging tirades that appalled colleagues, and his brittle ego was exposed one evening in 1994 at a press briefing in Tokyo when a U.S. embassy official announced that the remarks by the undersecretary should be attributed to an administration official. "*Senior* administration official," Summers instantly corrected him.

Summers had originally been in line to become CEA chairman, but his bid was blocked by environmentalists outraged over a memo he had signed while at the World Bank concerning pollution in developing countries. (Although the memo was written by another World Bank staffer, Summers took the heat for having signed it.) Ironically, the episode redounded to his benefit because he ended up accepting the Treasury undersecretaryship, a job with less prestige but plenty of responsibility for formulating specific areas of policy, unlike the CEA, a tiny agency that was little more than a bully pulpit for its members. Hence arose Blinder's lament about the lopsidedness of the clash with Summers over liberalizing international capital flows.

Summers's version of the debate with Blinder and Stiglitz was that he, at least, didn't favor a U.S. policy of prodding developing countries into allowing the inflow of more foreign money. Rather, he wanted those countries to grant greater access in their domestic markets to competition from foreign banks and financial institutions. Many Asian nations, in particular, made it hard for the likes of Chase Manhattan or Bank of America to compete directly against local banks for deposits and customers. Lifting such restrictions to allow foreign competition, Summers and others argued, would force these countries' financial systems to become more efficient and less corrupt; a local Thai bank would be less inclined to make shaky loans to friends of influential politicians if it had to compete with Citibank for access to deposits.

Summers acknowledged that some of his subordinates at Treasury might have aggressively advocated the department's traditional line, which was to broadly favor dismantling controls on international capital flows. But his own line was different, he contended: "There are enormous advantages for the U.S., and these countries, in having foreign participation in their domestic financial systems. So as a trade issue, we saw [removing barriers to competition] as something that should be very aggressively pushed. But it is possible for a country to have foreign participation in its financial system and still have capital controls. It is possible to have no capital controls and no foreign participation in the domestic financial system. The question of capital controls is a separate question from the question of foreign participation in financial services."

Blinder retorted that although Summers was technically correct, and that he agreed with Summers's point about competition, "our view was that the line was very blurry in practice" between pressing developing countries to allow competition from foreign financial institutions and pressing them to open up to hot foreign money.

Other former administration officials said ruefully that in retrospect, the Treasury and the IMF should have been far more vocal in warning developing countries against the risks of welcoming foreign funds before their banking systems had matured to the point that the money could be prudently lent. Even when such caveats were stated, the admonitions were muted. "I think what everybody felt— and I mean everybody, not just the government but all the financial markets, virtually all public policy thinkers—was to see the conceptual value and importance of these capital flows, and to also see the potential dangers," said W. Bowman Cutter, a White House economic adviser during the first Clinton term. "But the tendency was to overestimate the first and underestimate the second."

One emerging market was viewed by Blinder, Stiglitz, and their allies as a near-paragon of prudence in the financial realm: Chile, which maintained a set of rules designed to limit incoming short-term capital. Foreign investors and lenders were required to leave 30 percent of their money in non-interest-bearing accounts at the central bank for one year—in effect, a tax on the short-termers. But most IMF and Treasury officials looked askance at Chile's system of capital controls. Summers resisted the idea of encouraging other countries to follow Chile's lead, because such controls could easily be used to protect powerful domestic financial interests against the cleansing influence of competition. Asked at a World Bank seminar in late 1997 why Washington didn't favor more Chilean-type systems in emerging markets, Summers replied: "It's kind of like telling an alcoholic that a little bit of wine is good for your health. It may be true, but you don't want to tell him."

The high-water mark for the cause of globalizing money flows came at the September 1997 annual meeting of the IMF and World Bank in Hong Kong. The IMF had already been using its influence to urge countries to open their financial systems, and now—with U.S.

backing—the Fund was moving to formally override the preferences
of its founders, White and Keynes, for restricting capital movements.
The IMF's policy-setting Interim Committee, consisting of member
nations' finance ministers and central bank governors, declared:

> It is time to add a new chapter to the Bretton Woods agreement.
> Private capital flows have become much more important to the
> international monetary system, and an increasingly open and lib-
> eral system has proved to be highly beneficial to the world econ-
> omy. By facilitating the flow of savings to their most productive
> uses, capital movements increase investment, growth and pros-
> perity. Provided it is introduced in an orderly manner, and
> backed both by adequate national policies and a solid multilateral
> system for surveillance and financial support, the liberalization of
> capital flows is an essential element of an efficient international
> monetary system in this age of globalization.

Citing the turmoil in Southeast Asia, which had erupted only
three months before, the IMF committee noted "the importance of
underpinning liberalization with a broad range of structural measures . . . and to building sound financial systems solid enough to cope
with fluctuations in capital flows." But the statement concluded
with an "invitation" for the IMF Executive Board "to complete its
work on a proposed amendment to the Fund's articles that would
make the liberalization of capital movements one of the purposes of
the Fund."

Camdessus delivered a rousing endorsement of the move in a
speech at the meeting, in which he was careful to explain that the
Fund would not encourage countries to remove capital controls prematurely, nor "prevent them from using capital controls on a temporary basis, when justified." He continued:

> Certainly, there are risks in tapping global markets: Sometimes
> they react too late, and sometimes they overreact. No country—I

repeat, no country—is immune to these risks. But let us not forget that markets also provide tremendous opportunities to accelerate growth and development, as Southeast Asia itself so vividly shows. . . .

Freedom has its risks. But are they greater than those of complex administrative rules and capricious changes in their design?

Freedom has its risks. But is there any more fertile field for development and prosperity?

Freedom has its risks! Let us go then for an orderly liberalization of capital movements.

Some developing countries had already embraced the call with alacrity—or perhaps a better word is abandon. One, in particular, had already begun paying a steep price.

· 3 ·

WINNIE THE POOH
AND THE BIG SECRET

The IMF staffers who gathered in the office of First Deputy Managing Director Stanley Fischer on July 25, 1997, faced a vexing problem: Thailand didn't want their help.

Three weeks earlier, amid severe financial turmoil, the Thai government had abandoned its long-standing policy of maintaining a fixed value for the baht against the U.S. dollar, and the baht was sinking fast, having already lost 19 percent of its value in foreign exchange markets. Despite this frightening disintegration in the country's economic fortunes, however, Thai officials were refusing the IMF's overtures to start negotiating the terms of a rescue loan. The Thais were deeply reluctant to subject their economic policy-making to IMF approval, and there was no way for the Fund to impose itself on Bangkok. As an international organization whose members are sovereign nations, the IMF is forbidden from even sending a mission to a country unless it has been invited by the country's authorities.

Among the people seated around Fischer's conference table was an economist named Ranjit Teja, whose presence was a small but noteworthy illustration of how blissfully unanticipatory the Fund was about the carnage that would ensue from Thailand's financial crack-up. Teja, a thirty-nine-year-old Indian with a Ph.D. from Columbia University, had been promoted the previous month to a new job, chief of the division responsible for South Korea, and he had spent a few weeks boning up on the country's economy to prepare for a routine annual visit to Seoul in the autumn. But at the end of June he had been reassigned again, to Thailand, mainly because of his strong background in programs—that is, drafting and negotiating economic plans for countries seeking IMF loans. The notion that Korea would need a Fund program a mere four months hence seemed about as far-fetched as the chance of a snowstorm on that late July day.

Still, Thailand's woes were plenty worrisome, and as far as the IMF staffers were concerned, a program for Bangkok was an urgent necessity. The lower the baht fell, the closer Thailand's leading banking and industrial firms edged toward bankruptcy. Many of them had sizable foreign debts—which they were required to repay in U.S. dollars—and the burden of repaying those debts was escalating as the baht was descending. At the old rate of 25 baht per dollar, repaying a $1 million loan would have required 25 million baht; at that day's rate of 32 baht per dollar, the cost had risen to 32 million baht—a 28 percent increase. Deepening the alarm among the meeting participants was the prospect that the turbulence would spill over Thailand's borders and affect its Southeast Asian neighbors. Already, signs of financial contagion were sprouting. Earlier in the week, Indonesia's currency had sunk by 7 percent against the dollar in a single day. The Malaysian ringgit and Singapore dollar were also badly hit.

Frustrated by the Fund's inability to intervene in the rapidly deteriorating situation, Fischer decided the time had come to dispense with diplomatic niceties. The deputy managing director, who had been talking privately with Thai officials and believed they were coming around, ordered a mission to depart for Bangkok immediately.

"Just go," he said to the economists from the Asia and Pacific Department seated nearby.

"But they haven't asked for us," his subordinates protested, astonished at this proposed breach of protocol.

"Just go," Fischer replied, "and in the time it takes for you to get there, I'll persuade them."

Thus began the IMF's foray into what would soon be known as the Asian financial crisis. The Fund was not only surprised by the ensuing events but ill-prepared in certain respects. The Asia and Pacific Department was something of a backwater at the IMF, reflecting the prevailing view at the Fund that, in general, Asia was doing splendidly and needed little attention. The brightest and most aggressive of the institution's economists tended to gravitate to other departments, such as the ones overseeing Latin America or Europe, where the challenges were pressing and the assignments more glamorous. More important, the Asia and Pacific Department's staff had spent little time in the countries that would be hardest hit—Thailand, Korea, and Indonesia—because when countries are not subject to IMF programs, they are generally visited by missions only once a year, for a couple of weeks, as part of a surveillance process in which the Fund assesses the economy and gives advice, mostly on budget, tax, and monetary policy.

Thailand was the one Asian country where the IMF saw a crisis coming and was geared up to handle it. What went wrong, according to the Fund's version of events, was that the Thai government stubbornly refused to face reality. Thai officials repeatedly ignored private warnings from Washington to take preemptive measures aimed at easing the tremendous pressures threatening the stability of their currency and their economy.

True, but hardly the whole truth. Closely scrutinized, the Thai saga does not reflect gloriously on the IMF's role in either preventing or containing the country's tribulation. The Asian crisis would get off to a roaring start in Thailand, but the IMF would get off to a stumbling one.

* * *

The Bank of Thailand, like the central banks of many other nations, is an institution staffed with well-educated bureaucrats who deem themselves above the usual tugs of petty politics. Among the bank's employees in 1997 was Paiboon Kittisrikangwan, a University of Chicago M.B.A. whose job had been notable for its humdrum routine.

Thailand maintained a relatively fixed exchange rate of roughly 25 baht per U.S. dollar, and Paiboon's chief task was to manage the technical aspects of this policy. The dollar-baht rate, though fairly constant, wasn't rigid; it depended on a special formula that included a small weighting for the value of a few other currencies, such as the Japanese yen and German mark. So every morning, Paiboon or one of his colleagues would meet with senior Bank of Thailand officials to make a mathematical calculation of the appropriate baht-dollar rate for the day. If, for example, the formula dictated that the rate for the day should be 25.80 baht per dollar, Paiboon's department would stand ready that day to buy or sell unlimited amounts of U.S. dollars at that rate, plus or minus 0.02 baht. This was a fairly conventional system for an economy with many internationally oriented businesses that had a variety of currency needs at different times. From its reserves, the Bank of Thailand would sell dollars for use by banks and importers, who needed the U.S. currency for foreign transactions; at the same time, it would buy dollars earned by Thailand's exporters, who needed baht to pay their local workers and suppliers.

The system had held for more than a decade, and it was an integral part of the strategy that had helped make Thailand, a country of 66 million, a hotbed of growth. In the decade starting in 1986, the country's gross domestic product expanded at a compound rate of more than 9 percent a year, one of the highest in the world, reaching $182 billion in 1996. Exports grew at an even more phenomenal clip, rising 19 percent a year during the first half of the 1990s. Living standards for millions of Thais improved markedly as they streamed from impoverished villages to booming cities where jobs beckoned at factories and construction sites offering far higher pay than could be had in the countryside. Bangkok still had plenty of poor people crowded into slums and shacks, but a striking feature was its burgeoning middle class, whose members indulged their newfound spending power on automobiles with such gusto that the city gained notoriety for the worst traffic jams in Asia. The media were abuzz with the capital's rapidly proliferating department stores, restaurants, and high-rises, which were often—and deservedly—described as "swank" or "glitzy."

Much of the force driving the growth, at least in its early stages, came from heavy investment in factories by foreign multinationals, especially Japanese auto and electronics companies. For these investors and others, one of Thailand's attractions was the stable value of the baht. The fixed-rate policy reduced their worries about the value of their holdings and the costs of production fluctuating. The fixed exchange rate also made doing business simpler and more predictable for homegrown Thai exporters.

The system was particularly favorable for Thailand in the first half of the 1990s because during much of that time, the dollar was weakening relative to other major currencies, and with the baht linked closely to the dollar, Thai exports became less expensive on world markets. Thai-made clothes, shoes, auto parts, and electronics became better deals vis-à-vis similar products made elsewhere—and orders flooded in.

But the dollar began a powerful rebound in mid-1995, and the fixed-rate system started working inexorably against Thai exports, making prices for those same clothes, shoes, auto parts, and electronics less attractive. Compounding the problem was a downturn in the worldwide market for electronic components, of which the country had become an important manufacturer. In 1996, export growth went flat while imports continued to grow, and Thailand found itself saddled with an uncomfortably high trade deficit, with the current account gap rising to 8 percent of the country's GDP.

Large trade deficits are not necessarily damaging to a country's economy. A country can spend more hard currency than it earns as long as it can "run up a tab" without "maxing out on its credit cards," especially if it is making wise use of the incoming foreign money. In some ways, Thailand's trade deficit was a sign of strength; it meant that foreigners were willing to lend so much money to the country because of their faith in its future.

Indeed, by some traditional indicators, Thailand was not living beyond its means at all. Its government budget was in surplus, and inflation was comfortably below 6 percent. So by itself, the trade gap might not have been cause for undue concern. But Thailand had another problem as well—a financial system infected with a go-go mentality.

Among the system's most visible symbols was Finance One, which was run by Pin Chakkaphak, a graduate of the Wharton School of Business at the University of Pennsylvania, who affected a casual style that included occasional rollerblading jaunts through Bangkok's Lumpini Park. In the mid-1980s, he began building a financial services empire that quickly grew to $4 billion in assets, and he shrugged off worries about the independence with which his subordinates aggressively pursued business. "I don't believe in coordination," he was once quoted as saying.

Pin's firm was the largest of Thailand's finance companies. These companies weren't banks, exactly, but they were similar. They provided about 20 percent of all the credit in the country, and they specialized in lending to Thai consumers and businesses—on easy terms, with low interest rates and little money down—in some of the economy's hottest areas, including autos, property, and purchases of stock on margin. They raised large sums by selling interest-bearing "promissory notes" to the public, and they also borrowed substantial amounts from local banks and foreign investors, much of it in the form of very short-term loans. Thailand's commercial banks, which accounted for more than three times as much credit as the finance companies, were less aggressive, channeling a much higher proportion of their loans into manufacturing, but they also lent sub-

stantial sums to property developers. Overall, loans to private borrowers surged from $89 billion in 1992 to $204 billion in 1996.

Lucrative as this lending binge was when the stock and real estate
markets were soaring, it began to turn sour in 1996 when interest
rates rose, stock prices sank by 35 percent, and the economy slowed
due to sagging exports. Finance companies were saddled with $4.8
billion in margin loans to stock investors, many of which couldn't be
repaid. Most ominous of all was evidence that the property market,
where far more loans had been advanced, was grossly overbuilt.
That year, 600,000 square meters of office space came on the market
in Bangkok, more than half of it unleased, with another 900,000
square meters planned for 1997 and 1.3 million more planned for
1998—and most of the future expansion was already under construction. The most spectacular real estate boondoggle was a $1 bil-
lion-plus development on the city's outskirts called Muang Thong
Thani Estate, which was designed to house hundreds of thousands of
people and included high-rise condominium buildings, townhouses,
retail shops, and a sports complex. Sales were abysmal, and with
weeds growing high amid the unoccupied buildings, the desperate
developer—allegedly a major contributor to the ruling party—furi-
ously lobbied for government deals to move Parliament and part of
the Defense Ministry onto the property.

By early 1997, Thai banks and finance companies were reporting
increases in their nonperforming loans—loans on which payments
were at least six months overdue—which in May reached about 12
percent of all loans outstanding. Disturbing as the figures were, financial analysts in the region reckoned the true amount of dud loans to be
much higher, especially for the finance companies. The skepticism was
justified, for the government's oversight and regulation of the financial sector could generously be described as benevolent, if not lax.

A shocking case had come to light in mid-1996 involving the
Bangkok Bank of Commerce (BBC), the country's ninth-largest
bank, which was run by a former central bank official named
Krikkiat Jalichandra. The revelations showed that the central bank

knew in 1993 that nearly 40 percent of BBC's total assets consisted of nonperforming loans, many of which consisted of loans to Krikkiat's associates, other bank insiders, and influential politicians to finance speculation in real estate and corporate takeovers. Yet the central bank had refrained from taking any serious enforcement actions; although regulators had ordered BBC to shore up its financial position, they had not required it to disclose how deeply its capital had eroded. The head of the central bank, Vijit Supinit, would explain later that he wanted to avoid alarming the public and undermining confidence in the banking system.

Distressing as the BBC scandal was, it was modest compared with the bombshell that dropped on March 3, 1997, when an uncharacteristically grim Pin Chakkaphak stood before reporters and TV cameras to sign an agreement that effectively dissolved his empire by merging Finance One into one of the country's commercial banks, Thai Danu. (In a humiliating turnabout for Pin, the bank was one he had tried to acquire the year before.)

The news that Thailand's "takeover king" had himself been forced into a takeover was an unnerving sign of how bad things were for the finance companies as they struggled to recoup the loans they had made to the erstwhile highflyers of the property and stock booms. Many of the finance companies' depositors and creditors—both foreign and domestic—had assumed that the finance companies were immune to failure, because a number of the companies enjoyed close links with businesses owned by powerful politicians and their families. But now the jaws of financial hell appeared to be closing on Thailand, and scores of finance companies began experiencing heavy withdrawals by jittery depositors.

This was a fine mess Thailand was getting into. But the Thais didn't produce it by themselves. They had plenty of help from their admirers overseas, who provided much of the money that made it all possible.

* * *

Every year, IMF staff missions visit each member country—including the United States and other rich nations—to consult with government policymakers and conduct an assessment of the economy, known as an "Article IV report." In March 1996, an Article IV mission arrived in Bangkok and prepared a report noting that private capital flows into the country in 1995 were equal to 13 percent of gross domestic product. That was a much larger percentage than most other developing countries received at any time during the emerging market craze of the 1990s; and since only a small portion of it consisted of long-term investment in plant and equipment, it signified that Thailand was positively gorging on hot foreign money.

Thailand, like a number of other developing countries, had opened its economy to foreign capital with the encouragement of the IMF and World Bank, but it had needed little if any prodding. The Thai government, in fact, had long harbored dreams of turning Bangkok into a financial hub for the booming Asian region. On April 18, 1990, the Bank of Thailand outlined such a plan, stating that it would soon begin relaxing rules and regulations "to facilitate foreign capital flows and boost foreign investor confidence." The bank knew the plan entailed risks. In a letter to the Finance Ministry, the bank cautioned that lifting controls "must be accompanied by the strengthening of financial institutions to enable foreign investors to develop confidence in such institutions."

Unfortunately, the government never got around to achieving that goal. Instead, in late 1992—with IMF support—it created a new mechanism, called the Bangkok International Banking Facilities (BIBFs), aimed at enhancing Thailand's lure as a banking center. The theory was that banks based in Thailand (both Thai banks and the local branches of foreign banks), spurred by the incentive of special tax breaks, would attract money from around the globe that they could either relend abroad—say, in China or Indonesia—or lend at home in Thailand. The officials who concocted the BIBFs evidently assumed that much of the money would be relent outside of the country; instead, most of it ended up being lent to Thai businesses and converted into baht. The financial appeal, after all, was compelling all around, and the tax breaks only made it sweeter: Since interest rates in Thailand tended to be several percentage points higher than rates in the United States or Japan, foreign lenders got higher interest rates on the money they deposited in Thai banks than they could get at home. The Thai borrowers paid lower interest rates on the dollars they borrowed than they had to pay on regular baht loans. And since the baht was relatively fixed against the dollar, neither lenders nor borrowers had to make bothersome calculations about how much they might lose on a swing in the Thai currency's exchange rate. By 1997, these transactions totaled $56 billion, triple the 1994 level.

It's perfectly healthy for a country to borrow heavily if it uses the money in ways that improve its long-term capacity to generate goods the rest of the world wants, but many of the dollars flowing into Thailand ended up in the hands of companies like Finance One (which borrowed about $600 million from abroad) and the developers of Muang Thong Thani (whose parent company borrowed from foreign banks and sold stock to, among others, Mark Mobius's emerging-markets fund). As the Bank of Thailand would later admit: "It was inevitable, ... [given the] insufficient profitable investment projects to support such a large influx of capital, that much investment moved into the stock and property sectors."

So, were those IMF staffers who traveled to Bangkok in March 1996 worried when they finished examining the Thai economy? Not unduly. Their confidential report, which was submitted to top Thai officials and to the IMF board, said that the amount of short-term debt Thailand had incurred to foreigners was "high by both Thai and regional standards." That debt, and the current account deficit, "pose risks, and action should be taken to reduce them." They offered some advice that looks sensible in retrospect, given the circumstances at the time—namely, for Thailand to give up the fixed rate for the baht and adopt "a greater degree of exchange-rate flexibility."

But the report said nary a word about the overheated property market and precious little about the state of the banking system (though in fairness to the Fund, the Thai authorities refused to share their confidential data on the banks showing the extent of nonperforming loans). Perhaps most important, the report implied that Thailand would do just fine by sticking to its present course. It contained two scenarios—a "baseline" scenario in which the fixed rate for the baht was left in place, and an alternative in which Bangkok took the Fund's advice to adopt a more flexible exchange-rate system. Even under the baseline scenario, economic growth was projected to continue at 7 to 8 percent a year, with moderate inflation, over the five years covered by the forecast.

Of course, at that time, few if any analysts foresaw a systemic crisis in Thailand, and the government hadn't yet taken the steps that would put the economy in truly grave peril. But as 1996 wore on, Thailand's underlying weaknesses began to attract notice from some observers on Wall Street and in London and other financial centers. Even as mutual funds and foreign commercial banks continued to invest blithely in the country, the baht was coming under occasional selling attacks from a less beneficent quarter of the financial world—hedge funds.

"Predatory" is a word often used to describe hedge funds, and many of the industry's titans seem to relish the image. Louis Bacon, head of Moore Capital Management, once hunted water buffalo with a crossbow in Zimbabwe. Paul Tudor Jones II, head of Tudor Investment Corp., also enjoyed stalking game and owned a private hunting preserve on Maryland's eastern shore. Tiger Management's Julian Robertson named his funds after fierce cats—Jaguar, Puma, and Ocelot.

The fame of hedge-fund managers derives from another sort of predation—shooting down currencies and markets. George Soros, the Hungarian refugee who founded the Quantum Fund, earned more than $1 billion in 1992 by betting that Britain, then in recession, couldn't stop the pound from falling outside the limits set under a system designed to keep European currencies relatively sta-

ble against one another. Robertson similarly reaped handsome profits in a 1990 bet that Japanese share prices were due to tumble.

Hedge funds defy simple definition, because they number around
3,000 and engage in a wide variety of investment strategies. One
generality applies: They are open exclusively to the rich, which
means they can escape regulations designed to protect ordinary
investors. As their name implies, they often (though not always)
seek to hedge their bets, and one of the techniques by which they
both speculate and hedge themselves is "short-selling," which
involves making a bet that the price of something will fall. For example, the first hedge fund, which was established in 1949 by a man
named Alfred Winslow Jones, sought to create a balanced portfolio
that would be neutralized against the ups and downs of the general
stock market. Stocks that Jones believed to be cheap, he bought;
stocks he considered overpriced, he sold short. (A short seller bor-
rows stocks—or bonds, currencies, or other financial instruments—
then sells them at the current price, in the expectation that the price
will fall, making it possible to buy them later at a cheaper price and
repay the loan, collecting a tidy profit in the process. In other words,
instead of buying cheap and then selling dear, the short seller first
sells dear, then buys cheap.)

For all their fabled power to drive markets up or down, hedge
funds command much fewer dollars than other market players such
as commercial banks. But given their reputation for canniness,
hedge funds can help ignite or accelerate a run on a currency by betting on its fall, and that is what several of them, including Soros's
firm, were trying to do in late 1996 and early 1997 by going short
against the baht. Destructive though this sort of practice may seem,
hedge-fund managers contend that they provide a healthy disincen-
tive against bad government policies. As Soros wrote in *The Crisis of
Global Capitalism*: "[B]y selling the Thai baht short in January 1997,
the Quantum Funds managed by my investment company sent a
signal that it may be overvalued. Had the authorities responded, the
adjustment would have occurred sooner and it would have been less

painful. As it is, the authorities resisted and when the break came it was catastrophic."

Back in Washington, the IMF was watching the attacks on the baht with a mounting sense of alarm. Stung by accusations that it had failed to anticipate the Mexican peso crisis in 1994, the Fund had been beefing up its capacity to detect and head off crises. It equipped economists' offices with monitors showing up-to-the-minute market developments (the IMF building had been deplorably short on such equipment prior to Mexico), and staffers were expected to maintain much more regular contact with finance ministries and central banks during periods of market turbulence. The Fund created a website that displayed a vast array of figures on countries' key financial indicators, and member governments were strongly exhorted to provide timely data, so that financial markets could base their judgments on accurate information rather than rumor. Thailand was shaping up as a key test of the Fund's early-warning capabilities, and on January 31, 1997, a day after a particularly intense amount of baht short-selling, the Fund went to a stage of high alert, transmitting a letter signed by Camdessus to Finance Minister Amnuay Viravan.

A letter from the IMF's managing director in such circumstances is intended to convey a degree of great concern and galvanize the country's authorities to act before they lose control of the situation. The Fund believed the Thais should swallow their pride as soon as possible and substantially loosen the exchange-rate system for the baht. By trying to keep the baht at the fixed level of 25 per dollar, the Thais risked running out of the dollars held in the central bank's reserves, should too many baht-sellers come demanding greenbacks. Moreover, lowering the baht's value would cause imports to decline and exports to rise, thus reducing the trade deficit and making it less necessary for Thailand to run up a tab. In his letter, Camdessus referred to the recent spate of short-selling by hedge funds and gave this advice: "In the present circumstances, provided that policies succeed in calming markets in the next few days, I would not recom-

mend an immediate change in exchange-rate policy. However, I
urge you to move quickly and decisively to reform the present system, taking into account the need for greater flexibility."

To underline the urgency of the message, Stan Fischer sent a letter to Amnuay shortly thereafter conveying a similar warning, and
in March, the advice was reiterated by an IMF mission visiting Thailand to prepare the 1997 Article IV report. "We continue to believe
that the introduction of a more flexible exchange-rate arrangement
is a policy priority," the mission said in its confidential report to the
Thai authorities. "During our discussion you have indicated that you
intend to introduce greater exchange-rate flexibility at the appropriate time; we encourage you to do so promptly." The mission chief,
David Robinson, "was of a strong opinion that without [a devalua-
tion], the risk of the damage to Thailand was very high," according
to a report by the Nukul Commission, an official Thai panel that later
investigated the government's handling of the crisis, and Camdessus
also "pleaded for a baht devaluation" in a phone call with Rerngchai
Marakanond, the central bank governor.

The advice went unheeded, which highlights one of the fundamental paradoxes about the IMF. The Fund has immense power to
compel governments to accept its remedies when they seek its aid.
Not only can the IMF extend or withhold loans; its approval of a program for a country also confers a sort of "Good Housekeeping Seal"
signaling its economic endorsement for the World Bank, other foreign aid donors, and private investors and lenders to again put in
money. The Fund's refusal to provide the seal can doom a country to
a virtual cutoff of foreign aid and hard currency.

But in nations that aren't seeking its help, the IMF feels obliged
to tread lightly. Even when Fund economists grow concerned about
a country's economic shortcomings, they deliver their bluntest
warnings secretly to government authorities, and they couch their
public advice in extremely diplomatic language rather than "blow
the whistle." The approach is partly because they want to avoid
unnerving markets and igniting the very crisis they're trying to pre-

vent; in some cases, they're also concerned about arousing the wrath of powerful member nations.

This practice helps account for the IMF's ineffectiveness at preventing crises, and in Asia, the crisis-prevention system suffered from yet another problem—the lack of conviction among the staff that the countries' vulnerabilities were genuinely serious. When surveillance teams would express worries to officials of a country in the region, "They'd be politely told 'Go away,' and the country would grow seven percent," a former IMF economist recalled. "The teams would go back the next year and tell the country again there was a problem, and they'd be told 'Go away' again, and then the country would grow by eight percent. True, there were all these warnings given to the countries in letters and so forth. But in terms of the dialogue with these countries, we ratcheted down the concerns. They seemed to be surviving."

In a similar vein, another IMF staffer remembered the words Stan Fischer scrawled on a briefing paper for a Fund mission that was visiting South Korea in 1995 to prepare that country's Article IV report: "It's hard to argue with success."

The man the IMF couldn't convince to devalue the baht was an avid stamp collector, who had written books and articles about stamps under the pen name "Winnie the Pooh" because, as he once explained to a Bangkok newspaper, his nickname in Thai is Pooh, and his American friends called him Winnie.

His real name is Chaiyawat Wibulswasdi, and he was deputy governor of the Bank of Thailand, a position to which he had risen in 1995 after two decades at the central bank. Though he was the bank's second in command, he was, like Stan Fischer, the intellectual leader of his institution, especially in the realm of currency issues, where the central bank effectively exercised control over policy. A graduate of Williams College with a Ph.D. from MIT, the intense, bespectacled Chaiyawat was known at the central bank as a perfectionist who insisted on well-reasoned, neatly presented reports from his subordinates. He tended to be aloof, although he often became quite animated when asked about stamps.

Chaiyawat understood the IMF's case for a devaluation, but he disagreed with it strongly, as did many of his Bank of Thailand colleagues. For starters, they questioned whether a devaluation would hold for long, because hedge funds and other speculators would probably take the move as a sign of weakness—evidence that the government lacked the resolve to keep the baht from falling even further. "The issue was, would you find yourself in a situation where the baht keeps depreciating uncontrollably?" one central bank official recalled. "If you devalue the baht from 25 [baht per dollar] to 28, would you be able to hold it at that level? Would speculators be satisfied with the baht at 28? Would they be satisfied at 30? If they attack again, what would you do then?"

Furthermore, once the baht started to fall, its decline would call into question the solvency of the numerous Thai financial institutions and companies that had borrowed dollars from abroad. So Chaiyawat's strategy was to hold the line on the exchange rate and buy time in the hopes that the government could fix the country's underlying problems.

In the IMF's view, the Bank of Thailand was committing classic errors in currency policy. Many a government has learned the folly of hanging on to an unviable exchange rate until the bitter end. But the IMF's efforts to talk the Thais out of this approach were, in retrospect, misguided.

In a visit to Bangkok on May 22, 1997, Fischer and a couple of other IMF officials urged the Thais to devalue the baht by 10 to 15 percent and widen the "band" within which the baht was allowed to move. Chaiyawat objected that Mexico had tried a similar controlled devaluation a couple of years earlier—and failed to keep the peso from falling precipitously. The visitors from the Fund, however, were concerned that allowing the baht to float freely might produce even worse results, because no one could be sure where the currency would stabilize. A letter from Camdessus also urged the band-widening approach.

The IMF was advising Bangkok to adopt policies that the Fund itself would subsequently brand as foolish. A couple of years after this episode, the Fund would adopt the gospel that it is almost always futile for developing countries to ward off assaults on their currencies with band-widening and other halfway measures. Said Fischer when he was asked about the counsel he gave Thailand in May 1997: "It's very hard to know how to advise a country on how to get out of [a fixed exchange rate]. More and more, we just say, 'Let it go.' We're much more aware of how devastating the capital flows can be. What did the Europeans do [when a crisis hit the continent's currencies] in 1993? They broadened their band, and it worked. Well, that was sort of our thinking [in Thailand]. Now you see that we have these emerging-market countries, with devaluations of 50 to 70 percent. So in a country under attack, we're less inclined to think a devaluation of 15 percent plus a band-widening will do any good."

The IMF's influence with the Thais in May 1997 was weak, in any event. Worse, the Thais were holding back vital information. In meetings at the Bank of Thailand, Fischer asked for one key piece of data that the Fund would need if it were to come to Bangkok's aid—namely, the full details concerning how much hard currency the central bank held. The governor, Rerngchai Marakanond, declined to answer but said he would think about it. When the same question was put to Chaiyawat, he promised to call the IMF team at the airport after getting permission from Rerngchai to release the data. True to his word, Chaiyawat called, but he said the governor had refused to allow the disclosure.

The Fund knew Thailand's predicament was bad—but not how truly awful it was.

Thailand's revered late-nineteenth-century monarch Chula-longkorn—known to Americans as the Crown Prince in *The King and l*—built his children a small, elegant riverside pavilion, which later became part of the Bank of Thailand's complex of buildings. There, in the last week of June 1997, Rerngchai received an important visitor—Thanong Bidaya, who had just been appointed finance minister on June 21.

A few days earlier, Thanong had been in Hong Kong on vacation with his wife, enjoying a respite from his responsibilities as chief executive of a major commercial bank. But an urgent call came from Prime Minister Chavalit Yongchaiyudh, making an offer he couldn't refuse—the Finance Ministry portfolio, which had just become vacant. A novice to government, Thanong spent his first couple of days in office attending a cabinet meeting and a parliamentary session and delving into the details of the government's pending budget proposal. But now he wanted to find out how solid the country's financial position was, and he asked Rerngchai essentially the same question Fischer had posed a few weeks earlier: What was the exact status of the central bank's reserves?

Unlike Fischer, Thanong was in a position to demand an answer. It surpassed his worst suspicions: Of the more than $30 billion that the Bank of Thailand publicly claimed to hold in reserves of dollars, yen, and other hard currencies, only a couple of billion dollars was readily available for defending the value of the baht. The rest had been committed for future delivery in a series of complicated transactions during a pitched battle to fend off the hedge funds a few weeks earlier. Thanong managed to remain cool, but said he would have to go to the prime minister for a major decision on what to do about the country's fixed exchange-rate policy.

The information Thanong learned that day was dynamite. The Bank of Thailand had embarked on one of the most audacious currency defenses in history, a desperate maneuver in which the central bank nearly emptied its financial war chest and hoped that nobody else would figure it out.

One of the central bank's chief battlefield tacticians was Paiboon Kittisrikangwan, the young technocrat whose job of managing the baht's fixed exchange rate had once been so humdrum. He and his colleagues had started off in early 1997 reasonably well armed, with $38 billion in reserves of dollars and other hard currencies. That amount was many times more than any individual hedge fund or other speculator would be willing to gamble against the baht. So the Bank of Thailand appeared to be in a position to buy plenty of baht at the official rate of 25 baht per dollar from anyone betting on its fall—and by showing its determination to maintain a stable exchange rate, it hoped to discourage its tormentors. But throughout spring 1997, speculation against the baht intensified, reaching a crescendo in the second week of May, with the attackers including Soros's Quantum Fund, other hedge funds, and a host of traders at U.S. financial institutions such as J. P. Morgan & Co. and Goldman, Sachs and Co.

A central bank can defend a currency in several ways. Usually the most effective is to raise interest rates. A higher interest rate on, say, Thai government bonds or Thai bank deposits would increase their appeal to investors—who must buy baht in order to invest in them. But in spring 1997, the Bank of Thailand had already lifted borrowing costs and was reluctant to go much further; the economy was slowing, and many finance companies were scrambling to avert bankruptcy.

Another currency-defense method is to intervene in the foreign exchange markets, to pump up demand for the currency. In the Bank of Thailand's case, this would mean using its reserves of dollars to buy baht. The Bank of Thailand did a substantial amount of such buying, because under the fixed-rate system for the baht, it was obliged to exchange one dollar for every 25 baht that someone wanted to sell.

But the central bank's officials didn't want to rely on this sort of intervention exclusively. For one thing, buying baht reduced the amount of the Thai currency circulating in the nation's economy, which had the same effect as jacking up interest rates. For another, selling dollars from reserves risked inciting the speculators to redouble their efforts. Once the likes of Soros, Morgan, and Goldman saw that the Bank of Thailand's reserves were shrinking, they would gain confidence that the day of reckoning for the baht was nearing.

So Paiboon and his colleagues used other techniques to mitigate and disguise the effects of their baht-buying and dollar-selling. Much of it involved the "swap" market, where participants can buy or sell one currency for another with a promise to trade the currencies back after a certain number of weeks or months. It is not necessary to understand the intricacies of this market to comprehend the essence of what Paiboon did. He obtained dollars in the swap markets, thereby replenishing the central bank's reserves, and in the same transactions he unloaded baht, thereby replenishing the amount of baht circulating in the Thai economy. Problems solved! But there was a catch—because in each of these swap transactions, the central bank was entering into commitments to reverse the transaction a few months later.

The beauty was that the Bank of Thailand didn't have to disclose the commitments, so its published figures indicated that it still had ample dollars in the till. The downside was that the more this practice continued, the fewer dollars the central bank actually had that were readily available to defend the baht, because so much of its dollar stockpile was already committed to these future transactions. (The same was true of another of the central bank's stratagems for propping up the baht, which involved using the "forward" market, where it contracted to sell dollars a certain number of weeks or months in the future.) The long-shot hope was that the speculators would eventually give up, and the central bank could quietly and gradually put its finances in order.

The Bank of Thailand deployed enormous sums using these tactics, especially during the second week in May—throwing $4 billion into the market one day, $6 billion on another. Yet the hedge funds relentlessly pursued the short-selling attack. "The market is not afraid," Paiboon's department concluded on May 13.

May 14, 1997, was "an unforgettable day" for the top management of the Bank of Thailand, according to the Nukul Commission Report, which quoted former head Rerngchai as recalling: "Everyone panicked, and some even cried." On that day, the central bank threw $10 billion into the fray, using various markets, without beating back the speculators.

Only a handful of officials knew the dreadful secret—that once the official reserve figure was adjusted to reflect the dollars committed in the swap market, the Bank of Thailand was nearly out of hard currency. Rumors were swirling that the reserves were well below the official figure, but even senior government policymakers were denied access to the data by bank officials. "We said, 'You have to tell us!'" recalled one cabinet minister who was a member of a panel with oversight responsibility for some of the funds used in the baht defense. "They [Bank of Thailand officials] said, 'Legally, we don't.'"

The Bank of Thailand's obsession with secrecy was understandable. A leak of the information about the reserves would be akin to showing a weak hand to an opponent in a poker game. And the Bank of Thailand's hand was getting very weak indeed.

The central bank had one weapon left in its arsenal. On May 15, it deployed that weapon. Reversing its policy of liberalizing the Thai financial market, the Bank of Thailand ordered all twenty-nine local and foreign banks in Thailand to stop lending baht to anyone outside the country. The baht would cease flowing outside of Thailand unless there were a genuine, trade-related reason such as payment for imports.

The move inflicted acute pain on the hedge funds, to the tune of $400 million to $500 million in losses. Now it was virtually impossible for anyone to short the baht, since going short required borrowing the Thai currency. Traders in New York, London, and other financial capitals who had already sold baht short scrambled madly for the baht they needed to repay loans they had already borrowed. The interest rate they had to pay on their borrowed baht zoomed to triple-digit annualized levels, then to 1,000 percent, 1,500 percent, and even beyond. At a press conference, Chaiyawat declared sternly that speculators "have to pay the price." Stanley Druckenmiller, Soros's chief lieutenant, would later admit: "They kicked our butt."

The selling pressure on the baht eased in the following weeks, prompting some market commentators to conclude that the Bank of Thailand had triumphed. Prime Minister Chavalit called the central bank and promised to treat the staff to a victory party. But the celebrations proved premature. Thailand may have thwarted the foreign speculators, but an even bigger source of potential baht-selling lurked within its own borders.

On June 19, 1997, Finance Minister Amnuay, a vocal champion of the fixed exchange rate, resigned in a dispute over tax policy, triggering new worries about a baht devaluation. Suddenly, the floodgates opened anew. Hedge funds were no longer the main problem. Now it was Thai banks and corporations that were selling baht en masse, in a mad rush to acquire the billions of dollars they needed to pay short-term debts that were falling due soon. Their foreign creditors, who had once lent money so willingly, were demanding immediate repayment as their loans matured, and they were refusing to extend the loans further. Few of the Thai borrowers had bothered to hedge themselves against the possibility of a collapse in the baht (though they could have done so by paying for contracts in the currency markets to obtain dollars at a fixed exchange rate in the future). Their frantic baht-selling and dollar-buying weren't covered by the Bank of Thailand's antispeculator rules, and the central bank held nowhere nearly enough reserves to stem the run.

At a meeting presided over by Chaiyawat on Saturday, June 21, the bank's top policymakers glumly concluded that the fixed-rate system could not survive, and they prepared to let the baht's value float according to market forces. The following week was when Thanong, Amnuay's replacement as finance minister, discovered the true size of the reserves. A plan was hatched to announce the float at the earliest practicable opportunity.

At 4:30 A.M. on July 2, 1997, Bank of Thailand officials began phoning senior executives at commercial banks in Bangkok, telling them to come to a meeting at the central bank in two hours. A flash message announcing the float was transmitted to government news services at 7 A.M., and at 8:30 A.M., the Bank of Thailand broadcast a public-address announcement to its junior employees. At a press conference later that day, Rerngchai said; "I haven't slept for two months. I think that tonight I'll be able to sleep at last."

Still, the true size of the bank's reserves would remain a carefully guarded secret, at least for the time being, even from the IMF. Thai officials feared that if the markets realized how much of their reserves were tied up in swap contracts, selling pressure against the baht would know no bounds.

IMF officials were indignant over the Bank of Thailand's refusal to share the information, which they believed they had a right to know in light of their mandate to help maintain international financial stability. They tried to divine the amount by quietly querying market sources in Southeast Asia, but ended up with a wide range of estimates.

In an episode that still evokes chuckles and eye-rolling among some at the IMF, Chaiyawat finally revealed to Fischer in late July 1997 how much of the central bank's reserves were committed in the swap market—but only on the condition that Fischer not tell anyone else at the Fund.

The riverside pavilion built for King Chulalongkorn's children is informally known as the "Fish House" because of the aquatic inhabitants of the Chao Phraya river that throng to the area nearby. Visitors may entertain themselves by standing on a veranda jutting over the river and tossing pieces of bread, furnished by Bank of Thailand employees, attracting fish that reach several feet in length. This building served as the main site of the negotiations between top Thai economic policymakers and the IMF in the summer 1997 crisis, and fish-feeding proved to be a frequent pastime for Fund negotiators. When disagreements erupted requiring the Thais to consult among themselves, Fund economists were ushered to the veranda and given loaves of bread. It soon became clear that the two sides would have many disputes, prompting Hubert Neiss, who led the IMF mission, to observe to his colleagues, "We're going to need a lot of loaves."

Neiss's mission got off to a jarring start when it arrived on July 29. The officials who were presumed to be their main interlocutors in the negotiations (Chatu Mongol Sonakul, the chief bureaucrat at the Finance Ministry, and Bank of Thailand Governor Rerngchai) resigned only hours after the mission arrived. Thus the team generally sat around idle for three or four days.

The chilly reception from the Thais bespoke their ambivalence about accepting IMF support. In the days following the floating of the baht on July 2, Prime Minister Chavalit first sent emissaries to Japan and China to secretly request bilateral loans of hard currency, but they were refused. (In Japan's case, one reason was that the Thais would not disclose information about the swaps.) "The prime minister was stunned and depressed," recalled a cabinet minister who was with him when the news came. "He kept saying, 'Then we have no choice [but to invite the IMF] . . . are you sure the conditions will be okay?'" The Thais' misgivings were not assuaged by what they heard at the first meeting with Neiss.

Standard economic theory holds that when a country's economy appears to be headed into a slump, the proper policy is to pump up government spending and reduce taxes, thereby putting more money in people's pockets to cushion the effect of joblessness, and to cut interest rates, thereby stimulating borrowing and spending by consumers and businesses. But in the opening session with the Thais, Neiss made it clear that the IMF would require Bangkok to embrace a different policy: austerity. "The program," Neiss intoned, "is based on the restoration of confidence, which is based on tight monetary and tight fiscal policy." His words stunned the Thai negotiators, who felt that on budget and tax matters in particular, they were certainly not guilty of profligacy.

The IMF demanded, as a condition for its loan, that the Thai government take several measures aimed at producing a substantial budget surplus, including increasing the value-added tax (similar to a national sales tax) from 7 percent to 10 percent. Altogether, the IMF's conditions required Bangkok to raise taxes and cut spending by an amount equal to 3 percent of GDP. To put that in perspective for Americans, it's as if the United States raised taxes or cut government benefits by $300 billion in one year, or over $1,000 for every man, woman, and child in the country.

Negotiations were heated. Finance Minister Thanong, who came to the Fish House in the evenings after long budget sessions in Parliament, stormed at one point that "the time will come when no IMF staffer will be able to come to Asia." To his consternation, the IMF was insisting on an increase in bus fares, because of the costly government subsidy that kept fares low. The two sides finally agreed that only fares on air-conditioned buses would rise; fares on buses without air conditioning would remain subsidized, since the non-air-conditioned buses tended to serve the poorest riders. But the Fund held its ground on the basic issue and won agreement on a major tightening of fiscal policy, including the rise in the value-added tax.

Given the lessons taught at the IMF Institute, it's easy to understand the rationale behind the Fund's approach: Thailand was running a very large current account deficit, so it was living beyond its means; and since it had maxed out on its credit cards, the time had come to bring imports down into balance with exports. That, in turn, required dampening overall demand, and the most effective way to do that was to force the government to tighten its belt, even if the government's belt was already pretty tight.

But the IMF failed to grasp that Thailand needed no help whatsoever in reducing demand, because its economy was heading off a cliff. In 1998, Thai GDP would shrink by a whopping 10 percent, the result being that the country was "living within its means" far more quickly—and brutally—than the IMF had anticipated or anyone had wanted. Imports would shrivel so fast that the country ran a current account *surplus* of 12.7 percent of GDP in 1998. In other words, the last thing the Thai economy needed was higher taxes and budgetary stringency, since all that would accomplish was the intensification of an unexpectedly deep recession.

Officially, the IMF program for Thailand was based on a forecast of 3.5 percent growth in the nation's economy in 1998, though that figure was essentially a "political" forecast aimed at boosting public confidence. "In our hearts, we thought growth would be about zero," said one member of the Bangkok mission. But either way, the Fund was grossly miscalculating the depth of Thailand's woes. "We certainly didn't expect growth to be as negative as it turned out to be," the mission member said.

To its credit, the IMF changed its stance a few months later as the severity of the recession became more apparent, urging Thailand to adopt stimulative fiscal policies rather than contractionary ones. Staffers recalled, with some awe and relief, that Fischer told them the Thais should be encouraged to run a budget deficit—"something I never thought I'd hear us say," as one IMF economist put it. But not until March 1998 did Bangkok adopt the new expansive approach, and even then it was a while before government agencies reversed their budget-cutting modes. Meanwhile, unemployment rose to 6 percent in 1998, triple the level of two years earlier, and wages in urban areas shrank an average of 8 percent.

Why did the IMF miscalculate so badly? The main reason is that Thailand had another major problem that set its crisis well apart from the garden-variety current account type—the disastrous condition of its financial system.

The Fund was by no means oblivious to the existence of the banking system's troubles. Shortly after the mission arrived in Bangkok in late July 1997, its members were shocked to learn of the extraordinary lengths to which the Thai authorities had been going to keep the system from collapsing. To compensate for the steady withdrawals of deposits from the finance companies and some of the weakest banks, the Bank of Thailand had secretly lent about $20 billion to those institutions, at below-market interest rates. Those loans, moreover, went well beyond the standard central bank practice of serving as lender of last resort to healthy financial institutions that are suffering runs by panicky depositors. Although a central bank is supposed to lend freely to banks that are temporarily short of cash, the Bank of Thailand was propping up insolvent institutions that were so loss-ridden that they weren't genuinely viable as business concerns.

The Fund insisted that Thailand must stop the secret bailouts and start shutting down insolvent finance companies. But that triggered another battle—this one within the Fund itself, pitting the mission in Bangkok against much of the top brass at headquarters. At one point, the dispute became so tense that Carl-Johan Lindgren, who headed the IMF's financial-sector mission to Thailand, got calls in the middle of the night from colleagues in Washington, warning him that he was endangering his career because of the position he was taking.

Lindgren, a Finnish national, contended that closing insolvent finance companies meant that the Thais also had to take drastic steps to protect the surviving financial institutions. Otherwise depositors would become worried that more institutions might be closed, and total panic might set in, toppling bank after bank. Accordingly, he supported a plan for the Thai government to guarantee the claims of all depositors and creditors in all banks and finance companies. But this idea outraged many top Fund officials back at headquarters, who saw a guarantee as a giveaway to rich investors who had gambled on high-yielding deposits in shaky financial institutions. It would be a classic case of "moral hazard," they argued, in which people who had behaved recklessly would be saved from the consequences of their actions, thereby encouraging more recklessness in the future. But Lindgren persisted, asserting that although the guarantee might be costly, the cost of not issuing one would likely be much higher.

The debate with headquarters "was awful," said Anoop Singh, a deputy director of the Asia and Pacific Department, who as the number two member of the IMF mission was siding with Lindgren. "We had never worked this fast in any country. Deposits were flying out the doors of the banks. Over three nights, we were up in Bangkok, arguing with Washington."

Lindgren won. On August 5, the Thais suspended the operations of a total of fifty-eight finance companies, and a comprehensive guarantee was issued on deposits and liabilities of financial institutions. That decision now appears wise and farsighted, for the bank runs gradually abated.

The Fund's decision may have kept Thailand's banking system from utter collapse, but the closure of the finance companies left many small and medium-sized businesses without their traditional sources of funding. As a result, the financial system's woes crushed the country's economy far more severely than the Fund anticipated. Furthermore, and perhaps the worst of the fallout, the IMF program for Thailand misfired in achieving one of its overriding aims, which was to halt the slide of the baht.

"How does it feel to be a superpower?" Timothy Geithner, the U.S. Treasury's assistant secretary for international affairs, whispered jokingly to Eisuke Sakakibara, the Japanese vice minister of finance.

The occasion was an August 11 conference in Tokyo of donor countries and organizations that were planning to back up the IMF in its rescue of Thailand. Negotiations between the Fund and the Thai authorities were almost finished, and the Fund was planning to lend Bangkok $4 billion. Although that amount was 500 percent of Thailand's IMF quota, and thus considerably more than the country would qualify to receive under normal circumstances, by many standards it looked insufficient. It paled in comparison with the $50 billion package marshaled for Mexico in 1995, which included a $17 billion loan from the Fund and a $20 billion line of credit from the United States.

Japan now was eager to show that it could take care of its Asian neighbors the same way Washington had helped its most important neighbor in Latin America. So Tokyo was matching the IMF's loan with a $4 billion loan of its own, and other Asian nations were prepared to kick in another $6 billion. Including loans from the World Bank and the Asian Development Bank, the Thai package would total $17.2 billion.

The lighthearted comment by Geithner masked an underlying tension between the United States and Japan that would intensify in the coming weeks as the crisis unfolded. Washington wasn't adding a penny to the Thai package, and Treasury officials weren't enthusiastic about the support Japan and the other Asians were contributing, in part because they feared the IMF's central role in crisis-fighting might be undermined. Although the U.S. State Department and National Security Council had argued that Washington should make a modest contribution for the purpose of shoring up its image as a leader in the region, Treasury Secretary Bob Rubin had prevailed in rejecting the idea. He was concerned about a backlash in Congress, which during the Mexican episode had harshly criticized the Treasury's use of a special pool of money to extend credit to Mexico.

Accordingly, Japan stepped into the void left by the absence of U.S. support, happily seizing the opportunity to demonstrate regional leadership. The Thais were appreciative, according to Sakakibara, who recalled Finance Minister Thanong telling him at the Tokyo conference: "What happened today will surely find mention in the history of Thailand." Unfortunately, events a few days later deflated the high hopes the Asians had held at the Tokyo meeting.

The IMF board approved the Thai program on August 20, and at a press briefing the next day, Camdessus said: "I strongly believe that, yes, we have seen the worst of the crisis, provided this program is implemented with perseverance which should match the boldness of the measures which have been adopted. . . . I have no reason to doubt it, and as a matter of fact, I have been reassured by the reaction of the markets today." But within hours of his remarks, the baht was plummeting to an all-time low of about 34 to the dollar, and the Thai currency weakened even further in September, trading between 35 and 37 to the dollar. The reason for the bailout's miserable debut was that the Bank of Thailand had finally disclosed its big secret—the $23 billion in swap commitments it had made back in May. Suddenly, market experts realized the full extent of the depletion in Thailand's reserves, and they questioned whether the IMF-led rescue was sufficient to provide the hard currency the country needed to meet its pending foreign obligations. Referring to the newly disclosed swap commitments, Donald Hanna, the Asian regional economist at Goldman, Sachs and Co., told *The Asian Wall Street Journal*: "I think everybody was surprised. That's a lot of money."

The Thais hadn't made the revelation voluntarily. On the contrary, they were forced to do so as a condition of getting the IMF loan. In a series of phone calls to Fischer, Chaiyawat had raised strenuous objections, arguing that the disclosure would undermine confidence and provide valuable information to the hedge funds. But he had been forced to yield in the face of Fischer's explanation that there was no way the loan could be made otherwise, because of the adamant position of Rubin and Summers, who were insisting that the Thais, having brought on the crisis with their untransparent policies, now needed to show they were coming clean.

Many at the IMF, including some of its most highly placed officials, were sympathetic to the Thais' position and disagreed with Treasury on the necessity of making the disclosure immediately. It would be better to wait for a few weeks, some argued—say, until October. After all, the point of the whole package was to stop the panicky flight of capital, improve investor psychology, and restore confidence. Why subvert its purpose? "I do not dispute the general case for transparency in policymaking," said Gregory Taylor, the executive director for Australia and several other countries, in a confidential statement delivered at the August 20 IMF board meeting that approved the Thai program. "The practical issue here, however, is that Thailand has to traverse an extremely delicate transition from the current unsustainable position to a more secure one. During this transition, it is vital that market confidence be maintained. . . . Publishing the figures [about the swap commitments] may well trigger a reassessment by the market." But the United States was too powerful to be denied. "We felt we could not perpetuate a deception," Summers said. "I have no regrets about this, nor have I heard any regrets from anyone in this [Treasury] building."

It is impossible to say whether allowing Bangkok to keep its secret a while longer might have made a significant difference to the success of the IMF's program for Thailand. The program went even further off track in October and November 1997, with the baht plummeting to 56 per dollar in early 1998. The reasons were numerous; prime among them was the reluctance of Prime Minister Chavalit's government to take tough action by closing sick finance companies. Only after Chavalit's resignation in November 1997 did Thailand begin to demonstrate a genuine determination to clean up its financial system. And only after that determination became evident did the baht begin to recover, as investors perceived the government's willingness to pursue IMF-mandated reforms. A logical conclusion—though it can't be deduced with certainty—is that the baht would have weakened significantly regardless of the disclosure about the reserves.

Still, within the IMF, many felt that the U.S. Treasury badly misread the likely reaction of the markets to the disclosure. In a 1999 report on the effectiveness of the rescues it launched in Asia, IMF staffers wrote that the disclosure "was intended as a step toward greater transparency . . . but its timing weakened the impact on confidence that the announcement of the program could have had."

One of the IMF's virtues is that it is not above issuing mea culpas as long as a decent interval has passed. The report just cited is one example. In an effort to learn from its mistakes, the Fund studies its performance in handling problems and crises, and it often publishes the results. Its less than stellar job in Thailand has come in for a fair share of self-criticism in IMF publications.

Not that the IMF concedes, as some of its harshest critics allege, that it bears responsibility for all the misery that Thailand endured in 1997 and 1998. The country was surely destined to undergo a painful recession once its financial bubble had burst and billions of dollars in capital had fled the country. One can only imagine how much more pain Thailand would have suffered, and how much faster and further the baht would have fallen, if the Fund had not mobilized a sizable package of loans.

But the IMF admits that its excessive demands for fiscal tightening exacerbated Thailand's recession. In the 1999 report assessing the Fund's performance in Asia, the authors, a group of staffers from the Policy Development and Review Department, took their colleagues to task for underestimating the weakness of the Thai economy, a mistake that was repeated in Indonesia and Korea. The report noted that even though most independent economists had also failed to foresee the severity of the downturns, the Fund couldn't hide behind that excuse: "The fact that the IMF's projections were close to the consensus is not very reassuring . . . as the IMF should in principle have been able to anticipate events better than outside observers." The report's authors also wondered why the designers of the Fund's Asia programs had failed to learn from what had happened in Mexico: "The experience of Mexico, where growth declined from four percent in 1994 to minus six percent in 1995, might have led one to predict a much sharper slowdown in growth than was initially projected in the Asian crisis countries."

As for the IMF's crisis-prevention efforts, another report, authored by a panel of independent experts, leveled perhaps the most damning criticism—that instead of encouraging the Thais and other emerging markets to welcome foreign capital, the Fund should have been raising red flags about the risks. Citing the IMF staff's confidential recommendations to the Thai government in 1996, the panel faulted these because the staff "failed to caution on the dangers associated with the then prevailing system, which tended to encourage short-term foreign borrowing." The panel summed up the issue as it applied in Asia in general: "On the issue of capital account liberalization . . . the Fund's advice certainly did not help prevent the crisis."

The poor initial results of the Thai rescue cast a shadow over the Fund's prowess at halting crises at a time when more trouble was brewing. The Fund and the rest of the High Command would soon have bigger fish to fry—though few could envision it at the time.

After working until dawn one night in mid-August dictating a report to Washington on the program they had just agreed upon with the Thais, Hubert Neiss and Anoop Singh held a small celebration. "I went out and bought a little silver box for one of the secretaries, who had stayed up an entire night with no sleep," Singh said. "The box was inscribed 'Thai SBA [stand-by agreement], August 14, 1997.' Hubert opened a bottle of champagne. We did that partly to thank her, but in the back of our minds was that this was a unique event. And we would not have to repeat it."

· 4 ·

MALIGNANCY

On October 8, 1997, less than two months after approval of the Thai rescue, an IMF mission was dispatched to negotiate a program, including a substantial loan, for Indonesia. Jakarta was seeking the Fund's assistance because the Indonesian rupiah, which had initially held firm following the floating of the baht in July, was starting to drop sharply. This time, though, the nature of the IMF's support was supposed to be different from the sort that Thailand had received. The watchword for the Jakarta-bound mission was "precautionary."

Leading the mission was Bijan Aghevli, age fifty-two, deputy director of the Asia and Pacific Department. A native of Iran who came to the United States by himself at eighteen, graduated from Colorado State University, and earned a Ph.D. from Brown University, Aghevli had thick, swept-back hair and would be nicknamed "Radovan Karadzic" by Indonesian journalists because of his passing resemblance to the leader of the Bosnian Serbs. Jovial and charming at times, willful and arrogant at others, he had spent his entire career at the IMF (except for a two-year teaching stint at the London School of Economics), earning a steady stream of promotions on the strength of his keen intellect.

Aghevli had not been to Indonesia for years, and the mission he led was organized in considerable haste. Instead of the usual procedure, in which a team going into the field drafts a briefing paper and circulates it around the Fund for several weeks before finalizing its marching orders, Aghevli's mission had to throw its plan together in about three days, almost immediately after the Indonesian government signaled that it wanted a program; the Fund wanted to respond promptly to the Indonesians' request.

The lack of preparation didn't seem to be a major problem, in view of the precautionary character of the program that the IMF envisioned. As far as the Fund was concerned, the purpose of coming to Indonesia's aid was to convince financial market players that they were wrong to bet against the country, and that the fall in the rupiah was grossly excessive. Unlike Thailand, Indonesia had a comfortably large $20 billion in hard-currency reserves. In both public and private comments, IMF officials went out of their way to praise Indonesia's fundamental strengths and to suggest that the government of President Suharto needed to take only a few more steps beyond what it had already done, which included cutting spending on expensive infrastructure projects. "We're in a strange situation where it's not entirely clear why the markets have been so disturbed lately, and we see ourselves as supporting what the Indonesians want to do," a senior IMF official said at the time. "I think of this as sort of giving a seal of approval to their policies, and maybe providing them with some extra resources to show the markets that their policies really make sense."

Accordingly, the mission left Washington with the expectation of negotiating a program with the Suharto government that would contain relatively modest reforms. Part of the Fund's thinking was that it wanted to score a success to counteract the black eye it was getting in Thailand. "The desire was, let's have a show of [financial] force up front, for a responsible regime," recalled Michael Mussa, who was the IMF's chief economist. "Indonesia didn't have a particularly big current account deficit. It was just a question of confidence. And there was a lot of political support for the regime. The

U.S. had been a strong supporter, and the Germans and Japanese too. So there was a lot of sentiment for the idea that we should stop the crisis at Indonesia. There was also the perception that the program in Thailand wasn't working. The impact on confidence had been negative. We said, we didn't want to do *that* again."

All the more stupefying, therefore, was the disintegration that would befall the Indonesian economy over the next several months, amid a highly charged showdown in which the IMF was demanding that Suharto dismantle long-criticized monopolies and subsidies benefiting his children and cronies. The rupiah would sink to the rate of 15,000 per dollar in January 1998, 85 percent below the summer 1997 level of 2,400 per dollar. As the rupiah fell, so would the fortunes of this country of 200 million people—the fourth most populous on earth—whose quarter-century record of solid growth and rising living standards had been one of the developing world's most impressive success stories. Economic output would shrink by more than 14 percent in 1998, a rate of contraction that ranks among the most catastrophic suffered by any country in a single year since the Great Depression of the 1930s. Among Indonesian men who were working in 1997, 15 percent would lose their jobs by mid-1998, and millions of Indonesians would slip back into the poverty they thought they had escaped forever, as median daily wages fell by about 30 percent (adjusted for inflation) in rural areas and 40 percent in urban areas. The economic slump would fuel social unrest that would force Suharto to resign in May 1998, amid bloodshed that would claim over 1,000 lives. The departure of his autocratic regime would pave the way for Indonesia's first truly democratic election in decades and the flowering of free expression. But by mid-2001, the economy was continuing to sputter and the political scene remained chaotic, with violent ethnic and religious strife flaring in parts of the Indonesian archipelago.

The IMF and the U.S. Treasury would pin most of the blame on Suharto when the rupiah cratered in late 1997 and early 1998. They would accuse the seventy-six-year-old Indonesian president of undercutting efforts to restore confidence in his country's economy by breaking promises he had made to prevent his children and cronies from receiving favored treatment. Although Suharto deserved much of the culpability for what happened, misjudgments by the IMF and other elements in the High Command would play no small part. The story is disheartening on many levels. Disputes, philosophical differences, and bureaucratic battles within and between the staffs of the IMF, World Bank, and Asian Development Bank would hamper the efforts to diagnose Indonesia's troubles and mount an effective rescue.

Recrimination and debate continues to rage over who was right. The Indonesian crisis is a tale of error piled atop error, with each side's bad moves—both the Fund's and the Indonesians'—compounding the other's and dragging the country's economy to depths nobody had previously imagined possible.

In many ways, Indonesia's economic management prior to the crisis had been brilliant. Over the course of his thirty-year rule, Suharto had entrusted many important decisions to a group of technocrats, dubbed the "Berkeley Mafia" because several of them had received their economics training at the University of California. The leading technocrat was Widjojo Nitisastro, a soft-spoken professor to whom Suharto had turned in 1966 to devise an economic plan for lifting the country out of its deep impoverishment. They made an unlikely pair—Suharto, an army general who grew up on a farm in Java and was trained in military matters, and Widjojo, an intellectual who held a Ph.D. from Berkeley. But Suharto backed the efforts by Widjojo and his associates to shift Indonesia's economic policies toward the orthodox theories taught at the most prestigious Western universities and think tanks. The Berkeley Mafia dismantled much of the statist economic structure built by Indonesia's former President Sukarno, and imposed tough restraints on government spending and money creation to quell triple-digit inflation. Battling politicians and ministers who favored more nationalistic policies, they pressed Suharto to open the economy to foreign investment and trade and ease up on heavy government regulation. Their approach paved the way for a period of growth that averaged 7 percent a year from 1979 to 1996, with relatively stable prices. Millions of jobs were created as firms set up factories to produce clothing, shoes, toys, furniture, and electronics.

Although powerful rivals and special interests often outmaneuvered Widjojo, who held no official title beyond "economic adviser" after 1983, Suharto invariably relied on him when the economy hit a rough patch, as it did in the mid-1980s when the price of oil, a key export, collapsed. Widjojo's reputation for honesty was beyond reproach; he drove a modest car and worked in a seldom-redecorated office. Indeed, one reason IMF officials cited for their confidence in October 1997 was the announcement that Suharto was asking the seventy-year-old Widjojo for a return engagement to shepherd the government's response to the rupiah crisis.

Among Indonesia's most enthusiastic boosters—and surely its most influential—was the World Bank, which had lent about $25 billion to Jakarta during Suharto's three decades of rule and treated the country as a poster child of economic development. As it stated in a 1994 report on Indonesia, "The evidence clearly suggests that the poor have been doing well, and far better than in most other developing countries."

Journalists visiting Jakarta around that time could hear a compelling, up-by-the-bootstraps story about Indonesia from the World Bank's resident representative, Dennis de Tray. An Ohio native in his early fifties, the aristocratic-looking de Tray had spent much of his youth in Mexico City and Nairobi—his father was a veterinarian who researched animal diseases such as African swine fever—and when he returned to the United States to attend Cornell University, he was determined to settle in small-town U.S.A. and never venture abroad again. But after getting his Ph.D. in economics from the University of Chicago and spending twelve years at a think tank, he joined the World Bank's research department in 1983 and moved to the operations side a few years later. In the Indonesia job, which he got in 1994, his passion for the country's successful development was manifest.

De Tray and his chief economist, James Hanson, touted figures charting the country's progress that were downright inspiring. Indonesia's per capita income in 1970 had been two-thirds that of India and Nigeria, but by 1996 it had risen to $1,080, four and a half times that of Nigeria and triple that of India. Life expectancy at birth in Indonesia was sixty-five by the mid-1990s, compared with forty-nine a quarter century earlier; the adult illiteracy rate had fallen to 16 percent from 43 percent; infant mortality had shrunk to 49 per 1,000 live births from 114.

Visitors who wanted to see what all this meant for average Indonesians could trek to villages in the lush, hilly interior of Java, where residents would recount the ways their lives had improved. For example, whereas two or three decades before, most of their meals had consisted of corn or cassava (a starchy root with little nutritive value), now they were eating rice three times a day with vegetables, tofu, and often some egg or meat. Whereas they formerly lit their homes with kerosene lamps, now many homes had electricity, at least on Java, the country's most populous island. Whereas a family used to count itself lucky in the 1960s and early 1970s to own a bicycle, now many of them had motorcycles. Whereas it had been difficult to bring products to market or get to school on the bumpy dirt road running through the village, now that road was paved.

The country's most glaring problem was "KKN"—*korupsi, kolusi, dan nepotisme* (corruption, collusion, and nepotism)—and the World Bank had a long list of complaints about sweetheart deals in an array of sectors that were enriching people with presidential connections. De Tray, Hanson, and other World Bank staffers in Jakarta prided themselves in hectoring the government about these issues, writing about them in official reports, and encouraging the Western press to publish exposés.

By the 1990s, the Suharto family's avarice was so pervasive that almost any foreign firm investing in, say, a power plant or phone system or petrochemical factory had to hand over lucrative partnership rights to one presidential relative or another to grease the project's way through the country's bureaucracy. Bambang Trihatmodjo, Suharto's second-eldest son, headed the Bimantara Group, which was granted a television license, special concessions for overseas distribution of the state petroleum company's products, and high tariffs to protect a $2.2 billion plastics plant built jointly with German and Japanese multinationals. Suharto's daughters also became multimillionaires thanks to government-granted contracts to build power plants and toll roads, among other ventures.

As for the president's youngest son, Hutomo Mandala Putra, (nicknamed "Tommy"), he enjoyed the benefits of a monopoly on the distribution of cloves, which are used in the scented *kretek* cigarettes favored by most Southeast Asian smokers. And in early 1996, Tommy's conglomerate was awarded perhaps the most outlandish concession of all—the rights to build a "national car," called the Timor. Not only was the venture exempted from luxury taxes and allowed to undercut its rivals by importing cars and parts duty-free from its Korean partner, Kia Motors, but it also received $700 million in bank loans, reportedly thanks to jawboning by powerful officials. The cars bombed with consumers, which led to government ministries and local corporations being subjected to pressure to buy fleets of them.

This is not to say that a blood relationship to the president was required for favored treatment. Some of the largest fortunes in Indonesia belonged to tycoons with whom Suharto had long engaged in mutual back-scratching. Most of these men were of Chinese origin; the ethnic Chinese, who accounted for about 4 percent of Indonesia's population, owned a proportion of the country's wealth variously estimated at 40 percent to 70 percent, a source of considerable tension in Indonesian society. The richest was Liem Sioe Liong, who as a supplier to the Indonesian military in the 1940s and 1950s helped advance Suharto's career. Among the more than 200 companies that Liem controlled were Indofood, the world's biggest instant-noodle maker, and Bogasari Flour Mills, the world's biggest flour-milling operation, which held de facto monopolies in the Indonesian market thanks to government contracts, special import licenses, and subsidies. Liem's empire also profited from government concessions allowing him to carve out immense palm oil and timber plantations on the island of Sumatra.

Still, as repugnant as such dealings were in a country where tens of millions of people were barely surviving on a couple of dollars a day, many experts—including those at the World Bank—regarded the KKN problem as wasteful and lamentable but not fundamentally threatening to the economy's well-being. In this view, Suharto was no kleptocrat on the order of, say, Mobutu Sese Seko of Zaire or Ferdinand Marcos of the Philippines, whose crony-dominated rule had bled their countries dry. Thus the World Bank, while repeatedly admonishing the regime to address "governance" issues, maintained an upbeat outlook. Its president, James Wolfensohn, set the tone by traveling to Jakarta in May 1996 and delivering a cheery speech after having rejected a more cautious draft written by his staff. "If you weigh up the odds," Wolfensohn said, "I have a very strong sense that this country is addressing the right issues to ensure sustainable economic growth."

But that assessment overlooked a source of rot in the Indonesian economy—related to KKN, but not exactly the same issue—that posed a grave danger to the country's economic stability. The rot was in the banking system. Ironically, the keenest insights into the depths of this problem would come from within the World Bank itself.

Headquartered across 19th Street from the IMF, the World Bank is a considerably bigger organization, with a staff of 10,000. It lends about $20 billion a year to the governments of developing countries, and its loans have financed many heartwarmingly successful projects that help spur economic development and reduce poverty. A program it funded in southern India, for example, is credited with rescuing several million children from malnutrition simply by educating mothers there about how to nourish their offspring properly with readily available foods. World Bank loans helped spread high-yield farming techniques in India, Pakistan, and Indonesia—the "Green Revolution"—that turned those countries into dynamic agricultural producers. In Indonesia, the World Bank helped finance an expansion of the country's electric power system that increased the capacity of the state power company fivefold between 1978 and 1992, and it also funded a number of other widely praised projects that provided school textbooks, teacher training, and family planning services. The family planning project helped cut the country's fertility rate by 60 percent.

The World Bank has some serious weaknesses, however, chief among them its bureaucratic, inward nature, which has led it to fund projects without proper understanding of the gritty realities in the countries concerned. A notorious example was a road through the Brazilian rainforest it financed in the early 1980s, which attracted hordes of migrants who razed a vast area and spread deadly epidemics among the aboriginals. Another, related problem at the institution is a syndrome called the "approval culture," or "lending culture." For decades, staffers have gained stature and promotions by drawing up impressive-looking loan proposals at headquarters, pushing them through the elaborate approval process, shoveling the money out the door, and moving on to the next loan. Sometimes the resulting projects succeed in the real world; sometimes they don't. Despite strenuous efforts by World Bank presidents (including Wolfensohn) to eradicate the syndrome, it has persisted, and all too often success in the loan development process has mattered more to staffers' career advancement than the impact of the projects on client countries.

In August 1996, a team of about a half dozen World Bank experts on banking and financial issues traveled to Jakarta to evaluate a

three-year-old project seemingly imbued with the classic character-
istics of the approval culture. The mission was led by Lily Chu, who
had recently come to the World Bank by way of Harvard, where she
earned an M.B.A. and Ph.D. in finance.

The project the Chu mission came to assess, like all Bank endeav-
ors, was based on good intentions. It was supposed to help improve
management and operations at Indonesia's seven giant state-owned
banks, which accounted for nearly half the assets in the banking system and needed assistance—lots of it—in cleaning up their acts. They
were a large, weak link in a banking sector that had grown explosively—the number of banks increased from 108 in 1988 to 232 in
1993—following a deregulation of the industry. The underlying
soundness of the state-owned institutions was highly questionable
because the Suharto regime had influenced their lending decisions
over the years to funnel loans to favored businesses. So in 1993, the
World Bank had begun a project, funded at about $300 million, to
provide the state-owned banks with an incentive to bring their operations up to proper commercial banking standards. If the state-
owned banks put their finances on a stronger footing by decreasing
the amount of nonperforming loans on their books, they would get
an extra dollop of capital investment from the government.

But as the Chu mission found, the project was producing the
opposite impact from its intended one. Offering the state-owned
banks the dollop of capital encouraged the banks' managers to cook
their books so that it looked as if their balance sheets were improving. Instead of causing the state-owned banks to strengthen their
financial conditions, the project was causing matters to worsen.

More upsetting was what the World Bankers found as they dug
deeper into the files of the state-owned banks. The team discovered
case after case of the worst sort of banking practices imaginable.
Bank officers were granting fresh loans to borrowers that had
stopped paying interest on old loans. The documentation on many
loans was grossly irregular, suggesting that the loans were being
granted either out of complete incompetence or outright dishonesty.

For example, borrowers' accounting statements would show after-tax profits to be greater than pre-tax profits, or they would show profits exactly the same, to the rupiah, one year to the next. Loans were being granted in excess of projects' costs, evidently to cover "facilitation fees" that were being kicked back to the loan officers and their superiors.

Altogether, bad loans at the participating state banks exceeded 25 percent, and worse, the team concluded that supervisors and examiners at Bank Indonesia, the country's central bank, were turning a blind eye to these sorts of activities—presumably in exchange for bribes. Foreign and domestic bankers confided horror stories and market scuttlebutt about Bank Indonesia examiners taking under-the-table handouts.

Upon returning to Washington, the Chu team delivered a disturbing report about what it had found: The state banks were so riddled with bad loans, and the World Bank's project so counterproductive, that the remainder of the project should be canceled. Their recommendation sparked fierce opposition from some of the World Bank's old Indonesia hands, who argued that although the project might be badly flawed, canceling it would only damage the World Bank's relationship with the Indonesian government and eliminate its sole means of exerting leverage over the country's financial authorities on the banking sector's problems. Accusations flew on both sides: As far as Chu's critics were concerned, she was a typically bright but overly brash, inexperienced interloper with little understanding of how Indonesia worked. As far as Chu's partisans were concerned, her critics had "gone native" and lacked a deep grasp of banking issues. Chu lost; the project was not canceled until the Indonesian crisis was well under way.

Amid the bureaucratic firefight, the World Bank missed a broader lesson from the Chu mission: Indonesia's entire banking sector (not just the state-owned banks) was in such serious trouble that an intensive World Bank effort was needed to help the government address the weaknesses and prepare for a potential crisis in the system. A report by an internal watchdog unit would later castigate the World Bank's management for having "downplayed the evidence" in the Chu mission's findings and for having neglected to take aggressive action. This criticism, to be sure, not only was based on 20-20 hindsight but also failed to take account of the likelihood that the Indonesian government would have rejected whatever reform initiatives the World Bank proposed. Still, at least some blame for the lack of effort should have gone to what the watchdog unit called a "halo effect" that existed in relations between the World Bank and Indonesia because of the "enthusiasm associated with [the country's] rapid growth."

The "halo effect" was evident in the World Bank's strong institutional disinclination to believe Indonesia was seriously imperiled. On July 10, 1997, a week after the devaluation of the Thai baht, World Bank staffers submitted a report to the board, dismissing worries that Indonesia would succumb to the sort of currency sell-off that had just hit Thailand. "Indonesia is relatively well equipped to cope with any spillover effects of such a [regional] crisis because of the wide exchange-rate bands, increasing and high levels of foreign exchange reserves, a fiscal surplus, and initial steps being taken by Bank Indonesia to strengthen the financial sector," the report said. In a section about the "low-case scenario" of a "severe economic shock," the report said the probability was "currently very low" and conceivable only if a host of political, social, financial, regional, and trade risks "all materializ[ed] at once."

De Tray, the World Bank's resident representative in Jakarta, presented and defended the report at the Board meeting, although he didn't write it. "I have rarely been more wrong," he said later.

Sudradjad Djiwandono, the governor of Bank Indonesia, was the toast of Asia's financial elite in early summer 1997—indeed, he was one reason for the rosy report de Tray presented to the World Bank's Board. Here was a central banker who seemed to know the sensible way to respond when sellers of his country's currency flooded into the market. The drop in the baht was driving currencies downward all over Southeast Asia amid concerns that Thailand's neighbors were afflicted with similar problems, but Sudradjad adopted an approach that set him apart. Whereas his counterparts at the Bank of Thailand had run out of hard currency battling to defend the baht at a set value, Sudradjad, a mild-mannered, fifty-nine-year-old Boston University Ph.D., took a flexible stance while Bank Indonesia still had its $20 billion stash of reserves. As if casually shrugging that his pride wasn't on the line, he widened the range by which the rupiah could fluctuate against the dollar, to a 12 percent potential swing, on July 11. The results were hailed in a Jakarta-datelined *Wall Street Journal* article published July 21, which called the rupiah "an island in the storm"—its 3.4 percent decline in value that month was much smaller than those of neighboring countries' currencies—and credited Indonesia's "deft macroeconomic management." Bank Indonesia's policies were "a model for developing economies," Neal Saker, the regional economist for Socgen-Crosby Securities in Singapore, told the *Journal*, which added, "Most economists think the pressure on the rupiah is a temporary spillover from the regional sell-off, and that the rupiah will rebound as the speculation subsides."

But in late July and early August, the rupiah's drop accelerated as gloom in the region intensified, and after consulting with Suharto, Sudradjad decided the time had come for a bolder move. Much of the Indonesian business and financial establishment was on hand August 14 for the start of a two-day conference, entitled "A Commitment to Progress," commemorating the twentieth anniversary of the establishment of the country's capital markets. The president delivered a speech earlier than scheduled, apparently so that he could leave before Sudradjad spoke, because the central banker had a bombshell to drop: After more than a decade of keeping the rupiah closely linked to the dollar, a pillar of Indonesian economic stability, the central bank was scrapping the policy and would allow the rupiah to float.

Sudradjad's reasoning, which was widely endorsed then (by the IMF, among others) and seems sound now, was that it was crazy to squander the nation's reserves of hard currency fighting a losing battle to keep the rupiah tied in any formulaic way to the dollar. But, he recalled, "After my speech, I started already to become more worried, because a lot of Indonesian businessmen and women came up to me, and said, 'Mr. Governor, how could you do this?'"

Like their Thai counterparts, Indonesian corporations had borrowed heavily from foreign lenders, to take advantage of lower interest rates overseas. Whereas it might cost them 18 percent per annum or more to borrow rupiah from an Indonesian bank, they could borrow dollars from foreigners at less than 10 percent and convert the proceeds into the rupiah they needed. It was obviously economical—and, they thought, safe. The rupiah wasn't rigidly fixed against the dollar, but the central bank had kept the currency's rate of decline predictable, about 3 to 5 percent a year. So with the rupiah that Indonesian companies earned on their business transactions, they could repay their foreign loans and still come out ahead.

For foreign financial institutions, too, the deal looked too juicy to pass up, and in the 1990s, Indonesia's capital markets—which had always been fairly open—drew a rising tide of money from abroad, averaging 4 percent of GDP from 1990 to 1996, attracted by the twin appeals of high returns and Southeast Asian dynamism. Some of this money was lent in the form of bank-to-bank loans as in Thailand; much of it also went directly to Indonesian corporations in a complex array of forms including straight bank loans, bonds, and commercial paper.

But as rewarding as this game was for both sides, there was a huge catch: If the rupiah fell sharply, the burden for Indonesian borrowers of repaying their foreign loans would increase dramatically. Sudradjad asked the business executives he spoke with at the conference whether they had taken the prudent step of hedging themselves against a drop in the rupiah by purchasing contracts in the currency markets ensuring that they could obtain dollars at a reasonable rate. "It was shocking to me, because their answer so often was 'Of course not,'" he said.

Shocking was the right word. Nobody—not Bank Indonesia, not the IMF, not the World Bank—seemed to have the faintest idea about what had suddenly become a hugely troubling question: How many dollars would Corporate Indonesia have to obtain in the next few months to pay its foreign creditors what it had borrowed? Official debt statistics were available, of course, and they showed that the Indonesian banks and companies owed about $55 billion to foreigners. But it also mattered a great deal whether the Indonesian firms had gone to the expense of buying hedging contracts to cover themselves against the potential cost of a rupiah decline. Everyone knew that a key factor responsible for the Thai baht's fall was the dash for dollars by Thai companies that had borrowed heavily from overseas and failed to hedge themselves against currency fluctuations. So government officials, brokerage houses, and credit analysts in Jakarta began calling Indonesian corporate executives and marshaling data as fast as they could to determine whether Indonesia was similarly exposed.

The answers weren't comforting. Jakarta brokerage firm reports, which once were full of starry-eyed prognostications about endlessly expanding horizons in the country's rapidly growing market, were suddenly focused on whether Indonesian companies were at risk of being unable to pay off their dollar loans. The investment firm SBC Warburg Dillon Read published an analysis in autumn 1997 that ranked major publicly traded companies according to how much they had borrowed from abroad and what percentage of their debt had been hedged. A few, like H. M. Sampoerna, a maker of clove-scented cigarettes, had paid for full hedges. But many others had followed the example of Indofood, the giant noodle maker controlled by Suharto crony Liem Sioe Liong, which had borrowed $600 million from abroad without bothering to hedge itself at all, according to the report. "The demand for US$ to cover unhedged borrowings has been far greater than first thought by [Bank Indonesia], or by private sector analysts," the report warned. "Market sources suggest that as much as US $30bn could still be waiting to be covered. . . . [T]he implications for the IDR [the rupiah] are clear—and ominous."

In other words, Indonesia was vulnerable to a vicious cycle taking hold in the markets. Any unhedged Indonesian company owing debt to foreigners might feel compelled to scramble for dollars, for fear that if the rupiah fell further, the burden of repaying the debt would increase. And the scrambling for dollars would cause the rupiah to drop, which would induce more scrambling, and so on.

That basic scenario started playing itself out beginning in September 1997, as people and companies became increasingly aware of the danger and began trimming their exposure to a further drop in the rupiah. Some of these were foreign banks pulling short-term credit lines to Indonesian borrowers. Additional participants in rupiah-selling, though virtually impossible to trace, were members of Indonesia's ethnic Chinese minority, who were starting to worry about the prospect of social unrest and wanted to move some money abroad. The Chinese had been frequent scapegoats of the Muslim majority, most notably during the bloody tumult of 1965–1966 that eventually brought Suharto to power, as dramatized in the film *The Year of Living Dangerously*.

A distraught Suharto could not understand what was happening to the rupiah, which had been worth 2,400 per dollar early in the summer but closed below the 3,000 rupiah-per-dollar level on September 2 and dropped to 3,400 on October 1. Though not outspoken on the subject like Malaysian Prime Minister Mahathir Mohamad, who railed publicly about a plot behind the attack on Southeast Asian currencies, Suharto shared Mahathir's suspicions. "Many times he kept asking me, 'What is the role of all these speculators?'" Sudradjad recalled.

It was against this backdrop that Indonesia, once again surprising the markets, turned to the IMF in the first week of October, and the mission led by Bijan Aghevli rushed to Jakarta. Exactly how Suharto was persuaded to invite the Fund, and whether he understood what sorts of demands might be made on him, remain open questions. He was evidently told that the IMF program would be precautionary and that it was needed for confidence purposes. At the same time, several top members of Suharto's economic team were confiding to U.S. and IMF officials that they wanted the Fund to impose a number of reforms they had long favored, and some of these policymakers, notably the passionately upright finance minister, Mar'ie Muhammad, favored an attack on the monopolies and subsidies that had flourished thanks to KKN.

Suharto must have had some basis for believing that the Fund wouldn't be highly confrontational, because the IMF mission started off operating under a similar assumption. Its initial brief suggested that because the program was to be precautionary, the mission should give the benefit of the doubt to Indonesian negotiators, who were likely to be proreform anyway. But in the three weeks that it took to complete the negotiations, the Fund substantially changed course toward demanding extensive anti-KKN conditions from the Indonesians.

The reason for the turnaround was pressure from members of the IMF board representing Western industrial countries. Karin Lissakers, the U.S. representative, was particularly assertive. In addition to hearing from proreform Indonesian technocrats, the Clinton administration was getting an earful from nongovernmental organizations—primarily religious and labor groups, both Indonesian and Western—who wanted to see the IMF's leverage used to attack KKN. Administration officials began to educate themselves on matters such as how BULOG, the state agency responsible for the distribution of many key foodstuffs and raw materials, helped enrich certain Suharto cronies, and they realized that a bailout of Indonesia would be criticized if it appeared to tread too lightly on the problem. Thus they wanted reforms to extend well beyond the typical Fund program, which normally would be confined to fixing macroeconomic problems such as excessive government spending: "The mission went out [to Jakarta] with the usual recipe—tweak a little on monetary policy here and fiscal policy there," Lissakers recalled. "We stepped up the heat, the more we found out about the issues, hearing about these massive subsidies to cronies and family members." The Fund's traditional mandate didn't encompass such matters: "This was clearly pushing the outside of the envelope," she acknowledged.

The one G-7 member that objected to this line of thinking was Japan, whose vice minister of finance for international affairs, Eisuke Sakakibara, flew to Jakarta on October 16 to press the argument that Indonesia's crisis had little to do with crony capitalism and much to do with the vicissitudes of global capital. Sakakibara recalled that he "had a heated discussion" lasting about two hours with mission chief Aghevli, "but Aghevli did not give in. We failed to win concessions from Aghevli even though we threatened that the Japanese government would act on its own if its opinions were ignored."

Aghevli had largely accepted the view that the program should place heavy emphasis on structural reforms. But the pressure from Washington for more concessions from the Indonesians made life difficult for the IMF team in Jakarta, which constantly had to up the ante in the negotiations. Urgent messages to Aghevli's mission were streaming into Jakarta almost daily from Hubert Neiss, who was attending IMF board meetings at which Lissakers and others were urging additional conditions for inclusion in the program. Accordingly, instead of doing what negotiators normally do—start off with a tough position and gradually yield ground—Aghevli and his colleagues kept insisting on more conditions as time went by. Their Indonesian interlocutors generally liked the reforms on substantive grounds, but they were faced with the daunting challenge of obtaining Suharto's assent.

The pressure on the mission to reach a satisfactory deal increased from intense to acute when currencies and share prices all over Asia nose-dived the week of October 20. The strain would take its toll in a variety of ways, not the least of which would be wretched relations between the IMF and its supposed partners in the multilateral development banks.

The Grand Hyatt, Jakarta's premier deluxe hotel, looms over one of the most congested traffic circles in a steamy, smoggy city whose avenues are lined with boxy office towers and grandiose monuments. The IMF mission led by Aghevli stayed there in October 1997, setting up a command center on the exclusive Regency Club floors.

The IMF and the World Bank had started off cordially enough in working to resolve the Indonesian crisis. The Fund, recognizing the World Bank's expertise in financial-sector issues, asked it to send some of its financial specialists along on the mission, and among those dispatched to Jakarta were individuals with knowledge of Indonesia's banking system, including a member of Lily Chu's team who had worked on assessing the ill-starred state-owned bank project. The World Bankers joined the IMF team at the Grand Hyatt.

But once the group was in Jakarta, hopes of cooperation evaporated amid infighting, mistrust, and differences of opinion, not only between the Fund and the Bank but also between the two institutions and the Manila-based Asian Development Bank (ADB), which also sent specialists to Jakarta in preparation for its contribution to the Indonesia bailout. (Like the IMF and World Bank, the ADB is owned by governments.) "The mission from hell," one participant called it.

The World Bankers and the ADB staffers complained bitterly to their colleagues that the Fund was shunting them aside, keeping them in the dark and ignoring their perspectives. IMF staffers often refused to let their World Bank and ADB colleagues see draft versions of the Letter of Intent—the document spelling out the promises the Indonesian government would make in exchange for a loan—asserting that the material was confidential and couldn't be viewed by anyone outside the Fund. Even when the World Bankers themselves wrote memos at the request of the Fund, they were told they couldn't have their own material back because once handed over, the documents became confidential.

Logistical snafus exacerbated tensions. Although the IMF and Washington-based World Bank staffers were ensconced at the Grand Hyatt, their ADB colleagues labored under expense-account guidelines that couldn't accommodate the room rates there, so they had to book into a hotel across the busy traffic circle. That often made it difficult for the ADB team members to learn of key meetings, and as time went on, it was impossible to distinguish which meetings they were intentionally excluded from—and which they were inadvertently not invited to. The antagonism and mutual suspicion grew. To make matters worse, the word-processing software the IMF used was WordPerfect, but the software in the World Bank laptops was Microsoft Word, so the two institutions' computer systems couldn't easily exchange files and documents—a perfect metaphor for their broader breakdown in communications. The World Bank and ADB, meanwhile, battled constantly over which agency would have control over certain issues—with tempers flaring so openly that Indonesia's deputy finance minister, disgusted by the bickering, stormed out of a meeting.

So furious were ADB staffers over their treatment by the IMF that two of the bank's senior officials, Shoji Nishimoto and Paul Dickie, wrote to Hubert Neiss warning that the ADB would go it alone in the future rather than work with the Fund on joint missions. (In fact, the ADB ultimately did just that in Indonesia in late 1997 and early 1998.) "The ADB representatives were not notified of many of the discussions and were not kept informed of the overall progress of negotiations, and comments provided by the ADB participants were ignored," they said in their letter dated November 13. "Furthermore, we have not as yet received any documents pertaining to the Mission. Our experience in this Mission means that we would be very reluctant to participate in any future missions with [the Fund's Monetary and Exchange Affairs Department]."

The Monetary and Exchange Affairs Department (known within the Fund as MAE), which was the focus of many of the complaints by the World Bankers and ADB staffers, had its own mission chief in Jakarta, Reza Vaez-Zadeh, an Iranian national. The department is a small but rapidly growing part of the Fund specializing in financial-sector issues that began expanding in the 1990s in response to mounting concerns about the dangers that weak banking systems posed in many countries. The World Bank staffers from Washington were formally assigned to Vaez-Zadeh's unit and found themselves cut off from much of the central decisionmaking, since all bureaucratic communication had to go through Vaez-Zadeh, in keeping with practice at the hierarchical Fund. All of this was particularly irksome to the World Bankers because they believed their grasp of the situation in the Indonesian banking system—a grasp based on in-depth scrutiny of banks and loan documents—far exceeded that of the Fund's economists. The Fund had sent missions from Vaez-Zadeh's department to Jakarta before to look at the banking sector's problems, but those missions had focused predominantly on Bank Indonesia— talking to government bank regulators and poring over official reports on the health of the banks, gathering evidence that the World Bankers had concluded was of little use and tainted with corruption.

There were other flashpoints as well, in particular between the IMF's main mission from the Asia and Pacific Department, led by Aghevli, and the World Bank's resident representative's office, headed by de Tray. The IMF was clearly in control of the negotiations with the Indonesians, and de Tray's operation was fuming that it wasn't being consulted even though the World Bank was expected to contribute a hefty sum to the package. Part of the problem was that the IMF staffers were working into the wee hours at the Grand Hyatt, communicating with Washington by e-mail or phone, so they could get approval for decisions and receive their orders in the morning. What were they supposed to do, they wondered—invite the World Bank staffers living in Jakarta to spend the night in their hotel rooms writing memos together?

The spats were, in a sense, bureaucratic tempests, typifying the differences among these organizations—one hierarchical and built for speed, the other two diffusely managed and accustomed to long deliberations. But the feuding had a cost. An Indonesian official chided one World Bank staffer: "The patient is dying, and the three doctors are fighting."

For cynics accustomed to seeing well-connected Indonesians receive sacred-cow treatment, the announcement on November 1 of the just-finalized IMF program contained some remarkable news. Sixteen private Indonesian banks were to be closed for lack of solvency, and the list included several whose major shareholders were linked to the Suharto clan. Among them were Bank Andromeda, of which 25 percent was owned by the president's son Bambang; Bank Jakarta, which was owned by Suharto's half-brother Probosutedjo; and Bank Industri, part-owned by Suharto's daughter, Siti Hedijanti Herijadi, and Hashim Djojohadikusumo, her brother-in-law.

The bank closures were the central element in the IMF program, which provided Indonesia with a $33 billion package of loans, including pledges of $10 billion from the Fund, $8 billion from the World Bank and ADB, and $15 billion in backup credit lines from Japan, Singapore, the United States, Australia, and Malaysia, to be made available if needed. Besides shutting the troubled banks, the Indonesian government agreed to a number of structural reforms aimed at curbing the privileges enjoyed by Suharto Inc., including a phaseout of several BULOG import and marketing monopolies, with wheat, soybeans, and garlic becoming immediately open to imports. The cement cartel would be opened to competition by giving up its right to control retail prices, and the chemical industry would lose some of its tariff protection.

Many foreign analysts praised the bank closures in particular as a sign that Indonesia was being forced to change its ways, and in the first few days following the program's announcement, the rupiah rose by about 10 percent, to the 3,200-per-dollar range, though that was thanks largely to a surprise series of interventions to buy up quantities of the Indonesian currency by the Singaporean central bank as well as Bank Indonesia and other Asian central banks.

But toward the end of the first week of November, the reaction to the bank closures took an ominous turn. Anonymous lists of "good banks" and "bad banks" began circulating around Jakarta, often arriving by fax in bank and brokerage firms' offices, purporting to tell which banks were safe from closure in the future and which ones were likely to join the sixteen already shuttered. Before long, a full-fledged run on privately owned banks was under way. Bearing bags and boxes to hold cash, crowds thronged to withdraw their deposits from branches of the giant Bank Central Asia, owned by Suharto's pal Liem Sioe Liong, in the second week of November. Many depositors rushed their money from private banks to state-owned banks, figuring the state-owned ones, whatever their problems, were at least backed by the government; others showed up with bags of rupiah to deposit at the Jakarta branches of Citibank and other foreign institutions. By the end of November, privately owned Indonesian banks had lost 12 percent of their rupiah deposits and 20 percent of their foreign currency deposits, raising the alarming scenario of a series of cascading failures in which the inability of one or two banks to pay their obligations would cause the others to default, eventually leading to a systemwide collapse that would paralyze the nation's economy.

Sudradjad, who as central bank governor had resisted many of the bank closures, watched with a mixture of agony and frustration as the bank runs accelerated. "From the foreign market's point of view, the policy [of closing the sixteen banks] was credible because even banks owned by people close to the Suharto family were being closed," he said. "But domestically, people said, 'Wow, if more banks are weak, and even banks belonging to people in the president's family are being closed, then there must be others next.' It may sound crazy, but that's what I encountered. You're damned if you do, and damned if you don't."

The problem was not just that banks had been closed; it was the way they were closed. The IMF believed, understandably, that it had to close at least some banks, since the markets knew the banking system was riddled with bad loans, and permitting the sickest ones to continue to operate would have sent a terrible message. But shuttering banks can be done artfully, or it can be done ham-handedly.

When done artfully, bank closures work like successful cancer surgery, in which the surgeon removes all the malignancy from the patient's body at once and leaves nothing but healthy tissue. The key, though, is to be convincing about how healthy the remaining tissue is. If the public suspects that some malignancy remains—in other words, that some rotten banks have survived—closures may lead to bank runs because depositors fear more closures are on the way.

Franklin Delano Roosevelt pulled it off in his first fireside chat on March 12, 1933, after widespread bank runs had led him to order all U.S. banks shut for ten days while auditors went in to inspect the books. Although 7,000 banks were shut permanently, Roosevelt persuaded the public through the sheer power of his rhetoric that the surviving banks were sound. "I can assure you that it is safer to keep your money in a reopened bank than under the mattress," he declared. "Let us unite in banishing fear. . . . It is your problem no less than mine. Together we cannot fail."

Of course, this kind of trick is much easier in an advanced country like the United States than in a developing country like Indonesia, because in Indonesia the bank regulators' reputations for competence and honesty are open to serious question. Closing banks in such a country—especially one with a history of few closures, and especially one where more closures appear likely—requires strong measures to maintain public faith in the banking system. That may mean providing a government guarantee on all deposits, at least temporarily. Indeed, the Fund had endorsed just such a policy in Thailand, but many on the Fund staff and on the IMF board felt uncomfortable about supporting expensive taxpayer-backed guarantees on bank deposits, and they wanted to draw the line against them in Indonesia. On this score, the IMF's policy in Indonesia "now appears to have been ill-advised," as the Fund's 1999 staff report evaluating the Asian programs later acknowledged. This is about as close as the Fund gets to saying, "We blew it."

When the sixteen banks were closed, the Indonesian government—with IMF advice and support—announced that it would guarantee all deposits up to 20 million rupiah (about $5,000), the idea being to protect small depositors, who were far more numerous than rich ones (though they held a minority of the deposit base). That guarantee proved woefully inadequate to induce confidence in the system.

A major part of the problem was the widespread impression that the Fund hadn't persuaded the Indonesians to close all the banks that would need to be closed eventually. After all, the sixteen shuttered banks accounted for less than 3 percent of all deposits in the system, and they had been selected in a hectic process involving untidy compromises with the Indonesians, recalled Jack Boorman, director of the IMF's Policy Development and Review Department. "We were getting faxes on a minute-by-minute basis, with people poring over information from the banks," he said. "And one of the elements that drove that final decision was that we were looking at the owners of the banks. How far could we go? How many toes could we step on? How many could the governor of the central bank afford to step on? We needed to be as sure of our facts in the case of each bank as we could be under the rather chaotic circumstances. That's why it stopped at sixteen."

A related problem was Suharto's fault, not the Fund's. The President's son Bambang, aggrieved over the closing of his Bank Andromeda, was allowed to take over a smaller bank, Bank Alfa, in late November. He brazenly announced that he was transferring the original bank's assets there so that, "in short, Andromeda is only changing its name." He admitted that his bank had violated regulatory guidelines by lending $75 million to its owners and their affiliated businesses, including a petrochemical venture he was involved in, but he offered the excuse that 90 percent of Indonesian banks had done the same sort of thing.

Plainly, much malignant tissue remained in the banking system. Because the IMF was thwarted from excising all of it, the Fund should have anticipated runs by depositors fearful that their banks would be closed. But when the runs started, "there was not a clear and decisive strategy to deal with that problem," as Mussa delicately put it, because "it was not well thought out in advance of the program, by us or by them." At this point, blunders began to compound themselves.

One fairly obvious solution might have been adopted by the IMF and the Indonesians to restore confidence in the banking system; in fact, Mussa and some others at the IMF were hoping to see it happen at the time. A full government guarantee could have been announced on all bank deposits, and simultaneously, another batch of sick banks could have been closed, eliminating as much of the malignancy as possible.

But the opportunity for such a deal slipped away as Indonesia's crisis deepened in the second half of November and December 1997. First, Suharto became quite ill in early December after returning from an arduous overseas trip. The precise nature of his ailment was never disclosed, but his cancellation of public appearances for ten days terrified the markets, which drove the rupiah below 4,000 per dollar on December 5 and 5,000 per dollar on December 12. Under his iron-fisted rule, Suharto had arrogated so many of the levers of power to himself that investors became worried his death or incapacity would leave the country rudderless and exposed to clashes among feuding groups.

Another factor preventing a deal on the banking problem was that relations between the Fund and the Indonesian government were strained thanks in part to the shenanigans involving Bambang and the reopening of his bank. Sudradjad and his reformist colleagues had fallen into Suharto's disfavor; they were in no position to push for more bank closures or a 100 percent deposit guarantee, an idea Sudradjad strongly disliked anyway.

Just as important, the IMF itself was badly split. The Monetary and Exchange Affairs Department was vehemently opposed to a comprehensive deposit guarantee. After all, recklessly run Indonesian banks had been offering astronomical interest rates to lure deposits from rich Indonesians; using taxpayer money to guarantee such deposits would be validating—and encouraging—the most irresponsible sort of financial behavior. Moreover, in some cases, bank owners had been paying themselves and their cronies high interest rates on their own deposits—hardly the sort of people who seemed deserving of being protected against loss.

Here again was the problem of moral hazard, a classic trade-off that often confronts financial-crisis fighters—restoring stability now versus punishing the guilty and discouraging imprudence later. Gross injustices would be committed, and lousy precedents would be set, by guaranteeing deposits and letting some slimy bankers and depositors off the hook for their misdeeds. But as Mussa put it, "If the alternative is what we've seen happen to the Indonesian economy, that's *real* hazard."

That argument was advanced by others in the Fund, including Joshua Felman, a senior member of the mission to Jakarta, who became emotional over the issue, accusing the moral-hazard zealots of "using 200 million people as guinea pigs for your theories." Felman, colleagues recalled, got into pitched battles with Vaez-Zadeh and others in MAE. He conceded their point that a blanket guarantee of deposits would have costly long-run consequences. But he didn't accept their analysis of the Indonesian banking system as being essentially healthy and having only a few "bad apples" that needed to be removed from the barrel and tossed out. Indonesia's banks faced a "systemic" crisis, he argued, because the decay in the system was much deeper than the official central bank figures indicated—deep enough, anyway, that the richest and best-connected Indonesians knew better than to trust the banks with their money in the absence of full government backing.

Felman couldn't prove his point. He was not a banking expert, and he lacked the data to support his case. The World Bank's financial experts, who had good insight into the parlous state of the banking system, were attached to Vaez-Zadeh's team and not interacting with Felman, who belonged to the Asia and Pacific Department.

With the Fund divided, the issue was left to fester in December, when the crisis in Korea diverted much of the time and energy of the IMF and the rest of the High Command. Meanwhile, Indonesia's banking crisis was morphing into yet another problem.

In his office at Bank Indonesia, Sudradjad was sprawled in his chair, his arms outflung like Christ on the cross, when he was visited by an IMF mission member in late autumn of 1997. "There is this Catholic maniac on one side, and a Muslim maniac on the other side, and I am coming apart!" the central banker complained. The Catholic maniac to whom he referred was Camdessus, who represented the demands of the IMF hierarchy for high interest rates; the Muslim maniac was Suharto, who was ordering the central bank to keep cheap credit flowing to Indonesia's cash-starved banks and companies.

The dilemma was indeed acute. The bank runs, sufficiently serious by themselves for the state of confidence in the economy, were contributing to a mess in the money supply. Because so many depositors were withdrawing their money, Sudradjad was facing demands from commercial banks for emergency loans of rupiah. Making such emergency loans, as noted previously, is part of a central bank's function as lender of last resort in a crisis. But with so much rupiah being pumped into the banks, the money supply began to rise explosively—so much so that by the end of 1997, Bank Indonesia's currency department, which was having trouble increasing production of rupiah banknotes, resorted to releasing some plastic 50,000 rupiah notes manufactured a couple of years before as souvenirs for the country's celebration of its fiftieth anniversary of independence. (The notes failed to sell well as souvenirs but then served a function as legal tender.)

The money supply might seem an odd issue to focus on in a history of the Indonesian crisis, which in the popular mind was all about Suharto and his cronies. But monetary policy proved an important factor in Indonesia's downfall, for much of the ballooning quantity of rupiah wound up being sold for dollars on the open market and shipped to Singapore, Hong Kong, and other offshore locations by Indonesians desperate to get their money out of the country.

Who was engaging in this capital flight? That is impossible to answer precisely. But again, some of it can surely be ascribed to members of the ethnic Chinese minority, whose worries were understandably growing as Suharto's grip on power began to look ever more tenuous. Loose money wasn't what scared them, but it helped accelerate their exodus from the rupiah.

Within the IMF, arguments flared over the monetary issue in late 1997. Alarms were sounded by the "hawks," who favored using tight credit and high interest rates to combat currency crises; they included the Policy Development and Review Department and executive directors from the United States and some European countries. The rapidly growing supply of rupiah, the hawks feared, would surely lead to a further erosion in the value of the Indonesian currency against the dollar. Moreover, they asserted, Indonesian interest rates had to be kept high to maintain incentives for people to keep money invested in the country. Yes, Bank Indonesia had to supply cash to banks suffering runs, but the only way it could save the rupiah, in the hawks' view, was to drastically tighten the overall supply of credit, even if that meant interest rates would rise to stratospheric levels—100 percent or more—at least temporarily, until the situation settled down. "Don't give me this crap that [with interest rates so high] no Indonesian company can afford to buy a machine," one hawk recalled arguing. "You're in the middle of a currency crisis. What's important is, do you as an investor want to hold the rupiah until next Monday morning?"

Aghevli, Felman, and others in the Asia and Pacific Department disagreed. Interest rates were already punishingly high, they contended, pointing to the fact that some Indonesian banks, in their desperation for funds, were offering 75 percent annual rates. In response to the counterargument that they were looking at the wrong interest rates—state and foreign banks, which were flush with deposits, were offering between 15 percent and 30 percent— they retorted that pushing rates a lot higher wouldn't be credible to the markets, because with the banking system on the verge of collapse, everyone knew that the banks couldn't afford to pay such a high cost for their funds for more than a few days. "They would say, 'Monetary policy is fine,'" Karin Lissakers recalled, referring to Aghevli and his allies. "We would say, 'No, it's not.' We would sometimes have three or four meetings a week. It was never a question of dogma. It was a genuine intellectual debate."

Who won? The "Muslim maniac" did, in the sense that Sudradjad continued injecting more cash into the banks as the runs continued and the crisis atmosphere intensified. Figures would later show that the rupiah streaming from the central bank into the banking system in December and January was equal to almost 10 percent of Indonesia's GDP, and the amount of currency circulating in the economy rose by one-third. (Subsequent investigations would show further that large central bank loans were improperly extended to banks and companies with political clout.) Aghevli, bowing to the wishes of his superiors, pressed for a tighter credit policy—to little effect.

The massive emission of money fanned the flames of the crisis and increased downward pressure on the rupiah throughout December. But the underlying problem was the bank runs, which were still unaddressed. Since confidence in the banking system had all but vanished, no good monetary policy choice existed—as even some among the Fund's interest-rate hawks would later acknowledge. "Bank Indonesia was caught in a virtually impossible situation," Mussa said, because as bad as it was to let the money supply explode, "if it had allowed the banking system to fail, that would have been an economic calamity."

An internal U.S. Treasury memo written in early December summed up the unpropitious outlook for Indonesia, which was symbolized by a haze that had settled over much of Southeast Asia following an outbreak of fires in Borneo, Sumatra, and other islands. Suharto, the memo said, was "frustrated by the absence of any apparent improvement in Indonesia's situation following the creation of the IMF program," and it added: "Fears of social unrest are growing; ethnic Chinese . . . fear backlash if times get rough, memories of massacres of 1965 remain strong. Financial crisis is compounded by drought, prospect of food shortages and uncontained forest fires. The political atmosphere, like the sky above Jakarta, is dark."

The atmosphere was also dark 3,000 miles to the north, where another Asian economy was coming unglued.

· 5 ·

SLEEPLESS IN SEOUL

In a televised address on November 22, 1997, Kim Young Sam, the president of South Korea, warned his nation to prepare for "bone-carving pain." His words were well chosen. Korean financial markets were sliding into chaos, and the government had just announced it would seek an IMF bailout. The following year, recession would shrink gross domestic product by 7 percent, wages for the average Korean worker would drop by 10 percent after adjustment for inflation, and the jobless rate—in a country where lifetime employment was the norm—would climb to nearly 9 percent.

Five weeks before Kim's somber TV speech, a team of IMF staffers had just put the finishing touches on a confidential report that envisioned an entirely different scenario for the Korean economy. The document, dated October 15, 1997, minimized the chances that Korea would become engulfed by the sort of financial turmoil that had beset Thailand over the summer and had spread to Indonesia and Malaysia. The mission had been sent to Seoul to prepare Korea's Article IV report, the annual assessment of the country's economy. But the October staff report, instead of being submitted to the Executive Board in accord with the usual practice, was quietly stashed in the Fund's files, because its findings were so quickly overtaken by events. The report stated in its opening section:

> The situation in Korea is quite different to that in Southeast Asia, and our assessment is that the weaknesses in the financial sector are manageable if dealt with promptly. While there are obvious risks, macroeconomic fundamentals remain strong and the current account deficit is narrowing toward a more comfortable range. External financing is certainly tight but we have confidence in the authorities' ability to prudently manage the situation.

The report was not entirely rosy. Its authors fretted that "Korea's vulnerability will remain high unless significant enhancements are made in the efficiency and soundness of the financial system." They took note of problems plaguing Korean banks, which had been jolted earlier in the year by several major corporate bankruptcies. Nonperforming loans were considerably greater than official estimates, according to the report, which reckoned that as of mid-1997 about 6 percent of all loans fell in that category—"a cause for concern, but not alarm"—and urged the Korean government to promptly pass financial reform legislation.

The IMF mission forecast growth of 6–7 percent for the Korean economy in 1998. "We have confidence in Korea's ability to deal with the current difficulties," the report concluded, "and believe that they provide an excellent opportunity for galvanizing broad based public support for the development of a more efficient and sound financial system."

Clueless as it was, the IMF report provides a useful reminder that in stark contrast with the Thai case, where threats to stability had been apparent for many months before the collapse of the baht, the Korean crash struck like a thunderbolt. More than any of the crises elsewhere, Korea's would show how swiftly and unexpectedly a nation's economy—even one that has dazzled the world with its industrial prowess—can fall victim to the mercurialness of the Electronic Herd.

The first attempt to rescue South Korea (see Chapter 1) was launched over the Thanksgiving weekend of 1997. It was based on what U.S. Treasury officials liked to call the "Colin Powell doctrine." This was a reference to the former U.S. general's belief, made famous during the Gulf War, in the value of amassing an overwhelming force capable of defeating an opposing army quickly and decisively. It involved mobilizing a huge loan package in the hopes of quelling a financial market panic. Another key element in this IMF rescue effort was that the program went far beyond the typical austerity-oriented measures and aimed to fundamentally restructure Korea's economic institutions, in particular the cozy links among the nation's giant conglomerates, its banks, and the government.

But even as the High Command sought to forge a financial imitation of Operation Desert Storm, little did it realize how abruptly it would be playing the role of the Iraqi Republican Guard, routed and beating a hasty retreat.

Lest excessively harsh judgment be rendered on the IMF's upbeat Article IV report, it is worth bearing in mind that South Korea has a history of repeatedly confounding the doomsayers.

At the end of the Korean War in 1953, the population of South Korea consisted mainly of peasants living in thatched-roof huts. International food aid in the form of milk powder was handed out every few days in schools, and nobody saw much promise in the war-torn economy. Experts wrote off South Korea in the early 1960s as having one of the dimmest economic futures in East Asia; Burma and the Philippines looked as if they would be the region's stars. Cambridge University economist Joan Robinson hailed the industrial development of Communist North Korea as a miracle and predicted it would economically overwhelm the "degenerating" South. Even in the 1970s and 1980s, when South Korean industrialization was leaping ahead, skeptics questioned whether the country could vault into the ranks of advanced economies. Although Korean manufacturers had shown they could move up the value-added chain from wigs, toys, and clothing to steel, petrochemicals, and shipbuilding, that did not augur that they could take on the mighty Japanese in global markets for products like autos and computer chips. But the *chaebol*, the conglomerates that dominate the country's economy, defied the doubters time and again. Hyundai and Kia carved out respectable niches overseas for their cars, and Samsung achieved the stunning feat of becoming the world's top producer of dynamic random access memory (D-RAM) chips, the silicon circuits that store data in every sort of electronic device imaginable.

A large part of Korea's success was based on rock-solid fundamentals—a high savings rate, an education system that produced near-universal literacy, a society with an unsurpassed work ethic, and prudent management of fiscal and monetary policy. The other major factor was government intervention, which was aimed at building an export machine that could bring in the hard currency the resource-poor country needed to pay for imported oil and raw materials. The nation's banks, instead of competing as market-based institutions, were used by the state for channeling peoples' savings to the *chaebol*, with "policy loans"—credits granted at low interest rates to government-blessed projects—accounting for 60 percent of all loans in the late 1970s. Government bureaucrats set detailed targets for exports by product and market, and guided policy loans to firms that demonstrated their competitiveness, cutting off those that didn't. Even though the bureaucracy relaxed its grip on the economy in the 1980s and 1990s, the line between government and private enterprise remained blurry, sometimes jarringly so, as I learned in 1993 on a visit to Samsung Electronics' computer chip fabrication plant in Kiheung, south of Seoul. I was interested in understanding how Samsung had succeeded at its risky plunge into chipmaking, and an executive vice president of the company, Lee Yoon Woo, explained that the policy loans the government had steered to Sam-

sung were only a small part of the venture's huge cost. What really
mattered, Lee said, was that "the government wanted to support us"
because Samsung considered itself to be "working for the government"—a statement no red-blooded American corporate executive
would utter.

The Korean system, which was closely patterned after Japan's,
generated robust economic growth well into the 1990s—8.4 percent
in 1994, 9.0 percent in 1995, and 7.1 percent in 1996—and the fruits
were well spread among the nation's 45 million citizens. By 1996,
those former occupants of thatched-roof huts were enjoying annual
per capita incomes of $11,400, nearly 100 times the 1953 level and
two-fifths that of the United States.

Beneath the glitter of progress, though, the system was showing
significant strains by the middle of the decade. The banking system
had been denationalized and liberated to some extent from government control, but the Ministry of Finance and Economy still exercised influence over the selection of senior commercial bank
managers. The banks also retained many of their bureaucratic char-
acteristics, in particular a propensity to shovel loans almost indis-
criminately to favored *chaebol* customers. The debt loads of publicly
traded Korean companies were hair-raising by international standards, averaging more than 400 percent of shareholder equity. (U.S.
firms, by comparison, average only a little bit more than a dollar in
debt for each dollar in equity.) In part, this phenomenon reflected a
tacit understanding among Korean banks that if their *chaebol* clients
got into trouble, the bureaucrats would step in to protect everyone
against calamitous loss, with a government bailout if necessary.
Although heavy borrowing is sensible when the money is used pro-
ductively, Korea's overconfident tycoons were spending as if there
were no limit to the world-beating facilities they could build. From
1994 to 1996, spending on new plants and equipment rose by nearly
40 percent a year. In some cases, these expansion programs reeked
not only of excessive ambition but even megalomania.

The Ssang Yong Group, whose chairman, M. P. Kim, was a car

buff (he once owned a fleet of twenty vehicles, including a Jaguar, BMW, Mercedes, Lotus, and Lamborghini), invested $4 billion to enter the Korean automobile market, where three giants (Hyundai, Daewoo, and Kia) already dominated. Samsung, whose chairman also cherished a personal car collection, insisted on following its rivals into the crowded automotive industry as well—and reportedly got permission from the administration of President Kim Young Sam by locating its plant in Pusan, Kim's home base. The Halla Group, founded by Chung In Yung, the younger brother of Hyundai's legendary founder Chung Ju Yung, built a state-of-the-art shipyard on Korea's southwestern coast to rival the one run by the elder brother's *chaebol*. All of these ventures would eventually prove ill-advised, but profitability was of little concern to these industrialists, for whom shareholders were a mere nuisance. What counted was size.

The costs of all this debt-financed, hell-bent-for-leather industrialization began to emerge in early 1997 as some of the most heavily indebted *chaebol* went bankrupt. The Hanbo steel group went belly up in January, the first bankruptcy among the top thirty *chaebol* in more than a decade. Compounding the shock was the conviction of Hanbo's chairman and his son for diverting hundreds of millions of dollars from the group to bribe government officials and bankers in a maneuver to stay afloat. Next to go were Sammi and Jinro, followed in the summer by Kia, number eight in the *chaebol* ranks. The upshot of these soured loans was a substantial deterioration in the soundness of the banking system—not readily discernible, given Korea's nebulous accounting practices, but evident even to the luckless IMF mission that drafted the Article IV report in October.

Still, it wasn't as if Korea's economy was rotten to the core. Its exports were growing at double-digit rates in volume terms, inflation was comfortably below 5 percent, and the government had run a budget surplus for three of the prior four years. In some respects, the developments of early 1997 could be interpreted positively, as evidence that Korea was finally tackling its underlying weaknesses. The government had formerly coddled the *chaebol* as if they were too big to fail; now it was allowing some of the biggest to go under. Kang Kyung Shik, deputy prime minister and minister of finance and economy, was an ardent reformer who vigorously resisted pressure to rescue bankrupt *chaebol* from their folly, and he was pressing legislation to modernize the regulation of the banking system. But whatever the grounds for positive sentiment, they would be overwhelmed by a series of events that began to surface on October 17, 1997—just two days after the completion of the Article IV report— during a friendly game of golf.

The match took place at a golf course in Taipei, the capital of Taiwan, among a foursome that included Lee Kyung Shik, governor of the Bank of Korea, and Hsu Yuan Dong, governor of the Taiwanese central bank, which is called the Central Bank of China. The two bank chiefs spoke English with each other, but Hsu was conducting frequent, agitated conversations in Chinese over his mobile phone. "I knew it was something urgent, but I didn't know what," recalled Lee. "I thought, 'Is it a personnel issue?' I didn't know."

Although Lee said he didn't expect to be told, it is astonishing that his golfing partner did not inform him of events, because the implications for the Korean economy would prove devastating. As Lee learned the next day when he returned to Seoul, Taiwan had decided to abandon its policy of defending the value of its currency, the New Taiwan dollar, against the U.S. dollar, and would allow it to fall. Because Taiwanese products compete closely with Korean products on global markets, the move would undercut the price competitiveness of Korean goods—and that in turn would put enormous pressure on the Korean won. The forces of financial contagion were reaching northward and infecting the Korean economy.

Up to that point, contagion had been largely limited to Southeast Asia. Frustration among the Asians over the phenomenon was much in evidence at the September 1997 annual meeting of the IMF and World Bank in Hong Kong, where Malaysia's fiery Prime Minister Mahathir denounced currency trading as "unnecessary, unproductive, and immoral." But on the whole, the mood at the meeting within the High Command was one of relief that the crisis had not spread further. "There was lots of complacency [at the meeting]," recalled a senior European official. "People thought Thailand was well contained; the general perception was that things were well under control, and Thailand was a special case."

The causes of contagion are still a subject of considerable mystery and controversy among economists, but in Asia, several factors appear to have been at play. One is trade-related: The plunge in the Thai baht, by making it possible for Thai exporters to sell their goods more cheaply, reduced the competitiveness of similar goods exported by neighboring countries—so foreign exchange traders figured those countries' currencies would be dragged down too.

A more likely explanation for the contagion is financial—that is, the tendency of lenders and investors who find themselves facing losses in one country to start reducing their holdings in similar countries. Partly, this is attributable to what economists call the "wake-up call" phenomenon, in which members of the Electronic Herd start taking note of ominous parallels between a crisis-stricken country and other, similar countries. Partly, it is attributable to herding behavior, in which portfolio managers follow their competitors' investing patterns lest they be blamed for failing to spot a trend that was obvious to everyone else. But in Asia, even more powerful factors may have been at work.

Carmen Reinhart, the former IMF economist who visited Japanese banks when they were lending heavily in the region, compiled evidence showing that those same banks played a major role in fomenting contagion there. A study coauthored by Reinhart, who is now at the University of Maryland, revealed that Japanese banks scrambled to cut their loan exposure after the devaluation of the Thai baht. "People tend to think of 'hot money' as mutual funds, or hedge funds—which, of course, it is," Reinhart said. "But in Asia, bank lending was the key form of hot money." Although banks make long-term loans for specific projects, they also commonly make short-term loans to other banks, typically a couple of weeks to a few months in duration, in what is called the "interbank market." Under normal conditions, these loans are routinely "rolled over," or extended, when they expire. But once the crisis started, much of the rolling-over stopped; in other words, "Banks were saying, 'Not only will I stop new lending; you have to repay what you owe me today,'" Reinhart said.

Having been Asia's major capital suppliers, banks were also the largest capital withdrawers in 1997 and 1998, Reinhart noted, with the Japanese doing it earliest and in the greatest quantities. Japanese banks held $97 billion in loans to the five Asian countries hardest hit by turmoil—Thailand, Malaysia, Korea, Indonesia, and the Philippines—four times the amount lent by U.S. banks. Moreover, Japanese banks were most exposed to Thailand, where the crisis started, and as the deterioration in the value of their Thai loans hit their balance sheets, they became the first to pull out of Asia, calling loans elsewhere and cutting their exposures to the region by more than $10 billion between June 1997 and December 1997. European banks had lent large sums ($85 billion) to these five Asian countries, too, but most of their exposure was in Korea, and they began withdrawing from the region only after the Korean crisis had started. In the end, all rich countries' banks contributed to the problem. "Even if the banks were not the immediate trigger of financial contagion, their actions certainly made the spillovers, first from Thailand and later from South Korea, far more severe than they would otherwise be," concluded a 1999 study by Reinhart and Graciela Kaminsky of George Washington University.

Loans from foreign banks were indisputably Korea's Achilles heel. In contrast with Thailand's case, foreign capital inflows had played a modest role in the growth of highly protected Korea; Seoul maintained tight ceilings on foreign stock and bond purchases, for example. But Korea opened its financial system in the early 1990s to permit greater borrowing from foreign banks, and Korean banks usually did the borrowing on the interbank market, taking advantage of lower interest rates overseas and passing the funds on to their domestic customers. This was hardly prudent banking practice, since it meant that Korea Inc. was borrowing short-term money abroad—money that had to be repaid in hard currency—and lending it long-term to the expansion-crazed *chaebol*. Nevertheless, foreign banks rushed into this promising new market, led by the Europeans and the Japanese. From 1994 to 1996, Korea's liabilities to foreigners soared by more than $45 billion.

All of this financial maneuvering suddenly became a serious problem amid the firestorm that followed the depreciation of the New Taiwan dollar on October 18. The shock waves hit first in Hong Kong. Traders reasoned that if Taiwan couldn't hold its currency steady, despite having more than $80 billion in hard-currency reserves, then Hong Kong probably couldn't maintain the long-standing system by which it rigidly links the value of its currency to the U.S. dollar. Hong Kong stocks sank by 23 percent on the first four trading days after Taipei's move, and markets from New York to Sydney tumbled on the fear that a successful assault on the Hong Kong dollar would shatter a pillar of confidence in one of the world's most stable financial enclaves.

But as it turned out, the country leading the downturn in Asia was not Hong Kong—which steadfastly held the value of its currency by raising interest rates to extremely high levels—but Korea. Korean officials well remember when they began to realize their economy was facing a crisis of potentially epochal proportions: It was on November 4, a day after they had increased the ceiling for foreign ownership of stock in publicly traded companies, from 23 to 26 percent. "That kind of market opening used to draw about $1 billion or so of foreign money," recalled Lee, the former central bank governor. "But although some foreign money did come into the Seoul stock market at first, it was soon withdrawn." The won, which had been hovering at 915 to the dollar before the Taiwanese move, sank to the 1,000-per-dollar level by November 10.

Just that fast, the Electronic Herd was galloping away from everything Korean. Many of the foreign banks that had extended loans to Korean borrowers were canceling them and demanding repayment as they came due, departing from their previous practice of routinely rolling the loans over. The decline in the won unnerved them, since it was increasing the burden on Korean debtors to repay the dollars they owed. Another factor was jitteriness about the nation's banking system. In any case, it didn't take much for the foreign bankers to conclude that they ought to take their money and run. As one IMF official recalled:

> I was being called by a lot of banks in October and November, and it was amazing how little they knew about Korea. They'd ask, "Has Korea ever defaulted?" Well, the answer is no. They'd ask, "How recent is Korea's miracle? Isn't it all driven by foreign capital flows?" Well, it's not. I remember one indignant guy in New York saying, "We're a responsible bank; we cannot roll over our claims on a nontransparent country." And I thought, "Well, you certainly seem to have been able to *lend* to them!" In a panic situation, once something becomes an issue, no bank wants to be left out on a limb.

* * *

Amid rampant speculation in mid-November that Korea would be forced to seek IMF help, a plan was hatched to bring Michel Camdessus to Seoul for secret consultations with top Korean officials. The scheme to keep the press from learning about the visit by the IMF managing director was based on a simple proposition, recalled Kim Ki Hwan, who was then Korea's ambassador-at-large for economic affairs: "Most Koreans cannot tell one Western face from another."

Camdessus arrived at Seoul's Kimpo Airport on November 16 in the manner of a typical traveler, with no official welcoming party, on the assumption that nobody would pay attention. His Korean hosts used an ordinary commercial car, picked up Camdessus (and Hubert Neiss, who was accompanying him) near the airport taxi stand, and drove them to the Intercontinental Hotel, where they registered under Korean names.

The Koreans were taking this step with dread. In the hopes of avoiding a Fund program, Finance Minister Kang had sent one of his top deputies to Tokyo on November 11 to ask the Japanese Finance Ministry to grant a bilateral loan and to pressure Japanese banks to cease cutting their credit lines to Korean banks. But the deputy returned empty-handed. So two days later, Kang had gone to the Blue House, Seoul's presidential mansion, along with the central bank's Lee Kyung Shik and other top economic policymakers, to break the news to President Kim Young Sam that Korea would almost certainly have to request IMF support. For the president, whose five-year term was nearing its end, the pill was especially bitter to swallow. The year before, he had led his country during its triumphant entry into the ranks of advanced economies belonging to the Organization for Economic Cooperation and Development (OECD). Now he would exit amid unprecedented national humiliation, and his party's candidate to succeed him, Lee Hoi Chang, was sure to suffer in the election, which was a little more than a month away.

As mortifying as it was to approach the Fund with hat in hand, the one scenario Seoul feared even more was default. The problem wasn't the government's own debt—unlike the Latin Americans in the 1980s, the Korean government had borrowed little from abroad. The debts were private (as in Thailand and Indonesia) and were owed almost entirely by banks. But a default by a major Korean bank would surely trigger a run on the system, and in any case the Ministry of Finance and Economy had announced in August that it would back the foreign obligations of the country's banks (a move aimed at forestalling contagion). Byeon Yang Ho, a senior official of the Ministry of Finance and Economy, recalled that the Korean government never considered a default a viable alternative because of the concern that foreign banks would respond by refusing to grant even routine trade credits in the future: "We have to import most energy and raw materials—that's the fundamental structure of the Korean economy," Byeon said. "Once we default, there would be tremendous difficulty obtaining energy and raw materials. The whole economy would halt." Lee Kyung Shik emphatically agreed: "I always thought default would be the worst thing. If we couldn't borrow [foreign] money, the economy would be crushed, for maybe two or three years."

So with the realization that Korea's back was to the wall, Kang and Lee met with Camdessus and Neiss on November 16 at the Intercontinental. They couldn't go to the hotel's restaurant without possibly blowing Camdessus's cover, Kang recalled; instead, they ordered "room service and a few glasses of Scotch."

The two sides reached agreement that Korea would need an IMF-led package of loans totaling about $30 billion. On the subject of the conditions the Fund would demand, the Korean attendees said they were struck, in retrospect, that Camdessus barely raised issues he would harp on a couple of weeks later concerning the need for a root-and-branch transformation of the Korean economic system. The IMF chief did not speak of bringing the *chaebol* to heel or of terminating the incestuous ties between the conglomerates and their bankers. Instead, he praised the financial reform legislation that Kang was vigorously promoting in the Korean National Assembly.

Even so, Camdessus probed for hidden time bombs in Korea's financial situation, fearing that some ugly surprises might be lurking in the data as they had in the Thai case. One of his first questions was about the Bank of Korea's hard-currency reserves, which the central bank had publicly put at $30.5 billion at the end of the previous month. The reply was that there was enough to last until at least the end of the year, though Korea might run out in early 1998. Pressing further, Camdessus asked whether the Korean central bank had engaged in the sort of swap and forward market transactions that the Bank of Thailand had conducted; the reply was yes, but only about $6 billion worth. Camdessus was relieved. "He said that when [the IMF negotiated its program with Thailand], the Thais had almost no reserves. But Korea has at least one month and a half to go," Kang recalled.

In fact, Korea was in much deeper trouble than its official figures indicated, and the true shallowness of its reserves would come as a shock to the mission led by Neiss over the Thanksgiving weekend. Camdessus didn't ask—and the Koreans didn't mention—where the reserves were deposited, or whether they were immediately accessible in a crisis. That would prove to be quite an oversight, because much of the central bank's hard currency had been deposited in the overseas branches and affiliates of Korean banks, where it was already being used to meet debts falling due, and it couldn't be withdrawn quickly without wrecking the banking system.

Another critical piece of missing information concerned the full extent of Korea Inc.'s foreign obligations. Official Korean figures indicated that Korean firms had about $65 billion in payments falling due over the coming year. But as the Neiss mission would learn, the figure was much greater; the overseas affiliates of Korean banks and companies owed an additional $50 billion in debts.

The upshot was that until the last minute, the IMF was unaware of how vulnerable a seemingly prosperous country like Korea could be to a panic. To a large extent, the fault lay with the Fund's obliviousness to some of the obscure sources of potential instability that have arisen in an increasingly globalized financial system.

In calculating Korea's foreign indebtedness, the Fund's Article IV mission that visited Seoul earlier that autumn had used the standard measure, which included only the debt owed to foreigners by companies, institutions, and people resident inside Korea. It did not count the debt owed by Korean entities based overseas such as, say, the New York branch of Korea First Bank. But in a crisis, when foreign creditors start calling in their loans to anyone or anything Korean, all those debts suddenly require Koreans to fork over dollars to foreigners, and the demands on the central bank's reserves can become overwhelming. "We'd been asking the wrong questions before," admitted a member of the mission team. "We didn't worry about the foreign debt of nonresident Korean entities. But in fact, these entities were also borrowing overseas, and ultimately those debts came home to the Bank of Korea."

The Koreans also apparently failed to realize the danger posed by the debt. In fact, Korean officials were so confused about the issue that they produced wildly disparate figures during the course of the crisis. "We were asking for a rescue. There was no intention to hide anything," said Lee Kyung Shik of the Bank of Korea. "Nobody cares what the short-term debt is, as long as the situation is stable. It could always be rolled over, so we didn't care about it. But suddenly, when the reserves fell, the short-term debt became really critical. I was surprised, and they [IMF officials] were surprised, too."

The clandestine hotel meeting of November 16 ended with agreement on a plan: Korea's intention to seek IMF support would be announced on November 18, the day after the scheduled vote on the financial reform bills. Camdessus slipped out of Seoul on the morning of the seventeenth, still unnoticed by the press. But the plan hit a snag when the National Assembly voted down the bills—and Kang was abruptly dismissed as deputy prime minister and minister of finance and economy on November 19.

With the won sinking further by the day, President Kim immediately replaced Kang with Lim Chang Yuel, his trade minister, who looked as if he would prove much more troublesome for the IMF than the reform-minded Kang. A former Finance Ministry bureaucrat, the nationalistic Lim was no shrinking violet. In some of his first public remarks as finance minister, Lim suggested that Korea would try to survive without IMF aid, and he pressed for direct loans from the United States and Japan, asserting bluntly: "It is in their national interests to help. . . . If the Korean currency depreciates beyond its value, it will seriously affect the Japanese economy." Washington and Tokyo rejected the request from Lim, whose haughty words helped send the won plunging 10 percent, to 1,139 per dollar on November 20.

On that tumultuous day, the IMF's Stan Fischer arrived in Seoul, having coincidentally arranged to visit there during a swing through Asia. The Korean press caught wind of his presence and surrounded his hotel room, congregating to such an extent that he complained over the phone he was literally trapped inside.

Fischer finally waded through the throng of reporters and photographers to meet Lim over dinner. Lim seemed to be reconciling himself to the necessity of an IMF program, after having learned that the country's reserves were fast depleting. But Lim's attitude bespoke the state of denial then afflicting the Korean body politic. He asked how much growth the IMF would permit Korea to have, and Fischer replied that the Fund didn't have the power to control such matters. "The Korean people," Lim retorted, "will not accept growth of less than five percent"—a remark that prompted Fischer to assert he suspected Korea's growth in 1998 would be more like zero. (Even Fischer was evidently not contemplating the minus 7 percent that would actually materialize.)

The next day, the two men held another brief meeting, and within hours Lim finally made it official: Korea would seek an IMF loan. As for Fischer, he rushed to the airport to catch a flight for London and called Neiss from the car to order the dispatch of the Fund mission. Photographers dogged him all the way to his plane. The headlines in the following day's Korean newspapers—"National Bankruptcy" and "Humiliating International Trusteeship"—bespoke the nation's trauma over the turn developments had taken. In an editorial, the *Dong-Ah Ilbo*, a leading daily, lamented: "This is tantamount to losing our economic sovereignty."

Four days later, on the day before Thanksgiving, Charles Siegman, senior associate director of the Federal Reserve Board's Division of International Finance, was sitting at his desk a few minutes before 9 A.M. when a call came from Lee Keun Yung, the head of the Bank of Korea's Washington office. Lee wanted to see Siegman right away. Fifteen minutes later, an apologetic Lee was in Siegman's office. He was seeking the Fed's help, he said, because the Bank of Korea's usable hard-currency reserves were very low, with so much draining out of the country daily that default might be only days away. Siegman was taken aback: Earlier in the week, he and Fed chairman Alan Greenspan had met Lee for breakfast, together with Lee Kyung Shik, and the figures available then had seemed less dire. (Lee would later insist that the figures he gave Siegman that day were consistent with the ones provided at the breakfast; there may have been a misunderstanding.) Siegman said he would have to see Greenspan immediately and promised to get back to Lee.

The information, of course, was essentially the same as what Neiss would learn at the Korean central bank's Seoul headquarters that same day. But now it was being provided to the U.S. government, and it would soon galvanize Washington's top echelons—not only the economic bigwigs but the national security team at the White House and the State and Defense Departments as well. This was Korea, after all. Its economy was of far greater potential importance to the global financial system than Thailand's or Indonesia's, and it stood at one of the last remaining flashpoints of the Cold War. Within its borders were 37,000 U.S. troops, poised to help fend off any incursion from the erratic and fanatical regime to the north and providing a reassuring symbol of America's commitment to maintaining stability in Asia.

Upon hearing the news, Greenspan called Treasury Secretary Bob Rubin and, together with Siegman, headed to the Treasury for a meeting over lunch in Rubin's private dining room. Deputy Secretary Larry Summers was out of town that day, and participated only briefly by speakerphone, but the rest of the Treasury's international brain trust quickly gathered. Heading the list was David Lipton, the undersecretary for international affairs, a quiet, intense Harvard Ph.D. who had worked eight years at the IMF. Also in attendance were Tim Geithner, the assistant secretary for international affairs; Caroline Atkinson, deputy assistant secretary for international monetary and financial policy; and Daniel Zelikow, deputy assistant secretary for Asia, the Americas, and Africa.

The mood at the meeting was a combination of shock, worry, and anger. Why, the participants wondered, were the Koreans conveying the information about their reserves when it was almost too late? Was Seoul playing some sort of trick, to panic the United States into making an emergency loan?

Presiding over the discussion was Rubin, who mostly listened, asked questions, and scribbled notes on a yellow legal pad, as was his habit on such occasions. Famously deliberative, the fifty-nine-year-old Treasury secretary had made a fortune on Wall Street of well over $100 million by examining all the facets of prospective investments and basing his decisions on carefully calibrated judgments about whether the potential rewards outweighed the risks. At the Treasury, he applied the same cold-blooded logic to the making of economic policy.

Trained as a lawyer like his father, Rubin had spent two years at a top-drawer Manhattan law firm, but he found the work boring and joined Goldman, Sachs & Co. in 1966. There he worked closely with Goldman's chairman Gus Levy, a cigar-chomping, hard-drinking Wall Street legend whose "technique for management was yelling," as Rubin once put it. Rubin made partner in just four years, and he was one of Levy's favorites, despite having an almost diametrically opposite personality and taste in consumables. (Rubin's lunches of carrot sticks, salad, and mineral water would put a fashion model's diet to shame.) Seemingly impervious to the tumult around him in the Goldman trading room, Rubin's sunken eyes and angular features were the picture of studied calm almost regardless of the pressures he was under. And he was under plenty.

Rubin made his name in "risk arbitrage," which involves buying the stocks of companies being targeted for takeovers or mergers. Suppose, for example, Company A makes a $50-a-share bid to buy Company B, whose shares have been trading at $35, and Company B's shares rise to $48 on the news. Tidy profits can be earned by buying up massive amounts of Company B's stock at around $48 and reaping a small gain on each share when the deal is consummated. On the other hand, if the deal falls apart, a large stake in Company B would generate ruinous losses, since the stock would presumably fall back to its original price of $35. Thus each investment decision involves a fair amount of research—what, for example, do the antitrust lawyers say?—plus a bit of mathematics: Given all the possible factors that could derail the deal, how high are the chances it will go through at $50 a share or higher, and how high are the chances that Company B won't be bought at all? From these calculations, do the probable profits appear to outweigh the probable losses?

The risk-arbitrage desk that Rubin headed consistently earned fat returns, which was one of the factors that elevated him to the cochairmanship of Goldman in 1990. But beyond the riches, the arbitrage game instilled a mental calculus by which he came to approach almost all issues. As Rubin himself repeatedly put it, he liked to think "probabilistically." A decision might produce bad results—for example, a takeover stock might plunge in value, or the bailout of a country might flop—but that doesn't mean the decision was wrong, as long as the odds of profit and loss, or success and failure, were carefully assessed and weighed at the time, given all the information available. On the other hand, of course, it was crazy to proceed when the probable downside clearly exceeded the probable upside. In risk arbitrage, "You had to stick to your discipline and try to reduce everything in your mind to pluses and minuses and to probabilities," Rubin once told Clay Chandler of the *Washington Post*. "If a deal goes through, what do you win? If it doesn't go through, what do you lose? It was a high-risk business, but I'll tell you, it did teach you to think of life in terms of probabilities instead of absolutes. You couldn't be in that business and not internalize that probabilistic approach to life. It was what you were doing all the time."

As his Wall Street profile rose, Rubin, who was politically much more liberal leaning than most of his peers, became active in Democratic circles, and in 1992 he made a favorable impression on Arkansas Governor Bill Clinton, not least by helping to raise money for Clinton's presidential campaign. After Rubin moved to Washington in

1993 to chair the White House National Economic Council, he and Clinton quickly developed a tight bond, thanks in part to Rubin's advocacy of a budget deficit reduction strategy that helped lower interest rates and paved the way for the long U.S. economic expansion of the 1990s. Named to replace the courtly Lloyd Bentsen as Treasury chief in late 1994, Rubin struggled with the public responsibilities of the job; his speaking style tended to be disjointed, with frequent midsentence interruptions for caveats and modifications and retractions. But given the president's enormous trust in his judgment, nobody in the administration could approach his clout on economic matters, and his reputation for thoughtful analysis and imperturbability added to his luster. "In a way, he's like a Socratic professor," said Robert Boorstin, who was a senior adviser to the Treasury secretary. "He would listen, endlessly, and he would only interject when he really had something to ask or say. You always knew Rubin had something to say when he would start off with, 'Well, I don't know much about this, but...' And you knew he *really* had something to say when he would start off with, 'Well, I know a thing or two about this'—like when someone would start talking about the markets."

At the meeting about Korea the day before Thanksgiving, Rubin was in that cautious mode his subordinates had come to know well. Undertaking an all-out effort to rescue Korea looked like a losing proposition, such as buying the stock of a takeover target whose merger was almost certain to fall through. Korea was so close to default, its short-term debt was so large, and its reluctance to change its ways was so deep, that a huge bailout seemed likely to produce nothing but a costly fiasco. The only course of action the meeting participants could agree upon was to think hard about what to do and talk again the next day.

Assistant Secretary Tim Geithner tried to counter the sense of futility. Of all the members of the senior Treasury team, Geithner had by far the most Asia expertise. He had grown up in Thailand, India, and other foreign countries (where his father was a Ford Foundation executive), held degrees in Asian Studies from Dartmouth and the Johns Hopkins School of Advanced International Studies, and had served as assistant Treasury attaché in the U.S. embassy in Tokyo. Only thirty-six years old, he had risen like a shot through the Treasury's ranks, starting as a career civil servant in 1988 and impressing one superior after another with his rapid-fire analytical capacity and good-humored manner.

Geithner argued that Korea was too important a country, both economically and strategically, to be allowed to default. "But that's the kind of thing Rubin hates," he admitted later, "because you can't let some perceived imperative of action dictate your choices, and you may not have alternatives that are a plausible response to the problem. I don't think we concluded the meeting thinking that *nothing* could be done. There was a presumption that Korea would get an IMF program. But I think we concluded the meeting with everyone thinking that it was very dark."

That night, Summers—who was predisposed to be more activist than Rubin in situations such as these—called Geithner from his parents' home in Philadelphia, where he had traveled from New York for the holiday. Agreeing that U.S. policy needn't necessarily be doomed to inaction, the pair concocted a multipart strategy that they thought might be plausible. First, the United States would make a determined effort to persuade the Koreans to adopt a credible set of policy reforms that addressed the problems that had gotten them into this mess. Second, a package on the order of Mexico's $50 billion bailout would be marshaled—with IMF, World Bank, and Asian Development Bank money backed by a "second line of defense" that would include $5 billion from the United States, $10 billion from Japan, and billions more from other countries. Third, Japan would be pressured to send positive signals about its intentions to shore up its ailing banking system, because the frantic pulling of loans by troubled Japanese banks was compounding Asia's woes.

On Thanksgiving morning, the Treasury team held a conference call from their homes to discuss the idea. But within hours, the pressure on Rubin would grow even more intense, as the administration-wide conference calls proliferated. "It was the worst Thanksgiving Day of my life," recalled Sandra Kristoff, the senior director for Asian affairs at the National Security Council. "Not only were we having a traditional dinner, but we were also celebrating a family birthday, and we celebrated at my house. By the time I got off the phone, all the dishes were done, and everyone had gone home." Other participants on the calls—including Secretary of State Madeleine Albright—bemoaned their ruined dinners, though there were occasional breaks for people to spend time with friends and family.

In the calls, the national security and foreign policy heavyweights pressed the case that the United States could not walk away from Seoul at such an hour of need. "This president is not going to look like Jimmy Carter," admonished James Steinberg, the deputy national security adviser, referring to an episode in the 1970s when President Carter proposed a major reduction in the U.S. military presence in South Korea, sparking an uproar in Asia about Washington's commitment to the region. Steinberg worried that by failing to show strong support for Korea, the United States risked stirring an anti-American backlash in Seoul that could lead to pressure for the removal of U.S. troops. His boss, National Security Adviser Samuel "Sandy" Berger, wondered aloud about the danger that North Korea would foment "mischief" should South Korea undergo economic collapse; the reclusive Communists in Pyongyang might seize the opportunity of financial chaos in the South to launch provocative military adventures that could trigger a deadly conflict. The Central Intelligence Agency was tasked to step up monitoring of the North, as was General John Tilelli, the commander of U.S. Forces in Korea, who also participated in the call. Albright was perhaps the most emphatic in favor of a bailout, earning the derision of the Treasury team, who felt she was simplistically assuming that money alone would vanquish the crisis.

Rubin couldn't dispute Korea's strategic importance, but he made it clear he wasn't hearing proposals for resolving the problem that made sense to him. The Treasury chief's main concern was that the

IMF's credibility should not be squandered. The Fund's value to the international community, he explained, stemmed from its ability to instill confidence among bankers and investors. A badly botched rescue, he feared, could seriously diminish its capacity to instill that confidence in the future.

In the end, the two sides reached an understanding that appealed at least somewhat to Rubin's probabilistic mentality. As Steinberg recalled:

> The extreme version of the argument the national security types like me were making was that [a major bailout] was worth trying even if it was certain to fail. That isn't what we were saying; it's just the extreme interpretation. The extreme version of the Treasury argument was, don't do it unless it's certain to succeed. What was mutually arrived at was that it was no good to do something if it was absolutely futile. We accepted that there had to be some degree of probability of success, and Treasury accepted that it didn't have to be just a high probability. If there was some chance it would succeed—even if it was less than fifty-fifty—there was a political value in having tried.

* * *

Sharmini Coorey wasn't expecting that the IMF would send her to Korea, and certainly not on such short notice. A thirty-nine-year-old native of Sri Lanka, with a Ph.D. from Harvard, Coorey was in the process of moving in autumn 1997 to the Asia and Pacific Department from the Policy Development and Review Department, and she was expecting to work on the Philippines and Indonesia. But in late November, she was assigned to the Seoul-bound mission, to oversee the monetary policy portion of the program, even though she had never been to the country before.

Gary Moser was not expecting to be sent to Seoul either. A member of the Policy Development and Review staff, he had been working on a project to evaluate the Fund's skill at monitoring economies and detecting crises. But he was told he would be going to Korea (his first time, too) while on a weekend trip in mid-November to New York, where he was watching his daughter perform with a singing group at Carnegie Hall, and he had to rush back to Washington the day after the performance.

The Asia crisis was stretching the IMF thin, especially the Asia and Pacific Department. Hubert Neiss and his department colleagues had to dig deep to find people who were available for the Korea mission, and familiarity with the country and its current economic problems was preferable but not a prerequisite. Wanda Tseng, whom Neiss took as his cochief of mission, had worked on Korea in the late 1980s, and she kept abreast of the country's developments while working on China in the 1990s, but in 1995 she had left the Asia and Pacific Department to become deputy secretary to the Executive Board. Aside from Neiss and a banking expert who had participated in the Article IV mission in October, only one of the senior members of the mission staff, James Gordon, had spent time recently in Korea.

After arriving in Seoul on November 26, the IMF mission members had barely recovered from jet lag—and the shock of learning that Korea was nearly out of reserves—when formal negotiations began two nights later. The talks opened with a long statement by Choi Joong Kyung, director of the Finance Ministry's Financial Cooperation Division, who stood up, bowed deeply, and apologized for what had happened. "We are sorry, for having called [the IMF] in so late, and for having let the situation get so desperate," he began, according to one of the IMF staffers, who recalled: "I would say he was nearly crying. It was a very emotional point."

Apologies aside, the Koreans were not rolling over to meet the Fund's demands. On the contrary, they were ready with backup teams to research and rebut every proposal the IMF made for the program's conditions. No sooner would exhausted IMF staffers retire to bed than they would be wakened at three or four o'clock in the morning with word that the Korean negotiators were ready to resume talks on one point or another. Starting Sunday, November

30, Neiss and Tseng simply stopped sleeping and stayed up for three and four straight days, respectively.

The main elements of a draft Letter of Intent started to take shape over the weekend, with Washington following the negotiations closely by e-mail and telephone from Seoul. To some on the Fund staff, it seemed clear that Neiss wasn't getting the Koreans to agree to much. The Koreans made commitments to cure many of the problems in their financial system—improving oversight, openness, and transparency, for example—but the commitments were vague, without specific deadlines, or they repeated commitments the government had already made in other venues. The IMF wanted the government to close a number of merchant banks—firms similar to Thai finance companies, which were essentially unsupervised, and had lent aggressively to *chaebol* with which they were closely affiliated. But the Korean negotiators said they could consider closing only one. "No finance minister in Korean history has ever closed a financial institution," Finance Minister Lim Chang Yuel reminded the IMF team. As for interest rates, the initial drafts of the Letter of Intent suggested the central bank would raise the overnight borrowing rate, its chief monetary tool, only a few percentage points. That was a disappointment to many at the Fund who favored using high rates to make the country a more attractive place for investors to keep their money.

It soon became apparent that the deal Neiss was negotiating would fail to satisfy one intensely interested party—the U.S. Treasury. As one IMF economist recalled, "Treasury thought Neiss was giving the shop away." And though Treasury officials emphatically denied that they were dissatisfied with Neiss, their actions left little doubt about their concern. On Thanksgiving, the administration had taken the extraordinary step of sending a top U.S. official to Seoul to "monitor" the negotiations—Treasury Undersecretary David Lipton.

With a placid, blue-eyed gaze that masked a restless spirit, Lipton was the obvious choice for such a "parachute" job, though he had never been to Korea himself. He understood how IMF missions worked, having spent eight years at the Fund after getting his Ph.D. in 1981 from Harvard, where he was a frequent study-group colleague and tennis partner of Larry Summers. He also had some expertise in dealing with countries that had fallen into extreme financial distress.

In 1989, he left the IMF to join Jeffrey Sachs, another friend from Harvard's economics department, who had formed a small advisory group for economically troubled countries. The pair soon embarked on some lively adventures. In June 1989, for example, they spent all night in a Warsaw hotel drafting a radical economic program that had been urgently requested by Poland's Solidarity movement, two days after Solidarity had trounced the Communists in the country's first free parliamentary elections since the advent of the Cold War. Poland's economic outlook appeared almost beyond hope at that time, and the plan helped convince Solidarity leaders—who weren't sure they should take the risk of forming a government—that they stood a chance of making a successful transition to market-based capitalism.

At the Treasury, which he joined in 1993, Lipton was known for advocating "out-of-the-box" ideas. But although he had been associated with Sachs, one of the IMF's most outspoken critics, he did not share Sachs's vehement opposition to Fund orthodoxy on matters such as the need for crisis-stricken countries to keep interest rates high. Lipton was "Safe Sachs," as one IMF staffer joked when Lipton joined the Treasury.

Before leaving for Seoul, Lipton called Richard Holbrooke, the veteran American diplomat, for advice on Korea. Holbrooke said the most important point Lipton needed to grasp was how Korea's tragic history of invasion and subjugation by neighboring powers had shaped its attitude toward the outside world. "You've got to understand, for 4,000 years, Koreans have maintained their culture, and their nationality, even when they weren't a nation," Holbrooke told him. "They're hostile to intrusion from foreigners."

But the marching orders Lipton got from Rubin did not leave

much room to avoid offending Korean sensibilities. If the Koreans were willing to take decisive steps to change the way they ran their economy, the United States would help them, Rubin said. But if they weren't willing, then aid wouldn't work, and Lipton should make it clear that Washington couldn't help.

To Rubin, Summers, and their lieutenants, Korea's crisis was the inevitable result of the country's stubborn insularity and its slavish attempts to follow the Japanese economic model, with its system of cosseting banks to pump funds into industry. The Treasury's international staff had long urged Seoul to open up its financial sector—for example, to drop restrictions on competition from foreign banks, and allow Korean companies to borrow on international bond markets and sell more stock to foreigners. Lobbying by American financial services firms, which wanted to crack the Korean market, was the driving force behind the Treasury's pressure on Seoul. But the department argued that liberalization would benefit Korea; it would give small and medium-sized firms a chance to compete with the *chaebol* and make the entire Korean economy less dangerously dependent on bank loans. The Korean Ministry of Finance and Economy, in part to help secure the country's 1996 entry into the OECD, grudgingly acceded to some of the American demands, but with long phase-in periods. As Treasury saw it, Korea was now paying the price for its decisions and would have to take radical steps to show that the same mistakes wouldn't be repeated. So as in Indonesia, the United States wanted a program with conditions that surpassed the Fund's traditional boundaries.

The IMF staff was less enthusiastic about imposing structural change on Seoul. Whatever the merits of a wholesale makeover of the economic system, it wouldn't necessarily stem the panic besetting Korea, and in some quarters of the Fund, cynicism abounded about the Treasury's ulterior motives. "The U.S. saw this as an opportunity, as they did in many countries, to crack open all these things that for years have bothered them," said one member of the IMF's Asia and Pacific Department.

The general view on the staff was that "this is the Asian model, and it won't change," said Karin Lissakers, the U.S. executive director of the IMF. "But it was so clear, at least to the United States, that the real problems with Korea were structural and that the financial system was the point of vulnerability."

Lipton's presence in Seoul added another element of theater to the negotiations—and provided a symbol to the Koreans of how the United States was influencing the IMF behind the scenes. Lipton checked into the Hilton and, mistaken for an IMF staffer, escaped notice by the press at first, even though he was meeting often with Neiss and had to walk past reporters thronged in the hall near the elevator on the nineteenth floor where the IMF mission was staying. But after a day or so of anonymity, he opened his door to find a photographer lying in wait. He closed the door, waited for a while, and the photographer fell asleep. But when Lipton started to leave, the photographer jumped up and followed him, taking pictures. Soon Lipton's visage would be featured in anti-IMF and anti-U.S. cartoons in the Korean media. After being "outed," he changed rooms at the Hilton and registered under a false name.

In accord with his mandate from Rubin, Lipton was pressing both the IMF and the Koreans to strike as far-reaching an accord as possible. When Korean officials informed him shortly after his arrival that they had practically completed a pact with Neiss, Lipton told them they could announce anything they wanted, but until it was actually agreed with the IMF, it wouldn't have the backing of the United States. Toward the end of the negotiations, he had a dramatic 4 A.M. encounter with Chung Duk Koo, a top Finance Ministry official, who emerged from a meeting with Neiss to tell Lipton that Seoul had granted every concession it could possibly make. Lipton was unmoved, reminding Chung that he had met the previous morning with Finance Minister Lim and discussed the elements Washington believed were necessary to turn the economy around and needed in an IMF program. "I told the minister this morning, and I mean it, what we want in terms of change in your economy," Lipton told Chung.

Much of Lipton's effort was concentrated in obtaining firm, specific Korean commitments to speed up liberalization of the country's financial system. He also wanted a much tighter monetary policy. IMF staffers thought many of his proposals were sensible, but they bridled at others that they felt were focused more on serving U.S. interests than Korea's, in particular a demand for Seoul to allow greater business opportunities for foreign brokerage firms. Some on the mission team fumed that they couldn't get to see Neiss because when he wasn't locked in negotiations with the Koreans, he was spending so much time with Lipton. But Neiss himself, ever the diplomat, showed no irritation whatsoever with Lipton's intervention, and Lipton, for his part, had only kind words for Neiss. "I would meet with Hubert at, say, 2 A.M. or 4:30 A.M.," he recalled. "When I went to sleep, he would be in a meeting; when I got up a couple of hours later, he would still be in a meeting. The amazing thing was his equanimity."

Not that Neiss was impervious to the pressure. On the last night of the negotiations—Tuesday, December 2—he disappeared from the hotel in the wee hours of the morning, to the consternation of Tseng, who like Neiss had not slept since Sunday. "I was getting very worried," said Tseng, who finally tracked Neiss down and found that he had gone for a midnight jog. "He said he had just gone out on Namsam Mountain [a small mountain near the Hilton]. He said he went up to the top and saw Seoul and all the lights. He said he just needed to clear his head."

At 6 A.M. on Wednesday, December 3, Neiss—who had finally collapsed, fully dressed, for a couple of hours in his bed—was jolted awake by the sound of a phone ringing. It was Chung Duk Koo, from the Finance Ministry, who was downstairs waiting to go with him to the airport. Neiss hurriedly brushed his teeth; there was no time to shower or shave. Arriving that morning in Seoul to complete the negotiations was his boss, Michel Camdessus. In contrast with Camdessus's previous visit, all of Korea would be aware of his presence this time.

The IMF's managing director and his wife, Brigitte, did not look pleased as they stepped off the plane at Kimpo Airport in the early morning of December 3. The weather was frigid, and reporters were mobbing them so aggressively that Mrs. Camdessus became apprehensive. To ease the tension, Oh Jong Nam, a Korean Finance Ministry official who had been sent to welcome them officially, tried a joke: "Since it is so cold, I invited many reporters to warm the air, so don't be scared."

Camdessus's mood did not improve when Oh handed him the ministry's proposed schedule for the day. The managing director's arrival in a country at the end of negotiations usually means that the talks are essentially finished, the Letter of Intent has been readied for signing, and the champagne has been chilled for toasting. That, in fact, is what Korean officials were devoutly hoping for this visit; they tried to arrange a virtually content-free day filled mostly with press conferences, signing ceremonies, a courtesy call with President Kim, and a luncheon with the ambassadors to Korea from the G-7 countries, capped by a send-off for Camdessus to Tokyo, where he was scheduled to arrive that evening. The Koreans had been embarrassed a couple of times during the negotiations when they told the press they had reached agreement with Neiss, only to be forced to admit later that further bargaining was required. (Both sides professed to be furious over the mix-ups. IMF officials accused the Koreans of trying to bulldoze them into an agreement, and the Koreans accused the IMF of constantly raising new issues at the behest of the United States.) On the afternoon before Camdessus's arrival, Finance Minister Lim Chang Yuel suggested that he foresaw no further major obstacles. "The talks are virtually completed," he told reporters.

But they weren't. "I am here to negotiate," Camdessus said stiffly after glancing at the schedule handed to him. In fact, he did so much negotiating that day that he had to postpone his flight to Tokyo and send his wife to represent him at the ambassadors' luncheon. By all accounts, he got the Korean program "strengthened" considerably during his one-day whirlwind visit, extracting substantial further concessions from the Korean side.

It is not clear how tough Camdessus had originally planned to be. Several days before his arrival, while Neiss was still negotiating with the Koreans, Camdessus had participated in a conference call with a group of senior IMF officials in Washington who argued that the Fund should be insisting on stronger conditions. Informed during the call that the Americans were particularly dissatisfied, Camdessus retorted dismissively, "They're always unhappy." That comment left his listeners uncertain about whether he genuinely intended to disregard the U.S. concerns or was simply engaging in a show of bravado for his staff.

The Treasury was evidently worried that Camdessus would acquiesce to a quick signing of a Letter of Intent based on the concessions the Koreans had already offered. To head off that eventuality, Rubin phoned the IMF chief shortly after Camdessus's arrival in Seoul. What Rubin said, and how far he went in pressuring Camdessus, nobody will reveal. But this much is certain: Rubin delivered an extraordinarily blunt, unequivocal warning that the United States would not countenance what it regarded as a weak program. There was a chance, of course, that the Koreans would eavesdrop electronically on the call—but as far as the Treasury was concerned, such snooping would be a plus, not a minus, since it would help Seoul understand that Camdessus was under tremendous pressure to take a hard line.

The final negotiations on December 3 took place in Lim's Finance Ministry office instead of at the Hilton, because of the media frenzy at the hotel. One major dispute was over the short-term interest rates set by the central bank. To attract foreign investors, Camdessus said, those rates should be doubled from 12.5 percent to the legal limit of 25 percent—well above the 15 to 20 percent figure that the Koreans and the Neiss mission had been negotiating. Lim and his lieutenants voiced deep concern about the impact on Korea's highly indebted corporations, and argued that in Korea, higher rates wouldn't help much in luring capital from overseas because of the limited opportunities for foreigners to invest in the economy in the first place. But Camdessus stood firm, diplomatically presenting the case for higher rates as a way for the country to win back the confidence of the markets by restoring the credibility of the central bank. The Koreans finally backed down, recalled Lee Kyung Shik, the central bank governor, because the country's supply of usable reserves at that point was down to about $6 billion.

Finally, around 6:30 P.M., the two sides shook hands on a deal that would provide Seoul with a package of loans and backup credits totaling more than $55 billion. (The sum would rise as high as $60 billion in the next few days as the number of countries offering bilateral lines of credit increased.) The $21 billion IMF portion was the most the Fund had ever lent to a single country, and it was more than six times the amount Korea would normally be allowed to borrow. The Koreans had agreed to a slew of measures aimed at opening their economy to greater foreign involvement, increasing competition in the financial sector, and weakening the ability of the *chaebol* to pile on debt from compliant banks. Foreigners would be allowed to establish bank subsidiaries and brokerage houses in the Korean market by mid-1998, as the Americans had demanded. The ceiling on aggregate foreign ownership of publicly traded companies would be raised by year-end from 26 percent to 50 percent, and the ceiling on individual foreign ownership from 7 percent to 50 percent. The nation's opaque accounting practices would be brought much closer to international standards, with corporations required to submit consolidated balance sheets and profit and loss statements, part of an effort to discourage the complex webs of loans and cross-guarantees the *chaebol* had established among their subsidiaries.

Large financial institutions would be required to submit to audits by internationally recognized firms. The Koreans also backed down on the issue of closing merchant banks, announcing that nine insolvent institutions would be suspended from operating and given thirty days to draft plans for rehabilitating themselves or face closure.

As Camdessus and Lim emerged to face the cameras, Camdessus's buoyant confidence contrasted with Lim's sorrowful appearance. "I am pleased to announce that the Korean authorities and an IMF team concluded discussions in Seoul today on a strong economic program that provides for a decisive and welcome response to the country's present financial difficulties," the IMF chief declared. Lim, meanwhile, said that he had "come here to beg the forgiveness of the Korean people. . . . These pains and burdens are the cost our economy has inevitably to pay to revive and to recover our lowered credibility in the world financial society." In Washington, a Treasury official briefing reporters on the terms of the bailout crowed that the program "will bring about substantial changes in the Korean financial sector, which in turn have the potential to open up the Korean economy and move it toward one that is much more dependent on the operation of market forces."

The High Command was doing its best to turn the situation into a finale from "The Perils of Pauline," the silent movie adventures that typically ended with the tethered heroine plucked from the path of an onrushing train. The message to the outside world was, Breathe easy. The IMF and the rest of the High Command would provide the money needed to avert a potentially catastrophic default, and Seoul would be forced to change its crisis-prone system. Korea would be saved.

But Pauline was still firmly lashed to the railroad tracks.

· 6 ·

THE NAYSAYERS

Bob Rubin's concern about the IMF's credibility was well founded. The Fund's skill at resuscitating ailing economies was coming under severe question following the disappointing results in Thailand and Indonesia. The chorus of voices criticizing its approach to the crisis was growing louder.

The IMF, of course, was hardly unaccustomed to criticism. But for the most part, Fund officials had successfully rebuffed their critics and easily surmounted the political challenges they posed. To those on the left who complained about the austerity incorporated into IMF programs, the Fund replied that there is no reasonable alternative to making countries live within their means. To those on the right who accused the IMF of interfering in markets and propping up inefficient governments, the Fund countered that cash-strapped countries deserve to be helped through a painful adjustment period if they are willing to change their ways.

But as the Asian crisis spread, discord arose from within the economic mainstream, from people who shared the Fund's ideology of free markets, free trade, globalization, and the need for an official safety net. Some criticism was even coming from within the Bretton Woods institutions and top officials of the G-7. Among the dissidents were four of particular prominence who were raising significant issues that would weigh heavily on how the IMF conducted its affairs.

Sitting on a panel at a conference in summer 1997, Harvard Professor Jeffrey Sachs received a note from fellow panelist Larry Summers, the Treasury's deputy secretary. The note asked for Sachs's views on how the IMF ought to handle the budding crisis in Asia. "I wrote back, 'Stay home!'" Sachs recalled. "And Larry wrote back saying, 'No, really.' And I wrote back, 'Really!'"

The episode was vintage Sachs, who reveled in his role as gadfly-in-chief to the IMF. The Fund had endured slings and arrows from many distinguished academics over the years, but the brash, boyish-faced Sachs stood above them all in his capacity for making veins bulge and teeth grind. The owlish Martin Feldstein, Sachs's Harvard colleague, might chastise the Fund using scholarly terminology in the pages of *Foreign Affairs,* but Sachs pulled no punches in his op-eds. Shortly after the first IMF rescue for Korea was announced, he wrote in the *Financial Times:*

> It defies logic to believe that the small group of 1,000 economists on 19th Street in Washington should dictate the economic conditions of life to 75 developing countries with around 1.4 billion people. . . . Since perhaps half of the IMF's time is devoted to these countries—with the rest tied up in surveillance of advanced countries, management, research and other tasks—about 500 staff cover the 75 countries. That is an average of about seven economists per country.
>
> One might suspect that seven staffers would not be enough to get a very sophisticated view of what is happening. That suspicion would be right. The IMF threw together a Draconian program for Korea in just a few days, without deep knowledge of the country's financial system and without any subtlety as to how to approach the problems.

Such screeds were derided by indignant members of the Fund's External Relations Department as exercises in self-promotion, and indeed, Sachs' ego often did loom large. "Mr. Sachs is not shy about his academic accomplishments," a *New York Times* profile observed in 1989. "His curriculum vitae runs some 13 pages and contains such tidbits as the fact that he graduated third in his Harvard class of 1,650 students. He took pains in an interview to note that he is a member of Harvard's elite Society of Fellows."

Sachs first made his name not as a critic but as an adviser helping acutely distressed developing countries achieve economic turn-arounds. His stock-in-trade was an approach that came to be known as "shock therapy," which involved radically market-oriented reforms and—as the name implies—an initial period of dislocation and joblessness as a precursor to recovery. His first case was Bolivia, which was racked by an inflation rate that by 1985 had reached somewhere between 24,000 percent and 60,000 percent, depending on how it was counted, on an annual basis. Sachs, who was thirty-one at the time, was one of Harvard's youngest tenured professors (along with his friend, Larry Summers), and he was fascinated by the problem of hyperinflation. At a university presentation by a group of visiting Bolivians, he insisted there was a plausible way to stabilize the economy, and they invited him to come to La Paz and try. He accepted, and helped reform-oriented officials in the government devise a plan that included drastic spending cuts, the closure of money-losing state enterprises, the liberalization of prices and restraints on wages. Some initial results were excruciating—unemployment rose to 22 percent by 1988, and incomes, already miserably low, dropped to about $573 per person. But inflation shrank to 10 percent the year after the plan took effect, and the economy began eking out some growth after years of stagnation.

Sachs's next case was Poland, where inflation was running at about 50 percent a month in the late 1980s and the economy was sinking fast amid the collapse of communism. The leaders of the Solidarity labor movement, who were about to take power in 1989 and desperately wanted to bring their country into the Western main-stream, enlisted Sachs's advisory firm. Together with his colleague David Lipton, Sachs drafted a program that envisioned a breathtak-ingly ambitious break from Poland's socialist past, and promised Poles in speeches and television appearances that the plan would eventually bring growth and stable prices. The "big bang" came on January 1, 1990, when the government freed almost all prices to rise to market levels, slashed subsidies for lumbering state enterprises, and reined in wages and the money supply. As in Bolivia, inflation and unemployment soared at first, and workers' purchasing power shrank. But within a couple of years, as industrial efficiency improved and new enterprises sprouted, Poland became a star per-former among Eastern Europe's newly capitalist economies.

As these stories suggest, Sachs was no foe of the free market and was not reluctant to prescribe temporarily painful adjustments for the countries he counseled. But as his reputation grew, he clashed often with the IMF, which he viewed as insular, rigid, and resistant to considering novel approaches. And upon seeing the onset of the Asian crisis, Sachs went into overdrive, arguing passionately in aca-demic papers and op-ed articles that the Fund was fundamentally misdiagnosing the problem by putting so much of the blame on the Asian economies' internal weaknesses.

Although he acknowledged that Thailand, Indonesia, and Korea suffered from corruption, poorly supervised banking systems, and crony capitalism, these problems were long-standing and could not explain why so many countries were hit all at once, Sachs con-tended. He believed the crisis was similar to a bank run in which depositors rush to withdraw their money for fear that no money will be left in the vault. The crisis, he noted, was affecting only those countries that were most susceptible to such runs—countries where foreign bankers and other creditors suddenly woke up to the fact that there wasn't enough hard-currency reserves to cover all the debts they were owed in the near future. As Sachs wrote in a paper with his colleague Steven Radelet:

[T]he crisis is mainly the result of a self-fulfilling panic of creditors. Rational investors may have an incentive to pull money out of an otherwise healthy country if the other investors are doing the same thing. The key analytical question is when such a self-fulfilling panic can occur. In our view, the main condition is a high level of short-term foreign liabilities relative to [hard-currency reserves].

The crisis hit only countries that were in a vulnerable position, i.e. with high levels of short-term debt relative to [reserves]. No emerging market with low levels of short-term debt relative to reserves was hit, even those with high levels of corruption and weak banking systems.

The IMF didn't dispute that panic played an important role in the crisis. But Sachs contended it was such an overwhelming factor that the Fund's traditional austerity-oriented remedies—budget cuts, tight monetary policy, and so on—would only exacerbate the problem. The impact of the withdrawal of capital, after all, is recessionary, so as Sachs put it, "You don't need to contract on top of the contraction. Don't crunch fiscal policy. Don't send interest rates sky high. It doesn't restore confidence. It just makes the crisis worse."

What Sachs didn't know—and couldn't, because of the IMF's ironclad internal discipline—was that some of his analysis was echoed, at least to an extent, by Fund economists during internal debates over how to handle the crisis. In Korea, for example, some staffers from the Asia and Pacific Department fought hard against proposals by others in the IMF for sharply higher interest rates, insisting that such a policy would be counterproductive in a country where companies were so highly indebted. Wanda Tseng, cochief of the Seoul mission in November 1997, made such an argument in a high-level meeting some weeks later. One IMF economist recalled her saying, "If you raise interest rates, the corporations will go further into the red. External creditors will be even less willing to lend to Korean banks that are exposed to these corporations and will withdraw dollars even more. So the currency will depreciate further, and you'll worsen the crisis." The economist further reported: "Fischer was listening. And it did give people pause."

The Fund's interest-rate hawks conceded that raising borrowing costs would magnify the pain to economies in distress. But they argued that the alternative was worse—a currency plunging completely out of control. Since many Asian borrowers owed debts in dollars, a drastic weakening in the local currency would also cause widespread bankruptcies. So the best policy for a country in crisis, they argued, was to raise interest rates quickly to extremely high levels—upward of 60 percent or even 100 percent, if necessary—and hold them there, in the hope that the currency would soon stabilize. The high rates would provide irresistibly attractive yields for investors of all kinds to keep their money in local currency, and as soon as the panicky sell-off of the currency abated, rates could be eased back down.

Backing up the hawks were the most influential members of the Executive Board—Karin Lissakers of the United States, together with representatives of Britain, Germany, and other powerful countries. In informal meetings, these board members often berated dovish staff members when they felt interest rates weren't being raised enough in countries that had sought Fund rescues. (As previously noted, such a clash occurred in Indonesia.) "There were huge fights over monetary policy, partly because of ambivalence on the part of the staff," Lissakers recalled. "Some people said, if we jack up interest rates, we'll kill off companies. But you're dealing with a foreign exchange crisis. So pick your poison. You're going to have a terrible problem either way."

The IMF's doves were not as dovish as Sachs would have liked, to be sure. Tseng said she favored higher rates in Korea, just not as high as the hawks advocated. But some staffers later became bitter over the upbraiding they took for tight-money policies that were a source of much greater contention within the Fund than was known at the time. "On the one hand, we were being clobbered by Jeff Sachs, who was on Mars," one former IMF economist said. "And the Board was coming from the opposite direction, thinking we are all wimps. The U.S. Treasury guys were incredible hawks, wanting us to raise interest rates sky high. They hid behind our skirt. They were willing to let the Fund get all the blame, and never made it clear that if things were left to them, interest rates would have been raised substantially higher."

Regardless of who was responsible for the policies, Sachs contended that he was right to condemn them. The fact that several of the crisis-stricken countries had enjoyed strong recoveries in recent years only strengthened his conviction. "You got a sharp rebound in Asia from mid-1998 onward, and both sides in the debate claim vindication," Sachs said. "I argued that this was not a crisis of fundamentals; it was a crisis of confidence, and the crisis was so much more extreme than justified by the fundamentals that when it ended, you would get a sharp bounceback. The IMF says, 'Look how good we did'—looking, for example, at Korea. But my view is, why did you have to have a recession like that?"

The scene was the September 1997 annual meeting of the IMF and World Bank in Hong Kong, and Joseph Stiglitz was committing heresy—if not outright sedition.

Meeting privately with a group of East Asian finance ministers, Stiglitz, the World Bank's chief economist, was taking a position flagrantly at odds with the IMF's dogma that supported liberalizing the flow of capital around the globe. The fifty-four-year-old Stiglitz urged the ministers to press ahead with a plan some of them were considering to impose emergency controls on short-term funds flowing in and out of their countries. When the ministers fretted that such an action would draw the opprobrium of the IMF and the financial markets, Stiglitz suggested that they could dampen the impact on their individual economies by acting collectively.

The plan never came to fruition. But as the story suggests, Stiglitz was not bashful about breaking with his employer's sister institution. During his tenure at the World Bank, he refrained from using Sachs-like purple prose in his public utterances and writings; indeed, he usually avoided mentioning the IMF by name. But he managed to convey, quite publicly, his agreement with Sachs that the crisis was a panic and that the IMF's austerity programs were making it worse. In a February 1998 speech in Chicago, for example, he derided the use of high interest rates as an inducement for investors to stop withdrawing their money from a crisis-stricken country: "In many circumstances [high rates] will also create financial strains, leading to bankruptcies . . . making it less attractive to put money into the country," he said. His position afforded explosive force to his opinions; if Sachs was an irritant to the IMF, Stiglitz was a bull in the Bretton Woods china shop.

Bearded, with thinning salt-and-pepper hair and round wire-rimmed glasses, Stiglitz had a distinguished academic record that would win him a Nobel Prize in economics in 2001. Tales of his absent-minded-professor ways were legion. His ties were perpetually askew, and he often removed his shoes in the middle of meetings. But despite a twinkly-eyed good humor, he tended to press his arguments in internal debate with such unrelenting ardor as to limit his effectiveness as a policymaker; during his four years on the Council of Economic Advisers, he often exasperated even those who were siding with him, former colleagues recalled.

In a conversation shortly after he left the World Bank in spring 2000, Stiglitz explained his motivation for going public against the IMF. "I thought the adverse consequences of the [Fund's] policies were so great—people actually *died,*" he said, adding that the IMF refused to respond to his "private, quiet interventions," so "I felt from a moral point of view, one couldn't just remain silent." Manifesting the fervor that often rubs people the wrong way, he cited a history course his children had taken in which they learned about the Holocaust and the culpability of Germans who failed to speak out. "You have to think about that kind of issue," he said. "Clearly it was not the same kind of crime. But peoples' lives were being destroyed, and I believed unnecessarily so."

Stiglitz's battles with the IMF (later recounted in a best-selling book he wrote) were the most visible part of a larger rift between the World Bank and other elements in the High Command. Many World Bankers shared his views on the crisis, and they felt aggrieved because their institution—which, like the IMF, has an Executive Board dominated by the G-7—was being forced to contribute vast sums toward rescue packages as if it were some sort of giant automatic teller machine. World Bank officials recalled James Wolfensohn, its president, railing about "late-night phone calls" from Rubin and Summers, who would typically pressure him by saying they had prepared a package of so many billions of dollars including a portion from the World Bank—and that without the World Bank's contribution, the entire rescue would fall apart.

Since the mission of the World Bank is to alleviate poverty, there was a legitimate argument for it to lend money to countries in crisis, for purposes such as helping families keep their children in school. But the demands from the U.S. Treasury, which came with virtually no consultation, left no time for study or planning at an institution that traditionally took months or even years of deliberation before granting a loan. The main motive was clear—to beef up the dollar amount of the packages—so under duress from its main shareholders in the G-7, the World Bank provided the Asian crisis countries with billions of dollars in all-purpose, fast-disbursing "structural adjustment loans," which soared from 2 percent of its lending in fiscal 1996 to nearly 40 percent in fiscal 1998. "It was in all ways galling," said one of Wolfensohn's top aides. "It wasn't just that we disagreed with the macro tightness of the Fund packages; it was that our development lending was being diverted into this financial crisis-fighting function."

Still, as angry as the World Bankers were, many of them considered Stiglitz a loose cannon. His broadsides often seemed aimed at the World Bank as well as the Fund, notably speeches he gave questioning the "Washington consensus," the orthodox economic view that countries maximize their chances for prosperity by liberalizing, stabilizing, and privatizing their economies. He spent little time on internal issues and projects and remained distant from most of the staff. "He was playing the outside game, using the bank as a bully pulpit, seeing how far he could go," said David Ellerman, a close aide to Stiglitz at the World Bank. "In terms of looking at the detailed design of a program, and trying to shape it while it was still in the bank, Joe did very little of that. . . . He had personal sources of information, like Korean professors he knew, or people who'd been his students, guys who were now *chaebol* big shots. He almost took it for granted that the information he was getting from the Bank was degraded in some way. So even when he was in the bank, he wasn't really of the bank."

Stiglitz was proud of having been raised in working-class Gary, Indiana, where he went to a public school that taught skills such as printing and electrical work. After graduating from Amherst College and earning his Ph.D. at MIT, he taught at several major universities and ended up at Stanford in 1976. He soon became renowned for his pathbreaking research in a field called the economics of information, which explored how free markets could produce bad outcomes. Challenging the conventional assumption of most economic analysis that the private pursuit of individual gain always maximizes societal welfare, Stiglitz's work showed that unfettered markets function imperfectly under some circumstances because of the less-than-perfect information available to each participant. Part of his antipathy toward the IMF stemmed from his belief that the Fund had never used his findings in its theories about how economies work. "None of these ideas is incorporated into their model," he said. "They stopped [updating their model] in 1975."

One important paper Stiglitz wrote, for example, demonstrated that high interest rates had a serious, little-noticed downside: Companies suffer severe losses of net worth as they struggle to make interest payments, and once that happens, they find it difficult to recover and issue stock to new investors. Thus the damage from high rates is long-lasting even if the high rates themselves are temporary.

Stiglitz discussed the implications of his work in summer 1997 with Stan Fischer at a party at the Washington home of Jeffrey Frankel, a member of the Council of Economic Advisers. The two men went outside while other guests remained indoors. "I conveyed the sense I was worried [the IMF] was being excessively contractionary," Stiglitz recalled, "and Stan conveyed the view that if that turned out to be the case, they would have enough flexibility to adapt"—in other words, the Fund would urge crisis-stricken countries to switch to a more stimulative approach. "I replied that there are long lags and irreversibilities—that is, if you destroy firms, you don't re-create them."

Later, he said, he tried to organize a conference or seminar to which experts would be invited to discuss with IMF and World Bank officials the problems posed by the Fund's austerity-minded approach. But the IMF rejected the idea after Fischer received a phone call from a reporter asking about it. "I wasn't willing to have a public event at which Joe expressed his views and others expressed their views and we got this whole thing escalated up," Fischer said. In a voice at once measured and smoldering, he added:

> The notion that Joe has—that he was the only voice in the wilderness, and nobody else had thought of all this and that, is just wrong. Those debates took place, without Joe's intervention. It could have been done with Joe.
>
> On the argument that companies go permanently bankrupt because of high interest rates—there is a trade-off. He just ignores the fact that further devaluation also produces bankruptcies. It's not as if people at the IMF don't understand that if you have high interest rates it's bad for firms.
>
> There are institutional reasons why you don't want one Bretton Woods institution criticizing another publicly. I very firmly believe that our institutions stand or fall together. It took a lot to

refrain from responding to the World Bank's attacks, but we did the right thing.

* * *

The phone rang late on Saturday night, September 14, 1997, at the Tokyo home of Eisuke Sakakibara, the Japanese vice minister of finance for international affairs. The caller was Larry Summers, obviously angry and apparently in no mood for conversational niceties. "I thought you were my friend," he sputtered.

Sakakibara was no stranger to confrontation with high-ranking officials from Washington, but this time, he was in deep. Four days earlier, he had sent a confidential document to five Asian governments proposing that Japan and its neighbors establish an "Asian Monetary Fund" armed with tens of billions of dollars in hard currency, and now Washington had obtained a copy. For two hours that night, the fifty-six-year-old Sakakibara tried to mollify Summers, without success. As far as his American interlocutor was concerned, Sakakibara's plan posed a grave danger to the proper functioning of the IMF.

From his lively attire to his voluble manner and his zest for intellectual combat, Sakakibara was a breed apart from the stereotypically starchy Japanese bureaucrat. In a country whose elite civil service wields legendary control over policy, the ministry he served was the most eminent and powerful of all. The men (and they are almost all men) who staffed its offices were primarily top graduates of Tokyo University's law department, the pinnacle of achievement in an education system that subjects students to a grueling battery of exams at every step. But in contrast to the formal air that pervaded the ministry, where officials tended to ponder questions warily and respond with carefully hedged opinions, Sakakibara's style was to prop his feet up on his desk or coffee table and let fly a stream of provocative statements, interspersed with throaty cackles. Whereas dark suits and white shirts tend to be de rigueur among Japanese bureaucrats, Sakakibara often sported beige suits with green or purple shirts. Flaunting his familiarity with Western culture, he kept vintage wines on display in his office and made frequent references to his extensive experience in the United States, which included a year as a high school exchange student in Pennsylvania, a Ph.D. in economics from the University of Michigan, a spell on the IMF staff, and a visiting professorship at Harvard.

Yet as un-Japanese as he seemed on the surface, Sakakibara was a passionate nationalist who championed the view that his country must cling to its cultural values and reject the socioeconomic model that Washington tried to press on Tokyo and other Asian nations. The United States, Great Britain, and other individualistic, Anglo-Saxon societies might be ideally suited to the dog-eat-dog world of creative destruction in which the forces of the profit motive constantly eradicate weak enterprises and spawn vigorous ones. But that was decidedly not true of Japan, in Sakakibara's view, because of the importance Japanese attached to social harmony and the group rather than the rights of the individual.

Sakakibara's distaste for the untrammeled free market shone through in a book published in 1990, *Beyond Capitalism,* in which he made the case that Japan's "non-capitalist market economy" was perfectly designed to sustain the country's prosperity while preserving its social fabric. Although Japanese corporate executives competed fiercely to win customers by providing high-quality products and service, they didn't have to worry nearly as much as their American counterparts about pressure from shareholders for short-term profits, because the bulk of their companies' shares were typically owned by other companies belonging to the same corporate family, called a *keiretsu.* Accordingly, Japanese companies could put top priority on maintaining lifetime employment, which in turn elicited profound loyalty and dedication from their employees. As Sakakibara put it, Japan was "anthropocentrist"—meaning that instead of having people serve the interest of capital, the state made sure that capital was marshaled to serve the interests of the people.

The United States had no right to seek fundamental changes in this system, Sakakibara argued, even though the close-knit links among *keiretsu* members often made it very difficult for foreign firms to crack the Japanese market. Indeed, he noted that with the fall of communism, different forms of capitalism were now competing with each other—and at the time his book was published, Japan's seemingly boundless growth was stirring speculation that its system would triumph. The country's GDP, ranked twentieth in the world in 1965, had rocketed to second-largest and, based on the 4-plus percent growth rates posted in the late 1980s, awed some pundits into concluding that it would overtake the output of the flagging U.S. economy within a decade or two. Japanese industrial and financial giants were muscling aside American firms in one sector after another, their competitiveness fueled in part by cheap capital raised from their *keiretsu* banks. Sakakibara himself declined to predict that Japanese-style capitalism would displace the U.S. version; he saw each country's system as tailored to its national strengths and societal traits. But whereas Americans would presumably stick with their own economic practices, he said, "I personally like the Japanese system."

From his perch as vice minister, which gave him membership in the G-7 deputies, Sakakibara registered discontent with the way the Asian crisis was being handled by the IMF and the rest of the High Command. The Fund was too quick to blame the Asian economic model, he contended, when the real fault lay with forces beyond Asians' control. Like Sachs and Stiglitz—with whom he conferred often—he strongly disagreed that the turmoil was attributable to cronyism and excessively cozy ties between business and government; this was, he repeatedly insisted, "not an Asian crisis but a crisis of global capitalism." Although he never went as far as Malaysia's Mahathir in demonizing hedge funds and currency speculators—in fact, Sakakibara counted George Soros among his regular contacts—he sympathized with Mahathir's calls for much greater regulation over international capital markets. A U.S.-dominated IMF, he complained, was "trying to change the Asian system, without changing the international financial system."

Sakakibara saw an opening for an offensive in mid-August 1997, when the international rescue for Thailand was being cobbled together. Resentment was running high in the region over how the United States was insisting on including tough conditions in Thailand's IMF program while refusing to contribute money directly to the bailout. During the Tokyo conference at which Japan led a group of neighboring nations in providing Bangkok with $10 billion in loans to bolster its IMF rescue, Sakakibara recalled, "We sensed an intensity . . . that could be termed the 'unity of Asian countries.'" Together with his deputy, Haruhiko Kuroda, he began sketching plans to launch a gigantic hard-currency fund that would use a portion of the hundreds of billions of dollars in reserves held by Japan, China, Hong Kong, Singapore, and other countries in the region. Sakakibara and Kuroda had been considering the merits of such a fund ever since the Mexican peso crisis, when they noticed that Asian nations probably wouldn't qualify for IMF loans proportionate with the one Mexico received because their Fund quotas had failed to keep pace with their rapid economic growth. Now that contagion was spreading, they concluded, their idea required urgent implementation. An Asian fund would intimidate speculators into leaving the region's tigers alone, by showing that a big pool of dollars was readily available for any country that came under attack.

"In retrospect, it was all too hasty," Sakakibara admitted in a reconstruction of the episode that he wrote about in late 1999 for *Yomiuri Shimbun,* a major Japanese daily. That was putting it mildly. Sakakibara sent an "unofficial" outline of the plan to South Korea, Malaysia, Hong Kong, Singapore, and Indonesia on September 10, 1997. Although the documents didn't cite specific figures, Japanese officials let it be known they were contemplating tens of billions of dollars, and their hope was to reach agreement at the IMF–World Bank annual meeting to be held later that month in Hong Kong. The documents weren't intended for American eyes, but "our phones were lighting up with concerns from several Asian nations about the proposal," the Treasury's Tim Geithner recalled. American officials were enraged. Sending the proposal to the Asians without involving Washington seemed a rude departure from the normal conduct of the U.S.-Japanese alliance, which is based on the precept that the United States should maintain a strong presence in the Asia Pacific region (a major element being the 47,000 U.S. troops stationed on Japanese soil). Summers's phone call to Sakakibara was just one of several conversations in which U.S. officials expressed indignation to their Japanese counterparts that the rules of U.S.-Japanese engagement had been violated.

In that phone call, Sakakibara reminded Summers that the two men had discussed the idea for an Asian Monetary Fund at a meeting in Paris about a week earlier. But Sakakibara later admitted that he had omitted one crucial point in the Paris conversation: "I did not mention the possibility that the AMF might act independently of the IMF, since that option was still undecided." Soon thereafter, he added, he decided that "although the AMF would basically cooperate with the IMF, in certain cases the AMF would act independently."

That detail, of course, was what the United States objected to most of all—the prospect that countries under financial siege could circumvent the IMF by tapping into a separate pot of money. What incentive would such countries have to correct their underlying weaknesses if they could obtain sizable amounts of money with few or no strings attached—and what would stop them from inciting even larger crises down the road by continuing to run irresponsible policies?

The U.S. counterattack against the AMF began swiftly, with a letter dated September 17 from Rubin and Greenspan to their Asian counterparts, followed up with visits to Asian capitals by Tim Geithner and Ted Truman, the director of the Fed's Division of International Finance, to lobby against Sakakibara's plan. Tokyo could claim some supporters among Asian countries, including Malaysia, the Philippines, and Thailand. But Australia opposed the idea, and Chinese officials dealt it a serious blow by telling Japanese emissaries that China could take neither a positive nor negative position—in effect, a veto by the region's geopolitical heavyweight. Other Asian policymakers may have played one side off against the other; Japanese and U.S. officials both claimed to have garnered backing for their positions from Hong Kong and Singapore.

Tensions over the issue were sufficiently high that some of the Asians wanted to exclude U.S. officials from the meeting of deputy finance ministers called to discuss the plan on September 21 during the IMF–World Bank conclave in Hong Kong. The Americans hadn't contributed to the Thai rescue package, so why, Washington's critics asked, should they be allowed into the meeting? Japanese Finance Ministry officials, who were chairing the meeting, considered the argument but compromised by allowing Summers and Truman and Stan Fischer to attend as "observers." In any event, Chinese representatives continued to withhold endorsement of the Japanese plan, and the idea was shelved at that point.

Still, Sakakibara's efforts forced a shift in U.S. policy. Even if the AMF was going nowhere, Asian officials liked the idea of mustering vast new sources of funding for countries in crisis. And although the Clinton administration was loath to commit direct U.S. contributions to such rescues—the risk being a fiercely critical reaction from Congress—Washington found itself obliged to go along.

Initially, U.S. officials took the position that rescue funds should be provided almost entirely by the IMF and other multilateral institutions. The Rubin-Greenspan letter of September 17 stated that although "it is important to increase substantially the resources available to the international community to respond to crises," the money should come via the IMF rather than via bilateral loans. The IMF's member countries, they noted, were already scheduled to approve an increase of about $90 billion in Fund quotas, which would substantially fatten the Fund's war chest of hard currency. In addition, the Fund—whose rules made it awkward to provide jumbo loans quickly to member countries—could establish new procedures to make such loans easier to approve in emergencies. "This in turn should help reduce the likelihood that substantial bilateral resources would be necessary in future cases," the Rubin-Greenspan letter said.

But the Asians were not convinced that the IMF and other multi-lateral lending agencies had enough financial firepower without bilateral money to back them up. In a memo to high-level administration colleagues dated September 30, Geithner reported, "The original Japanese proposal to establish an Asian Monetary Fund faces significant resistance within the region, but there is still substantial support for establishing some type of financing mechanism for mobilizing bilateral resources in support of future IMF adjustment programs." The approach outlined in the Rubin-Greenspan letter was "likely to prove insufficiently compelling to avoid some regional financing mechanism," Geithner said. "Our best case outcome would probably be an ad hoc arrangement for mobilizing bilateral resources alongside IMF programs."

Accordingly, the United States agreed to a new strategy for dealing with the crisis that combined beefed-up IMF rescues and the promise of bilateral aid as a backstop, an approach that was adopted in November at a meeting in Manila of deputy finance ministers from Asia and the United States. The so-called Manila Framework ensured that the IMF would remain as the center of the official response to crises in the region, killing off Sakakibara's AMF. It included an agreement to establish a new type of IMF loan facility, called the Supplemental Reserve Facility, that would provide larger amounts of money more rapidly than traditional Fund loans. Moreover, the IMF and other multilateral agencies like the World Bank would provide the bulk of the up-front money in a rescue, but bilateral loans would provide a "second line of defense" that could be tapped by a crisis-stricken country if the first line proved inadequate. Acknowledging defeat of the proposed AMF, Sakakibara said, "We were taught a valuable lesson on the influence the United States wields in Asia."

Just as the AMF fight was winding down, Sakakibara found himself on the defensive over a new, more serious bone of contention between Japan and the United States—the state of the Japanese economy. By the time of the Manila meeting, economic conditions in Japan were reaching a frightful low, prompting outcries that, as the country accounting for two-thirds of Asia's GDP and the single largest source of its capital, Tokyo was doing its neighbors a terrible disservice at the worst possible time.

The 1990s had made Sakakibara's paeans to Japanese-style capitalism look more than a trifle overstated. The country's banks were stuck with hundreds of billions of dollars in bad loans, thanks to a collapse in real estate prices in the early part of the decade that sharply reduced the value of the collateral many borrowers had put up. The Nikkei stock index, which had peaked close to 39,000 at the end of 1989, had fallen to well under half that level; this exacerbated the banking system's troubles because Japanese banks, unlike banks in most industrialized countries, had bought stocks directly and used them as a major part of the capital cushions they maintained to protect against loan losses. (The practice of banks buying stocks was one of the features of the *keiretsu* system.) The anthropocentrism of the Japanese system was still working to a large degree—companies were taking all manner of measures to avoid mass layoffs—but now Japan's economic strengths had become its weaknesses. *Keiretsu* ties between banks and their corporate clients, which kept the banks from foreclosing on many struggling debtors, meant that the economy was prevented from ridding itself of unhealthy firms and renewing its vigor by creating new ones.

The economy, after staging a recovery in 1996, slumped anew following an April 1997 tax hike, and the Nikkei, which was trading above 20,000 in June, dipped to the 15,000 level in mid-November. Now the banks were in worse shape than ever, with their capital cushions evaporating and hopes fading that cash-strapped borrowers could repay their loans. The strains became more evident as the banks, once envied the world over for their financial might, found themselves unable to borrow dollars without paying anywhere from half a percent to four percentage points more than their healthy foreign competitors. Ominous cracks in the system materialized on November 17, when for the first time since the turmoil immediately following World War II, one of Japan's nationwide banks, Hokkaido

Takushoku Bank, went under, followed a week later by Yamaichi Securities, one of the "Big Four" Japanese brokerage firms. Prime Minister Ryutaro Hashimoto won a temporary reprieve from the relentless drumbeat of bad news by announcing a surprise income tax cut on December 17, declaring, "We can't trigger a worldwide depression beginning in Japan."

To U.S. officials, the sickness of the Japanese economy—and its impact on Asia—made Sakakibara's criticisms of the IMF all the more irritating. Notwithstanding his claims that the Fund's policies were fanning the flames of the crisis, Japanese banks were the ones running for the exits in the greatest numbers.

Despite the bitter fight over the AMF, Sakakibara ultimately joined forces with the U.S. Treasury often during the Asian crisis. The United States and Japan held a like-minded view on one major issue—the desirability of providing large-scale packages of official money when rescues were needed. Within the G-7, that position was coming under harsh attack.

Hans Tietmeyer's beef with the IMF was different from that of Sachs, Stiglitz, and Sakakibara. Tietmeyer, president of the Bundesbank, Germany's central bank, believed that by providing huge bailout packages, the Fund was violating the basic tenets of financial sobriety. Specifically, it was creating moral hazard by encouraging bankers, portfolio managers, and other members of the Electronic Herd to take excessive risks on the assumption that IMF rescues would protect them from the consequences of default.

German central bankers are well-known for playing the Defender of the Faith role on such matters of financial rectitude, and Tietmeyer, who once studied for the Catholic priesthood, fit the stereotype neatly. A bald, big-boned man with thick white hair on his temples and piercing blue eyes, he had grown up in a small Westphalian village near the Dutch border that he once described as having "strongly influenced me with its Catholic church culture, mixed with a dose of Prussian discipline." He was the second of eleven children, and his father was a relatively low-paid civil servant responsible for administering the town finances, so young Hans, who was thirteen when World War II ended in 1945, had to procure his own resources for getting an education. Starting in high school, and later as an economics student at the University of Cologne, he worked on a farm, at a factory, in construction, and even in a coal mine.

Tietmeyer entered the Economics Ministry in 1962, working for Ludwig Erhard, the father of West Germany's postwar miracle, whose reverence for stability in prices and currency values resonated deeply with a nation still seared by memories of the hyperinflation that preceded the rise of Nazism. When the Social Democratic government of Helmut Schmidt fell in 1982 and was replaced by Helmut Kohl's right-of-center Christian Democrats, Tietmeyer, a conservative, became state secretary at the Finance Ministry, where he was Bonn's chief international economic diplomat and its representative in the G-7 deputies. Then in 1989, he was named to a top post at the Bundesbank, the guardian of the almighty deutsche mark and the world's standard-bearer for central bank independence, and he became its president in 1993. His refusal to sacrifice the mark's stability, despite pressure from fellow Europeans for easier credit and faster growth in the continent's dominant economy, helped enshrine his reputation for uprightness and constancy. "When he comments with raised finger on the evils of debt, inflation and sloppy currencies, the words 'Thou shalt not' hover, constant if unspoken," the *Economist* magazine said.

A similar aversion to quick fixes underlay his opposition to large bailouts and the moral hazard they engendered. "Although rescue operations of this kind may afford relief in the short run, for the future they involve the risk of a recurrence of unwelcome behavior on the part of market players," he wrote in the Bundesbank's 1997 annual report. His concerns were widely shared within the German government and by other northern European nations, and critics elsewhere also echoed the argument, notably conservative analysts in the United States and Republican members of Congress. But as a powerful G-7 insider, Tietmeyer was the world's most influential decrier of moral hazard.

The principle of moral hazard is easiest to grasp in the case of insurance. People who insure their autos against the cost of collisions are likely to drive a bit more carelessly than they would otherwise, and people who insure their homes against fires are likely to be a bit less cautious about removing flammable material from their attics—because they know that even if something terrible happens, they will be reimbursed for their loss. The problem becomes particularly acute when an official agency is providing the guarantee. Government deposit insurance, for example, makes people less concerned than they would otherwise be about whether their money has been deposited in banks that are lending imprudently— and as a result, some banks make riskier loans than they should.

As the crisis in Asia unfolded, Tietmeyer and his colleagues at the Bundesbank and the German Finance Ministry were still seething over what they regarded as an egregious case of moral hazard on an international scale—the 1995 bailout of Mexico. Part of the problem was that the rescue had come as a total surprise to them. The Clinton administration, anxious to halt a panicky flight from the peso, was losing a battle in Congress to provide Mexico with billions of dollars in loan guarantees, and on the night of January 30, 1995, with Mexican reserves nearly exhausted, the Treasury persuaded Camdessus and Fischer to announce a $17.8 billion IMF loan for Mexico the following morning, to supplement a $20 billion line of credit from the Treasury's own special pool of lendable funds. The furious Germans and British, who had not been consulted even though the loan was more than three times the amount that any IMF borrower had ever received, sought to register abstentions on the vote in the Fund's Executive Board after the board had okayed the loan—as strong a diplomatic signal of disapproval as they felt they could send without undermining the rescue.

Quite apart from their anger over the lack of consultation, the

Germans fumed that the IMF loan to Mexico was essentially going to bail out Wall Street. It was a point the Clinton administration could not deny. American investors and brokerage firms had bought tens of billions of dollars worth of short-term Mexican government bonds, called *tesobonos,* and the rescue package was providing Mexico with enough dollars to ensure that it could avoid defaulting on any of those bonds. Washington's defense was that the alternative—allowing default—would have dealt an incalculable blow to U.S. interests and conceivably to the global economy in general. Mexico had become one of the shining stars of market-oriented reform in the developing world, and that model would be severely tarnished if the country became an international financial pariah. Moreover, administration officials argued, a Mexican default would risk causing other countries to succumb to crises, with ill effects all over the Western Hemisphere if not beyond. But in Tietmeyer's view, the deal virtually invited investors and lenders to shower money on emerging markets as if the downside didn't exist. "The generous involvement in Mexico must remain an exception," he thundered.

The German protests about moral hazard were a source of considerable contention within the IMF. The prevailing view was that Tietmeyer and his colleagues were overstating the problem. In the first place, as Camdessus repeatedly noted, many private investors were taking heavy losses on their emerging-market holdings. Moreover, there was little if any hard evidence that the Mexican bailout had caused excessive amounts of capital to flow into Asian countries such as Korea; the overwhelmingly dominant factor was that the region was booming.

But perhaps the most compelling counterargument to the Germans was that appalling consequences were likely in store for millions of people if bailouts were not provided. Should the world turn its back on a country in distress for the sake of deterring reckless behavior in the future? Wasn't that somehow analogous to denying medical treatment for a car-crash victim who has been driving too fast? At an IMF conference, the Fund's chief economist Michael

Mussa acknowledged that the Mexican bailout might have made investors and lenders a tad more cavalier. But he added, to laughter from the audience, "And if we hadn't rescued 800 people from the *Titanic,* we would have taught everyone an even more valuable lesson about the dangers of ocean travel!"

The Germans, like the Japanese, eventually fell in line with the U.S.-led consensus on how to handle the crisis, partly to avoid worsening the turmoil. But their concerns about moral hazard could not be dismissed lightly, and when the crisis spread to Russia, there would be no disputing that investors had placed large bets on the expectation of a bailout for a country deemed too strategically important to fail. Although Tietmeyer and his colleagues strongly supported the need for IMF programs, they inveighed against "Powell Doctrine" packages. Instead of providing massive amounts of taxpayer money, they argued, the international community should insist on "involving the private sector"—a code phrase for inducing banks and investors to accept part of the burden for resolving a crisis by reducing or stretching out their claims.

The ultimate German taunt was that the Powell Doctrine was a fraud—that the flows of private capital moving across borders had grown so vast that they would almost always swamp the packages that the IMF, the World Bank, and the G-7 were capable of putting together. Sure, the $50 billion rescue for Mexico was large enough to assure all the holders of *tesobonos,* plus all the other foreign holders of Mexico's short-term debt, that the country would have enough dollars to pay all its obligations. But Mexico would prove to be the only example of the official sector mobilizing truly overwhelming financial force to stem a crisis. In other cases, the markets would see that even large packages were insufficient to cover all possible capital outflows.

By that logic, the only surefire crisis-beating strategy is to involve the people controlling those outflows, and make sure they are part of the solution rather than part of the problem. The logic, which Tietmeyer tirelessly propounded, would prove particularly compelling in Korea.

· 7 ·

THE BOSUN'S MATE

Within the IMF, staffers later recalled, one person saw more clearly than most that the rescue for Korea announced on December 3, 1997, wouldn't work, and that a different strategy was required. That person was Michael Mussa, the Fund's chief economist and head of its Research Department.

Mussa could be counted on to relieve the tedium of IMF meetings with a savagely funny line (for example, his remark about Camdessus seeing the glass half-full even when there wasn't any glass)—or, in some cases, with plain odd behavior. He once broke into song at a board meeting, regaling the bemused executive directors with a rendition of "My Wild Irish Rose." After returning to work from a long absence due to a heart ailment, he was cheerfully blunt about its severity: "My condition is category three/four," he told colleagues. "There is no category five."

Balding, bespectacled, and a lifelong bachelor, Mussa was born in 1944 and grew up in Long Beach, California. His father, a native of France whose education ended in the eighth grade, was a leader in the Screen Set Designers and Decorators Union. Mussa attended the University of California at Los Angeles and earned his M.A. and Ph.D. at the University of Chicago, where he later joined the business school faculty. But he developed a yen for public policy after a stint as a member of the Council of Economic Advisers in the Reagan administration, and he joined the IMF as chief economist in 1991. Economics, by the accounts of his friends and associates, was his life's great passion, aside from his private collection of fine wine. Socially awkward, he tended to stand nervously sipping a drink at social gatherings, unless he was stimulated with a remark or question about economics—in which case he suddenly became the life of the party, using anecdotes and analogies to illustrate his points. He often used such story-telling devices to good effect in internal debate, and during the Korean crisis, he told this story about his cousin:

> On the eighth of December 1941, my cousin John volunteered to join the U.S. Navy. He was then not quite old enough, and he lied about his age. He was assigned to the aircraft carrier *Lexington*.
>
> He was serving in the engine room, during the Battle of the Coral Sea, when they took two torpedoes from Japanese naval aircraft. The crew fought for at least eighteen hours to keep the *Lex* afloat. But ultimately the order came down to abandon ship. And John said that as they were climbing up the gangway out of the engine room, there was a 200-pound bosun's mate standing on deck, pounding on the rail with a billy club, commanding, "One at a time! One at a time! One at a time!"

Something like that bosun's mate—something to restore order—was what Korea needed, Mussa reasoned as the country's crisis unfolded. Foreign banks were clambering all over each other to abandon ship, so unless order was imposed on them, the country's economy was doomed. Simply throwing together a large package of loans wouldn't work. The amount of money the international community could reasonably muster for Korea wouldn't suffice to reassure all the foreigners holding short-term Korean debt that they could get their money back. They would keep jumping overboard in a panic unless prevented from doing so. Korea posed no worries about *solvency*—it had an economy churning out a half trillion dollars a year in goods and services, so full payment could be made eventually on the debts Koreans owed to foreigners, which totaled just 30 percent of that half-trillion-dollar GDP. But the country was in quite a *liquidity* bind.

At meetings in November 1997 with Fund staffers preparing to head to Seoul, Mussa suggested a plan in which Korea's financial problems would be handled much as New York City's were in 1975. That is, creditors holding short-term debt owed by Korean banks would be induced to exchange their claims for longer-term bonds. Foreign banks would be told to calm down, that they would eventually get their money back, but they couldn't get it back right away, so they would simply have to wait over a longer period. They would become "involved" in resolving the crisis, as the Germans liked to put it. Instead of being bailed out, they would be bailed *in*.

In fact, something quite similar to this solution would ultimately be adopted, but only after the world's eleventh-largest economy had come within a whisker of being forced to default. The final resolution of the Korean crisis is now viewed as a triumph for the High Command, and in a way it was. But the tumultuous series of events that preceded it is evidence for the tenuousness of the High Command's grip on the global economy, and shows how close the Committee to Save the World came to being the Gang Who Couldn't Shoot Straight.

On the night of December 3, following Camdessus's press conference in Seoul where he announced the completion of negotiations with the Korean authorities, exhausted IMF mission members began work on one final task—writing a report on the program for the Executive Board, which would meet at 9 A.M. on December 4 to approve it. Some went back to their rooms and crashed, and Neiss had to fly to Washington to attend the board meeting. But Wanda Tseng and a handful of hardy others stayed up for yet another all-

nighter (her fourth straight) at the Hilton. "I don't know how I managed. And I don't remember how I managed," she said, adding that
her miseries intensified when her computer froze during the night,
requiring an assistant to scroll through the Letter of Intent and type
it into her own computer.

Computer malfunctions would be the least of the mission's woes.
Far more serious was the growing concern that the rescue plan,
unveiled to such fanfare, was itself dangerously prone to failure.

The $55 billion package of loans consisted of two distinct por-
tions. The multilateral portion, totaling $35 billion, came from the
two Bretton Wood institutions—$21 billion from the IMF and up to
$10 billion from the World Bank—plus $4 billion from the Asian
Development Bank. The remaining $20 billion, which was to come
on a bilateral basis from governments of wealthy countries, was the
second-line-of-defense money—funds that were available if the
multilateral loans proved insufficient. This portion had been thrown
together in great haste during the last days of the negotiations.
"Some unfortunate finance minister from one country—I won't tell
you which one—was woken at 2 A.M. [to see if his country would
agree to contribute]," one IMF official recalled. "The executive director for that country said, 'I can't wake him at such an hour.' We said,
'Do you want your country in or not? The minister will be pretty
mad if you're not in because you didn't wake him up.'"

The IMF economists at the Hilton compiled a chart showing that
Korea would obtain enough hard currency to avoid default if it
received all the loans in the package, including the IMF money
(which was to be disbursed in tranches a few billion dollars at a
time), plus the $20 billion second line of defense. But after they sent
a draft of their report to Fund headquarters, their work started to
unravel. Bijan Aghevli, home from Indonesia, called from Washington in his capacity as deputy director of the Asia and Pacific Department to say that the report needed to be changed because of its
assumption that the $20 billion in the second line would be lent to
Korea. Board members from the rich countries contributing the sec-

ond line couldn't vote for a program that so clearly assumed the money would be used, Aghevli explained.

The mission members in Seoul were thunderstruck, for without the $20 billion, the projections in the report showed the Koreans falling short of the reserves they needed to meet all their obligations. This posed an urgent problem: The Executive Board was due to meet in a matter of hours to approve the plan; it was close to midnight in Washington, and the staff report was supposed to be delivered to board members' homes at 5 A.M. Eastern Standard Time. Under IMF procedures, the board cannot approve a program that is "not financed"—that is, in which the projections show a likelihood of a country lacking the ability to pay its bills. "You will have to tell the Board that the program is not financed!" members of the Seoul team told Aghevli, who tried—with limited success—to calm them down.

The problem over the second line of defense was, at bottom, a problem with one country—the United States. The Treasury Department was still nervous about drawing attacks from Congress for even suggesting that it would use its emergency cash fund for lending money directly to bail out a country, and it wanted numerous conditions imposed on the use of the money. To this day, the prevalent view among non-U.S. policymakers involved in the Korean rescue is that the Treasury never intended to permit disbursal of the second line. "It was a funny thing about the second line," said one IMF executive director. "The line was 'there'—but it wasn't there."

Treasury officials would later insist that they were prepared to disburse U.S. funds to Korea if the situation had become sufficiently dire. But they also admitted that the second line was, as one of Rubin's former aides put it, "an experiment in trying to make something look as real as possible without ultimately having to spend the money. It had a sort of Catch-22 quality to it: If you don't need the money, you don't get it. And if you do need it, then you probably haven't met the conditions for disbursal."

Aghevli and the Seoul mission team concocted a makeshift solution to their problem as the clock ticked down. Essentially, they cooked the books. They didn't fake the numbers, of course, but they changed the assumptions. To compensate for the loss of the $20 billion in second-line money, the report assumed that 80 percent of Korea's foreign creditors would roll over their loans instead of demanding immediate repayment as they had recently been doing. With that assumption plugged in, the chart showed Korea able to pay its obligations. Never mind that few staffers thought the assumption had a high probability of being achieved in the near term; at least the numbers added up.

The episode may have amounted to little more than a bureaucratic snafu. In a sense, the report *had* to assume that the rollover rate for the bank loans would rise sharply; the whole point of the IMF's plan was to restore confidence. But the last-minute number crunching did not augur well for the rescue the IMF board would approve that morning. In effect, the board was endorsing a program in which key Fund staffers had very little faith. In their report, the mission team inserted an unmistakable caveat about the bailout's chances for success: "It is difficult to estimate with any certainty the likely development in capital flows over the program period, given the uncertainty surrounding the rolling over of private sector short-term debt." Translated from Fund-ese, this meant staffers feared the IMF's money would end up being used to pay off foreign banks that were unwilling to keep their money in Korea.

Stan Fischer was subdued but guardedly optimistic when he faced the press in Washington on Friday, December 5. "The early reactions have been promising," he said, noting that in the two days since the completion of the negotiations, the won had appreciated about 2.5 percent, and the Korean stock market had rebounded by 15 percent. "While these immediate reactions are welcome, they will be sustained only if the Korean economic program is rigorously implemented and is seen to be rigorously implemented by the markets."

This would be the public position of the IMF and the Treasury: We've done our part. The Korean program is solid, and the rest is up to the Koreans themselves. If they fail to demonstrate sufficient commitment to IMF-mandated reforms, the markets will punish them accordingly. So the following week, when the bottom fell out, official fingers in Washington quickly pointed at Seoul.

Beginning December 8 and continuing for five days, the won plummeted by the 10 percent limit each day, ending up at 1,712 per dollar on December 12, and markets around the world went into a tizzy. The Koreans were blamed for demonstrating an obvious lack of enthusiasm for revamping their economic system. The chief evidence that Korea still "didn't get it" was the reaction of presidential candidate Kim Dae Jung, who held a slight lead in the polls for the December 18 election. The day after the rescue was announced, Kim—despite having joined his rivals in signing a pledge to support the program—said that if elected he would renegotiate the terms, and soon thereafter his campaign took out ads in major newspapers attacking the deal. Washington's frustration deepened when the Finance Ministry disclosed on December 9 that it would invest $1 billion in two large ailing commercial banks and take control over them rather than shut them down. "It was one of a series of dubious decisions that have been surrounded with a lot of ill-thought-out pronouncements," an unidentified American official told *The New York Times*. The Treasury publicly rejected Korean pleas for a speedup of disbursements from the international rescue package, with Rubin stating pointedly: "I think they've got a strong program with the IMF and I think the key is for them to implement that program and implement it effectively."

The Koreans' actions were unhelpful, and the political uncertainty over the looming December 18 election surely increased the difficulty of regaining financial confidence. But what really hurt market sentiment was growing evidence that the bailout, large as it was, didn't provide Seoul with sufficient hard currency to deal with the potential near-term outflow of capital. The precipitous downturn in the won had begun when *Chosun Ilbo*, a leading Korean daily, published a leaked version of the December 3 IMF staff report, which laid bare how low Korea's reserves had fallen, and how high the country's short-term debt was. Particularly shocking was one table showing that usable reserves had shrunk to $6 billion on December 2, and another indicating that the foreign debt falling due over the coming year was as high as $116 billion, instead of the $65 billion officially reported, once the data included debts owed by the overseas branches and subsidiaries of Korean companies. This information became public only because of a leak to the press; unlike the Thais, the Koreans were not forced to disclose it by the IMF or the Treasury or anyone else. But the impact was devastating to confidence in much the same way as the impact on Thailand when Bangkok revealed in August 1997 how much it had spent on forward commitments to defend the baht.

Now the markets could see more clearly than ever how close Korea was to running out of reserves and how vulnerable it was to a rush for the exits by its creditors. Some market participants had already drawn the conclusion that the rescue package was insufficient; they had peered through the hype of the $55 billion "headline" figure and noticed some squishy elements, such as the second line of defense and the World Bank's pledge to lend "up to $10 billion." The data in the IMF document enabled them to discern that Korea was not getting a sufficient injection of reserves compared with the hard-currency obligations of Korean firms. As Guillaume Lejoindre, director general of Credit Agricole Indosuez in Seoul, told Agence France Presse on December 12: "The calculation is simple. Korea is to receive $9 billion from the IMF and other multilateral institutions between now and the end of the year. The short term debt due at the same time is difficult to calculate precisely, but it is around $20 billion. The country still has $4 billion to $5 billion in reserves, but they can't let it fall to nothing. The money isn't there."

The Thompson Financial Services Company, the world's largest bank credit rating agency, expressed similar sentiments, downgrading Korea's sovereign risk rating on December 11 with a warning about the "increasing prospect of the recent IMF emergency package being insufficient to meet the country's short-term financial obligations."

As such assessments proliferated, the panic among foreign banks deepened, and their willingness to roll over short-term loans to Korean borrowers virtually ceased. John Dodsworth got a close-up view of the process from the offices of the Bank of Korea, where he helped staff the IMF's "drain watch." A British citizen, Dodsworth had been sent by the IMF to India in June 1997 as the Fund's resident representative, and he recalled his six months there as "interesting but quiet." Around December 10, he got orders to fly to Seoul—not that he had ever worked on Korea or been there before. He arrived around December 15, missing a Christmas visit from his three children, and returned to India for only about five days. "I finally told my wife, 'Pack up. We're moving to Seoul,'" said Dodsworth, who was eventually named the Fund's resident representative there.

In the evenings at the Bank of Korea, Dodsworth and other members of the drain-watch team, which included American economists Gary Moser and Rob Kahn, looked on in dismay as the central bank scrambled to respond to the flood of requests for hard currency that were coming in from Korean commercial bank branches around the world. Usually these requests took the form of faxes, saying that the commercial bank making the request had an obligation coming due that a foreign creditor had refused to roll over. And usually the Bank of Korea would accede to the request by lending reserves, although in some cases, central bank officials would call in a top executive from the commercial bank to appear in person—in the middle of the night—to explain the request in more detail. "The second or third evening I was there, someone came in from a commercial bank, and all of a sudden a Bank of Korea employee started screaming at him,"

Dodsworth recalled. "This guy had seen too many of these things, of people coming and asking for [reserves], and he just snapped."

The IMF tried to maintain a brave face, insisting that the program was finally starting to work even as all market indicators continued to point toward disaster. At a briefing for reporters on December 16, a senior Fund official said that the Korean authorities—as well as the presidential candidates and the nation's broader body politic—had finally recognized the seriousness of the situation and were demonstrating the sort of firm commitment to the program that was required:

> We had during the last few days a significant change in Korea. You had conflicting signals from Korea just after the adoption of our program; you had the impression that the government was only half-heartedly committed to it, that after signing [letters promising to back the program] the candidates could have second thoughts. Now all of that is changed, for the candidates, and the government.
>
> We are impressed that not only is the government complying with the program but they go beyond it, and in the right direction. We asked for the suspension of nine merchant banks, and fourteen have been suspended so far. We asked for liberalization of financial operations, for foreigners to operate in the money market and bond market—all of that is speeded up.
>
> We are not going to change this program when the ink is not yet dry.

But behind the scenes, despair was taking hold among top policymakers. Alarmed members of the Clinton administration's foreign policy establishment were once again demanding that the United States take whatever actions were necessary to save Korea, including backing a new and bigger international bailout. But Rubin dug in his heels more firmly than ever. "What Bob said at that point was, 'If you go with *another* package, and that one doesn't work either, then you're *really* in trouble," recalled Daniel Tarullo, the president's chief international economic policy adviser.

Talk of the unthinkable—allowing a Korean default—was quietly spreading. At a meeting among senior Treasury and Fed officials over lunch in Rubin's private dining room, Greenspan asked that the agencies' staffs examine the possible consequences of a default more thoroughly than they had previously. He wanted to know how awful the impact would really be; for example, how much further would the won be likely to fall? The Fed chief had a strong libertarian streak, having once been a leading disciple of Ayn Rand, the philosopher whose "objectivist" theories disdain large government. So his question about the impact of default was no mere matter of wanting to be sure that the High Command was prepared for the worst. He considered government bailouts inherently distasteful and preferred to let debtors and creditors sort out their own problems. The failure by a major country to pay its obligations might be the best outcome for the financial system, he thought, because if lenders paid the price for having made irresponsible decisions, the moral-hazard problem would be obliterated and justice would be served. The only question was, would the system destabilize completely?

Similar sentiments were voiced at the IMF's board meeting on December 16 by Onno Wijnholds, the executive director representing Holland and several other countries. Wijnholds, who shared Greenspan's desire to see the moral-hazard problem addressed more forcefully, said, "While not fit for publication, I would be interested in staff's assessment of default."

In fact, the Fund staff had been contemplating that issue, in a top-secret document addressed to Stan Fischer that came to be known as the "Plan B" memo. Dated December 12 and drafted by Matthew Fisher, a British economist in the Policy Development and Review Department, the memo outlined several options for resolving the Korean crisis and explored their pros and cons. One option

involved increasing the size of the bailout and speeding loan disbursements to Seoul faster than originally contemplated—which
had the obvious disadvantage that the money might simply fly out of
the country into the vaults of the foreign banks just as the initial
bailout money was already doing.

A second option was default, in which the Korean government,
recognizing that its reserves were insufficient to fulfill all obligations,
unilaterally ordered Korean banks and companies to suspend making payments on their debts to foreigners and imposed controls on
all outflows of capital except for trade-related transactions. Although
this option was carefully considered as a possible least-bad choice,
the disadvantage for Korea was that it would risk wrecking the
country's creditworthiness for the foreseeable future, and the disadvantage for the world as a whole was that it would risk sparking
massive contagion, with the Electronic Herd bolting out of Latin
America and every other emerging market just as it had in Asia. The
chances that this would happen were unknowable and unquantifi-
able, but as one Fund economist who was involved in the Plan B discussions said, "You could tell yourself a story that this could deliver
the most severe shock to the world economy since the 1930s."

The third option involved using the IMF and the G-7 to perform
the role of the 200-pound bosun's mate on the USS *Lexington*. This
was the "bail-in," which was elegantly simple in theory but laden
with practical complexities.

The basic idea of the bail-in was that government officials in
Washington, Tokyo, London, and other world capitals would use
"moral suasion" to induce Korea's foreign bank creditors to stop
pulling their money out of the country. It was in the banks' own
interest, after all, to call a collective halt to their panic, roll over their
loans, and accept a stretched-out payback of their claims, since
default would be averted if everyone participated. But one obvious
problem with this plan, which is also known as a "standstill," was
that it would require a high degree of government intervention and
coordination. It wouldn't work unless creditors could see they were

all being treated more or less equally. Creditors might accept the argument that they had a collective self-interest in refraining from demanding immediate repayment, but the whole scheme would fall apart if the perception took hold that certain claimants were getting a better deal than others. Thus governments would have to ensure that the banks acted together.

Camdessus and Fischer favored the idea of trying a bail-in, an option also supported by the Bundesbank's Tietmeyer and his German government colleagues. In a G-7 deputies meeting at New York's Kennedy Airport on November 26, the German deputy, Jürgen Stark, had argued for approaching the banks and admonished that a Mexican-style bailout should not be repeated in Korea, but he was rebuffed by the others.

The idea of bailing in Korea's bank creditors was also being bruited about within the U.S. government. The chief advocate, who initially proposed it before Thanksgiving, was the director of the Fed's Division of International Finance, Edwin "Ted" Truman, a curmudgeonly former Yale professor. Truman, fifty-six, was a force to be reckoned with at the Fed, where he had worked since 1972. Much admired by Greenspan for his encyclopedic knowledge and experience in international financial issues, and by his subordinates for his devotion to public service, Truman was also saddled with a temper that sometimes got the better of him when he was confronted with lesser intellects who didn't grasp the power of his logic with sufficient speed. The targets of his outbursts even included members of the Fed's seven-person Board of Governors, who resented him for his reluctance to share information with them and acting as if his only fealty belonged to the chairman. Although not a physically imposing person—five feet, seven inches, balding, with thick glasses—Truman didn't shy from raising his voice in board meetings to discourage lines of questioning he disliked. "Ted thought he was guardian of the gate," said one former board member. "Governors were political types who came and went, and he was the protector of the institution, and he knew what was best."

Truman, perhaps better than any other senior U.S. policymaker, appreciated the art of twisting bankers' arms to save countries from financial crises. He had been the top lieutenant on international matters for former Fed chief Paul Volcker during the Latin American debt crisis of the 1980s, which was first addressed with a strategy called "concerted lending." When countries such as Mexico, Brazil, and Argentina had trouble paying the debts they owed to foreign banks, Volcker and Jacques de Larosiere, the IMF managing director at the time, would apply heavy pressure on the banks to provide new, longer-term loans, as would Volcker's counterparts in other wealthy countries—provided, of course, that the debtor country reached agreement with the IMF on the conditions of a program to put its economy in order. The idea was to buy time for the countries to resume growth and make sure that the banks, which were being saved from default, bore a fair share of the burden involved in the rescue. Although Volcker never explicitly said he would use his powers as a bank regulator to exact retribution from a bank that refused to follow his moral suasion, the implication was not lost on bank executives.

Korea was a nearly ideal candidate for a bail-in, Truman believed, because most all its foreign creditors were banks, which were easier to organize and more susceptible to government suasion than, say, mutual funds holding bonds. But the plan faced resistance from two very powerful men—Alan Greenspan and Bob Rubin.

Greenspan had his libertarian reasons for objecting; as the nation's chief bank regulator, he was loath to take any action that smacked of using his powers to coerce private-sector institutions, which were supposed to be accountable to their shareholders. More important, the Fed and Treasury chiefs were dubious that the bail-in would work, and they were fearful that if it did, it might produce catastrophic side effects. They knew the markets had changed a great deal since the 1980s, when banks were virtually the only conduits for private international capital flows. They were unsure whether the banks that had lent to Korea would bow to the exhortations of government officials, and they reasoned that the banks might react to being concerted in Korea by withdrawing en masse from other emerging markets. "The main question was, would doing this cause more dominoes to fall?" said Truman, who recalled that Brazil and Russia were most frequently mentioned as countries from which foreign banks might flee.

In other words, the High Command might be damned it if did and damned if it didn't. A unilateral stoppage of payments by Korea would surely risk contagion, but so might an effort to prevent default that involved bailing in the banks. Meanwhile, Korea's reserves were dwindling lower by the day.

At the Jefferson Hotel, where Rubin lived, the top policymakers in the Treasury and Fed gathered for dinner on Thursday, December 18, the day of the Korean election. The idea of bailing in the banks, participants recalled, was not even discussed much. The main option before the group was whether to increase the size and speed of the bailout, which would involve accelerating the IMF disbursements, inducing the World Bank to lend faster, and disbursing the second line of defense. Summers and Lipton made the case for this approach, but others argued that extra bailout money would do little more than ensure that more frightened bankers got their loans repaid.

Rubin mostly listened and asked questions, his skepticism evident. As usual, he was weighing the idea probabilistically, in terms of whether it would substantially improve the odds of a favorable outcome. "The Jefferson dinner was the classic Rubin decisionmaking paradigm," Geithner recalled. "Rubin's view was, he's totally happy to take the risk if it's a prudent risk. If $5 billion of U.S. money is going to make the difference between success and failure in Brazil or Korea, he would invest the money; a serious country should be willing and able to make that kind of investment. But the key question is what the probability is that it will increase your chances of success."

The dinner meeting broke up in a bit of disarray as Geithner and Truman, who carried pocket electronic devices that could transmit financial newswires, began catching some of the early reports from Seoul about the pending electoral victory of Kim Dae Jung. The president-elect's initial comments did not inspire confidence and were causing renewed turbulence in the markets. The won, which had rallied earlier in the week, was falling again, to about 1,630 per dollar. The outlook was bleaker than ever. As Summers recalled: "That dinner sort of ended with everyone agreeing that default's a terrible alternative; pouring more money into Korea so the banks can take more money out is an untenable alternative; so let's all wrack our brains and see what we can come up with."

Kim Ki Hwan had been waiting patiently for several days to travel from Seoul to Washington. Now, on December 19, he was arriving in the U.S. capital on a mission that he desperately hoped would save his country's economy.

Kim was not a government official, exactly, though he bore the title "ambassador-at-large for economic affairs." Fluent in English and distinguished-looking with wavy silver hair and glasses, Kim was a lawyer who had been recruited by the Ministry of Finance and Economy earlier in the year to help represent the government's interests overseas. He was traveling to Washington at the behest of Finance Minister Lim, with whom he had dined a few days before, to plead with the Treasury for a new rescue plan.

Instead of leaving for Washington immediately after the dinner with Lim, he had deliberately arranged an appointment with Summers for Friday, December 19, because the Korean presidential election was scheduled for the eighteenth. He wanted to know the identity of the next president before making his pitch. "The Korean government had lost so much credibility, I felt making any request in the name of the existing government would not be enough," Kim recalled. "That's why I decided to visit right after the election. So I got on a plane right after voting. I didn't know who had won. When the plane landed at Kennedy Airport, that's when I learned who would be our next president. I had a person from the ministry make a call to the Korean consulate in New York. He said, 'It's going to be DJ!'"

The victory of "DJ"—the affectionate nickname for Kim Dae Jung, which helped differentiate him from the current president, Kim Young Sam—was a development for which Kim Ki Hwan was not fully prepared. Before leaving Seoul, he had met with the ruling-party camp, but he had not had a chance to meet with DJ's people. And although Kim Ki Hwan felt fairly sure he could speak on DJ's behalf, he couldn't be entirely certain. DJ, after all, was a populist, a man who had become famous worldwide for his struggle to rid South Korea of military dictatorship. In 1971, while running against President Park Chung Hee, DJ had been permanently injured when a truck "accidentally" ran his campaign vehicle off the road; a couple of years later, he was kidnapped from a Tokyo hotel by Korean security agents and nearly murdered. Put on trial for allegedly fomenting riots, he was sentenced to death, spent years in prison, and was eventually exiled to the United States. Following the overthrow of military rule in 1987, he had resisted joining the ruling party, and he maintained close ties with Korea's militant trade unions.

While on the plane to New York, Kim Ki Hwan had decided on a name for the plan he wanted to pitch to the Treasury—"IMF Plus." Since he was intending to ask the Treasury a big favor, he thought he should offer something in exchange—namely, additional and faster reforms of the Korean economic system than had been pledged in the December 3 IMF program. The question was, would DJ endorse such a policy? During his campaign, the president-elect had backed off from his initial denunciations of the IMF program and had pledged to support the reforms. But to assert that DJ would go even further down the reform path—especially given the likely pain for his working-class constituency—was a claim Kim Ki Hwan was not prepared to make on his own.

When I learned the next president would be DJ [Kim said], I thought, "I have to get his endorsement." So as soon as I arrived in Washington, I made several calls to Seoul. I contacted an influential legislator in DJ's party, and he in turn got in touch with DJ's secretary. The reply came from the secretary. He said, "Oh, Ambassador Kim, we are all behind you, and we wish you all success for your mission." That call came just a couple of hours before I left my hotel to go to the Treasury.

Actually, the way it happened was this: I had been waiting for the call in my room. But you cannot deny yourself a call from nature. When I came back, there was a voice mail saying the president-elect assures me you have our full support. So I felt I could tell the Treasury I speak for both governments—incoming and outgoing.

To prepare for the meeting with Summers, Kim had met Lee Kyung Shik of the Bank of Korea on December 16 and had obtained a table showing how much hard currency the central bank had left and how many days would pass before default was likely. But by his arrival in Washington on the nineteenth, he worried that the figures might already be outdated. So he called Lee, asking for a more up-to-date version. Concerned about security, Lee replied that he would have someone in his Washington office deliver the data by hand. "When the guy gave me that data, his hand was shaking," Kim said. "He said, 'The situation is truly bad, and I hope you succeed.' The table showed that if nothing were done, our foreign exchange reserves as of December 31 would be minus $600 million to $800 million."

At the meeting with Summers, Kim explained how precarious Seoul's reserve situation was, and he made two requests. First, he asked the deputy secretary to use his influence so that the IMF would speed up its disbursements of rescue loans to Seoul. Second, he asked for the U.S. government to persuade American banks and other international banks to roll over their loans to Korean banks. "On the first request, Mr. Summers indicated he was quite willing," Kim said. "But on the second question, he played a little poker face on me. He said, 'You know our system. Our government cannot tell banks what to do.' I said, 'Well, if you cannot tell *your* banks, would you please tell the Japanese to tell *their* banks.' That is something he said he would consider."

Toward the end of the meeting, Summers asked where Kim would be that evening, and Kim replied he would be at his hotel. Hopeful that favorable word would be forthcoming, Kim waited for a call, but having heard nothing by 9:30 P.M., he rang Summers's office and was told the deputy secretary was in a meeting. About fifteen minutes later, however, Tim Geithner phoned back with what sounded like promising news: The Treasury was dispatching David Lipton to Seoul, on a plane leaving Washington the following day at 1 P.M.

The meeting with Kim Ki Hwan, according to Summers, was "very consequential." The promise that Korea's new president would seize the mantle of reform provided the basis the Treasury needed for one last attempt at forging a new rescue. On the morning of Saturday, December 20, Summers and the other top Treasury policymakers held a marathon conference call with Rubin, who—in a characteristic manifestation of sangfroid—had flown off for a fishing vacation in the British Virgin Islands.

Although a final decision would take a couple more days, the Treasury was at long last coming around to the view held by Mussa, the Germans, Ted Truman, Camdessus, and Fischer, who had been quietly lobbying the G-7 after weighing the options in the Plan B memo. The conclusion was simply inescapable: Korea would default without an initiative to bail in the banks. Even Greenspan finally agreed, despite his distaste for government-imposed solutions, that the potential consequences of default were simply too great to risk.

But now the question was whether the banks would go along or whether they would react by pulling loans all over the world, engendering an even bigger crisis. John Reed, chairman of Citicorp, told Summers that the scheme had a fifty-fifty chance of success.

Furthermore, there was almost no time left, as Kim Ki Hwan's data from the Bank of Korea suggested. The Christmas holidays were just around the corner, and once commercial bank CEO's left town for the ski slopes or beach resorts, the chances of persuading them to act collectively were almost nil. A substantial amount of Korea's short-term debt was coming due the last week of the year, and if the bankers holding those claims insisted on immediate repayment instead of rolling them over, Seoul would be forced into default. Help for Pauline was on the way, but she was still on the railroad tracks, and the onrushing locomotive was fast approaching.

That was the urgent message from another power center in the U.S. government, the Federal Reserve Bank of New York, which is by far the most important of the twelve regional banks in the Federal Reserve System. The New York Fed supervises most of the largest banks in the country, and it also serves as the central bank's watchdog for financial markets and handles the day-to-day dealings in the money markets through which the Fed controls interest rates.

The New York Fed's president, William McDonough, was the second most powerful Fed official after Greenspan, and unlike Greenspan, the sixty-three-year-old McDonough was itching to use the moral suasion his office commanded to convince the banks that it was in their collective interest to avert default. Over the weekend of December 20–21, in calls to Washington, he argued for convening a meeting of bankers as quickly as possible before the holidays. "I said, I've got to have the meeting on Monday, because otherwise there won't be anyone to talk to," McDonough recalled.

With his silver hair and square jaw, McDonough exuded the polished charm one would expect in a high-ranking central banker, though he had been raised far from the lap of luxury. The son of Irish immigrants who moved to the west side of Chicago, he lost his mother at age ten, and his father, who sold insurance, died the following year. He went to Holy Cross College in Massachusetts on a U.S. Navy ROTC scholarship, majoring in economics. Then came five years in the Navy, during which he continued his economics training with a master's degree from Georgetown University, and six years in the State Department. He joined First Chicago National Bank in 1967, where he spent more than two decades and rose to the rank of vice chairman. With this background as a top commercial bank executive, he felt he understood how the minds of bankers worked and how to persuade them of what was in their self-interest.

At McDonough's behest, top executives from six of America's largest banks—Citibank, J. P. Morgan & Co., Chase Manhattan, Bank of America, Bankers Trust, and Bank of New York—filed into the stately offices on the New York Fed's tenth floor on Monday morning, December 22. The meeting was to make sure the top banks would be prepared to move fast to start the process toward a collective agreement aimed at stopping the hemorrhaging from Korea. Policymakers in Washington were still debating what sort of approach to take with the banks. Some favored a strong-arm stance to ensure that the banks rolled over their loans; others argued that tough words would only backfire. The approach favored by McDonough and Terrence Checki, a New York Fed executive vice president responsible for international issues, was to avoid giving the bankers the feeling they were being locked in a room and handcuffed; rather, the idea was akin to inviting them into the room and suggesting they try on the handcuffs to see how they feel. "You've got to put them in a position where doing 'the right thing' is demonstrably in their interests and that of their shareholders," McDonough said. "You don't want to make a guy stand up at his annual meeting and say, 'We did this for the good of mankind.' You want him to feel that he'll be able to stand up and say, 'We did it because otherwise we would have had a loss, and we believe Korea's debt is fully collectible.'"

At the meeting, McDonough confined himself to explaining his personal view, which was that if the banks refused to roll over their loans and stretch out their claims, the IMF and the High Command would have to refuse to take any further steps aimed at preventing a Korean default. His words to the bankers went roughly as follows:

This is not an official position of the U.S. government. But let me tell you what my view is, and what I'm advising my colleagues in Washington, which is, it is unconscionable for taxpayers' money, whether from the IMF or bilateral funds, to be used to repay private-sector creditors. So my advice to my colleagues in Washington is, there should be no additional public-sector money for Korea unless you guys reschedule the debt. That's my position. It doesn't mean it will be followed, because it is not yet U.S. policy. But I wanted you to know that, because the flow of funds is such that we're talking about a Korean default next week if this matter is not resolved.

The bankers asked a number of questions and expressed several reactions, according to people who were present. But one of the most striking, and widely voiced, was this: Why had it taken so long for a meeting such as this to be called?

Upon hearing that David Lipton was returning to Seoul, Ambassador Kim Ki Hwan didn't waste any time. He knew Lipton would be seeking the commitment of president-elect Kim Dae Jung to a host of reform policies, and he feared that if Lipton heard a lot of equivocating, American support for the "IMF-Plus" plan might be lost. The Korean envoy wanted to make sure that DJ was well-briefed on what to say, because after all, the president-elect didn't even know what IMF-Plus was. "I felt I had to beat Mr. Lipton back to Seoul," Kim said with a sly smile. So early Saturday morning, December 20, Kim left Washington to catch an earlier flight back to Seoul from New York, which enabled him to land in the South Korean capital Sunday afternoon. Lipton's flight would not arrive until 6:30 Monday morning.

Back in Seoul, Kim Ki Hwan reported immediately to Finance Minister Lim, who agreed that it was "inevitable" for Korea to accept further reforms, and said that DJ should hear directly what had happened at the meeting with Summers. An appointment was arranged for Kim Ki Hwan to meet DJ at the president-elect's home early Monday morning, around the same time as Lipton's plane was scheduled to land. In fact, as Kim walked into DJ's house, he passed a number of aides who were watching a TV screen showing a live broadcast of a bedraggled Lipton arriving at Kimpo Airport, wearing jeans and a blue-and-red sports shirt. "When I made my report to the president-elect," Kim Ki Hwan recalled, "I said, 'Mr. President-elect, I am sure the U.S. embassy will call you shortly, asking for an appointment with Mr. Lipton.' And I said, 'You've got to do IMF-Plus.' I didn't exactly say it was a promise I had made to the U.S. Treasury. The president-elect asked me, 'What does that involve?' I said, 'Well, [Finance Minister] Lim should report to you.' But I gave him four or five examples of what my conception was."

Fortunately for Kim Ki Hwan, who had never met DJ before, there were some powerful advisers within the president-elect's camp who favored breaking the power of the *chaebol*. Indeed, DJ's main economic adviser, You Long Kuen, a provincial governor and former Rutgers economics professor, had been trying since the election to convince the Treasury and IMF that the populist DJ would prove far more willing than the existing government to endorse those kinds of reforms. He soon got the chance to show he was right.

Lipton's meeting with DJ took place at the headquarters of the president-elect's political party, the National Congress for New Politics, an unassuming eighteen-story office building that was draped with a banner declaring, "Thank you. I'm going to revive the economy. I will work hard. Kim Dae Jung, President-elect."

A key question about DJ, as far as the U.S. Treasury was concerned, was whether the aging crusader for democracy was willing to accept the dislocations—including job losses—that would inevitably accompany the closure of weak banks and uncompetitive *chaebol* units. Korea had a law against layoffs, and some of the unions that had provided DJ's strongest support were already demonstrating against a proposed easing of the law. But the Treasury hoped that DJ, as a leader with a history of championing labor rights, would be ideally situated politically to persuade workers of the need for sacrifice.

Lipton didn't demand that DJ accede to layoffs, although he came close, suggesting that Korean unions could save their jobs only by accepting much lower pay. He told the president-elect that he felt the subject of labor was "key to Korea's situation," and that if the unions wanted to have a high level of employment, they would have to "exercise wage flexibility." Citing his own experience in Poland, Lipton reminded DJ that in that country, too, a jailed dissident leader with ties to labor, Lech Walesa, had come to power in the midst of a financial crisis and saw that short-term pain would lead to long-run gains. "I said that while unemployment rose in Poland, there were a lot of jobs created, and unemployment is now below the European average," Lipton recalled.

Kim Dae Jung replied that his first priority was to make needed adjustments in the Korean economy, and that everyone—including labor, business, and government—would have to share in that adjustment. Job security, he said, must come second. Watching a news account of the encounter on television, Kim Ki Hwan sighed with relief. "As far as I could tell," he said, "it was all music to Mr. Lipton's ears."

It was the timing, not the content, of the G-7 deputies' conference call that Jürgen Stark found so objectionable. With less than twenty-four hours remaining before Christmas, Stark, the German state secretary for finance, "did not appreciate" being stuck in his office on the phone until well after midnight, another official recalled, especially since he thought the conversation should have taken place weeks earlier.

On Monday, December 22, out of the blue, Larry Summers had delivered an important message to his fellow deputies: The New York Fed was approaching large U.S. banks about rolling over their

loans to Korea, and the United States was now urging its G-7 partners to do the same, in what would be a massive bailing in of Korea's
creditors. This sort of "private-sector involvement" was, of course,
exactly what the Germans had been advocating. So although a couple of the deputies voiced qualms, Stark said the idea was fine with
him, as long as all banks involved were treated equally. But he
warned that he couldn't be sure he could implement it, because
some of Germany's top bankers might not be reachable. Christmas is
a holy time of year in any Christian country, but that is especially
true in Germany, where families traditionally retreat to their homes
starting Christmas Eve to decorate the tree—often with candles,
which requires considerable time and care—and don't expect to be
disturbed until after the twenty-sixth. The point, Stark said, was that
the plan shouldn't have waited until the last minute.

During the conference call on December 23, the deputies and
Stan Fischer hammered out the details of a statement that would be
released on Christmas Eve, stating that the Fund, Korea, and a number of advanced industrialized countries had reached agreement on
a new plan: The IMF would speed disbursement of $2 billion to
Seoul on December 30, well ahead of schedule, and the World Bank
and the Asian Development Bank would disburse $3 billion and $2
billion, respectively. Moreover, the countries contributing to the second line of defense—including the United States—would "support"
a disbursement of $8 billion from the second line (though in the
end, the second line would never be tapped). In return, Korea
would accelerate many of its promised reforms and undertake new
ones, under the terms of a revised Letter of Intent, which Hubert
Neiss was already negotiating in Seoul.

But the statement contained a new catch: The aid for Korea was
being provided "in the context of a significant voluntary increase in
rollovers or extensions of the maturities of existing claims by international bank creditors on Korean financial institutions." In other
words, just as McDonough had admonished, the Fund would help
Korea avoid default only if the banks played their part by agreeing to

a standstill—calling a halt to their withdrawals of money—and accepting a payback of their loans over a longer period of time.

As Stark had feared, organizing the standstill over Christmas proved a monumental and nerve-racking challenge. To get in touch with Martin Kohlhaussen, chairman of Commerzbank and a leader of the Association of German Bankers, German Finance Ministry officials had to go through Chancellor Helmut Kohl's office, where an officer in charge—in the German equivalent of the White House Situation Room—tracked down a private phone number for Kohlhaussen's vacation home in the Bavarian Alps. In France, Stark's counterpart, Jean Lemierre, had little trouble getting the banks' top executives to agree to the standstill, given the French tradition of government intervention, but rounding them up wasn't easy. Upon being reached at home, one CEO told Lemierre, "Look here, I'm opening oysters [a traditional Christmas Eve treat in France]; I'm not going to talk about Korea," to which Lemierre replied: "Look here, you *are* going to talk about Korea."

In New York, McDonough convened a second meeting of U.S. bank executives on the morning of December 24, with John Reed of Citicorp participating by speakerphone from Colorado. Once again, McDonough told the bankers the realities as he saw them: Either they reschedule the debt, or Korea goes into default. "They were sort of looking around," the New York Fed president recalled, "and I said, 'I bet it would be convenient if I just go have a cup of coffee. Why don't you guys talk.' And when I came back, the best of all possible worlds had happened. They said, 'Not only will we reschedule, but we think a public announcement that we're supporting the policy would be a great idea.'"

Some of the bankers present recalled a more contentious discussion, in which participants demanded to know why Wall Street investment banks weren't being roped into the standstill, and others complained anew about being solicited at the eleventh hour.

The plan was still touch-and-go. New York Fed officials informed the bankers that William Rhodes, vice chairman of Citicorp, was being asked to coordinate the effort by international banks to halt the run on Korea, but they acknowledged that Rhodes wasn't in New York. "They said he was on an island somewhere, which tells you how completely screwed up all this was," one banker said.

In fact, Rhodes was on vacation in Barbados, but he was the obvious choice for the job. During the debt crisis of the 1980s, he had headed or worked on committees of major banks in negotiations with Brazil, Mexico, Argentina, and numerous other countries, and he still maintained an extraordinary number of contacts in the executive ranks of financial institutions around the world. Rushing back from Barbados just before Christmas, the sixty-two-year-old Rhodes spent the next several days on the phone cajoling his fellow bankers. In the process, Rhodes said, he gained a scary insight into how Japan's financial weakness was threatening its neighbors:

> The pulling [of credit lines from Korea] was still going on at $1 billion a day. I called [Japanese Vice Finance Minister] Sakakibara, and he said he alone could not get Japanese banks to hold. So the first step was to get the major banks to stop pulling. Over the weekend of the twenty-seventh and twenty-eighth, I got all of them—either the president, chairman, or vice chairman of major Japanese banks. Some I knew, some I didn't. I had to promise that I would get the European and U.S. banks to hold. Some of the banks, like Long Term Credit Bank, which was already in trouble, said, "It's hard for us to do this." I really had to put my name on the line. I finally got everyone to agree not to pull.
>
> This was a sign of the Japanese banking crisis. The world had changed. [Tasaku] Takagaki [the president of the Bank of Tokyo-Mitsubishi] told me, "Bill, this is not like the days when we worked together in the eighties."

In the end, thanks to a lot of luck—not to mention ruined Christmases—the world's bankers behaved in much the same way as Mussa's cousin John and the other sailors on the *Lexington* under the stern gaze of the 200-pound bosun's mate. There is much more to the story, but in a nutshell, most of the banks—or enough of them, anyway—stopped panicking and rolled over their loans. To ensure that they did, and to protect against cheating, the IMF and the central banks of wealthy nations established a worldwide monitoring system, supervised by the Fund's Matthew Fisher and the Fed's Ted Truman. Crucially important to the operation was a mass of data that the IMF drain-watch team and Bank of Korea staffers in Seoul had painstakingly assembled, showing how much each Korean bank owed to foreign lenders, to which foreign institution the money was owed, and when the debt was coming due. Every business day, a report was sent from IMF headquarters to each major central bank in the G-7 and other wealthy nations, showing which of their country's banks had rolled over loans and which hadn't; each central bank also received a report of how the other countries were doing. Top finance ministry and central bank officials—in the United States, Rubin and his aides—had to call the CEOs of banks that were balking, to reiterate that a default could be catastrophic.

In a sense, the international banks got away with murder. They had foolishly injected billions of dollars of short-term loans into a country with a shaky financial system, yet they were suffering no losses. On January 28, 1998, after an intense month of negotiations, the banks reached a broad agreement with Korean officials to reschedule $22 billion of short-term interbank debt owed by Korean banks. In exchange for the interbank loans they held, the foreign banks received equal amounts of bonds, fully guaranteed by the Korean government. Moreover, those bonds paid attractive yields— 2.25 percent over the London Interbank Offered Rate (LIBOR) for one-year bonds, 2.50 percent over LIBOR for two-year bonds, and 2.75 percent over LIBOR for three-year bonds.

The Korean people, of course, were not so fortunate, especially the 1.5 million who found themselves out of work in 1998. For a brief insight into the misery and heartbreak such a statistic entails, consider Hong Kwan Pyo, a former elevator company manager who, before the crisis, was a contented member of Korea's middle class, enjoying vacations at ski resorts and living with his wife and nine-year-old son in a spacious three-bedroom apartment in suburban Seoul. Hong's company went bankrupt when the economy crashed and builders halted construction projects. His wife and son moved in with her parents, and Hong, too humiliated to face his wife or his in-laws, became a homeless inhabitant of a park near Seoul's main train station, selling magazines on the street and vowing that he would not see his family until he raised the $4,000 he needed to start a small outdoor food stand. "I will stay away until I am able to stand up with nobody's help," Hong told Mary Jordan of the *Washington Post*. But he admitted that the wait was painful—so much so that one day, he went to his son's school and hid in the shadows just to catch a glimpse of the boy. "I cried all the way back here," he said.

Since Hong had to suffer for his country's economic excesses, why not the banks that helped fuel those excesses? The answer is that meting out justice in the midst of the Korean crisis would have been hard to square with the goal of maintaining financial stability, as Rubin noted in a speech he delivered as the Korean crisis was abating in January 1998: "We would not give one nickel to help any creditor or investor . . . [but] any action that would force investors and creditors involuntarily to take losses, however appropriate that might seem, would risk serious adverse consequences. It would cause banks to pull money out of the countries involved. It could reduce the ability of these countries to access new sources of private capital. And perhaps most tellingly, it would cause banks to pull back from other emerging markets."

Defenders of the outcome in Korea can reasonably ask how much worse the situation might have been—and how many more stories like Hong's might have materialized, not only in Korea but elsewhere—if the country had defaulted, or if losses had been imposed on the banks. In the end, at least, Korea got what an IMF rescue is supposed to provide—a breathing space to set its economy right, and enough hard currency to keep its economy functioning—

thanks to the fact that the banks had finally been stopped from draining the money out faster than the IMF could pour it in.

Still, the question asked by the bankers at the New York Fed on December 22 remains: What took so long?

Many criticisms have been raised about how the Korean crisis was handled. But perhaps the most significant one is whether the High Command should have sought a bail-in right from the start, instead of a bailout. If the banks had been concerted into a standstill much earlier, and reached a collective agreement to stop pulling credit lines when the crisis was just beginning to unfold, a lot of unfavorable developments might have been avoided or minimized. Korea might have suffered a less severe crisis and, consequently, a milder slump. The IMF might have enhanced its image with a rescue that was successful from the get-go instead of damaging its credibility with a bailout that initially flopped. The Fund might also have avoided making demands for deep structural changes in the Korean economy that delved into sensitive political questions and went far beyond ensuring that Seoul could restore financial stability. The structural reforms Korea accepted were surely beneficial to its long-run health, and some were arguably necessary for the resolution of the crisis, to persuade the markets that the country would be a safe place to invest in for the foreseeable future. But they weren't as helpful in crisis-fighting as the more direct approach—halting the panic among the banks.

In fact, officials of the Clinton administration Treasury have drawn flak at economic conferences from a number of bankers who say they wish the standstill proposal had come around Thanksgiving, in conjunction with the first rescue attempt. Rubin, Summers, and their subordinates insist that such timing would have been terrible. In early December, they contend, the markets would have reacted with disbelief to the news that Korea was on the brink of default, and the banks would have either refused a request for a standstill or reacted to such a dramatic initiative with a bigger panic. Moreover, the December 18 election was crucial; only after the nation's political future was clear, and Kim Dae Jung had delivered a ringing endorsement of economic reform, could the markets feel confident in Seoul's commitment to tackle its fundamental weaknesses.

Readers may or may not be persuaded by that argument. But its implications help illuminate how Korea's rescue depended so heavily on luck, and how close the High Command came to standing by helplessly as a default ensued.

Imagine what might have happened if a few events had gone differently. Suppose, for example, that the Korean election had been scheduled for a month later, mid-January instead of December 18. The country was on the verge of running out of reserves on New Year's Eve based on the funds it had received in the first rescue, so it would have defaulted before it had the chance to elect new leadership and demonstrate its commitment to reform. If, as the Treasury argues, the change in the country's political environment was so essential to the late-December rescue, it is a matter of great good fortune that the election came in time to arrange the bank standstill.

What would have happened if the election had not been scheduled as early as it was? Bill McDonough's response to the question was to raise his palms toward the ceiling, smile broadly and say, "God is good!"

No doubt. But only those with extraordinary trust in Divine Providence would wish to depend on it for the safety of the global financial system. Indeed, back in Indonesia, Providence was about to bestow a much less favorable outcome.

· 8 ·

DOWN THE TUBES

President Clinton was in his office aboard Air Force One, flying back to Washington from a fund-raising dinner in New York, when the White House signal room operator put through a phone call to President Suharto shortly after 9:30 P.M. Eastern Standard Time on January 8, 1998. A handful of top U.S. officials listened in on the call anxiously, which reflected the serious concern the administration felt about the budding upheaval in Indonesia.

Hard on the heels of the Korean crisis, Indonesian financial markets were registering the full force of the compounding blunders that had been committed by the IMF and the Suharto regime in the closing months of 1997. The rupiah had dropped below 6,000 per dollar on January 2, which put the value of the Indonesian currency 60 percent below its level of the previous summer. Four days later, when the IMF was reported—inaccurately, as it turned out—to disapprove of the Indonesian government's new budget, the rupiah-dollar rate hit 7,600. On the day of Clinton's call to Suharto, the exchange rate touched the incomprehensibly low level of 10,000, causing ordinary Indonesians to strip supermarkets and grocery stalls bare of rice, cooking oil, flour, sugar, instant noodles, and just about every other conceivable commodity, as rumors flew that a ban on food imports and large-scale rationing would soon be imposed to save their nation's free-falling currency.

Washington had long eyed the Indonesian market as a potentially rich source of demand for U.S. products and services, but the country's crisis threatened much more than just the loss of a few billion dollars in exports. Indonesia has the world's largest Muslim population, so the State Department, the Pentagon, and the National Security Council were worried about the political implications of what was happening there. The brand of Islam practiced by most Indonesians is moderate and tolerant, but if hard times were to give rise to a more fundamentalist regime, the country might turn hostile toward the United States, and in particular toward the U.S. military presence in Asia. A stable, strong, and unified Indonesia helped keep Southeast Asians at peace with one another and with China; a weak and fractured Indonesia might generate tensions that would draw China into a conflict. Suharto's repressive mode of governing, which included jailing dissidents and brutally quelling civil disturbances, was offensive on human rights grounds, but its avowedly secular nature had helped keep the peace in a nation of widely disparate ethnic groups—more than 300 of them, by some counts—that included Hindus, Christians, Buddhists, and animists.

In the phone call between the two presidents on January 8, Suharto started by thanking Clinton for his attention to the crisis, not only in Indonesia but in Southeast Asia generally. Clinton replied that he had been watching the situation very carefully, and that he was appreciative of the role that Indonesia played in the region. But he said that Suharto's reform plan, though initially receiving a positive reaction in the markets, was producing the opposite effect now because of the perception that the reforms would not be implemented.

Clinton praised Suharto for showing courageous leadership in the past and said it was vital that he demonstrate similar leadership on economic reform now. The U.S. president urged Suharto to work with Michel Camdessus, who was due to arrive in Jakarta the following week to finalize a new IMF program for Indonesia. Clinton added that he was dispatching Larry Summers to Jakarta immediately to meet with the Indonesian president and his economic team.

Suharto responded with a long, somewhat discursive interpretation of his country's troubles, including a complaint that foreign speculators were to blame for torpedoing the rupiah. Although the Indonesian people would accept sacrifice if they could be sure the result would be positive, he said, he was reluctant to adopt austerity measures, such as cutting fuel subsidies, when citizens could not understand the reasons.

Clinton said he understood how speculation can get going in one direction. But the only thing Suharto could do, he added, was to change market psychology by embracing reform. Closing a bank and then permitting it to reopen didn't help, Clinton observed.

Suharto said he absolutely agreed with the need to restore confidence. He tried to justify the favoritism shown his son Bambang concerning the closing of Bank Andromeda, stating that one bank among those shuttered had been allowed to reopen because it filed a successful lawsuit. As Indonesia's president, he said, he was obliged to respect the court's decision.

The phone call from Clinton would be quickly followed by similar calls from other world leaders, including German Chancellor Helmut Kohl and Japanese Prime Minister Ryutaro Hashimoto, and private meetings with Camdessus and Stan Fischer. The dominant message was that Suharto could lead his country out of its mess, but doing so would require demonstrating a renewed commitment to IMF discipline and structural reforms of the KKN-riddled economy. That included taking actions that would leave no doubt about Suharto's willingness to change his ways and eliminate the most egregious practices that were enriching his children and cronies. Many of Suharto's interlocutors, if not all, were anticipating a highly positive impact if he followed their advice.

On January 15, 1998, Suharto would make a dramatic gesture toward acceding to the IMF proposal. He would sign a "strength-

ened" IMF program containing promises to eliminate or curb virtually all of the most prominent examples of KKN. The front pages of
newspapers the world over would splash photos the next day of
Camdessus with arms folded, standing over Suharto as the president, seated at a table, put his name to the Letter of Intent.

This program would fare even worse than the first, and once
again, Washington would fault Suharto's evident distaste for reform.
"It's not that he tried the program and the program has failed; he's
not tried the program," a senior Treasury official said heatedly in
February. But the January 15 program would go down in flames
before Suharto had any chance to undermine it, and its failure
would come as a stunner to the IMF, underscoring the weakness of
the grasp that the Fund had on the forces buffeting Indonesia's
economy.

For Indonesia, the news that Clinton had called Suharto offered a
ray of hope that the international community would somehow rally
together to lift the country from the morass into which it was rapidly
sinking. The rupiah began to recover as word spread that the IMF
had begun intense work on a new program. A team led by Bijan
Aghevli was joined in Jakarta by Fischer on January 11, and
Camdessus was on the way. By January 14, the Indonesian currency
would rise to 7,300 per dollar—still weak compared with precrisis
levels but moving in the right direction.

Summers's meeting with Suharto, which took place on January
13, was not promising. For much of the session, the elderly president
lectured the American wunderkind on his country's economic
accomplishments. To colleagues, Summers joked later that if the
conversation had been a baseball game, they would have had difficulty getting out of the first inning, "because it was always Suharto's
turn at bat."

But reaching agreement on the structural reform package proved
astonishingly easy for the IMF, especially considering that the Fund

wasn't offering Indonesia any new financial support. Aghevli and other top staffers spent an entire night hammering out many of the measures with the technocrats and other reformers in the government, and Fischer met a couple of times with Suharto to obtain his assent on most of the items, leaving a couple of sticking points for Camdessus, who arrived on January 14.

The package read like the World Bank's wish list for reforming every rotten, wasteful distortion in the Indonesian economy, and for Dennis de Tray and his Jakarta-based team, who played a central role in drafting the structural conditions, it was a triumph. "Tommy" Suharto's National Car project would lose all of its subsidies, and his control over the clove trade would be abolished. B. J. Habibie, the nationalistic technology minister, would lose government funding for his cherished project to build commercial aircraft. The president's daughters would suffer the cancellation of power-plant projects they had invested in. Tycoons close to Suharto who controlled cartels or monopolies over the trade in palm oil, plywood, paper, and a host of other products would be forced to face the chill winds of competition. Such measures might not be crucial to the performance of the Indonesian economy, de Tray and his colleagues knew, but they were of immense symbolic significance to average Indonesians, who were becoming fed up with the excesses of the elite. Instead of grudgingly allowing piecemeal reforms as in the past few months, Suharto now had a chance to get ahead of the curve and show his country—and the world—that he truly "got it."

One huge, unanswerable question looming over the negotiations was whether Suharto really intended to deliver on the program, with all the financial pain it would entail for his loved ones and lifelong allies. Fischer believed that the IMF had sound reasons for assuming that the presidential pledges were genuine, because Suharto intended to sign the Letter of Intent personally, instead of leaving it to the finance minister and central bank governor as is the usual custom. "We were told by a senior politician in the region that we must have Suharto sign—it won't mean anything if the finance minister signs," Fischer said. "But if Suharto signs, that's it." Camdessus, for his part, went to Suharto's house for several hours on the evening of January 14, going over the accord line by line, making sure the president understood exactly what he was signing. Suharto assured Camdessus that he had already summoned his six children to explain what he was being asked to do, and they had urged him to take whatever steps were necessary for the country's good.

But another question was whether putting all these reforms in an IMF program made sense. Paul Volcker, the former Fed chairman, didn't think so. At the time the negotiations for the January 15 program started, the Indonesian government had asked Volcker, whose height of six feet, seven inches reinforces his giant stature in policy-making circles, to fly to Jakarta and offer some advice. Leafing through a confidential draft of the IMF's conditions, Volcker was surprised to see items such as the termination of the clove monopoly. "I'd never read an entire Fund program before," Volcker recalled in his gruff baritone, "but it was a long plane trip. And I'm half asleep, and I get to page forty-six or something, and there I see [the provision dismantling the monopoly on cloves]."

What did spice monopolies have to do with restoring financial stability? Volcker demanded of IMF officials when he arrived in Jakarta. "They said, 'You don't understand. It's run by Suharto's son, and if we don't do anything about it, nobody will say we're serious,'" recalled Volcker, who was still not entirely convinced of the merits of the Fund's approach. "People have different philosophies," he said. "The Fund's business is macro policy, and that's the stuff you can change. How programmatic you can be, in things that go into basic cultures and economic structure—whether that's productive or counterproductive, well, it's a continuing issue, that's all I'll say."

But no amount of skepticism could halt the momentum in favor of a full-bore attack on KKN. Reformers in the Indonesian government were generally pleased with what was happening. Some worried that by targeting the businesses of the people close to Suharto, the program risked backfiring, because even if Jakarta delivered on most of the measures, the president's failure to deliver on a few politically sensitive ones would become the focus of attention. But most were glad for the opportunity to achieve measures they had long favored, and within the IMF, there were few doubts that the package was going to take the world—and the markets—by storm. A thrilled Camdessus met with the joint IMF–World Bank mission, thanked members for their hard work, and told them Suharto's concessions had far surpassed what he was expecting. "I am confident that in a few days, this will be over and you will be home with your families," he said.

One of the Washington-based World Bankers, Florence Cazenave, demurred. In meetings over the previous few days, colleagues recalled, she had expressed worries that the anti-KKN and structural reform measures in the package did not deal with the issues most worrisome to the markets. The program, she argued, should focus on addressing the problems of the banking system and the foreign debt burden of Indonesian corporations. "I would love to go home," she said at the meeting with Camdessus, "but we have still not started on the problems of the financial sector."

For most of the others, though, it was unimaginable that the reform plan's announcement would be followed by anything other than a rise in the rupiah. "We had produced one of the most comprehensive reform packages in history," said de Tray. "There was a real sense of euphoria. We thought, 'If this doesn't surprise the market, nothing will.'

"And by God, nothing did."

The room was packed, and the excitement level high, as Camdessus stepped before the TV cameras and microphones at mid-morning on January 15, 1998, to unveil the "much strengthened and reinforced" program that Suharto had just signed. Speaking in almost rhythmic cadence, with pauses for emphasis before the crucial verbs and adverbs, the IMF managing director announced the highlights:

Budgetary and extrabudgetary support and credit privileges granted to IPTN's airplane projects [run by Habibie] will be *discontinued*.

. . . all special tax, customs, and credit privileges for the National Car project will be *revoked*, effective *immediately*.

. . . BULOG's . . . monopoly over the import and distribution of sugar as well as its monopoly over the distribution of wheat flour will be *eliminated*.

. . . The Clove Marketing Board will be *eliminated*, by June 1998.

. . . the cement, paper, and plywood cartels will be *dissolved*.

. . . by February 1, all formal and informal barriers to investment in palm oil plantation will be *removed*.

Roberto Brauning, an IMF external relations officer, watched an Indonesian reporter whose eyes, Brauning recalled, "kept getting wider and wider" with the enumeration of each reform that Suharto had accepted. The reporter, and many of his Indonesian colleagues, burst into applause at the end of the managing director's statement.

After the press conference, Aghevli and three other IMF staffers went to lunch in a hotel restaurant and, in a celebratory mood, ordered a bottle of wine. "We were all very pleased," Aghevli recalled. But the team's sense of exhilaration abruptly vanished when Aghevli called on his mobile phone to find out how the rupiah was faring in the currency markets and learned that it was dropping sharply. "I couldn't believe it," Aghevli said.

The rupiah fell 6.5 percent against the dollar that day, another 5.4 percent the next day, and plummeted to 15,450 rupiah per dollar on January 23. For anyone who has wondered what it means for an economy to "melt down," this period of Indonesia's crisis offered some phantasmagoric illustrations.

Prices fell completely out of whack amid the precipitous cheapening of the currency. An obvious example was taxi rides; you could flag down one of the luxurious, air-conditioned cabs that service the tourist trade, let the meter run as you spent four hours shopping or zipping to meetings, and with the rupiah-dollar exchange rate in five digits, the cost would be the equivalent of $3 to $4. You could order a double cheese, medium pizza with pepperoni from Domino's (yes, there are Domino's outlets in Jakarta), and the cost in rupiah would be less than $1.

Enterprising traders were buying up caseloads of internationally branded goods like Camay soap and Marlboro cigarettes—a pack of Marlboros went for the equivalent of about 20 cents—and shipping them for resale to neighboring countries, where they could fetch three times the price. But that was for goods previously imported; prices of newly imported goods were soaring beyond the reach of ordinary Indonesians. Auto dealers were raising the prices of cars two or three times a week, and some were insisting on waiting until delivery to finalize prices.

And life was getting harder for the newly unemployed, whose numbers were reported to be approaching 1 million and rising fast. Riots were erupting in several East Java towns because of anger over the rising price of rice, cooking oil, and other staples. Runs on banks were intensifying, and foreign companies were quietly preparing their employees for a possible reprise of *The Year of Living Dangerously*. "You keep $1,000 in U.S. dollars per family member, so you can bribe your way out of the airport if necessary," a Canadian business executive reported. "You keep open return tickets out of Jakarta. You keep provisions of one to two weeks for your house, and you keep a bag packed."

IMF and World Bank officials were at a loss to explain why the markets were reacting with such savage negativity to a program that was designed to exceed expectations. "I'm surprised, because I think this is a very strong program," Aghevli said two days after the program's announcement. "I think it may just take time for the market to digest the news and realize the enormous significance of these reforms." One theory was that currency traders and investors were skeptical that the sweeping measures would be implemented—not because Suharto had said or done anything in particular since Janu-

ary 15, but because his credibility had sunk so low. That interpretation, of course, pointed the finger at Suharto, though it also implied
the Fund was pitifully insensitive to market sentiment by including
so many structural measures that only undermined confidence.

Nobody can discern with precision the motives of the thousands
of people who were unloading the rupiah at the time. A look at
news reports and investment analyses from January 15 and 16
shows that some foreign exchange analysts in the region were
indeed questioning Suharto's commitment to the promises he had
made. Others cited political factors and concerns about social unrest
that remained unaddressed; Suharto, after all, still didn't have a
clear successor, and if he were to die or be forced from office, the
potential for bloodshed was high.

But the most oft-cited and specific complaint about the IMF program was that it contained no hint of any plan for tackling a primary
source of worry about the rupiah—the increasingly crippling foreign
debt of Indonesian companies. In a comment echoed by a number of
other market analysts, Manmindar Singh, a senior economist at
Nomura Research Institute in Singapore, was quoted as follows by
Dow Jones International News on January 15: "The downside of the
reform is it is short of policy on how to resolve the problem of corporate debts. The market will not go anywhere as long as the issue
remains unresolved."

Here, it might seem, lay one of the keys to pulling Indonesia out
of its death spiral—taking steps that would ameliorate the corporate
debt problem—and the obvious question is why the IMF sidestepped
the matter in the January 15 program. Part of the answer is that the
Fund, for all its expertise in macroeconomic policy, has few specialists in corporate finance. But more important, the issue posed thorny
dilemmas that underscore the difficulty of coping on the fly with
crises of globalized capital.

The argument for taking action on the corporate debt issue was,
in broad terms at least, the same as the argument for the deal that
had saved Korea just a few weeks before, on Christmas Eve 1997—

namely, a self-fulfilling panic had taken hold. Everyone could see that most of Indonesia's private companies and banks would be unable to obtain enough dollars to repay their foreign creditors what they owed in the months to come. For example, Indofood, the company controlled by Suharto crony Liem Sioe Liong, had borrowed hundreds of millions of dollars from abroad without hedging itself. The company was presumably in a position to repay its debt the previous summer when the rupiah was at 2,500 per dollar, but if the rupiah were to fall to 10,000, the amount of rupiah it needed for repayment would quadruple. The extraordinarily cheap value of the rupiah was aggravating fears of corporate insolvency, and vice versa. So unless the markets got some kind of assurance that debtors would be given time to work out their debts and avert cutoffs of credit, the panic would continue apace.

The World Bank's Cazenave had been raising this issue, as noted previously, and some IMF economists, Josh Felman in particular, were also arguing prior to January 15 that the subject had to be addressed. At the very least, Felman contended, the portion of the debts that Indonesian banks owed to foreign banks should be handled with a standstill similar to the one in Korea, because Indonesian banks, like the Korean ones, were suffering from a refusal by foreign creditors to roll over credit lines. This debt constituted less than half of the country's obligations to foreigners, but it was arguably the most important part. A bank that has defaulted on its debt isn't able to provide the kinds of services that keep the economy functioning, such as letters of credit, foreign exchange transactions, and so forth. If the High Command could use its muscle to help Korea get some relief from the pressure being exerted by foreign financial institutions, why couldn't it do the same for Indonesia?

But the majority sentiment within the Fund and the G-7 was against such action: Indonesian firms should sort out their own problems with their foreign creditors. In the first place, Indonesia was different from Korea because so much of its overseas debt consisted of obligations owed directly by companies such as Indofood

rather than by banks. And saving those companies from their creditors would pose monumental moral-hazard problems. The Indonesian government, for example, could help the companies by
guaranteeing payment of the additional debt burdens the companies
faced as a result of the drop in the rupiah. But why reward such
companies, especially when so many of them—presumably counting
on being bailed out if the going got rough—had failed to hedge
themselves? The cost to the Indonesian taxpayer would be both
staggering and unjust.

The U.S. government was particularly opposed to anything that
resembled a bailout of Indonesian companies. "This was the third
rail"—that is, an untouchable idea, said the Fed's Ted Truman. "Can
you imagine—having the Indonesian government take over obligations of private Indonesian corporations to foreign banks?"

One other option, even more radical, was a government edict to
halt the panicky outflow of funds and impose capital controls that
would bar all payments abroad by Indonesian companies at least
temporarily, until a longer-range plan could be developed to stabilize
the economy. Some IMF staffers in Jakarta urged such a step around
the time of the January 15 program, arguing that the country's crisis
had gone beyond conventional remedies. But the drawbacks were
glaring, not the least of them the fact that Indonesia's corrupt
bureaucracy would allow a lot of money to escape anyway. At a
meeting in early January, Stan Fischer told Fund economists that the
leading shareholders—meaning first and foremost the United
States—would never go along.

The debate over what should have been done to save Indonesia
continues to swirl today. But here's the punch line: The IMF eventually did take measures (albeit limited ones) to address the private
debt problem, and it also took a couple of other steps that it had been
resisting, the most important being to reach agreement on a full
guarantee of bank deposits to stem runs by depositors. The problem
was, these corrective moves came after the failure of the January 15
program, and at that point, confidence in the country's economy

had been dealt a blow from which it would never recover. It must be added that Suharto made a bad situation worse; about a week after January 15, the Indonesian leader began dropping hints that he would choose B. J. Habibie, his technology minister, as his next vice president and presumed successor. That sent a strong signal Suharto was turning away from his reform pledges, since Habibie was a well-known economic nationalist whose government-backed project to build an aircraft had been among those targeted by the Fund.

Perhaps the most overdue measure, a comprehensive Indonesian government guarantee on bank deposits (set for a minimum of two years), was announced on January 27, 1998. The moral-hazard zealots at the Fund had been fighting this proposal since late 1997, but by this stage, the bank runs were so ruinous as to leave little room for debate. Later in the spring, the IMF would work out a plan that enabled Indonesian banks to reschedule their interbank loans from foreign banks, as the Korean banks had done. And at the same time as the deposit guarantee was initiated, the Fund agreed with the Indonesians to start a process aimed at rescheduling corporations' foreign debts. (The corporate debt plan was by no means a miracle cure; in keeping with the concerns of U.S. officials and others, it was devoid of any government subsidy that would make it very attractive for Indonesian companies and their creditors to participate.)

It is instructive to spin a small fantasy about how the Indonesian crisis might have worked out differently. Imagine what might have happened if the comprehensive deposit guarantee had been issued in, say, mid-November 1997, so that the bank runs would have been contained and Bank Indonesia would not have felt obliged to flood the banking system with cash. Suppose, too, that a plan for rescheduling the interbank debt of Indonesian banks had been implemented earlier in the crisis, along with something resembling the limited corporate debt scheme that was eventually adopted. Finally, suppose the IMF had insisted on fewer structural reform conditions in its Indonesia program.

Would the rupiah still have crashed? If it hadn't, would Suharto have manifested greater fidelity to the structural reforms—or would he have reneged on his promises anyway? Would a virtuous cycle have taken hold, or would a vicious one have continued?

The virtuous-cycle fantasy may be just that—a fantasy. Once the rupiah started to slide in earnest in late 1997, Indonesia's economy may have been doomed, simply because fears of social and political unrest became so intense and so self-fulfilling. The wealthy ethnic Chinese who supported Suharto's regime, and benefited from it, may have been impossible to restrain from moving their money overseas, because they were so spooked by concerns about the president's mortality—his political mortality as well as his physical mortality.

Still, the IMF's tardiness in dealing with issues such as the deposit guarantee and corporate debt is a subject of considerable ruefulness among its staff. "In hindsight, the [Indonesian] program did not move quickly enough to address the problems of corporate debt," stated the staff report assessing the three major Asian rescues of 1997–1998. Second-guessing also abounds as to why so much emphasis was placed on detailed anti-KKN reforms. Following a sober reappraisal of this and other cases, the Fund has suggested that in the future its programs will include such structural measures only when they enjoy the heartfelt support of the country and its leaders. In endorsing this new approach, Horst Köhler, Michel Camdessus's successor as managing director, declared, "I will not have another Indonesia."

In any event, after the flameout of the January 15 program, the IMF and Suharto were repeatedly at loggerheads, and the rupiah's value fluctuated between 7,500 and 15,000 per dollar for weeks. The High Command became increasingly convinced that the aging leader would never abandon the KKN system, a perception that gained force when the Indonesian government issued rules in March and April 1998 circumventing the promises to dismantle the plywood cartel and the clove monopoly.

Suharto, meanwhile, was flailing around for answers to his country's problems that transcended the conventional orthodoxy of the

IMF. His search for solutions would lead to one of the most curious episodes of the crisis.

Steve Hanke was in Istanbul, Turkey, delivering economics lectures at Bogazici University in late January 1998 when a fax arrived requesting that he fly to Jakarta. The fax came "from Suharto's people," he said, offering no further elaboration.

A few days later, Hanke, a professor of applied economics at Johns Hopkins University, was in Indonesia for the first time in his life, staying with his wife Liliane at the Shangri-La Hotel under the name "Simon Holland." Most evenings, he went to Suharto's home, where the fifty-five-year-old Hanke entranced the aging president with a plan for saving Indonesia's economy. Word spread swiftly that Suharto had a new *dukun,* or medicine man, and the pair indeed seemed to be hitting it off. "See, Professor?" the Indonesian strongman chortled one evening, waving a copy of *The Asian Wall Street Journal,* which carried pictures of both men on the front page. "You're a crony now."

Hanke brimmed with the resentment of a man long treated as a bit of a crank by many of his professional colleagues. A pipe smoker who sported silk ascots and kept half-moon glasses perched on his nose, he had a penchant for hyperbole, exacerbated by his frequent abuse of the word "literally." In conversations, he sometimes fumed that unless Indonesia adopted the policies he favored, the country was "literally going to blow up" or "literally going to go down the tubes"—conjuring up, albeit unintentionally, images such as a mass eruption among the archipelago's many volcanoes.

The policy Hanke championed was a currency board, a monetary system that is analogous to putting an economy—or at least its money supply—on autopilot. A nation that adopts a currency board rigidly pegs its currency to another major currency, usually the U.S. dollar—and the operative word is "rigidly," because a currency board affords no wiggle room, unlike the more flexible systems that linked the Thai baht and Indonesian rupiah to the dollar prior to their crises. For example, when Argentina established a currency board in 1991, the value of the peso was set at $1 per peso, and if anyone wanted to trade in pesos, the central bank was bound by law to hand over an equal amount of dollars. Further, it was required to back the supply of pesos in circulation with dollars held in its reserves, so the peso supply could increase only if reserves increased. In adopting a currency board, a government essentially admits that it has lost all credibility with financial markets, so to restore faith in its currency, it hands over its monetary controls to a credibility-laden foreigner (in Argentina's case, Alan Greenspan, the man in charge of the world's supply of dollars).

One huge downside—and the main reason few economists share Hanke's ardor—is that the central bank completely surrenders its power to respond to booms and busts. Even when the economy slumps and joblessness soars, the monetary authorities can't pump up the money supply and drive down interest rates if doing so would violate the rules of the currency board.

In Hanke's view, such drawbacks amounted to nothing more than minor nuisances. "All these economists who've never studied any of these things in depth, and have no historical perspective, and very little empirical perspective, come in here with all the litany of reasons [currency boards] won't work," he once told me. "The fact is, they've always worked. There are no cases where they haven't."

Indonesian economic policymakers were dumbfounded, and the IMF was alarmed, by Hanke's sudden emergence as an influential adviser to Suharto, who publicly disclosed his interest in a currency board by declaring on February 9 that "we must quickly fix the currency at a certain rate" (he was widely rumored to be aiming for something like 5,500 per dollar.) The American interloper got a spacious office suite in Bank Indonesia, where he spent his days poring over mounds of monetary data, and he became an instant celebrity on the streets of the capital, with strangers pressing to shake his hand in restaurants. Some evenings, a government car would arrive at the Shangri-La to whisk him to Suharto's home; other evenings he would go with one of the presidential cronies, usually timber baron Bob Hasan, and there he would discuss the merits of currency boards with Suharto, who spoke English but occasionally relied on an interpreter. "At night was when the real business got done," Hanke recalled. "About seven, [Suharto] would start, and it was a steady stream of people coming in there. It was obviously very informal, but that was his preference for doing real business. I had complete access to him; I could see him any time I wanted to. It was very worrying for the opposition"—that is, top Indonesian economic policymakers, many of whom didn't seem to be welcome at Suharto's soirees.

Among the items on Hanke's résumé—about which he said he duly informed Suharto—is the chairmanship of the Friedberg Mercantile Group, a Toronto-based international investment firm that profited from short-selling Southeast Asian currencies, including the rupiah, in 1997. Characteristically, Hanke cited his real-world experience as evidence for his superior insight. "I'm always amused by these economists who never traded a currency in their life telling us how currency markets work," he said. "I know what I'm doing. I know what causes currencies to blow out and what causes a currency crisis. And I also know what fixes the crisis."

The chest-thumping notwithstanding, Hanke could tell a persuasive story about how the success of currency boards had dramatically increased their acceptance among once-disdainful mainstream economists. He first became aware of the idea in autumn 1983 when Hong Kong was stricken by a panic that sent money flying out of the country following China's indication that it would reclaim the territory from Britain at the end of London's lease in 1997. The crisis quickly abated when British Prime Minister Margaret Thatcher—whose economic adviser, Alan Walters, was a friend of Hanke's—established a currency board that locked Hong Kong's currency irrevocably to America's, at 7.8 Hong Kong dollars per U.S. dollar.

Hanke's enthusiasm grew as he researched the concept, which

appealed to his hard-core free market view that governments should restrain themselves as much as possible from economic fine-tuning. He advised Argentina on its currency board and took great pleasure in the speed at which the country recovered from hyperinflation once control over the money supply was effectively removed from politicians' hands. The Argentine case was followed by several others in which currency boards generated sharply lower inflation and interest rates, including Estonia in 1992, Lithuania in 1994, and Bosnia-Herzogovina and Bulgaria in 1997. In Bulgaria, whose government Hanke also advised, the IMF itself insisted on a currency board as a condition for a loan, much to the satisfaction of Hanke, who felt his crusade was finally starting to win converts in high places.

But the IMF and the rest of the High Command viewed Hanke's proposal for an Indonesian currency board as economic snake oil, as evidenced by the name "Hanky-panky" with which he was derided in some quarters of the U.S. Treasury. Although officials at the Fund and Treasury say they carefully examined the merits of introducing a currency board to steady the rupiah, they concluded that Indonesia was ill-suited for such a plan. "We had a serious discussion about it— it wasn't treated frivolously—and it turned out we were all pretty strongly against it," said David Lipton, who tended to be more sympathetic toward unorthodox proposals than were other U.S. officials. "We thought they [Suharto and his inner circle] were grasping for an easy way out that simply didn't exist, and that they wouldn't be able to behave in the ways that would be required in order to make a currency board successful."

A primary reason it wouldn't work in Indonesia, IMF and Treasury economists argued, was that Suharto had shown no inclination to restrict the supply of money, as a currency board would require. With the banking system on its knees, they reasoned, the government surely wouldn't be able to resist the temptation to funnel emergency rupiah loans to cash-starved banks, especially well-connected ones, even though such transactions would be forbidden under a currency board. Another problem was that Indonesia did not hold sufficient reserves of dollars to back the value of all its rupiah.

Finally, the Fund and Treasury suspected that once the rupiah was fixed at, say, 5,500 per dollar, Suharto's family and friends would take advantage of the opportunity to spirit their money out of the country at a favorable exchange rate, using their connections to obtain the remaining dollars in the central bank before it ran dry. Although Washington had no evidence suggesting that the currency board would be used for that purpose, U.S. and IMF officials thought the potential for such abuse existed.

On February 11, Camdessus sent Suharto a private letter warning him against proceeding with Hanke's plan. The second $3 billion tranche of the Fund's $10 billion, three-year loan for Indonesia was scheduled for consideration by the Executive Board in mid-March, and Camdessus's letter left little doubt that a currency board would cause the Fund to cut off money to Jakarta. "[I]f a currency board were adopted, we would not be able to recommend to the IMF Board the continuation of the present program because of the risks to the Indonesian economy," Camdessus wrote.

Hanke saw Suharto's pursuit of a currency board as motivated purely by an understandable desperation to shore up the rupiah—and an understandable displeasure that the IMF's prescriptions were failing in that regard. In one of their early meetings, he recalled, the Indonesian strongman fretted about the inflation that would likely ignite as the result of the rupiah's collapse. "He said, 'They'll riot in the streets, I'll have to bring in the military, and it could potentially get quite bloody,'" Hanke said. "He also said he was very worried about radicalization of the Muslims."

At first, it appeared as if Suharto might disregard the IMF's threat. In mid-February, he asked Hanke to draft a comprehensive economic plan, including a currency board, and told him that Indonesia was prepared to throw out the IMF just as it had thrown out the Dutch colonialists after World War II. Hanke triumphantly reported at the time that Suharto knew "he holds the trump card—because if this thing [Indonesia] goes down the tubes, all of Asia's going down the tubes." In other words, the IMF wouldn't dare pull the plug on Jakarta.

But the pressure on Suharto was relentless, with frequent phone calls from Clinton, Kohl, and a host of other world leaders warning him to follow the IMF's counsel to shelve the currency-board plan. Their governments were advancing bilateral loans to Indonesia to help cash-starved Indonesian companies finance their exports and imports, plus shipments of rice to ease a looming famine in Indonesia's interior, which had been stricken by one of the worst droughts in years. With its hard-currency reserves depleted, the country needed every dollar to ensure that it could buy food from abroad. A furious Hanke concluded that the Clinton administration was trying to get rid of Suharto: Why else would it block a currency board, the only plan that could save his country's economy and hence his presidency?

In late February, Indonesian economic policymakers let it be known that the currency-board proposal would be deferred for the time being, and in early March, Suharto said that although he was "carefully and cautiously contemplating" a currency board, "whatever measure we shall take, we need the support of the IMF." Reduced to working on a plan that never seemed to be getting off the ground, Hanke returned to the United States, still hoping that Suharto would implement his proposal.

Hanke spoke one last time with Suharto in late April, by phone, from Hong Kong. The Indonesian president told him he would have to abandon the currency board once and for all, because Indonesia simply didn't have enough dollars in reserve to make it work. Hanke insisted that this should not necessarily prevent a currency board from going forward, because there were ways of launching a board with less than "full coverage," and he offered to fly to Jakarta immediately to work out the technical details. But Suharto showed no interest in that idea, and—according to Hanke—said "there is another problem," namely that the U.S. Pacific Fleet had been dispatched to conduct exercises near Indonesia.

That conversation, of course, reinforced Hanke's conviction that the United States wanted to see Suharto ousted. Hanke's logic—that U.S. officials were deliberately blocking the currency board because they knew in their hearts it would work wonders—may have been cockeyed. But his conclusion was not utterly divorced from reality. In fact, some powerful forces in Washington were hoping for a speedy end to the Suharto regime.

Ever since taking over at the Treasury, Bob Rubin and Larry Summers had exercised significant influence over many foreign policy debates, often to the disgruntlement of the State Department, the Defense Department, and the National Security Council. This was a natural consequence of the end of the Cold War and the priority the Clinton administration attached to economics in its conduct of global affairs. Concerns about missile throw weights and guerrilla insurgencies had lost importance, in relative terms, to matters such as cracking import barriers and generating healthy demand for job-creating U.S. exports. So economic agencies such as the Treasury, the U.S. Trade Representative's office, and even the lowly Commerce Department were assuming far greater roles than before in setting the foreign policy agenda. The Asian crisis in particular had turned Rubin and his Treasury team into heavyweight players on the diplomatic stage, because nobody else in the administration could compete with their grasp of the complex financial issues at stake. The president's faith in Rubin, moreover, made it extremely daunting for other administration officials to take disputes with the Treasury Secretary to the Oval Office.

But in Indonesia, Treasury's intrusion into the foreign policy sphere reached new heights, especially in the months following the failure of the January 15 program, when the rupiah continued to sag and the Indonesian economy imploded. During this period, Rubin and Summers, who had always preached the paramount importance of sensible macroeconomic policies and sound financial fundamentals, concluded that Indonesia's crisis had so deteriorated that necessary remedies fell far outside the Treasury's traditional realm of responsibility. "I was astounded," said Sandra Kristoff, the National Security Council's chief Asia specialist. "Rubin was saying, 'I am no longer confident that economic reform alone will work. There has to be political reform as well.'"

Treasury's new approach was based on the following rationale: A change in economic policy alone wouldn't do much to convince investors to bring their money back into the country. Funds would return to Indonesia only if people felt assured that the country afforded a stable long-term environment, both in political and economic terms. The conditions for such stability were obviously not present in a country with a history of violent political transitions and no rule of law, run by a seventy-six-year-old autocrat whose hold on power was looking increasingly shaky, and with little consensus about the choice of his successor. Some among Rubin's brain trust were blunt in asserting what all of these concerns really meant— namely, that Indonesia's current leadership was emerging as the chief obstacle to economic recovery. "I wrote memos saying, 'As long as Suharto is in charge, this [attempt to restore confidence] is going nowhere,'" said Robert Boorstin, one of the Treasury chief's counselors.

Admittedly ignorant about Indonesian politics, Treasury officials consulted outside experts, notably Paul Wolfowitz, a former U.S. ambassador to Jakarta who was dean of the School of Advanced International Studies at Johns Hopkins University—and who happened to be David Lipton's next-door neighbor. Wolfowitz believed that Indonesia's political stability depended not only on the question of presidential succession but also on whether the regime could broaden its support sufficiently to unify the country in facing the economic crisis. That meant Suharto had to reach out to some of his internal critics, perhaps even bringing into a new government the leaders of the opposition parties and movements whom the president had previously treated as subversive. The Treasury adopted some of Wolfowitz's reasoning, arguing that in the absence of political change, further IMF support for Jakarta would simply be wasted. Suharto didn't appear capable of embracing political reform, as indicated by his backtracking on some of the conditions in the January 15 program. In the Treasury's view, those seemed poor circumstances under which to continue disbursing the Fund's money; blithely handing large-scale aid to Suharto would risk further damage to IMF credibility.

Reinforcing the Treasury's hard line was the assessment that, unlike the crisis in South Korea—a much larger economy—Indonesia's meltdown appeared to pose little risk to the global financial system as a whole. Whereas in Korea, the world might have been shocked by a single, dramatic moment of default, many Indonesian companies had gradually stopped servicing their foreign debts because they couldn't afford to pay, and the country's creaky, corrupt bankruptcy system allowed little chance for foreign creditors to press claims in a timely manner. Indonesia might be sinking deeper by the day into national insolvency, but international investors seemed capable of differentiating it from Korea and Thailand, whose financial markets and currencies were rebounding nicely in the first four months of 1998.

The Treasury's new stance sparked an uproar at the State Department and the Pentagon and among some at the NSC, who were viscerally opposed to any move that smacked of trying to undermine Suharto. "There were nearly fisticuffs in Erskine's office," recalled Kristoff, referring to White House chief of staff Erskine Bowles. It was one thing for Rubin and Summers to dominate debates over international economic policy, but now they were venturing into areas in which they were amateurs.

"They thought we were a bunch of ignoramuses poaching on their turf," said Boorstin. "And we thought they were willing to give any amount of money to anyone under the naïve assumption that it would actually stabilize the country."

Members of the foreign policy team conceded that Suharto had become a hindrance to economic recovery, but they dismissed as fanciful suggestions that his power was threatened or that the country could stabilize without him. "Suharto will be here three years from now," Stanley Roth, the assistant secretary of state for East Asia, predicted flatly in one of the White House donnybrooks.

Roth and other foreign policy officials drew a stark contrast between Indonesia and the Philippines, whose dictator Ferdinand Marcos had stepped aside under U.S. pressure in 1986. Whereas a clear alternative had existed to Marcos—Corazon Aquino, the popular widow of a slain opposition politician—no one in Indonesia other than Suharto appeared capable of holding the fractious archipelago together. The State Department and the Pentagon worried that if Suharto were somehow forced out, the country would be engulfed in bloodshed, with the powerful military perhaps split between rival factions, leading eventually to civil war. Furthermore, even if Suharto's ouster were desirable, any move that appeared to be encouraging it would surely prove destabilizing, with the Indonesian president circling the wagons and turning antagonistic toward the United States. Stapleton Roy, the U.S. ambassador to Indonesia, denounced as a fantastic conceit the suggestion that Washington could tell a leader as proud as Suharto how to run his country's internal political affairs.

The battle between the two sides reached a crescendo over a plan hatched in late February to send a special presidential envoy to Jakarta to meet Suharto. The White House settled on Walter Mondale, the former vice president and former ambassador to Japan, whose stature, U.S. officials hoped, would convey the message to Indonesians that the United States wanted at least to try to help their important country. Long, intense debates were held to discuss the nuances of what Mondale should say—the Treasury favoring a tough message, the foreign policy types a more muted one.

The debates proved largely a waste of time, for Suharto wasn't of much mind to listen. On March 3, Mondale—accompanied by Lipton—arrived at the presidential palace in Jakarta for his audience with Suharto, who treated his visitors to a forty-minute monologue on Indonesia's economic development.

Mondale's message was that the United States wanted to see Indonesia recover, and if Suharto acted in a way that would cause that to happen, Washington would be supportive. But when Mondale admonished Suharto on the need to comply with IMF conditions, the Indonesian president made it clear that "he thought that the IMF wanted to overthrow him and didn't like him," Mondale said. Nor was Suharto receptive to Mondale's suggestions about how the Indonesian president, who was just starting his seventh term in office, ought to fill his new government with honest faces from outside his inner circle.

Still, Mondale was able to persuade Suharto to open a dialogue between Indonesia's economic policymakers and Lipton. "If you don't trust the IMF, how about working more closely with our [U.S.] officials?" he urged. This was, in a way, an odd suggestion, since Lipton came from the department most hostile toward Suharto. But the upshot was one final crack at repairing relations between Washington and the Indonesian leader. Neither side wanted to risk a total rupture; Suharto needed the IMF's hard currency to ensure that Indonesia could continue to import vital goods, and Washington wanted to avoid social chaos in the world's fourth most populous country. Rubin was willing to "take another shot at finding a workable set of policies that Suharto could sign on to," Lipton said, although the Treasury chief considered it "a low probability of success option."

Lipton traveled back to Jakarta in mid-March, as did Hubert Neiss, who took over responsibility for Indonesia from Aghevli at a time when ties between Jakarta and the IMF were reaching a low point. The Fund had delayed disbursement of the second $3 billion tranche of its loan pending Suharto's choice of a new cabinet, and Suharto responded on March 14 with a gesture widely interpreted as thumbing his nose at the international community, appointing a "crony cabinet" that included one of his daughters and timber baron Bob Hasan. But the Clinton administration and the IMF found one reasonably reform-minded policymaker in the new cabinet—

Ginandjar Kartasasmita, who had been named to the key post of coordinating minister for economic affairs. Following negotiations with Ginandjar, a new IMF program was announced on April 8 that allowed Indonesia to receive its $3 billion tranche in three dribbled-out portions, $1 billion per month. Among the most important elements of the new program was a tight credit policy with clear rules against excessive money creation—an approach pushed hard by Lipton—and this helped the rupiah strengthen in April.

But Indonesia's economy was still reeling from the blows of January, and Suharto's hold on the presidency was loosening far more quickly than outsiders like Stanley Roth had realized. Even as Lipton and Neiss were discussing the terms of the IMF's new program, student demonstrations demanding Suharto's resignation were spreading on college campuses in major Indonesian cities. Although the students stood little chance by themselves of toppling the regime, their protests were a sign of the combustibility building in the country's political atmosphere.

The ignition spark came on May 4. On that day, as the IMF disbursed the first $1 billion monthly tranche under the new program, Suharto simultaneously announced increases in the price of many types of fuel, including a 25 percent boost in kerosene and 71 percent for gasoline, to comply with IMF conditions aimed at curbing costly government subsidies. In doing so, he was taking action several months before he was required to under the program, instead of allowing the prices to rise gradually, according to IMF and World Bank officials. One possible explanation for Suharto's move is that he hoped to sow among the populace discontent with the IMF, whose anti-KKN conditions had become a rallying cry for his critics.

Whatever his reasoning, antigovernment riots soon intensified, with college students defying army orders to keep their demonstrations restricted to their campuses. On May 12, four students at Trisakti University in central Jakarta were killed by sniper fire. Three days later, blazes swept shopping centers throughout the capital, killing hundreds. Students occupied the grounds of Parliament on

May 18; the next day, Parliament officially asked Suharto to resign, and the following day, even U.S. Secretary of State Albright went public to say that the time had come for him to go. The Indonesian leader finally handed the presidency to his handpicked successor, B. J. Habibie, on May 21.

One interpretation of the Indonesian crisis is that Suharto's suspicions were essentially correct—that is, the West was seeking his overthrow, and the IMF was used as an instrument to achieve that aim. But the events previously described do not support so extreme a thesis, despite the desire among some in the U.S. government to see the Indonesian leader step aside in spring 1998. Even the U.S. Treasury fell in line behind the third IMF program in April, and all the evidence suggests that the efforts by Lipton and Neiss to make the program a success were sincere.

It is fair to say—as Camdessus has publicly acknowledged—that the IMF programs had the effect of helping to foment Suharto's ouster, even if that was not the intention, because by demanding such extensive reforms, the Fund threw a spotlight on the ugly, corrupt aspects of his regime and inflamed popular sentiment against him. But this perspective on the Indonesian story misses the big picture. Up to the time of the January 15 program, the IMF and the High Command, including the Treasury, were desperately trying to ameliorate the crisis, and little thought was being given to an Indonesia without Suharto. His downfall was not the result of a Machiavellian scheme to topple an autocrat; it was the upshot of an international rescue attempt gone badly, embarrassingly, and tragically awry. In the end, Suharto fell because the economic prosperity that underpinned his legitimacy as a ruler had crumbled, and although his departure from office may have been a good thing, the economic developments that caused it were anything but.

Mercifully, the worst fears of the Clinton administration's foreign policy team proved unfounded. Post-Suharto Indonesia has suffered from the feeble leadership of two presidents—Habibie and his successor, Abdurrahman Wahid—and separatist movements, emboldened by the country's weak government, have violently pressed their causes, which has helped keep the economy in a sickly state. But the country has not undergone the horrors of civil war, at least not as of early 2003.

As for the economic impact of Indonesia's collapse beyond its borders, the Treasury was right to conclude that the repercussions would be modest. But the crisis was moving next to a country with nuclear weapons, where the fallout would be felt far and wide.

· 9 ·

GETTING TO NYET

David Lipton landed at Moscow's Sheremetyevo Airport on Wednesday, August 12, 1998. The visit was a hurried one, cooked up the previous weekend over the phone with Larry Summers while Lipton was driving to North Carolina to pick up his children from camp. The Russian leadership, the two U.S. Treasury officials agreed, needed a warning to prepare for the worst.

A $22.5 billion IMF-led rescue package, negotiated with Russia in mid-July, was failing to achieve its aim of stanching an outflow of capital from the country. Russian stocks, the highest of flyers among emerging-market investments a year earlier, had fallen 48 percent in the four weeks since the IMF program's approval. Investors were dumping Russian treasury bills at a rapid pace, and the government had been forced to cancel its weekly sales of the bills because it didn't want to pay the 100-plus percent interest rates the markets would have demanded. The turmoil threatened to undo one of the most cherished accomplishments of President Boris Yeltsin's regime, the stability of the ruble against the U.S. dollar.

To Lipton's consternation, most of Russian officialdom seemed only dimly aware of how close the country was coming to the financial abyss. Two of the most important policymakers were on vacation: Sergei Dubinin, chairman of the central bank of Russia, was in Italy; Anatoly Chubais, Russia's top negotiator with the IMF, was in Ireland. And several of the officials who were in Moscow, including Finance Minister Mikhail Zadornov and Prime Minister Sergei Kiriyenko, were taking false comfort, Lipton thought, from projections indicating that the government had enough rubles and dollars to pay its debts coming due over the next few weeks. What they didn't seem to understand, Lipton told them, was that confidence in the country's financial soundness was falling alarmingly fast, just as it had in South Korea, and although the central bank still held hard-currency reserves of about $11 billion, ruble-holders might suddenly demand so many dollars as to wipe out those reserves, leaving the country with nothing to pay its foreign obligations or sustain the ruble's value.

A world of difference separated this Moscow trip of Lipton's from one he had taken nearly seven years earlier. At that time, he was working with Harvard's Jeff Sachs, and the two of them arrived in Moscow on November 6, 1991, the very day Yeltsin named Yegor Gaidar to the posts of finance minister and deputy prime minister. Technically, Russia was still part of the Soviet Union at the time, but the USSR was on the verge of breaking up, and Gaidar—a thirty-five-year-old, fervently market-oriented reformer—was committed to a damn-the-torpedoes approach for converting Russia's lumbering state-run economy to capitalist principles as quickly as possible. Because Lipton and Sachs had advised the Polish government on its rapid transition from communism, their views were of intense interest to Gaidar, who met them late at night in his office on his first day as finance minister. No one held any illusion that the new government in Moscow had an easy job, but Lipton and Sachs—and their Russian interlocutors—had a sense of great hope and expectations. The moment seemed laden with possibilities for sweeping aside the wreckage of the Soviet system and building a vibrant free-market economy in its stead.

But now, in August 1998, that vision lay in tatters amid the cor-

ruption, criminality, and tax avoidance that infected Russian capitalism, and the country's venture in free-market economics was nearing a nightmarish climax. Lipton saw no painless way out; part of his
message was that if the Russians were counting on an additional dollop of IMF money on top of the disbursements already scheduled,
they should forget it.

The urgency of Russia's plight became clear to Lipton when he
met with Sergei Alexashenko, the deputy chairman of the central
bank, who had a much better grasp than other top Russian officials
of the reality that the country would soon be forced to make
extremely unpleasant choices. The two men met at the central bank
for an hour and a half on Thursday, August 13, discussing figures
showing that the demand for dollars by people exchanging their
rubles had depleted the central bank's reserves by $2.4 billion over
the previous eight business days. At the end of the session, Lipton
told Alexashenko that he would like their aides to leave the room so
they could talk alone.

"I want to ask you one question," Lipton said when the others
had stepped outside. "How many more days can you hold out?"

Alexashenko sighed. "It could all accelerate very fast," he replied,
referring to the outflows of capital. "I don't think more than three to
five days, perhaps a week."

Almost anyone in the world of international finance will know
instantly how close to the mark that comment was, for it came four
days before August 17, 1998, an infamous date in financial markets.
Most Americans were paying attention to another major development that took place that day—President Clinton's grilling before a
federal grand jury and his admission in a speech to the nation that
night that he had conducted an "inappropriate" relationship with
White House intern Monica Lewinsky. But that same day, Russia
announced it was devaluing the ruble and effectively defaulting on
its treasury bills. The implications for the global financial system
were profound: At long last, the IMF and the rest of the High Command were saying "no." They were standing by and allowing a

country to cease paying its full obligations to creditors, instead of throwing fistfuls of dollars to prevent such an eventuality from occurring.

Gosudarstvennye Kratkosrochnye Obligatsii, or "state short-term obligations," known by the acronym GKO, was the name of the treasury bills upon which Russia suspended payment. Therein lies a tale about how Boris Yeltsin's Russia, with no malice intended, created a threat more destabilizing to the West than anything the fiends of communism had ever concocted during their decades in the Kremlin. Global capitalism had survived KGB spies, MiG fighter planes, and SS nuclear missiles. Yet of all the acronyms to emanate from Moscow in the twentieth century, the GKO would come closest to bringing the capitalist system to its knees. Had Marx and Lenin lived to witness the events of 1998, they surely would have relished the irony.

That the "no" of August 17 applied to Russia meant that the move packed a special wallop, for unlike the Asian-crisis countries, Russia had an extensive and recent history of IMF programs.

During the 1990s, the Russians had usually heard "yes" when it came to seeking aid from the IMF, to the point that the mantra "too big and too nuclear to fail" pervaded the attitudes of many market participants about the country. Russia, after all, was a hard supplicant to refuse, with its tens of thousands of atomic missiles that might fall into the wrong hands should a hostile government come to power in Moscow, and its lethal military technology that might be sold abroad should the country's need for dollars become sufficiently acute. Beyond the country's geopolitical importance, top officials of the IMF, as well as the governments of the United States and other major powers, genuinely believed that loans to Russia could produce substantial benefits by advancing the cause of reformers who were battling to ensure that the country would hew to the capitalist road. But in assessing these efforts to encourage Russian reform, when IMF money continued to flow to Moscow throughout periods of glaring financial high jinks and economic mismanagement, it is reasonable to wonder whether Russia was set up for the colossal letdown of 1998 because it had been told "yes" too many times in the past.

The IMF's role in Russia was part of a new mission it and the World Bank had been handed in the early 1990s—helping to guide and finance the conversion of the Soviet bloc to the free market. Many experts were calling at the time for the West to mobilize tens of billions of dollars for Moscow in a Marshall Plan-style reconstruction program, but the administration of President George Bush made plain its reluctance to provide such vast sums, especially amid America's record budget deficits and sluggish economy. So the Fund and the World Bank were charged with doing the best they could on a task that was unprecedented in scope and complexity. The countries involved had spent decades under central planning, with every price and factory production target set by the state. They lacked the basic components of market economies, including viable commercial banking systems, stock and bond markets, and laws to protect private property and enforce contracts.

The transition strategy the two institutions favored was "shock therapy," which involved dismantling the Communist command-and-control system and liberalizing prices and markets as rapidly as possible, much as Poland had already done. Among the reasons for swift, radical change rather than gradualism was the decrepit condition of Soviet industry, a vivid example of which was a huge factory making ZIL trucks that a team of World Bank economists visited in 1990. The ZIL assembly line was producing vehicles that looked like 1950s models, and the real eye-opener came when the visitors went to the roof, where they saw thousands of trucks parked outside—painted either light blue, for commercial sales, or brown, for the military. "One of our guys commented on how large the inventory was," recalled John Nellis, a World Bank private-sector specialist, "and one of the Russians who was guiding us said, 'That is not inventory, those are mistakes'—things that came off the line so wrong, they can't even be fixed. The idea that this system could be reformed with some tinkering around the margins seemed to us nonsensical."

The Western advocates of shock therapy found a highly receptive audience in the top officials Yeltsin picked to run the newly independent Russian Federation shortly after his famous stand atop a tank in August 1991, which thwarted an attempted coup d'état by hard-line Communists. Known as the "young reformers"—most were in their thirties—their leaders were Yegor Gaidar, a short, moon-faced intellectual who became finance minister and deputy prime minister; and Anatoly Chubais, a tall, redheaded former chief economist of St. Petersburg with ruthless skill as a political infighter. They were itching to bulldoze the state-run apparatus and establish Western-style markets together with a property-owning class that could serve as a bulwark against a Communist revanche. Nellis had these observations:

> When you went to Russia in those days, you met some extraordinary people. You could meet some dinosaurs, who were saying, "This will all settle down, all this fervor will die away, and we'll reestablish socialist orthodoxy." And you could also meet people like Chubais who were saying, "We have a small window of opportunity." At that time, there were a lot of people in the parliament recommending daily that Chubais should be fired, and when someone asked him whether it bothered him, he said, "I try to act as if I have only two weeks left in office, so I have to think of what I can do in fourteen days to make sure the Communists never come back." That was a lot more pleasing to us than the people who said, "We're going to reestablish the Brezhnev regime."

The first hard jolts of shock therapy coursed through the Russian economy shortly after New Year's Day 1992, when the government ended controls over the overwhelming majority of prices, and soon thereafter Russians were allowed to establish private retail shops and import foreign goods. The next big step was privatization, in which the government sold some 15,000 factories and enterprises, employing nearly two-thirds of the labor force, from 1992 to 1994. Millions of Russians received vouchers from the state, which they could use to buy shares in newly privatized companies or, if they preferred, sell for cash.

The resulting transformation of the Russian economy was dramatic, yet it was only a half-finished revolution. The majority of privatized companies remained under the control of their Soviet-era managers—known as "red directors"—because the voucher system gave special rights to an enterprise's workers and managers to buy their firm's shares. Many of these enterprises suffered from inefficiency, bloated payrolls, and outright theft by their red directors, yet few of them underwent the drastic restructuring they needed because the red directors had little desire to change the status quo. Furthermore, the institutions necessary for the proper functioning of capitalism—in particular, a legal system capable of enforcing contracts effectively and impartially—remained rudimentary at best.

Meanwhile, as the living standards of ordinary citizens suffered, the young reformers found themselves on the outs with Yeltsin, who over the next few years would alternately hire them and fire them as his enthusiasm for reform waxed and waned. Old-guard apparatchiks who obtained positions of power managed to keep enterprises afloat by funneling them government loans and other subsidies—the predictable result being a towering budget deficit, an explosive rise in the money supply, and an inflation rate of 842 percent in 1993 and 224 percent in 1994.

Led by Chubais, the young reformers made a bold foray in 1995 at putting the Russian economy back on the right track, and they got help in the form of a $6.8 billion loan from the IMF. The IMF program was aimed chiefly at taming inflation; the Fund's long-standing doctrine holds that economic *stabilization* is an essential condition for economic *growth*—a sound principle, since in a climate of unstable prices, interest rates tend to be inordinately high and business firms tend to shy from expanding their operations. In accord with Fund demands, the Russians imposed strict limits over the printing of rubles and slashed subsidies by two-thirds, thereby shrinking the budget deficit from 10 percent of GDP to about 5.7 percent.

The outcome was gratifying: Inflation quickly subsided, and in a potent symbol of the government's commitment to stability, it pegged the ruble loosely to the dollar, ending a long and debilitating slide in the currency's value. But once again, the success was adulterated. To help fund the government's operations, and to win powerful allies for Yeltsin against the resurgent Communists, Chubais permitted rigged auctions to be held in late 1995 in which some of Russia's newly rising business tycoons grabbed control of some of the state's most valuable assets—huge mining and oil producing enterprises—at absurdly cheap prices. The winners of the auctions, known as the "oligarchs," gained wealth and influence over government policy that would rival the caricatures of capitalist elites conjured up by Marxist propagandists during the height of the Cold War.

The IMF essentially held its nose at this outrageous giveaway of public property and continued monthly disbursements of its loan. The auctions didn't technically violate any of the program's conditions, and as a Fund staff report noted at the time, the Russians were "fully complying with the quantitative targets of the program" in areas the Fund cared about most—namely, inflation and the budget deficit. "The realistic view on Russia is that outsiders' ability to influence things is limited," Stan Fischer said in explaining that decision years later. "You can move things in one direction or another. But you're fighting huge domestic forces. We tried to use the leverage we had to move them in the right direction. Whether the West is better off walking away, whether the IMF is better off walking away—that's a judgment you have to make all the time. On balance, I think we tilted things in a better direction than they would have been otherwise."

The IMF's tolerance for Russian transgressions underwent even more severe tests starting in 1996, a presidential election year in

Russia. When the IMF approved a $10 billion program in March (the second largest, at the time, after Mexico's), suspicions naturally arose that the Fund, by providing resources that Moscow could spend on government activities, was being used by the G-7 to help Yeltsin overcome a stiff challenge from his Communist opponent. IMF officials dismissed the criticism, arguing that the three-year loan, granted under the terms of the IMF's Extended Fund Facility (EFF), was fully justified on economic grounds. Russia's macroeconomic results under its 1995 program had been splendid, they noted, and now the time had come to consolidate the gains it had made in stabilizing its economy. So the program contained a battery of conditions aimed at moving the economy to the next stage of reform, such as creating a modern banking system. It also contained tough targets for the budget deficit—4 percent of GDP in 1996, 3 percent in 1997, and 2 percent in 1998.

But Russia's performance made a mockery of the program's ostensible purposes. Even after Yeltsin won reelection in July 1996, the government failed to deliver on promises to shore up tax collection and impose fiscal discipline. The deficit for 1996 ended up at 8.4 percent of GDP—more than double the target level—and for 1997, 7.4 percent of GDP. Although the IMF occasionally suspended monthly disbursements of its loan, it usually granted waivers allowing Moscow to continue receiving the funds—in effect, easing the targets. To justify these moves, Fund officials contended they were only showing realism and flexibility. Furthermore, the Clinton administration and the rest of the G-7 heartily backed the overriding strategy of nudging the Russians in a positive direction and helping the beleaguered reformers. Within the Fund's private councils, however, officials such as Michael Mussa were voicing misgivings about the leeway afforded the Russians in late 1996 and 1997. "We kept lowering the hurdles; now we've dug a hole in the ground and *buried* the damn hurdles!" the Fund's chief economist fulminated at one meeting.

Behind the huge deficits lay a deeper problem—the warped

manner in which Russian capitalism was functioning. Even though the government had cut off many direct loans and subsidies to enterprises in its effort to quell inflation, uncompetitive enterprises were still managing to stay in operation by using a vast web of dealings involving barter, finagling, and bribes. This system was aptly dubbed the "virtual economy" by American scholars Clifford Gaddy and Barry Ickes, because instead of buying and selling for cash at prices that reflected genuine supply and demand, Russian businesses and government agencies were conniving in all sorts of noncash transactions that enabled them to stave off factory shutdowns and unemployment.

In this never-never land, factories "paid" their suppliers by swapping goods they made for the raw materials and inputs they needed—tractors for steel, for example, or plastic for electricity. Workers were often "compensated" with goods in lieu of paychecks; an underwear factory gave its workers brassieres, and a crystal factory handed out cartons of shot glasses on payday. The government "levied taxes" by obtaining goods it needed from companies—buses, say, or military uniforms—in exchange for documents that reduced the recipient's tax liability.

Theoretically, an economy can function reasonably well under a barter system, but not so if the prices of the goods being bartered diverge significantly from their true value. In Russia's virtual economy, the "official prices" charged by enterprises in barter deals were invariably much higher than the prices at which they sold for cash (twice as high or even more in many cases), which meant the enterprises were only pretending to make products that were competitively produced and priced. Instead of adapting to the brave new world of the free market, Russian firms were insulating themselves from the market. Instead of restructuring and providing goods that people would willingly pay decent amounts of cash for, they were using other methods to obtain the resources they needed to continue operating—for example, persuading friendly officials at the state gas monopoly to provide gas in exchange for bartered goods.

The gas monopoly, in turn, was willing to provide gas to keep the factories running because it could count on powerful politicians protecting it from having to pay taxes. This system was rife with opportunities for managers, middlemen, and government officials to enrich themselves in all sorts of improper ways, and it is small wonder that Russia became a hotbed of rent-seeking, organized crime, and capital flight.

The IMF and World Bank tried to dismantle the virtual economy, or at least some of the more egregious parts of it. The Fund demanded as a condition of its 1996 loan that Moscow stop issuing "KNOs," or treasury tax offsets, by which government officials obtained goods and services their agencies needed by canceling vendors' tax bills. But no sooner had KNOs been discontinued than officials began issuing a new type of tax dodge called a "monetary offset" (MO) that involved the use of banks as middlemen. And after the Fund shut down MOs as a condition of continuing monthly disbursements, the Russians came up with "reverse monetary offsets," or RMOs, which technically complied with the conditions of the program but violated its spirit. The virtual economy, in sum, was more ingrained and systemic than the Fund realized, because the Russian body politic had become so wedded to it. The system flourished thanks to the failure to develop a healthy rule of law in Russia that might have protected the rights of creditors to collect their debts and forced unviable businesses to restructure or die.

Amazingly, none of this seemed to matter much at the time, for emerging-market fever was catching on in Russia. In 1997, with inflation at a relatively low 11 percent, the ruble stable, the Communists vanquished, and the $10 billion IMF program in place, Russia became one of the world's prime destinations for international portfolio managers looking for high-yielding paper to fatten their returns. Portfolio investment in Russia surged to $45.6 billion, or roughly 10 percent of the country's $450 billion GDP. Russia-dedicated mutual funds sprang up and found themselves deluged with foreign cash as the stock market, which began 1997 with its main index below 200, peaked at 571 in October. Western investment bankers traveled to regional capitals such as Omsk and Yekaterinburg, where, having braved Russia's notoriously rickety air transport system, they demonstrated even greater appetite for risk by making syndicated loans and snapping up the bonds of local governments. The flood of incoming money reduced the IMF's leverage over Russia, and it also reduced the Russians' incentives to take bold reform steps, but it continued nonetheless.

By early 1998, downtown Moscow was brimming with new offices and planned expansions for the financial titans of Wall Street, London, Frankfurt, and Zurich. Credit Suisse First Boston, which employed 300 people in its Moscow operation, was getting ready to move into a new nine-story building near the Kremlin. Dresdner Bank unveiled an elegant Moscow mansion as the new headquarters for a Russia staff of 180. Deutsche Bank held a soiree at the sumptuous Metropole Hotel to celebrate its plans for turning its representative office into a full subsidiary, with a staff of about 150 offering a wide range of financial services for domestic and international clients. Merrill Lynch, which employed 25 people based in the glittery Marriott Hotel, announced plans to move into new digs to accommodate a doubling of its Moscow-based personnel.

Reckless though they were, financial market participants may be forgiven for reaching the conclusion that the IMF would always bail out a friendly Russian regime so long as it demonstrated a minimal commitment to reform. Moral hazard may have been a poor explanation for why foreign investors thronged to emerging markets like Thailand and South Korea, but there was no gainsaying its importance in luring the Electronic Herd to Russia.

Policymakers in Washington could only wince at the "too big, too nuclear to fail" syndrome that had taken hold among investors. In spring 1998, David Lipton attended the annual meeting of the European Bank for Reconstruction and Development, where, he recalled, he became "particularly alarmed" over a term he heard commercial bankers using. The bankers were referring to Ukraine, because of its close resemblance and proximity to Russia, as "the latest moral-hazard play."

Boris Berezovsky, the oligarch whose empire included oil refineries, airlines, and a television network, had injured himself in a snowmobiling accident, so he couldn't meet Michel Camdessus when the IMF managing director visited Moscow in mid-February 1998. But most of his fellow oligarchs showed up at the central bank of Russia to hear what Camdessus had to say. Shocked over the speed with which financial crises had decimated Asia, the IMF chief wanted to spread the word among Russia's elite that Moscow must show the markets its readiness to slash the budget deficit and rid the economy of pernicious practices. Russia was vulnerable, he warned the oligarchs, and since they were the country's biggest property owners, it was in their interest to support economic reform and pay taxes on time and in cash. With Yeltsin, too, he was blunt. "Mr. President, I've just come from Indonesia," Camdessus said. "And I want to tell you, what I've seen there can happen here."

Russia's weak point was different from Asia's. Whereas the Thai, Indonesian, and Korean crises stemmed from the debt incurred by private banks and companies, Moscow's problem was its government budget deficit, which had totaled $33 billion in 1997. But like the Asian-crisis countries, Russia had become hooked on short-term foreign capital. Specifically, Moscow depended on foreigners to buy large quantities of its GKOs.

On behalf of the GKO, this much must be said: It was preferable to the alternative. Russia needed a way to cover its deficit without printing large quantities of rubles, which would rekindle hyperinflation. So the government, as part of its anti-inflation drive, began selling GKOs in substantial volumes to investors in 1995, and with IMF encouragement, it loosened the rules in 1996 and 1997 to allow foreigners to buy and sell GKOs freely.

Big-time financial crapshooters at foreign hedge funds, brokerage firms, and commercial banks were heavily invested in GKOs, to the tune of about $20 billion in early 1998. The chief attraction was the yield, which offered returns in the 20–30 percent range (on an annualized basis) during this period, and the short maturity—often three months—which made the risk seem low. The downside for investors was that interest and principal were payable in rubles. But Moscow had succeeded brilliantly in holding the ruble stable against the dollar since 1995, and the government attached top priority to keeping the currency fluctuating within a band around 6.2 rubles per dollar. In many respects, GKOs were similar to the high-yielding, fixed-currency deals offered by, say, Thai bank certificates of deposit that international investors found so irresistible during Thailand's heyday of foreign capital inflows. They would pay off beautifully—as long as the country wasn't forced to devalue. And they had an added, uniquely Russian enticement—namely that the IMF appeared to view Moscow's financial soundness as a matter of the utmost importance.

But starting in late April 1998, foreigners' appetites for GKOs and other Russian securities diminished appreciably, as the forces of contagion hit Russia with the same fury that had undone the Asian economies. The plague came from two distinct sources, one of them trade-related. The recession in Asia's biggest economies dampened world demand for oil and gas, Russia's most important export, causing the price of crude to fall by nearly half from the early 1997 level. As a result, Russia's trade balance, as measured by the current account, fell to a deficit of $1.5 billion in the first quarter of 1998; it had posted a surplus of $3.9 billion in the same period the year before. This shortfall deprived the country of a critical source of hard currency it needed to bolster confidence among investors concerning its ability to maintain the ruble's fixed exchange rate.

Second, Asian financial markets, which had rallied in early spring, reversed themselves, casting a new pall over emerging markets worldwide. From February to May 1998, as evidence mounted of continued economic weakness in Japan, the yen lost more than

10 percent of its value against the dollar, and since the yen's drop undermined the competitiveness of neighboring countries' products, other Asian currencies—including the Korean won and Thai baht— receded in May as well. Rumors that China would devalue its currency, the yuan, raised the specter of the region undergoing a fresh round of depreciations. The Herd's skittishness, in short, had returned with a vengeance, and Russia was its primary focus of anxiety. From the last week of April until the third week of May, Russia's main stock index—already down considerably from its 1997 highs—fell by more than one-third.

Among emerging markets, Russia was particularly pregnable because as market jitters intensified, the more intractable its budget problem became—which of course caused the jitters to intensify even further. The vicious cycle in which the country was caught is known among economists as "exploding debt dynamics."

Most countries running perennially large budget deficits suffer some adverse economic consequences, but the cost often manifests itself gradually and subtly. The U.S. federal deficits during the 1980s and early 1990s, for example, made interest rates moderately higher than they would otherwise have been, stunting American economic growth by some amount of indeterminable magnitude. But Washington's budget woes never produced the financial blowout that some had feared.

Russia's deficit was not only proportionately much larger, at 7.4 percent of GDP in 1997, but the government's reliance on short-term borrowing subjected it to heavy costs with every uptick in interest rates. Having raised so much money on the GKO market, the government had to shell out a major portion of its expenditures on interest payments—nearly one-quarter of its total spending in the early months of 1998. And since the Finance Ministry had to borrow more than $1 billion each week by selling GKOs to replace the ones that were maturing, its interest expense was susceptible to steep increases as GKO investors demanded higher yields. That is exactly what happened in May 1998, when the ministry, after rais-

ing money on the GKO market at an interest cost of about 25 percent in April, had to offer yields exceeding 60 percent to entice buy-
ers in the final week of May.

Against this backdrop, IMF officials working on Russia began
receiving frantic entreaties from investors in spring 1998. Jorge Mar-
quez-Ruarte, the Fund's mission chief, complained to colleagues
about getting one phone call in his Moscow hotel room after midnight from a man who opened the conversation jocularly by saying,
"I know you guys don't sleep anyway."

IMF staffers were indeed accustomed to being disturbed at all
hours of the night, but these sorts of calls stuck in their craws. The
callers were Western investment managers who had plunged enthusiastically into Russian stocks and bonds in 1996 and 1997. Now that
Russian markets were sinking fast, these investors were imploring
the IMF to mobilize a *bolshoi paket*—a "big package"—for Moscow.
Even though Russia was still in the third year of the $10 billion EFF
loan it had received in 1996, advocates of the *bolshoi paket* argued
that a new IMF program, with tens of billions of dollars more in
loans, was necessary to keep Russia's debt dynamics from reaching
an explosive finale. With market tremors causing interest rates to
rise, and higher rates causing the budget deficit to widen, and wider
deficits generating more tremors, the potential cataclysm was plain
for all to see. If large numbers of GKO holders concluded they were
unlikely to be repaid and started cashing in their GKOs for dollars,
Russia would quickly run out of the $10 billion to $15 billion that it
held in hard-currency reserves, with frightful implications for the
ruble and the country's stability.

Other senior members of the IMF's Russia team received similar
pleas from financiers—also often at absurdly late hours. "They were
saying, 'It's got to be a big package, or everything will blow up!'"
recalled one of these economists. "One guy got to the point where
he was calling me three, four times a day."

The case for the *bolshoi paket* went something like this: Russia was
to a large extent the victim of circumstances beyond its control. The

contagion effect from falling oil prices and Asian markets explained why investors were pulling money out of the country. Furthermore, saving Russia from financial calamity was especially urgent because the reform movement had just regained control of the government and was being given one final chance to redeem itself. In one of Yeltsin's trademark shockers, he had sacked the old bull Viktor Chernomyrdin as prime minister in March 1998 and replaced him with Sergei Kiriyenko, a gentle-faced thirty-five-year-old with a background in business and strong free-market credentials. A *bolshoi paket*, by assuring investors that Russia had plenty of dollars to meet its obligations, would put the country on a virtuous cycle of market calm and lower interest rates, thereby giving the Kiriyenko government time to launch an ambitious reform program. Without it, Kiriyenko was doomed.

But the counterargument went like this: IMF rescues were supposed to go to countries that were genuinely committed to putting their economies on a sound footing. Russia's history suggested that giving it another IMF loan would be akin to handing a shot of vodka to an alcoholic. As serious as Kiriyenko might be about reform, opposition from the oligarchs, the red directors, and the Communist-dominated State Duma would thwart his efforts. So even if an international rescue restored calm temporarily, the country would still be operating a virtual economy, still running enormous deficits, and still borrowing huge sums of money—which would eventually put it right back in the same fix it was already in. Russia could save itself, of course—but with actions, not another large international loan.

Skepticism toward the *bolshoi paket* ran high among the staff of the IMF's European II Department, which was responsible for the countries of the former Soviet Union. Many in the department believed that Russia lacked both a widespread consensus for the far-reaching reforms that were needed and an effective government for accomplishing them. Yeltsin's support for reform, they noted, was episodic; he would deliver impassioned speeches on occasion and appoint a few reformers like Chubais to top posts, but then he would undermine the effort, often because of complaints from the oligarchs or other powerful parties who considered their interests threatened. The reform movement itself increasingly resembled a "Potemkin village" that was maintained to impress the West—in particular the U.S. Treasury and the IMF—and to disguise the fact that its members had little power to implement change. The Russian negotiating teams with whom the IMF dealt often seemed interested in only one goal—figuring out what modest fixes in the system would suffice to obtain the next monthly disbursement under the $10 billion EFF.

Reflecting the mood within European II was an indignant fax that Martin Gilman, the IMF's resident representative in Moscow, sent to William Browder, the head of an investment advisory firm who authored an op-ed in *The Wall Street Journal Europe* in late May calling for a $20 billion IMF-led loan package. "I find your views curious, to say the least," Gilman wrote. "If the situation really is as you describe, perhaps it would be appropriate for you and other investors to both save Russia and profit in the process by providing the '$20 billion' yourselves."

Gilman and other members of the IMF's European II department privately nicknamed the proposed package the FIEF, or "Foreign Investor Exit Facility." The black humor underlying the term evinced the fear that the Fund's money, instead of bringing tranquillity to Russian markets, would end up providing the dollars for which wealthy investors could cash in their Russian securities before the country went bust. Since many of those investors had been pocketing returns upward of 50 percent per annum on their GKO investments—yields that supposedly reflected the high degree of risk involved in buying such securities—the prospect of an IMF bailout protecting them against loss was especially galling.

The sour attitude in European II was a source of amusement to economists elsewhere in the IMF, who felt their colleagues had bent over backward for years to accommodate the Russians. "There was a quality of the jilted lover" to the attitude of the economists in European II, one senior staffer recalled. "After ten times saying, 'We're really confident they [the Russians] are going to do it this time,' this group had swung from one side to the other."

Facing such resistance, the Russians resorted to going over the heads of the IMF staff and appealing directly to the Clinton administration. Chubais, serving as Yeltsin's special envoy, arrived in Washington shortly before the Memorial Day weekend of 1998, accompanied by Sergei Vasiliev, Yeltsin's chief of staff. Russian financial markets had just taken a serious turn for the worse following the government's failure to obtain any bids in the privatization sale of a state-owned oil company. On Saturday, May 30, the Russians visited the home of Deputy Secretary of State Strobe Talbott and then Summers's home in Bethesda, Maryland, where they met with a small group of Treasury officials over orange juice and bagels.

Chubais warned that a devaluation, which would make imports much more costly, would rekindle triple-digit price hikes, wrecking one of the reform movement's most important economic achievements—the taming of inflation and the establishment of a sense of stability in the value of the currency among the population at large. He also offered a strong testimonial about the reform credentials of Kiriyenko, who wasn't well-known to the Americans, assuring them that the new prime minister had good intentions.

Summers had prepped his troops with a simple message: "We want to keep the markets calm and the Russians scared." But Chubais succeeded in deepening the Americans' own sense of fright over the nasty tumble the markets had taken. So the Treasury team embraced his suggestion that although Russia didn't need funds immediately, the United States could issue a statement indicating the West's willingness to come to the rescue should the situation deteriorate further. The Americans were also heartened by Chubais's assertion that the Kiriyenko government was willing to prepare significant further reforms. (As a downpayment on the new reform push, Yeltsin had just fired the head of the nation's tax service and replaced him with Boris Fyodorov, a liberal economist renowned for his advocacy of harsh punishments for tax cheats.)

On June 1, IMF staffers in Washington picked up their morning papers to read that the White House had issued an unusual Sunday statement, in Clinton's name. The United States "endorses additional conditional financial support . . . as necessary" from the IMF and the World Bank, "to promote stability, structural reform and growth in Russia," the statement said.

As far as members of the European II department were concerned, Clinton's statement left them no room to continue fighting against the *bolshoi paket*. If there was ever a chance for Russia to restore market confidence without a large pot of new money, the White House rhetoric had obliterated it. "Once that announcement was out there, it was the end of the debate," said one senior IMF staffer. "It affected expectations in financial markets, and they would not have been satisfied after that had money not been forthcoming." Asked whether he and his colleagues had been upset by the White House move, the senior staffer replied: "Well, you know, we accept the world as we find it. Presidents do make statements, and we live with that."

President Clinton was in the Oval Office shortly after 1 P.M. on July 10, 1998, when the White House signal operator put through a call from Boris Yeltsin. Negotiations between Russia and the IMF staff on the terms of a new program were stalled on several issues, and Yeltsin was pulling out all the stops, calling not only Clinton but the leaders of Germany, France, and Britain as well as Camdessus in an effort to break the impasse.

Russian markets were in the midst of one of their deepest swoons of the year. During June, the government had been forced to sell GKOs at annualized yields of 40–65 percent to obtain the rubles necessary for paying off principal on maturing GKOs and interest on outstanding ones. In early July, yields had topped 100 percent; moreover, the borrowing was for shorter and shorter terms (some of the GKOs auctioned had maturities of one week), reflecting Moscow's desperation for cash. The central bank's reserves had dwindled by more than $3 billion as investors swapped their rubles for dollars.

Clinton told Yeltsin he had just returned from a trip to China and was paying a lot of attention to the IMF recommendations concerning the Russia program. An impatient Yeltsin broke in and got straight to the point. This is an urgent situation, he told Clinton. If things don't go well with the IMF, Russia's reforms would be over. It would be "basically the end of Russia," he blustered, the consequences "catastrophic." He needed a decision by July 16, Yeltsin said, adding that not just his credibility was on the line, but that of the whole international community, including the United States.

Clinton said he knew Yeltsin had talked to Camdessus, and he told Yeltsin he had to take major steps to shore up Russia's tax system; he had to use all of his leadership powers to get the necessary legislation through the State Duma, and if he couldn't get the Duma's approval, he should use all the powers of his presidency to implement the measures anyway.

Yeltsin retorted that he was doing a lot—he had gone after Gazprom, the state gas monopoly, and forced it to pay taxes. He would do the same with other major tax debtors as well, he vowed. Clinton tried to recover the initiative in the conversation, asking how quickly Yeltsin could get the Duma to act once an IMF program had been announced. It would be good for members of the Duma to recognize how serious the crisis is, Clinton said. The American president said he understood how difficult parliaments could be, given his own nettlesome relations with the U.S. Congress, but when a country's future is on the line, a leader has just got to do the right thing.

Yeltsin replied that Clinton was right, adding that he would go to the Duma and tell its members, just as Clinton had put it, that they should set politics aside and do the right thing. In response, Clinton expressed the hope that Yeltsin could move fast. If Yeltsin promised to get the Duma to act quickly, Clinton vowed, he would go to the wall for Yeltsin with the IMF, but Russia had to come across with its part of the bargain.

Okay, Yeltsin replied, he would take care of the Duma, and he was counting on Clinton's leadership.

A television screen flickered in a large conference room on the twelfth floor of the IMF's headquarters building, as a rare videoconference briefing of the Fund's Executive Board began on July 13, 1998. Appearing on camera from Moscow was John Odling-Smee, director of the IMF's European II Department, who was explaining the agreement he had just struck with the Russian authorities on the terms of a rescue package. Under the plan, Russia would be lent a total of $22.5 billion over the following eighteen months, with $12.5 billion to come from the IMF in 1998 and another $2.5 billion in 1999, plus $6 billion from the World Bank and another $1.5 billion from the Japanese Export-Import Bank.

The video transmission was mediocre, giving an oddly reddish tint to the sandy hair of the fifty-five-year-old Odling-Smee. But the reception was clear enough that several directors detected a notable lack of enthusiasm in his voice as he read off the list of items in the Letter of Intent the Russians had signed. "He looked uncomfortable," one of them recalled. "I felt he didn't believe in the program." Another concurred: "More than usual, he was finding this rather difficult."

Tall and aristocratic, Odling-Smee exuded the urbanity and wit one would expect in a man with a hyphenated name who graduated from Cambridge, taught at Oxford, and spent much of his career in the British Civil Service, where he rose to the position of deputy chief economic advisor in Her Majesty's Treasury. His colleagues admired his analytical and managerial talents but professed to have cracked little of his English reserve. (The wildest exploit recounted about him was that at a Robert Burns evening held at the home of a Scottish friend, he read one of Burns's poems in Russian.) About the tone of his presentation of the July 1998 rescue for Russia, he maintained that at the time, he believed the program had a better-than-even chance of working. He added, however, "No one in this building felt 100 percent sure it would restore confidence."

The numerous strings attached to the program reflected the ambivalence that many in the Fund and the High Command felt about extending yet another loan to a country with such a history of vacillating on reform. Moscow pledged to bring the budget, excluding interest payments, into a surplus equal to 3 percent of GDP in 1999. Specifically, it promised to collect tax arrears from the government's twenty top debtors, including oil companies, which would be automatically denied access to the country's pipelines for exporting petroleum until they paid their taxes. This condition was a tighter version of a similar provision in previous Letters of Intent that the Russians had been circumventing—a revealing indication of the problems involved with making reforms stick. Moscow had issued an exemption from the pipeline ban for oil companies whose products were pledged as collateral for foreign loans, an exemption that turned out to benefit nearly all of the country's petroleum industry and thereby subverted the whole purpose of the provision. "Any measure that looked effective, there was always a loophole," one IMF economist recalled bitterly. So now the IMF was insisting that the ban on pipeline use be applied to tax deadbeats with no exceptions.

The program also contained a relatively novel element—a requirement that many of the reforms the Russians were promising must take the form of legislation approved by the State Duma, instead of presidential decrees. The issue was a major bone of contention between Russia and the Fund. For much of Russia's half dozen years as an independent country, Yeltsin had frequently exercised the right to govern by decree, evoking mounting criticism that he was running roughshod over democratic principles and making no effort to forge a national consensus around a domestic program. The Russian reformers argued they had no choice but to rely on decrees, given the Communist domination of the Duma, and they warned that insisting on Duma approval of reforms would only increase the risk of an adverse market reaction to the IMF rescue.

But after going along with ignoring the Duma for years, the Fund was demanding legislative support for reform, in part because Russian enterprises were citing lack of Duma approval as one reason they were ignoring tax laws.

The announcement of Russia's deal with the IMF on July 13 evoked an initial roar of approval on financial markets. Russia's main stock index, which had fallen by more than half since April, rocketed upward by 17 percent on July 14, a record in percentage terms. Yields on GKOs, after climbing to well over 100 percent the week before, receded to nearly half that level. The IMF scheduled an Executive Board meeting on Monday, July 20, to approve the program, and Yeltsin announced he was going on vacation.

The euphoria quickly subsided as new strains arose between the Fund and Russia in the days leading up to the board meeting. On July 17, the Duma balked at tax legislation submitted to fulfill conditions of the Fund program, and the Kremlin nullified a provision that Chubais had negotiated to trim government pension payments. To show that the IMF would refuse to overlook Moscow's backsliding, Camdessus brokered a deal to cut the first disbursement under the program from $5.6 billion to $4.8 billion, with the other $800 million to be disbursed in September provided Moscow fulfilled its promises by then.

As skeptical board members listened over an informal lunch at the IMF on the day of the board meeting, Chubais, who had flown to Washington especially for the occasion, pleaded for their understanding. He explained peculiarities in the Russian economy that, in his view, helped account for why Russia was taking so much longer to put its house in order than had other former Communist countries such as Poland. One of the factors, he said, was the importance Soviet leaders had placed on building up the defense industry, which meant the economy was saddled with vast numbers of military-oriented factories that were hard to shut down. Another was the Soviet planners' decisions to place large amounts of production in remote locations like the Arctic north, even though transportation costs were prohibitively high by conventional capitalist standards. Responding to questions about the prospects for Duma passage of the reforms pledged under the IMF program, Chubais said that the odds were favorable so long as Yeltsin made a personal effort to convince parliamentarians that the country faced a historic crisis.

In a meeting that lasted into the early evening, board members sharply questioned staffers in European II about the viability of the program, but, as one executive director put it, "Finally, we had to approve. Our political masters had already approved the deal." The board members from G-7 countries, who caucused separately that day, agreed they were being forced to vote for something they didn't think would work. "You had the strong feeling, would the Russians respect you in the morning after the vote?" said another director. "And the answer was no."

But the vote, of course, was yes, prompting a relieved Chubais to tell his Russian colleagues, "Now we are safe." It was a gamble—in many ways, an entirely justifiable one—by the G-7. A financial collapse in Russia would risk not only contagion infecting other emerging markets but also political unrest in the world's second-largest nuclear power. The rescue provided at least some hope that the Kiriyenko government would get a few months' breathing room, which might be just enough to push through some serious reform measures. Sure, the Duma would probably show contempt for the program—and in fact, the parliamentarians went on summer recess in late July after passing only the least controversial portions. But Kiriyenko and his ministers were champing at the bit—and they quickly obtained presidential decrees accomplishing much of what the Duma rejected, including quadrupling the land tax and raising individuals' pension contributions (although the decrees soon came under constitutional challenge in the courts).

A crucial question remained: What about the foreigners who had recklessly poured money into the country—especially the GKO holders, who had been enjoying such obscenely high returns on their investments? Had their midnight phone calls to the hotel

rooms of IMF officials paid off? Would the *bolshoi paket* go simply to
ensure that they could cash in their GKOs for dollars a few weeks or
months down the road? Or would they somehow be bailed in and
induced to help the country survive financially, as South Korea's
creditors were? The answers would come in one of the most dispirit-
ing episodes of the crisis.

Among the investment banks that thronged into Russia in the
1997–1998 period, one stood out for the splashiness of its presence:
Goldman, Sachs & Co., Bob Rubin's old firm, which celebrated the
opening of its new Moscow offices on June 18, 1998, by hosting a
gala event at the baroque House of Unions, once a private club for
Russian nobles. Adding a geopolitical sheen to the gathering, Goldman flew in former U.S. President George Bush, who imparted some
cheery words after meeting with Yeltsin. "Certainly Russia has big
economic problems today," Bush told the crowd of financiers, industrialists, and government officials. "But never underestimate the
power of freedom and free markets. I am optimistic. I believe Russia
is going to thrive."

The opulence of Goldman's party was matched by its aggressive-
ness in pursuing business with major Russian companies and government agencies that were seeking sources of foreign capital. Amid
the hot market atmosphere following the 1996 reelection of Yeltsin,
competition raged among Western investment banks for the fees
they could earn by selling bonds issued by Russian borrowers to
mutual funds, pension funds, and insurance company investors in
the United States, Europe, and Asia. Goldman proved adept at winning lucrative business with clients such as oligarch Mikhail
Khodorkovsky, whose Menatep group and Yukos oil affiliate borrowed hundreds of millions of dollars from foreign institutions in
deals that Goldman arranged.

As the IMF rescue was moving toward finalization in early July
1998, four senior Goldman executives brainstorming at the firm's

New York headquarters came up with a proposition they thought would appeal to their most important Russian client of all—the government. That very evening, a Goldman representative who had been planning a trip to Moscow took off armed with an outline of the proposal to present to Russian officials. Some of the Russians, including Finance Minister Mikhail Zadornov, were leery, but others embraced it enthusiastically. To hear IMF and Russian officials tell it, the Fund kept a discreet distance from the Goldman scheme, providing its blessing while treating the details as matters the Russians and Goldman should negotiate between themselves. Only later, after Goldman's plan went forward, would Fund officials recognize what a misfortune was brewing.

Goldman's plan appeared rooted in sound financial reasoning. The firm was proposing that Russia could do essentially the same thing that Korea had done—that is, change its very short-term debt into longer-term debt, thereby dispelling the panic in the financial markets. Whereas in Korea's case, the short-term debt consisted of loans from foreign banks, Russia's short-term debt consisted of GKOs, whose owners were proving increasingly reluctant to buy new bills when the old ones matured, despite the opportunity to earn yields of 50–100 percent. Over the next few months, the Russian government would face such a burden paying interest on GKOs and redeeming maturing ones—the projected outlay in rubles was equivalent to about $32 billion in the second half of 1998—that its ability to obtain the money it needed to fulfill its obligations was open to serious doubt.

The obvious solution, as Goldman saw it, was for Russia to offer GKO holders a deal, in which they would give up their high-yielding GKOs and receive in return long-term bonds paying lower interest— the sweetener being that principal and interest would be payable in dollars rather than rubles. Goldman had already demonstrated its prowess at marketing these sorts of dollar-denominated bonds, called Eurobonds, to foreign investors; the firm managed a $1.25 billion sale of such bonds for the Russian government in June. So with the same adept salesmanship, Goldman could rid Moscow of its most dangerous, destabilizing financial problem—the near-term costs of paying off the GKOs. Russia would still have to pay stiff interest of about 15 percent per annum on the Eurobonds—and it would have to pay in dollars—but at least the terrifying specter of imminent catastrophe would recede.

But one key element present in the Korean case was missing. No official force or suasion was being mustered to prod Russia's foreign creditors into participating in the debt exchange. The Western hedge funds, banks, and other investors who owned GKOs numbered in the thousands, and they could not be summoned for meetings at the Federal Reserve Bank of New York, or even called on the phone by government officials, to be persuaded that it was in their collective interest to surrender their short-term claims for long-term ones. Such an approach had worked in Korea because bank executives are susceptible to that kind of pressure. In Russia, the only alternative the High Command could see was for short-term creditors *voluntarily* to accept the GKO-for-Eurobonds exchange. (Technically, of course, Korea's creditors acted "voluntarily," but Russia's would be subjected to no governmental pressure whatsoever.)

Over the July 18–19 weekend, Goldman executives at the firm's London office watched documents pour out of fax machines as GKO holders sent in forms stating how much of their GKOs, if any, they were willing to exchange for Eurobonds. The results, announced on July 21, were disappointing: Investors holding only about $4.4 billion in GKOs, around one-third of the total held by foreigners, had agreed to the exchange conceived by Goldman, which offered them the choice of taking either a seven-year Eurobond yielding 14.88 percent, or a twenty-year Eurobond yielding 15.12 percent. In sum, Russia was still stuck with a huge short-term debt problem.

What went wrong? Why didn't most foreign investors go for the deal? An important part of the answer is that foreign investors had undergone an attitudinal change, now that the IMF was coming through with the *bolshoi paket*. Since the Fund had shown once again that it would stand behind Russia, high-yielding GKOs seemed a lot less dicey, and many GKO holders decided they ought to hang onto them, at least for the few weeks or months until they matured. "I spoke to a ton of investors during this period," said Al Breach, a Moscow-based economist who worked as an adviser to the Russian government at the time of the exchange, "and it was so clear. The market went from shit-scared to greedy. People were saying, 'Why should I exchange [GKOs for Eurobonds]? The ruble will hold, so why should I give up these returns?'"

That, indeed, was a commonly expressed view among market participants at the time. Shortly after the announcements of the IMF rescue and the Goldman plan to make its exchange offer, *The Wall Street Journal Europe* reported: "With the threat of a ruble devaluation now waning, some debt analysts wondered what incentive investors had to exchange the high-yield ruble denominated GKOs for safe and stodgy Eurobonds. One trader said the swap could mean trading 'a bronco for a mule.'"

Similar sentiments appeared in the "Emerging Markets Daily" published by Merrill Lynch on July 16. The report advised investors owning GKOs that they ought to consider trading in some of their holdings for Eurobonds. But it also contained the revealing comment that GKOs posed "little risk of devaluation with the new IMF loans." Investors holding GKOs maturing in the next few weeks would be particularly foolish to participate in the exchange offer, according to the report, which added: "Remember also that the IMF loan virtually assures a stable exchange rate, at least through the summer."

In other words, thanks to a bailout loan provided courtesy of the world's taxpayers, a bunch of punters in the international money markets decided it was safe for them to continue collecting ruinously high interest payments from the Russian government for a few more weeks or months, instead of accepting a longer-term, lower-interest payback that offered the country at least a chance of getting its economic act together. Of course, it is unfair to blame these investors for acting in their own self-interest, but their shift from "shit-scared to greedy" following the unveiling of the IMF rescue suggests something is rotten in the state of the international financial system.

The events of August 17, 1998, were now approaching. Greed would soon revert to shit-scaredness. And by many accounts, the Goldman deal exacerbated Russia's problems, because of a bizarre set of chain reactions that ensued.

Goldman evidently underestimated—and the IMF definitely failed to foresee—that issuing several billion dollars worth of new Russian Eurobonds would cause an imbalance in the market. Together with a couple of smaller deals and the Goldman GKO-for-Eurobond deal, the supply of Russian Eurobonds more than tripled, from $4.3 billion to nearly $14.5 billion, in about six weeks. Just like wheat, pork bellies, or any other product, bonds tend to fall sharply in price when their supply dramatically increases, and that is what happened to Russian Eurobonds, which went from trading at around 100 cents on the dollar in June to 80 cents at the time of the Goldman deal to about 50 cents in mid-August.

The price drop in the Eurobonds proved problematic because Russian banks had bought many such bonds with dollars borrowed from abroad. As the losses on their bonds mounted, the Russian banks got margin calls from their creditors—that is, demands to pay the loans back before the value of the collateral (the bonds) fell any further. The margin calls, in turn, triggered a mad scramble by Russian banks to pay their creditors off—which meant that a massive amount of capital was flowing out of the country, with rubles being exchanged for dollars in large quantities. "What we didn't know was how the Russian banks had this significant exposure to Russian Eurobonds," a senior IMF economist said. "When there were margin calls [on the banks], that precipitated a lot of outflows."

Many of Goldman's competitors remain bitter over what they contend was the firm's reckless behavior in initiating the GKO-for-Eurobonds deal, which earned Goldman a reported $56 million in fees. The IMF, too, has come in for plenty of criticism for giving Goldman the green light. "Both the Russian Finance Ministry and the IMF seemed tone deaf to the realities of the market for Russian securities," contended Charles Blitzer, the head of emerging-markets research at Donaldson, Lufkin, and Jenrette in London. "They just wouldn't take seriously warnings that the [Goldman] exchange could backfire. Why did the crisis happen in August? Why didn't the Russians get three months of breathing room to do what they promised? I think the exchange was the key thing."

For their part, Goldman officials maintain that the opposite is true, that the exchange might have saved Russia if many more investors had accepted it, since that would have reduced pressure on the Russian government to pay interest and principal on the GKOs still outstanding. The Russian government, they note, encountered grave difficulty servicing the GKOs in the first few days of August.

Maybe Goldman's explanation is right, or maybe its detractors' account is. Whichever version has more merit, the havoc that befell Russian markets so soon after the IMF rescue was another blot on the Fund's record. By the week that David Lipton arrived in Moscow to deliver his warning, most of the $4.8 billion the Fund had disbursed to Russia was gone, handed over by the central bank to investors exiting the country's market. The crowning blow came in a letter to the editor by George Soros, prominently published in the *Financial Times* on Thursday, August 13, after Russian stock prices had dropped by more than one-quarter in six trading days and yields on GKOs had soared to about 150 percent. Soros, who had been trying unsuccessfully behind the scenes to organize an emergency loan for Russia that would have combined private and Western government funds, proposed in the letter that Russia should devalue the ruble by 15 to 25 percent, and then impose a currency board. His letter began: "Sir: The meltdown in Russian financial markets has reached the terminal phase. . . . "

Trying to grab a week's vacation on the Greek island of Mykonos in mid-August 1998, Stan Fischer was having difficulty finding much time to relax. His only other holiday that summer, a week's trip to Martha's Vineyard with his family in early July, had been ruined by constant conference calls about the terms of the *bolshoi paket,* which forced him to spend hours atop a sand dune talking on a cellphone. ("Stan," his wife teased him, "do you know how ridiculous you look?") Now the IMF deputy managing director was anxiously keeping an eye on the deteriorating condition of Russia's stock and bond markets. On the evening of Thursday, August 13, he bought the *Financial Times* and turned immediately to Soros's letter. "That was it. I knew we were done for," Fischer said.

Fischer called Camdessus, who was on vacation in France, and told his wife that they would have to return to Washington over the weekend, several days earlier than planned. The airplane on which they flew was equipped with phones, so Fischer was able to spend much of the flight making calls. To ensure that other passengers couldn't overhear his conversations, Fischer had to sit under a blanket—an arrangement that, he conceded, "was not very dignified." But then, the world financial system was on the eve of one of the most traumatic episodes in its history.

Sergei Dubinin, the bearded, heavyset chairman of Russia's central bank, was also on vacation that week, in Italy, and he too made immediate plans to cut his holiday short when he saw Soros's article. As he rode into Moscow from the airport on Friday, August 14, Dubinin observed Muscovites lined up by the scores at the city's ubiquitous currency exchanges, clamoring for dollars. Up to that point, ordinary citizens had shown few signs that the crisis was affecting their behavior, but now the news media were reporting that two major banks, SBS-Agro and Inkombank, had defaulted on their obligations, and rumors of a collapse in the banking system were causing hordes of people to switch their savings into greenbacks. At some currency exchanges, rubles were trading at eight to the dollar, more than 20 percent below the government's target rate. "We can play games against the market, against the banks even,"

Dubinin said. "But we can't do anything if the entire population wants to change rubles into dollars."

On Friday evening, Dubinin met with other top central bank officials, and the group unanimously concluded that trying to maintain the ruble's value against the dollar had become fruitless. A meeting was arranged for about 9 P.M. to inform Kiriyenko of the decision, which was legally the central bank's responsibility. For the thirty-five-year-old prime minister, the move would be hugely awkward politically, Dubinin and his aides knew, especially since Yeltsin had issued a ringing pledge that very day on national television that "there will be no devaluation of the ruble." The central bank offered a small face-saving suggestion: Kiriyenko could decide exactly which day of the following week to announce the devaluation. After a short discussion, the prime minister adjourned the meeting until the following morning.

On Saturday, about a dozen of Russia's top policymakers met at the prime minister's dacha to confront the fact that under the circumstances of runaway interest rates and an evaporation of market confidence, continuing to pay interest and principal on the GKOs was no longer sustainable. They considered two alternatives, each abhorrent in its own way. Under the first alternative, the central bank would simply create the rubles needed for debt service—which would technically meet the government's legal obligations to its creditors, but at the cost of an explosion in the money supply that would likely rekindle hyperinflation. The group quickly rejected this option, said Sergei Alexashenko, the central bank's deputy chairman, because "it would have meant the loss of all macroeconomic stability."

The second option was in effect a default on the GKOs, under which the government would renounce its obligation to make interest and principal payments on the short-term bills and instead give their owners longer-term bonds—in other words, force them to accept a deal similar to the Goldman exchange offer (though on worse terms). "It was a bad solution, but at least it meant we could keep the basics of macro stability," Alexashenko explained. Devaluation of the ruble would have to accompany this move, the group agreed, because the announcement of the default would surely intensify the panicky rush to convert rubles into dollars—of which the central bank lacked a sufficient supply.

Now the questions facing the Russians were difficult: How badly, and how permanently, would their country be punished by international investors for its violation of the market's code that a debtor must never, ever renege on its obligations? And, as the only internationally recognized arbiter of countries' financial conduct, could the IMF help mitigate the impact of the default by issuing sympathetic or even supportive rhetoric? Or would the Fund take a critical stance and worsen Russia's plight?

The first signals came when Odling-Smee flew into Moscow from Washington Saturday night. Immediately after dropping his bags at his hotel, he headed to the Liberal-Democratic Club downtown for a dinner meeting with Chubais; Gilman, the IMF's Moscow representative; and former Deputy Prime Minister Gaidar, who was working as an adviser to the government. Chubais, who himself had just rushed back from a holiday in Ireland, was understandably in a funk. When Odling-Smee suggested that the Russians concentrate on "damage control," Chubais shot back: "It's not damage control. It's disaster control." Gilman later had stark comments about the session: "Here we were dealing with a completely new situation. Never had a country defaulted on its own treasury obligations in this fashion. We were trying to figure out the implications. There was a lot of concern about runs on banks, runs on the currency, a breakdown of institutions, a scarcity of goods. No one knew what the social and political consequences would be. We all had the feeling we were standing on the edge of a cliff."

The Fund officials' initial reactions to Russia's plans for default and devaluation came as something of a relief to Chubais and Gaidar. Odling-Smee said such moves were probably "inevitable," given the predicament Moscow was in. The main point of the dinner, though, was not to negotiate but to consider the possibility that some alternative might exist besides the default-devaluation route. Although the IMF was neither willing nor able to provide a last-ditch emergency loan, Odling-Smee raised a tantalizing suggestion: Perhaps the G-7 would be willing to lend a few billion dollars more on a bilateral basis. Chubais questioned whether any real purpose would be served by making inquiries along those lines; on his last trip to Washington, he said, he had been told that G-7 largesse was strictly limited to what was contained in the July package. But Odling-Smee, though not in any position to promise G-7 bilateral funding, told the Russians that in his judgment, the prospect of default put a whole new cast on the situation, and it was worth at least pressing to find out whether the G-7 would be worried enough about the consequences to come across with more money.

This slender hope was dashed, however, in a G-7 deputies' phone call that was joined by Fischer, who was horror-struck at the economic and political devastation he thought likely to follow a Russian default—both in Russia and beyond. Fischer raised the idea of a $20 billion loan for Russia from the G-7, in effect proposing a Mexico-style package, large enough to buy out all the foreign GKO holders just as the Mexican rescue had been large enough to buy out all of the *tesobonos*. But the G-7's willingness to lay any further wagers on Russia had run out. Hardly had Fischer begun to present the suggestion than Germany's Jürgen Stark interrupted him. "Stan, stop here," Stark said. "Who will pay for it? Germany will not pay for it. We are not in favor of any additional money, either bilateral or IMF."

With no chance of another rescue, the Russians were racing on Sunday, August 16, to refine the details of their default-devaluation plan. Rumors were beginning to sweep Moscow that drastic measures were afoot, and if the markets opened on Monday morning without a government announcement, pandemonium would surely erupt. The broad consensus among Finance Ministry and central bank officials was that the government should close the GKO market on Monday and Tuesday and announce the terms for an "involuntary" exchange in which foreign GKO holders would receive one type of bond and domestic holders a different one. The bond for foreigners would pay a low interest rate, perhaps 3 percent, but it would have a sweetener of being payable in dollars. The bond for residents of Russia would provide an initial cash payment, but it would be denominated in rubles. (Russia would not default on all its official debts; the government's Eurobonds, for example, would continue to be serviced in full.)

Late Sunday afternoon, Kiriyenko and Chubais flew by helicopter to Yeltsin's dacha to obtain his formal blessing for the decisions taken at meetings of which the president had been blissfully ignorant. To preserve Yeltsin's sense of presidential authority, Kiriyenko and Chubais offered him a choice about how the ruble should be devalued. The Russian currency could be allowed to float—that is, sink—against foreign currencies, without limit. Alternatively, it could be allowed to trade within a wider range than before, so that instead of staying in a band 15 percent above or below 6.2 rubles per dollar, it would move in a range of 6 rubles to 9.5 rubles per dollar. Yeltsin chose the latter alternative, which allowed him to claim, albeit with tortured logic, that he was sticking with the same currency system and abiding by his no-devaluation pledge.

But on Sunday evening, as the Russians were putting what they thought were the final touches on their plan, it blew up. Around nine o'clock, Odling-Smee arrived at Kiriyenko's office in the White House with bad news: The IMF had grave concerns and wanted Moscow to postpone its announcements to give time for cooperative consultations with the country's creditors. The Russians were outraged. Their impression, based on their earlier conversations with Odling-Smee, was that although the Fund obviously wouldn't welcome the default, it was prepared to accept the government's broad plan and would issue a statement that would help limit the fallout. Indeed, in phone calls with IMF staffers early Sunday from Paris, where he was returning from vacation, Camdessus had struck a sympathetic note, acknowledging that Russia clearly lacked the resources to pay off the GKOs and that printing rubles would be a shortsighted way out of the mess. But now, at almost literally the eleventh hour, the Russians were faced with the prospect that the Fund would issue condemnatory rhetoric that would worsen the country's image as a deadbeat and international pariah, making it all the more difficult for Moscow to obtain hard currency in the future. "It was a very unpleasant surprise for us," Dubinin recalled.

Based on his most recent conversation with Camdessus, Odling-Smee said the IMF's view was that the unilateral nature of the default plan was unacceptable. Instead of simply dictating the terms to GKO holders, Russia ought to first try hammering out a mutually agreeable approach, the Fund insisted, and as a sign of its good faith, the government should convene an emergency session of the Duma to enact further reforms.

Why was the IMF suddenly adopting a tougher stance so late in the weekend? Maybe Camdessus came under pressure himself from the U.S. Treasury; maybe some other factor was at work; maybe signals were mixed and wires crossed. In any event, the view that the Fund's position had changed "is the way it appeared to the Russians," Odling-Smee acknowledged. "I don't think it was necessarily the managing director's mind that was changing. It may be that I didn't convey properly what he said, or the Russians misunderstood."

Kiriyenko told Odling-Smee that, having obtained the president's approval for the planned actions, he could not change course now. And there was another problem: Too many people knew what the government was contemplating. The oligarchs had gotten wind of the discussions and had been briefed—an outrageous favor to special interests in one sense, but according to Russian officials, their main motivation was to ensure that the oligarchs would use the media outlets they owned to help prevent panic among the general population.

Shortly after midnight, an emotional, exasperated Chubais went to Odling-Smee's room at the Metropole Hotel, where he talked to Camdessus directly in Paris. He told the IMF chief that Russia needed a supportive statement from the Fund, lest the country become totally isolated and vulnerable to lawsuits by creditors. When Camdessus insisted that the government reconvene the Duma, Chubais retorted that it was impossible. After leaving the hotel, Chubais spent a wild night pleading Russia's case with other Western officials, including Summers, Lipton, and others. At 5 A.M. Moscow time, he called Aleksei Mozhin, Russia's IMF executive director in Washington, frantically trying to track down Fischer.

Monday, August 17 dawned with both sides—the Russians and the IMF—unsure of what the other would do. At an early morning meeting in Kiriyenko's office, Chubais reported to other top policymakers about the adamant position taken by Camdessus. A decision was made: Although the ruble devaluation would go ahead as planned, and Russia would announce its intention to restructure its GKO debt, the precise terms of the restructuring would be deferred. "These measures are tough ones, quite radical ones," Kiriyenko told the media. "But they are inevitable ones."

To the Russians' relief, Camdessus's statement later that day contained no condemnatory language, and he even left open the possibility that the IMF would deliver the second tranche of its loan to Moscow in September:

> As a preliminary reaction, I am of the view that, in the new context created by these measures, it will be especially important for the Russian authorities to take all necessary steps to strengthen the fiscal position. The authorities should also spare no effort to find a cooperative solution to their debt problems, in a close dialogue with Russia's creditors.
>
> More generally, it is important that the international community as a whole, both public and private sectors, show solidarity for Russia at this difficult time.

Global financial markets initially shrugged off the Russian developments on August 17. Stocks and bonds in emerging markets fell, with a couple of countries' stock markets hit hard—notably Turkey's and Hungary's, down 5.4 percent and 3.2 percent respectively. But European markets, following an early plunge, recovered on the strength of a rally on Wall Street that sent the Dow Jones industrial average up nearly 150 points. News reports in the following day's papers explained the Dow's move as a technical bounce following several weeks of declines.

It was a delayed reaction.

"Thank you for standing by," an operator's voice said, speaking to an audience of institutional investors and traders on Wednesday, August 26, 1998. "Welcome to the Deutsche Bank Russian debt restructuring and global implications conference call."

Nine days had passed since August 17, and global financial markets were starting to catch on to the implications of what had happened in Russia. Germany's main stock index was down 7.2 percent. Stock indexes in emerging markets all over the world, particularly in Latin America, had suffered double-digit losses. The market for U.S. bonds such as convertibles and high-yield corporates was undergoing one of its most brutal downturns in memory, and bonds of emerging-market countries had fallen so far out of favor that, on average, purchasers of those bonds were demanding four full percentage points in additional yield than before August 17.

Many market participants were upset that the IMF and the rest of the High Command had failed to prevent Russia from defaulting and devaluing the ruble. But few were so unhappy as the host of the Deutsche Bank conference call, David Folkerts-Landau, the bank's global head of emerging-markets research. And now, Folkerts-Landau was going to strike back, by issuing a chilling prediction about the likely contagion effects of the Russian default. Other emerging markets, notably Brazil, were seriously imperiled, he warned, because "the rules of the game have changed substantially. . . . If you're a rational investor and you saw what happened to domestic currency investors in Russia, you know now that could happen to you in Brazil."

When Folkerts-Landau talked, people in the world of emerging-markets investing listened. A dashing, bearded native of Germany who attended school in England as a teenager, the forty-nine-year-old Folkerts-Landau held a Ph.D. from Princeton and boasted a fifteen-year career at the IMF capped by the directorship of the Fund's Capital Markets Group. At the Fund, Folkerts-Landau had impressed some of his colleagues, while irritating others, with his relentless drive and cocksureness. When he left the IMF in late 1997 to join Deutsche, he lured about a half dozen IMF economists to work with him, and he quickly established himself as a leading authority in divining the likely actions of the Fund, the G-7, and emerging-market governments. But now, in the wake of August 17, he had egg on his face—and losses to account for.

Deutsche Bank was one of the largest foreign holders of GKOs, with about $290 million of Russian treasury bills in its portfolio; indeed, on the very day of Folkerts-Landau's conference call, the bank would lose its cherished triple-A credit rating from Standard & Poor's, mainly because of its exposure to Russia. When the IMF was readying its *bolshoi paket* in July 1998, Folkerts-Landau had assessed the likelihood of a ruble devaluation at near-zero, and he continued to believe during the first half of August that Russia would be bailed out in the end because of its geostrategic importance. Many of his clients—the Soros and Tiger hedge funds among them—had invested in GKOs partly on the basis of his advice and were facing horrendous losses, just as Deutsche was. But Folkerts-Landau was aggrieved about another matter as well.

For five days—Wednesday, August 19, until Sunday, August 23—Folkerts-Landau had bargained with Russian officials in Moscow over the deal that GKO holders would receive. He had gone there at the invitation of the Russian government, which asked Deutsche Bank and J. P. Morgan & Co. to participate in the negotiations as part of an effort to consult cooperatively with creditors instead of unilaterally imposing the terms of how they would be repaid. But the talks had failed to produce an acceptable deal for GKO holders, in Folkerts-Landau's opinion, and for this he blamed his former colleagues at the IMF.

Folkerts-Landau had sought a plan that would have given each GKO holder securities yielding 40 to 50 percent. This was "a solution that we perceived as being fair to the Russians, fair to the foreign investors, and fair to the domestic holders of Russian securities as well," he told the conference call. "It was our sense that by Saturday [August 22] there was an—I wouldn't say an agreement—but there was an understanding that things were moving along on these lines. Then the Russians ran this plan on Saturday, late Saturday evening by the IMF. This is where the problems began."

IMF officials in Moscow, Folkerts-Landau complained, had scuttled the deal—using the Fund's leverage as the only likely external lender to Russia in years to come—because they believed the government probably couldn't afford to pay the 40–50 percent interest rates that the plan envisioned. Ridiculing their calculations as faulty, he said: "There are two ways to interpret this. One of them is to say there was a certain amount of maliciousness involved. But the most charitable way is that I have taken most of the financial expertise with me into London out of the Fund, these people that I have hired."

Fund officials indeed weighed in against Folkerts-Landau's plan, and according to their version of events, they didn't have to convince the Russians that the plan was financially unsustainable. Although a couple of Russian officials favored it, including Deputy Prime Minister Boris Fyodorov, others were opposed, including top policymakers in the Ministry of Finance. As Daniel Citrin, who was the IMF division chief for Russia, explained: "Our basic position with the Russians was, 'Once you've done this [restructured the GKO debt] and created havoc in the capital markets, you'd better do something that will fix the problem, and don't do something now that you can't afford in six months so that you have to do everything all over again.'"

The Russians announced their final terms on August 25, the day before the conference call. Holders of GKOs would trade in their securities for a variety of new ones, all of which would yield less and mature later, with payment mostly in rubles. They would get a three-year note paying 30 percent interest, a four-year note paying 30 percent interest (until the fourth year, when the interest rate would drop to 25 percent), and a five-year note paying 30 percent interest (until the fourth and fifth years, when the interest rate would drop to 25 percent and 20 percent respectively). As a sweetener, they would get 5 percent of the value of their GKOs in cash, and if they wished, they could exchange one-fifth of their GKOs for dollar-denominated bonds, maturing in 2006, paying 5 percent interest.

Only 30 percent interest, and even less in some years? "This was a plan that we could not live with," Folkerts-Landau said. Having lost that battle, Folkerts-Landau wanted to make clear why contagion was inevitable now, especially in countries such as Brazil that shared some of Russia's weaknesses, now that "the rules of the game have changed" with the IMF allowing Russia to default. As he told the conference call:

> If a country has a significant volume of domestic debt outstanding [that is owned by foreigners], if that country is forced into the arms of the IMF . . . I believe that we should assume from here on out that any such program will ask that the foreign holders of domestic debt [take a major loss]. . . .
>
> Clearly, one had the right to be surprised in Russia and face a write-down there. I would think that anybody being caught this way in Brazil probably deserves all he gets.

It is tempting to condemn Folkerts-Landau for the remarks he made during the conference call. To put it crudely, he was telling his fellow foreign investors that because Russia was forcing them to accept a lower interest rate than they wanted on their securities, they should yank their money out of other countries' markets. Russia had offered them the opportunity to exchange their GKOs voluntarily in July, and many of them had passed up the chance because they figured they could earn fatter returns. Now that their bet on the too-big, too-nuclear theory was going sour, Folkerts-Landau was leading them to the conclusion that the time had come to hit the panic button.

But Folkerts-Landau's comments reflected the reality of modern global capital markets. He was articulating what thousands of members of the Electronic Herd around the world were thinking and saying. He was right, too: Russia's default *had* changed the rules of the game, and market psychology had been fundamentally altered as a result. Investors felt as if they had been whacked by a two-by-four in Russia, and though they may have deserved what they got, they naturally concluded they ought to flee from other places where they might suffer another whacking.

With greater elegance and less vehemence than Folkerts-Landau, George Soros made a similar point in a newspaper op-ed a few days later. Financial markets, Soros wrote, "are rather peculiar in this respect: They resent any kind of government interference but they hold a belief deep down that if conditions get really rough the authorities will step in. This belief has now been shaken."

· 10 ·

THE BALANCE
OF RISKS

For economic policymakers seeking a change of scenery to refresh their minds and souls, few sights can match the snow-capped peaks of the Grand Teton range looming through the panoramic window of the Jackson Lake Lodge in Jackson Hole, Wyoming. The lodge is the site of an annual conference, held in late August, at which top Federal Reserve officials gather along with a few dozen other economic policymakers, analysts, and journalists. Since that time of year tends to be uneventful, the conferences usually allow the attendees to indulge in battery-recharging activities, with mornings devoted to sessions on big-think economic topics, and afternoons free for hiking through the Tetons or river-rafting or tennis-playing. But sometimes pressing matters intrude, and Fed officials conduct important business informally on the sidelines. The August 1998 conference, titled "Income Inequality: Issues and Policy Options," began ten days after the Russian default and devaluation, and the policymakers present, who included Fed chairman Alan Greenspan, were exceptionally preoccupied with current circumstances.

On both evenings of the three-day conference, ghastly data arrived at the lodge from Fed staffers in Washington and New York showing the toll the events in Russia were taking on financial markets. On Thursday, August 27, the Dow Jones fell 357 points, its worst trading day of the year to date; Germany's DAX index dropped 4.5 percent; and Tokyo's Nikkei shed 3 percent. Latin America suffered even worse punishment, with Brazil's main stock index down 10 percent, Argentina's 10.6 percent, and Mexico's 6.1 percent. The following day, the Dow lost another 114 points, closing its worst week in nearly a decade; London shares lost 2.2 percent to hit a seven-month low; and although Latin American stocks recovered a bit of their losses, the Nikkei slid another 3.5 percent. Emerging-market bonds also took a pounding as investors fled in droves to the safety of U.S. Treasury bonds.

Unbeknownst to most of the attendees, a small drama was unfolding among the Fed officials and staffers attending the conference. At Greenspan's behest, members of the Fed's Board of Governors and presidents of the regional Federal Reserve banks, who sit on the Fed's main policymaking panel, were quietly called aside for meetings, up to five people at a time. Peter Fisher, the number two official at the New York Fed, was deputized to tap people discreetly on the shoulder and convey the message that Greenspan wished to see them in the lodge manager's office. Keeping the meetings secret was a challenge, because the manager's office is located between the men's room door and a bank of pay phones, where a number of reporters and brokerage-firm economists tended to congregate. Sometimes, the clandestine parleys proved awkward to convene. Alice Rivlin, who was Fed vice chairman, recalled that after dinner one evening, "the chairman sort of shooed my husband out of the way, which he didn't take kindly to. Wives are used to that. Husbands don't take kindly to it." But Greenspan urgently needed to consult with his colleagues about an idea he had.

Up to that point, the global financial crisis had proved more of a stimulant than a drag on the U.S. economy. Disconcerting as it was, the turmoil in emerging markets produced many gains for American firms and workers, mainly because of the favorable impact on inflation and interest rates. Prices for petroleum, metals, and other commodities were dropping worldwide in response to falling demand in Asia, the result being lower raw-material costs for American companies. With the overall U.S. price level rising at a mere crawl, banks and other private lenders were reducing interest charges to borrowers, since they could afford to be less concerned about inflation eroding the value of the money they were lending. Also helping to lower interest rates, especially the rates charged on home mortgages, was money pouring into the United States seeking shelter from Asia and other troubled markets.

Not all sectors of the U.S. economy were benefiting; some manufacturers were losing export sales and laying off employees because of the recession afflicting much of Asia, a major market for U.S. products such as airplanes, heavy machinery, and software. But in the year since the July 1997 devaluation of the baht, the crisis had made a positive overall contribution to the robust U.S. growth rate. Indeed, unemployment in early summer 1998 stood at lower levels than any seen in nearly three decades. Homebuying and homeownership were hitting records, and the job market was tight, with employers in some metropolitan areas sending recruiters to poor inner-city neighborhoods offering free transportation to jobs in the suburbs.

Accordingly, Fed officials had been growing increasingly worried in the first half of 1998 that inflationary pressures might be building beneath the surface, and they were engaged in a serious debate about whether to drive interest rates up and cool down the economy. The Federal Open Market Committee, the Fed panel responsible for monetary policy and interest rates, meets every six weeks in Washington, and at its meetings in spring and early summer 1998, the group's interest-rate hawks pressed for action. They argued that even though inflation seemed a distant worry given what was happening to commodity and import prices, those benefits probably wouldn't last long. With the economy booming, the danger was increasing that wages would surge and shortages would develop, sending prices upward. So the hawks wanted to use the Fed's most powerful lever, its control over the overnight interest rate charged by banks, to push up borrowing costs. This was no small matter; an increase of a percentage point or two in interest rates, if poorly timed, can squeeze the life out of the economy and throw millions of Americans out of work. The hawks did not prevail, the main reason being that Greenspan felt unready to move. The Fed chief was not so certain that a tight labor market would lead to inflation as it had in the past, because the American economy had entered a new phase in which companies, thanks especially to computerization, were posting enormous gains in productivity that offset their higher payroll costs. In public statements concerning its policy through July 1998, the Open Market Committee disclosed that it was maintaining a bias in favor of higher rates—meaning that although it wouldn't raise rates immediately, it was likely to raise them in the not-too-distant future, and might even do so in the period before the next meeting if inflationary pressures showed clear signs of emerging. "There were a lot of factors that would argue for a rate increase," recalled Thomas Hoenig, president of the Kansas City Fed. "Our finger was poised to push, but we waited."

But the calculus changed when financial markets crumbled in August. Now the risks were clearly rising that the crisis would hobble U.S. economic growth rather than spur it, and even the hawks were backing off their calls for higher rates. In the hopes of restoring calm, Greenspan wanted to explain to the markets that the central bank's posture was changing. Since the fear of a Fed interest-rate boost was one factor weighing on investors, the chairman figured he ought to clue the markets into something that wasn't known publicly—that at a meeting of the Open Market Committee in mid-August, the Fed had dropped its bias in favor of tightening credit, due to the deterioration in the world financial situation. His proposal, which was the focus of the secret, informal meetings at the Jackson Hole conference, was to convey this news in a speech he was scheduled to deliver on September 4 at the University of California at Berkeley. The Fed chief's colleagues endorsed his plan to speak forthrightly, even though the Open Market Committee's policy was to withhold announcing the details of its deliberations until its next meeting. "We were worried," Rivlin said. "The speech needed to signal willingness on the part of the Fed to think about something other than U.S. inflation. There was the possibility of an unraveling of U.S. financial markets, which suddenly seemed much more important."

Greenspan's speech at Berkeley came on a Friday night at the end of a week in which the Dow tumbled as low as 7,539, a dizzying 19 percent below its July 17 peak. "It is just not credible that the United States can remain an oasis of prosperity unaffected by a world that is experiencing greatly increased stress," the Fed chairman said, adding that the Open Market Committee concluded in its August meeting that "the risks had become balanced" between inflation and recession. When the New York markets opened after the Labor Day weekend, investors rejoiced over Greenspan's clear acknowledgment that the central bank was backing off from its tilt toward tight money, and the Dow jumped 380 points.

But for all of the Fed chief's forethought, the impact of his comments proved remarkably short-lived. The next two days, the Dow dropped a total of 405 points, and the carnage was even worse abroad. On September 10, Brazil's stock market skidded 15.8 percent, Mexico's 9.8 percent, Germany's 4.3 percent, and France's 4.6 percent. A fresh wave of selling hit the markets for corporate bonds and emerging-market bonds as well.

The global crisis was now entering its most critical phase, in which American financial markets would undergo bouts of such extreme disarray as to imperil the normal functioning of the U.S. economy and raise the prospect of a worldwide slump. With happy-go-lucky American consumers bingeing on imported electronics, clothing, and autos, the United States was by far the strongest source of demand in a world riddled with trouble, so the spread of crisis symptoms to American shores posed the threat of recessionary pressures gathering force globally. The IMF was in no position to be of help to an economy the size of America's; responsibility for keeping the crisis from worsening was now passing directly to U.S. officials and the policy levers they controlled.

The danger to wealth, jobs, and livelihoods is only part of the reason that many in the High Command, and many scholars and private analysts as well, look back on the late summer and autumn of 1998 as one of the darkest they can remember for the world economy since World War II. At times, the events that transpired during this period cast into doubt the progress of Western-style capitalism. The "end of history" proclaimed when the Berlin Wall fell suddenly seemed much less final amid a plethora of signs suggesting that the advancement of free market ideology, which had appeared so inexorable throughout much of the 1990s, was on the verge of going into reverse.

Pro-Western forces in Russia were in full retreat following Yeltsin's sacking of the Kiriyenko government on August 24, and speculation abounded that socialist policies would be revived under the prime ministership of Yevgeni Primakov. In Hong Kong, hitherto proud of its reputation as the world's most freewheeling market, the government launched a vigorous effort to bolster the Hong Kong Stock Exchange in late August by using billions of dollars of public funds to buy shares, following a round of attacks by currency traders betting on a collapse in the Hong Kong dollar.

The most serious challenge to market dogma came from Malaysia's Prime Minister Mahathir, who on September 1, 1998, exacted revenge on the speculators he despised by imposing capital controls that strictly limited the amount of money people could take out of the country. It is one thing for countries to maintain controls limiting the *inflow* of foreign money, as Chile had done, but quite another to block the exit door. U.S. Treasury officials, while trying to avoid inflaming the situation with confrontational rhetoric, were beside themselves. Privately, they blustered that Mahathir's act of apostasy would backfire by causing the Malaysian economy to undergo an even more wrenching downturn as the inflow of foreign money dried up in response to the government's restrictions. "Malaysia's going to provide a good negative example to everybody," a senior Treasury official predicted. "And in that sense, what they've done may turn out to be a constructive contribution."

Even more startling was the implicit endorsement of Mahathir's policy by one of globalization's most articulate defenders. Paul Krugman of MIT made the case in *Fortune* that capital controls (or exchange controls, as they are also known) may be the least-bad alternative for countries hit by crises. Capital controls had worked poorly in Latin America during the 1980s, Krugman acknowledged, partly because of abuse by corrupt officials, who held considerable power to decide which companies and investors had legitimate business reasons for moving money overseas and which didn't. But, he wrote, "Extreme situations demand extreme measures." Asian countries faced an impossibly cruel dilemma between holding interest rates high and letting their currencies plummet, so in Krugman's view, the time had come to consider exchange controls—"a solution so unfashionable, so stigmatized, that hardly anyone has dared suggest it."

Such subversion of global capital's guiding principles added an apocalyptic air to the more urgent problem facing the High Command of keeping the world financial system from coming apart at the seams. Unsurprisingly, top policymakers often found it difficult to hide how rattled they were during this period, though at times they resorted to gallows humor to maintain their equilibrium. Walking up the Capitol steps one day in September 1998, Summers turned to Howard Schloss, the Treasury's assistant secretary for public affairs, whom Summers called "Spinner," and asked half-jokingly, "Spinner, have you ever tried to spin a world depression?" At a G-7 deputies meeting in London on September 14, Sakakibara recalled, Summers passed him a note that read: "Eisuke, the world is going to hell. We've got to cooperate."

Summers later insisted that he would not use such colorful language in a note; perhaps, he said, he wrote that "these are big prob-

lems and we've got to cooperate." Whatever the precise words he
wrote, the perception of a hell-bound world economy was widely
shared. "I'm impressed how quickly people forget how frightening
those days were," said Jack Boorman, director of the IMF's Policy
Development and Review Department. "They were frightening
indeed."

Bob Rubin managed to get away for a brief Alaska fishing vacation
in late August 1998, hoping to snag some salmon and get a respite
from the pressures of Washington. While casting his line on a pic-
turesque inlet, his cellphone rang, with word that President Clinton
wanted to speak to him at 1 P.M. The Treasury secretary agreed, but
as luck would have it, he hooked a salmon just as Clinton's call
came through from the White House switchboard, and he wanted
to reel in his catch. So, he asked, could the president call back in a
few minutes?

The scene was emblematic of what was transpiring inside the
Clinton administration at the time—a White House raring for action,
and a Treasury Department trying to play it cool. The president was
growing extremely frustrated watching the global crisis worsen, and
he wanted to get more personally involved in trying to alleviate it.
Gene Sperling, his top aide on economic issues, received numerous
notes from Clinton about the crisis during this period, especially
after the publication of op-ed articles by economists urging radical
measures of one sort or another, which would prompt the president
to demand: "Are we considering this?"

Clinton had been suggesting for some time that he ought to
deliver a major speech on the crisis. He had a political motive, of
course, because the Lewinsky scandal was threatening to overwhelm his presidency, and he wanted to dispel the impression that
he was less than fully devoted to matters of state. But he put his case
in substantive terms: The markets would take heart knowing that
the leader of the largest and richest economy on the planet was

closely following the mounting economic strains and was prepared to take all necessary countermeasures. He was particularly enamored of a proposal to convene a global summit of world leaders, an idea he chatted about frequently on the phone with his political soulmate, British Prime Minister Tony Blair. But Rubin was trying to keep Clinton's instinctive activism in check. It was not that the Treasury secretary was trying to hog responsibility and claim the crisis issue as his department's exclusive purview; rather, he fretted that dramatic statements by the president might backfire by raising unrealistic expectations and spreading more alarm than comfort.

Still, Clinton was determined to do something—the only question was what. On the evening of September 7, 1998, Labor Day, he summoned his top advisers for a two-hour meeting in the Yellow Oval Room in the residential quarters of the White House. After a few introductory remarks by Rubin, Summers weighed in with an analysis that the rhetoric in Greenspan's Berkeley speech the previous Friday evening had already "galvanized" the markets. But the president wanted more. Although he put enormous faith in Rubin's judgment, he was chafing at the caution of the Treasury team, and he raised the idea of the world leader summit. In a sign of the tension pervading the meeting, Sperling stepped in to knock down his boss's proposal, since he happened to oppose this one himself, and he knew the Treasury chieftains feared losing their credibility with the president if they played the role of naysayers too much. The world summit idea, Sperling argued, was "dangerous for two reasons." First was the expectations problem: If the summit proved unable to produce a meaningful result, the consequences could be extremely damaging to market sentiment; even if a "deliverable" were formulated in advance, it would probably leak, diminishing any positive impact. Second, the summit would be a logistical nightmare, requiring weeks of planning—and who knew what sort of shape the world would be in by the time the leaders met?

Clinton relented. "You don't want to exchange something that will give you two weeks of good feeling for two years of pain," he admitted. "We don't need to do something that will raise grandiose expectations." But he was determined to give a speech, and a suitable venue was soon arranged—the Council on Foreign Relations in New York, on the following Monday, September 14.

The nub of the speech, its most crucial passage, would include a phrase that the Treasury had concocted: "Clearly the balance of risks has now shifted." Specifically, the president would observe that "for most of the last thirty years, the United States and the rest of the world has been preoccupied by inflation," but "the industrial world's chief priority today plainly is to spur growth." To make sure the markets got the message, the Treasury hatched a plan for the G-7 finance ministers and central bank governors to issue a communiqué containing similar words the night before Clinton's speech, so he could hail their action. This would show the world that the governments of the major industrial powers were united in fighting the crisis—a display of resolve that it was hoped would reverse the erosion in market confidence.

To the untrained eye, the proposition that "the balance of risks has now shifted" might seem innocuous, or perhaps even blindingly obvious in light of the events materializing at the time. But the phrase represented a daring statement, mainly because it held potentially major implications for monetary policy. It suggested, albeit obliquely, that the Fed—and other independent central banks around the world—should make absolutely certain they were avoiding excessively tight credit stances and should tilt toward lowering interest rates to ensure that their economies did not slump.

The Clinton administration had faithfully refrained from commenting on Fed policy ever since coming to power, an approach that had paid handsome dividends, because markets sensed that Greenspan held a free hand to do what he thought best. Historically, occupants of the White House and the Treasury have jousted in public with the Fed, especially when they felt it was holding interest rates too high, but Rubin and Summers firmly believed in keeping any differences with Greenspan over monetary issues strictly confined to their private conversations, lest public feuding brew disquiet among investors that could inflict even worse damage on the economy. Determined to avoid any step that might ruin their reputation for respecting the Fed's independence, Rubin and Summers consulted closely with Greenspan on the "balance of risks" terminology and secured his blessing (indeed, the Fed chairman used similar words himself about the U.S. economy in his Berkeley speech). The phrase, after all, did not formally commit the Fed or other central banks to do anything in particular; they were free to decide according to their own perceptions whether they were appropriately weighing the dangers.

But G-7 unity proved to be a questionable proposition. When the "balance of risks" phrase was sprung on the European central bankers over the weekend immediately prior to Clinton's speech scheduled for Monday, September 14, they rebelled—in a move that threatened to undercut the U.S. administration's plans.

The clash materialized on the top floor of an eighteen-story round building in Basel, Switzerland, the headquarters of the Bank for International Settlements (BIS), where the chief stewards of the world's money supply gather almost every month of the year for a Sunday evening dinner and Monday afternoon meeting. Stimulated by fine wine, haute cuisine, and a view over the Rhine River, the dozen or so principal attendees conduct conversation in the strictest of privacy, with the press kept at bay, as is true of meetings of the G-7 deputies—whose conclaves these rival in their capacity for shaping the course of the global economy.

Unlike the G-7 deputies, who hail from finance ministries, the diners at the BIS monthly meetings belong to the priesthood of central banking and might be called its College of Cardinals. They include the chairman of the Fed (or, if he can't attend, the vice chairman), the governor of the Bank of England, the president of the German Bundesbank, the governor of the Bank of Japan, and their counterparts from France, Italy, Canada, the Netherlands, Belgium, Sweden, and Switzerland. The president of the New York Fed also has a seat at the table (giving the United States the privilege of being the only country with two representatives), and so does the BIS general manager, a former Bank of England official named Andrew Crockett. With no formal agenda for the dinner meetings, the participants are free to bring up whatever subjects they like. (Topics may include the BIS itself, an institution established in the 1930s to handle German reparations from World War I that now serves as a clearinghouse for bank regulators and holds hard-currency reserves for a number of member central banks.) To enhance candor, the dinners exclude even the top central bank staffers who have accompanied their bosses to Basel; the only interlopers are special invited guests such as the IMF managing director. The most valuable feature of the parleys, participants widely agree, is the camaraderie and bonds of personal trust that develop. These are people who need to know each other well, since they can never be sure when they may have to communicate over long distances to prevent financial calamities from getting out of hand.

By the time of the Sunday dinner on September 13, 1998, a few of the central bank governors in Basel were dimly aware of the proposal for the G-7 to issue the communiqué about the shift in the balance of risks. But most were still in the dark. Greenspan wasn't there—Vice Chairman Rivlin attended in his stead—and the task of presenting a draft of the communiqué to the governors fell to Ted Truman, the Fed's top bureaucrat on international matters. Gingerly, for the governors were savoring brandy after the meal, Truman entered the sanctuary on the eighteenth floor—a breach of etiquette for a staffer, though it mattered little in this case, since Truman had announced he was retiring from the Fed to join the Treasury as assistant secretary for international affairs, and this was his last BIS meeting.

The Bundesbank's Hans Tietmeyer said flatly that he would not sign the communiqué, and other Europeans, notably Britain's Eddie George and France's Jean-Claude Trichet, resisted as well. Tietmeyer simply didn't agree that the crisis menaced the world economy, and the worst thing economic policymakers could do, he argued, was to aggravate the uproar in the markets by issuing rhetoric that smacked of official trepidation. He also opposed any moves that might put pressure on European central banks to ease credit, because the continent's growth indicators were reasonably healthy, and an overly lax interest-rate policy could undermine market confidence in Europe at a time when it was preparing to launch the euro and the new European central bank on January 1, 1999. Finally, as another participant at the meeting put it: "When one says 'there is a change in the balance of risks,' it means something in terms of monetary policy, and there was certainly among some of us some uneasiness about the executive branch going into territory that was not the territory of the executive branch."

At that point, Washington's original timetable—according to which the G-7 would release its communiqué Sunday night, followed by Clinton's New York speech Monday—was shot to hell. Now the question was whether the U.S. initiative might turn into a divisive fiasco, with the press getting wind of the discord in Basel and trumpeting stories about fissures in the G-7 ranks.

The U.S. side was poorly prepared for this turn of events. Rivlin had not even been briefed on the communiqué before going to Basel; Greenspan knew it was in the works but didn't expect such a flap to erupt. After dinner, the U.S. representatives—Rivlin, Truman, and New York Fed President Bill McDonough—called Treasury in Washington to find out what was going on and reached Tim Geithner, who filled them in and said Summers was on his way to Dulles airport to attend a G-7 deputies meeting in London. A Treasury operator broke in to ask if she should intercept Summers at Dulles. "No, I've been with Mr. Summers at Dulles," Rivlin replied drily. "If you intercept him, he'll miss his plane."

At the next afternoon's meetings at BIS headquarters, with the hour drawing close for Clinton to begin speaking in New York, the U.S. side proposed alternative language for the communiqué, but Tietmeyer still balked at signing. The Bank of England's George, evidently concerned about the potential for a damaging rupture in the G-7's public facade, suggested to U.S. officials that there was only one way to resolve the impasse: Greenspan must call Tietmeyer. That is what happened—and although nobody will reveal what Greenspan and Tietmeyer said to each other, it did the trick, with Tietmeyer agreeing to sign the communiqué even while continuing to grumble about it. To the immense relief of Clinton administration officials, the communiqué hit the newswires a few minutes after the president's speech—not the timing they had hoped for but close enough to appear well-orchestrated.

Again, in a pattern similar to that following Greenspan's Berkeley speech, markets rallied—at first—with the Dow closing up 150 points and London stocks rising by a like amount. Press and market commentary about the G-7 communiqué was full of speculation that the industrial powers were preparing to cut interest rates in coordinated fashion, as they had occasionally done during the 1980s. The G-7 finance ministers and central bank governors, after all, not only agreed in their communiqué that "the balance of risks in the world economy had shifted," but they "emphasized their commitment to preserve or create conditions" for growth and "noted the importance of close cooperation among them at this juncture."

But the air started leaking from the coordinated-rate-cut balloon the day after the Clinton speech, when Tietmeyer made it clear he had agreed to no such thing. "It would be wrong to see [the communiqué] as favoring a general lowering of interest rates," he told reporters. "In Europe, no reason can be seen to relax monetary policy." Likewise, Greenspan told a congressional questioner late on September 16 that "there is no endeavor to coordinate interest rate cuts," and the following day, a rout was under way in the markets, with the Dow closing down 216 points, the Nikkei skidding to a twelve-and-a-half-year low, and French, German, and Brazilian stocks dropping about 5 percent.

The High Command was surely justified in acknowledging that the balance of risks had shifted, and doing so in a high-profile venue made sense as a signal that its leaders were not oblivious to the need for possible action. But the effort offered some useful lessons in the pitfalls of trying to impress the Electronic Herd with verbiage. "The [G-7] statement was intended to calm things down, but I think it raised expectations," said one Fed official. "It wasn't *intended* to signal a coordinated rate cut. I think they were trying to sound warm and fuzzy, and in the process, they may have had the effect of appearing to promise something they had no intention of delivering."

The balance of risks would soon shift even further.

A fairly long list of good-sized countries looked as if they might need IMF help in late summer 1998. A July 30 memo from Assistant Treasury Secretary Tim Geithner to Rubin and Summers enumerated the likely recipients: Ukraine was "almost certain" to require $2.3 billion to $2.5 billion. Turkey, South Africa, and Malaysia were "quite possible" candidates for Fund programs, with needs ranging from $1 billion to $5.5 billion each. Brazil and Nigeria had "some possibility" of requiring aid, with a Brazilian rescue, it if came, "likely to be much more" than the $8.7 billion the country would be allowed to borrow under normal IMF rules.

But where would the money come from? That question helped wrack the nerves of the High Command at a time when worrisome developments were already popping up all over the globe. After having approved so many large loans for Thailand, South Korea, Indonesia, and Russia, the IMF was running low on hard currency; the Fund estimated the amount available for new lending at somewhere between $3 billion and $8 billion. Meanwhile, the U.S. Congress was balking at legislation that would enable the IMF to replenish its coffers. The Senate had passed legislation that would provide the $14.5 billion U.S. portion of a major increase in Fund quotas, plus a $3.4 billion U.S. contribution toward a new credit line for the Fund. But the bill faced powerful resistance in the House of Representatives. So the time had come to think about unorthodox ways of bankrolling the Fund—or, as Geithner wrote, "we need to consider options for dealing with requests for Fund support that might exceed current projections, taking into account the possibility that funding by Congress turns out to be inadequate, significantly delayed, or not forthcoming at all."

The IMF's quotas—the contributions from members—were worth, on paper, about $200 billion. But much of that was in the form of currencies not readily used in international transactions, and of the hard-currency portion, much had been disbursed or committed to the programs in Asia and Russia. That left about $38 billion, which would seem ample except that it included a substantial sum the IMF was obliged to keep on hand. The IMF, after all, works like a credit union, with member countries entitled to withdraw their contributions almost at will. Accordingly, Fund officials feel they must maintain a cushion—they put it at a minimum of $30 billion to $35 billion in mid-1998—in case one of its rich members exercises its right to take some or all of its quota out (as the United States did in 1978 during a dollar crisis).

That arithmetic produced the estimate of $3 billion to $8 billion being available for new lending. To be sure, the IMF's financial status wasn't quite as dire as those numbers suggest. In a pinch, the Fund could draw on a special credit line, called the General Arrangements to Borrow (GAB), which is furnished by the world's richest countries (the G-7 plus a handful of others, such as Switzerland and the Netherlands). But about a third of the GAB had already been used for the Russian rescue, leaving $14.3 billion, and as Geithner wrote in his memo, that might not be enough to cover all the possible demands on the Fund. Furthermore, few of the countries on his list of trouble spots would qualify for loans financed by the GAB, which was established to deal with threats to the stability of the global financial system.

No amount of cajoling and table-thumping by Clinton, Rubin, and Greenspan had succeeded in persuading the House that the failure to approve the IMF funding bill was endangering the world economy.

"Cutting off the water to the fire department when the city is burning down" was one of their favorite analogies for the congressional impasse, but that argument failed to impress some members who had taken note of the results in places like Moscow and Jakarta.

Strange bedfellows comprising House opponents included Bernie Sanders, a Vermont independent who calls himself a "democratic socialist" and boasts a 100 percent rating from the Americans for Democratic Action, and Ron Paul, a Texas Republican who favored shutting down the Federal Reserve and the Internal Revenue Service. Left-wingers like Sanders were critical of the IMF for failing to demand that borrowing countries improve their treatment of workers, the environment, and human rights. Right-wingers like Paul accused the Fund of interfering in markets and creating moral hazard.

The administration encountered particular difficulty with the GOP conservatives opposing the bill, since among their number were influential members such as the House Majority Leader, Dick Armey of Texas; the Majority whip, Tom DeLay, also from Texas; and James Saxton of New Jersey, chairman of the Joint Economic Committee. They derided the Treasury's contentions about the urgency of getting cash to the IMF, noting among other things that the Fund held $32 billion worth of gold. "The bottom line," Saxton declared, "is that the IMF is not destitute."

Saxton was on to something. The IMF had viable alternatives to avoid going broke—and as Geithner's memo showed, the Clinton administration was prepared to use them if necessary, although doing so would have incurred some political and economic costs.

The memo listed several options that "could be used in combination with each other." The IMF could indeed sell some of its gold, although that was probably the worst idea for raising money, according to Geithner, because "the more this option is exercised, the greater the effect on gold prices, the less return on sales." He gave low marks to another idea, having the IMF borrow money on private financial markets, because it would dilute member countries' control over Fund policies.

But the memo was less negative about other possibilities. Maybe $10 billion more could be squeezed out of the IMF's cash on hand, Geithner wrote. Since Treasury and IMF officials had loudly insisted that the Fund needed to maintain a $30 billion to $35 billion reserve cushion, using that money for loans would presumably require "some understanding among countries" to refrain from exercising their right to withdraw their contributions. Or perhaps the Fund could borrow on a bilateral basis from Japan, Germany, or the BIS. Although the lenders "would almost certainly exact a price," the Fund had engaged in such borrowing in the past when its resources were low, Geithner noted.

Much sound and fury accompanied the congressional debate about IMF funding in 1998. But although proponents were understandably anxious to see the legislation pass, the prospect of the Fund running completely dry was remote. The High Command had much more stress-inducing issues with which to contend.

For market players like David Tepper, August–early September 1998 was a time for getting out of the markets while the getting was good. Balding and mustachioed, Tepper ran a hedge fund called Appaloosa Management from a nondescript brick building in Short Hills, New Jersey, about forty-five minutes from Manhattan. The firm was one of the biggest in the hedge-fund business, with about $1.5 billion in investors' money, thanks to Tepper's reputation for spotting trends quickly. When Russia announced its default and devaluation on August 17, Tepper recalled in his staccato New Yorkese, "I knew you couldn't screw around." So in the days immediately following Russia's move, the forty-year-old Tepper ordered his traders to begin drastically trimming Appaloosa's portfolio, especially emerging-market bonds and U.S. corporate bonds.

"The problem was, you had had this idea that with the IMF, there was some safety net underneath the market," Tepper said, "but if Russia could default, why couldn't Brazil default, and why couldn't

Mexico default, and why couldn't others default?" And if those countries' bonds were going to fall because of default worries, the same seemed likely to happen to, say, the double-B-rated bond of a U.S. company that has to offer a yield sufficiently attractive to compete with the likes of Mexican and Brazilian bonds for investors' favor. "If you're doing portfolio management, and there's a 25 percent probability something's going to [negatively] affect the price of something you hold, you sell. No matter what," Tepper declared. "I don't give a shit if it's affected or not at the end of the day. It's just a probability game. So we moved pretty fast in August."

Tepper's reaction was shared by thousands of people who trade bonds on Wall Street and other financial centers, which explains why the bond market in the United States "seized up" in fall 1998 like an auto engine that has run out of oil, and very nearly created the conditions that would have forced the American economic expansion to a halt. The stock market's woes during this period were obvious and well-publicized, but policymakers like Rubin, Greenspan, and Summers weren't concerned much with falling share prices. Their major worry was the bond market.

The bond market is where, in today's world, most U.S. companies of any appreciable size borrow the bulk of the cash they need to run their operations day to day and year to year. They issue short-term commercial paper, maturing in two or three months, to pay their workers and suppliers while awaiting payment from customers. They issue longer-term notes and bonds to finance the purchase of new equipment or the construction of factories. They can borrow from banks, too, of course, and many do. But over the past couple of decades, a shrinking portion of the corporate loans provided in the United States has come from banks. Even mortgage loans, though handled by banks initially, are usually financed by bond investors who buy the rights to receive large batches of mortgage payments from homeowners and property owners. Some 70 to 80 percent of all corporate and mortgage lending is now funneled through the capital markets, which generally offer cheaper rates. So when investors refuse to buy all but the super-safest of bonds, as they did in autumn 1998, the consequences can be just as ominous for Main Street as for Wall Street.

Bonds are normally conservative, almost boring investments, rising and falling only modestly in price. A bond, after all, is supposed to provide a guaranteed stream of interest and principal payments, unlike a share of corporate stock, which provides returns that vary depending on the company's earnings or expectations thereof. To be sure, some bonds—Russian GKOs, for instance—are far from conservative, and their prices soar and plunge in tandem with fears about whether the issuer can make the payments due. But most bonds, issued by countries and companies for which nonpayment isn't much of a concern, rise and fall mainly because of changes in prevailing interest rates.

For a simple example, consider a $1,000 bond issued by a relatively solid U.S. company with a 10 percent coupon (that is, paying $100 in interest each year). It would become less valuable—and would fall concomitantly in price—if interest rates went up a couple of percentage points, because bonds with similar maturities, from issuers of similar creditworthiness, would become available with yields of 12 percent (that is, paying $120 on each $1,000 invested). Conversely, the bond would become more valuable—and would rise concomitantly in price—if interest rates fell a couple of percentage points, because it would compete with similar bonds coming on the market with coupons of only 8 percent. This illustration should help explain why the business pages of newspapers often tell readers that "bond prices move inversely with interest rates." And it should help explain why the bond market typically fluctuates much less than the stock market—because interest rates are the main influence, and they tend to rise and fall gradually.

But all these dynamics spun totally out of whack in August, September, and October of 1998, which an IMF report would later describe as "a period of turmoil in mature markets that is virtually without precedent in the absence of a major inflationary or economic shock." The result was a near standstill in the issuance of many types of bonds, crunching credit dangerously tight.

Smack in the midst of the upheaval was the trading room of Salomon Smith Barney, a cavernous, windowless chamber on the forty-second floor of a downtown Manhattan office tower where about 400 men and women worked at long rows of desks with flashing computer monitors, yakking over the phone about "crossover paper" and "stripped-spread Brady's" and "Treasury bond arb positions." Salomon ranked among the largest of Wall Street's broker-dealers; it was a major intermediary between banks, insurance companies, hedge funds, mutual funds, pension funds—just about any institution looking to buy or sell a few million dollars worth of bonds, stocks, currencies, options, interest-rate swaps, or other financial instruments. The firm's profitability depended on the ability of its traders and salespeople to gauge the appetite among institutional investors for these securities, and in autumn 1998, the appetite for bonds—with the notable exception of U.S. Treasuries—dwindled to virtual nothingness.

Among the people on that trading floor was John Purcell, a managing director in Salomon's bond trading operation, whose recollections provide insight into the process by which Russia, a country with only about 1 percent of the world's GDP, exerted such a profound impact on markets. The dapper Purcell, who earned a master's degree in economics from Ohio University in 1984, was fluent in trader jargon. But in explaining what happened that autumn, he often reverted to the simple language of gut feelings as he recounted a chain of events involving linkages and interactions among different types of securities, firms, and markets that nobody anticipated—either in the markets or in the High Command. "Russia from an economic standpoint was not very significant, but it affected the psyche of investors fairly substantially, because a lot of the things they believed in sort of fell apart," said Purcell. "There was a very visceral and emotional element to this."

One factor that initially confounded Western portfolio managers after August 17, he said, was a step the Russian government took that canceled foreign-exchange contracts they had with Russian banks. The contracts were supposed to protect foreign investors in Russia against a fall in the ruble by ensuring that they could exchange their rubles for dollars at the old fixed rate. But Moscow essentially invalidated those deals, on the grounds that the country's banking system would collapse if the banks were forced to fulfill their obligations. "So that's problem number one: Investors thought they had a hedged trade, but guess what? They don't have a hedged trade anymore," Purcell said. "Suddenly they realize they're standing in midair. Things they thought couldn't happen are happening, like defaults on local currency debt."

Also staggering was the scale of losses on some Russian bonds, which fell in price by 30 percent or more in a matter of days, followed by the bonds of other emerging-market countries whose creditworthiness was now in more serious doubt. "In the old days, if a bond went down 10 to 15 points, that was pretty bad, but it might only happen in one or two instances. Now whole asset classes were going down 20 and 30 points," Purcell said. "You're an insurance company or money manager, and you just had a piece of your portfolio—not a big piece, but a piece—blow up. It's one thing when that happens in isolation, but now it's happening in a whole bunch of different places."

Severe losses would have been manageable, except that many of the investors in securities like GKOs and Russian Eurobonds, especially hedge funds, had borrowed heavily to finance their purchases. This sort of leveraged investing is widespread in the bond markets; an investment firm can increase its overall return because the yield on its bonds almost always exceeds the interest on its loan. Alas, the catch is that its bonds are pledged as collateral—and when their value plummets, margin calls come from creditors demanding repayment.

Salomon had lent substantial sums to hedge funds, so it was compelled to place margin calls to them. Other financial firms were doing the same, and that is how a sell-off of "bad" bonds begat a sell-off of "good" bonds. Investors hit with margin calls were compelled to unload higher-quality issues to satisfy their creditors' claims, and when the higher-quality paper came under selling pressure too, the urge to cut and run grew even more intense.

A phobia of risk pervaded the markets, most clearly evinced by the widening "spread" between the yields on U.S. Treasury bonds and other types of bonds. Treasuries are regarded as the safest invest-ment in the world, because the chance that the U.S. government would fail to pay interest or principal is as near to zero as conceiv-ably possible. So the spread between Treasury yields and yields on other bonds is a classic measurement of how cautious investors are being—that is, the amount of extra return they require as compen-sation for the danger of default. The wider a bond's spread, the greater the market's concern about its riskiness.

By mid-September 1998, the spread on "junk" bonds—bonds issued by American companies with relatively low credit ratings—reached nearly 6 percentage points above comparable U.S. Trea-suries, up from about 2.75 percentage points at the end of 1997. The spreads on Mexican and Korean bonds roughly doubled, to about 10 percentage points above Treasury yields, and the average spread for all emerging market bonds widened to more than 17 percentage points. The result of this widening of spreads, and surge in yields, was that it became prohibitively expensive for most companies and governments to consider raising money in the bond market because of the interest cost they would have to pay.

But rising spreads and interest costs were only part of the problems that were causing bond markets to reach a state of disfunctionality.

Around Labor Day, a mutual-fund manager called Salomon wanting to sell $50 million of thirty-year bonds issued by a major telecommunications company. Ordinarily, such a transaction would be a matter of routine, because those particular bonds were widely traded—indeed, they were a benchmark for much of the corporate bond market—and the mutual-fund manager wanted to get

Salomon's bid for the bonds so he could compare it with bids from three or four other broker-dealers. But besides Salomon, nobody else would bid.

In other words, gridlock was setting in—or, as traders and economists put it, illiquidity. The market lacked the lubrication that comes with many intermediaries standing ready to buy and sell. Broker-dealers were much more reluctant than before to take bonds off investors' hands, unless they were reasonably sure they had another customer lined up to buy them. To the extent they were willing to trade at all, they insisted on prices that were much more advantageous to themselves. Trading shriveled as a result, and investors confronted the depressing reality that the numbers flashing on their computer screens almost certainly understated the losses they would suffer if they tried to sell their holdings.

Perhaps most disturbing was what was happening to U.S. Treasuries. Because they are backed by the full faith and credit of the United States, Treasuries are almost invariably snapped up by the billions of dollars during crises of all sorts, as investors engage in a "flight to quality" while shunning riskier issues. That was true during autumn 1998 as well but to an alarming extreme. Investors were so spooked by the illiquidity in the markets that they were putting a premium on particular types of Treasury bonds that could be sold with the greatest ease and speed, in case they needed to raise cash in a hurry.

Heather Neale, a trader who worked with Purcell, punched a few keys on a computer to bring up a row of numbers showing the prices and yields on a recently issued thirty-year Treasury bond. This is an "on-the-run" bond, so called because having just been issued, it's being actively traded. Then Neale punched a couple of other keys to bring up similar numbers for a thirty-year Treasury issued a couple of years earlier. This is an "off-the-run" bond, which no longer trades much because investors have salted it away in their portfolios. As expected, the prices of these two bonds had adjusted so that the difference in yield (the spread) between them was minuscule—it's normally about five to seven "basis points" (a basis point is one one-hundredth of a percentage point). After all, investors buying a bond backed by the U.S. government aren't likely to care much whether it matures in twenty-eight years or thirty years.

But in autumn 1998, investors did care. "If you get a chart comparing spreads in on-the-run and off-the-run, you'll see they exploded," Neale said. Specifically, the spread widened to 35 basis points in October 1998. Put another way, investors at that time were willing to sacrifice about a third of a percentage point in yield to buy a highly liquid thirty-year Treasury instead of a less liquid one. That may not seem significant, but in the world of bond markets, it signaled an intense fear of holding anything that couldn't be dumped immediately.

Unsurprisingly, considering the mood among money managers, "Guys on the floor were telling me, at the beginning of October, that there wouldn't be any bonds sold [that is, issued by corporations] until the end of the year," said Jeffrey Shafer, a senior Salomon executive. In fact, the amount of high-yield corporate bonds issued in U.S. markets fell in October 1998 by about 85 percent from the monthly average of the previous spring.

Purcell provided this encapsulation of the atmosphere in the markets:

> There's a huge flight to quality, because money managers might need to raise cash in the event of withdrawals. So what's your willingness to commit any money to the market? Zero. Who wants to buy a new corporate bond when all your analysts are too busy investigating the blowups you've already got in your portfolio?
>
> You're trying to figure out, what does anything mean anymore on this planet? All the relationships [between bonds] that we knew about are suddenly meaningless. And you don't have a lot of confidence in the whole global economic picture. You're thinking, things could really spiral out of control.

· 11 ·

PLUMBING THE DEPTHS

As the executive vice president heading the markets group at the New York Fed, Peter Fisher held chief responsibility at the U.S. central bank for overseeing and monitoring the health of the nation's financial markets. Six-foot-three, with a graying crown of thick, curly hair and horn-rimmed glasses, he was the son of Roger Fisher, a retired Harvard Law School professor and author of a bestseller about negotiating tactics called *Getting to Yes*. A lawyer by training who had spent his entire career at the New York Fed, Peter Fisher had a pleasant sense of whimsy, as evidenced by a practice he instituted concerning the timing of the Fed's daily interventions in the financial markets. The New York Fed's trading desk used to contact Wall Street bond traders at exactly the same time every morning to purchase or sell large amounts of Treasury bills—a closely-watched operation, eagerly awaited on the Street, by which the central bank regulates the nation's money supply and influences the level of interest rates. Shortly after being promoted to the executive vice president's job, Fisher decreed that each weekday a little after 10 A.M., a New York Fed staffer would shake a single die in a leather cup and roll it onto the table—the number, one to six, determining the number of minutes after 10:30 that the Fed would contact the bond dealers. He described the exercise as part of his effort to achieve "maximum flexibility."

At 5 A.M. on Monday, September 21, 1998, an alarm clock awakened the forty-two-year-old Fisher at his Maplewood, New Jersey, home, and as is his custom, he promptly checked a small electronic device by his bedside to see how overseas markets were faring. In the weeks since the Russian default, the bad news had come thick and fast, and this morning, he was anticipating another onslaught. The results in Asian and European stock markets confirmed his fears. Hong Kong had closed down 3.7 percent, Singapore 3.3 percent, and Tokyo's Nikkei index had plunged to a new twelve-year low. In mid-morning trading, Frankfurt was down 3.7 percent, Paris 3.9 percent, Milan 4.4 percent, London 2.3 percent, Madrid 4.9 percent, and Amsterdam 6 percent. Within hours, the Dow would be following suit, and market sages would appear on TV screens explaining the day's developments as a reaction to the imminent release of a videotape showing President Clinton's grand jury testimony on the Monica Lewinsky matter. This market commentary struck Fisher as idiotic: Why, he wondered, would anyone blame the Clinton videotape for moves in markets as far-flung as Singapore? Then again, Fisher had a pretty good idea what was really behind the sell-off.

The previous day, a Sunday, he had paid a secret visit to Long-Term Capital Management, a hedge fund in Greenwich, Connecticut, to examine its books. Virtually unknown to the American public, Long-Term was a major player in global financial markets, but after enjoying wondrous success in the mid-1990s, it now was on the brink of going bust. Word was spreading fast on Wall Street about Long-Term's plight—indeed, several firms had sent people to Greenwich over the weekend to study the books to see if they should take a stake in Long-Term or buy part of its holdings, but the outlook for such a rescue was dim. Fisher had been staggered by the potential damage that a collapse of Long-Term might mean, because of its deep and tangled transactions with brokerage firms and banks. Virtually every stock, bond, and other security in its vast portfolio was pledged as collateral to the firms with which it traded, and a default by Long-Term would leave those firms suddenly holding a huge quantity of securities to unload. With many of those same firms, moreover, Long-Term had engaged in a huge number of trades in the derivative markets, which involve agreements to make payments based on the movement of a particular stock or bond. In essence, these trades provided the firms with insurance against losses on other positions they had taken in the markets, and if Long-Term suddenly ceased to exist, they would likely sell out those positions in great haste.

As Fisher saw it, the slaughter under way in Asia, Europe, and New York on September 21 was but a foretaste of the selling pressure building as Wall Streeters who sensed what was coming scrambled to get out of the way. Once a default occurred, he feared, the strain on the markets might be so extreme as to cause a full-fledged breakdown.

The Long-Term saga has been told before, and many of its most colorful aspects are well known—in particular the firm's star-studded list of partners, who included a former Fed vice chairman and two Nobel Prize-winning economists whose theories of how markets are supposed to behave provided the basis for much of Long-Term's trading strategy. Still, the essential facts about Long-Term's meteoric rise and fall remain flabbergasting: The firm had opened its doors only four and a half years earlier, and its staff never exceeded 190 employees. Yet its profits of $2.1 billion in 1996 were greater than those of McDonald's or Disney or Xerox or Gillette; and the $140 billion in assets it held rivaled the largest financial institutions in the world. At its peak, Long-Term had $7 billion in capital (the accumulated investments and profits of its owners), which surpassed that of Salomon Smith Barney and nearly topped that of Merrill Lynch. But it all went up in smoke in a period of about five weeks, bringing the global crisis closer than ever to shattering U.S. economic stability.

Irony abounds in the story of Long-Term, for its founder, John Meriwether, and his academic accomplices prided themselves on having figured out a way to incur minimal risk while raking in returns of about 40 percent a year for their investors. They weren't speculating on pork bellies or Internet stocks; nor were they betting the bulk of their money on the overall direction of particular markets. They invested in a wide range of markets and financial instruments, with the aim of putting their eggs in numerous baskets, and in general, for every bond or stock they bought long, they sold another one short, so the losses on one investment would be offset (and, they hoped, exceeded) by gains on another. Their portfolio, they believed, was almost ideally insulated against any broad change in the economic climate and protected against the pitches and tosses of financial markets.

Meriwether, a onetime high school math teacher from an Irish Catholic neighborhood in Chicago's South Side, had first demonstrated his magic at Salomon Brothers, which he joined in 1974 at age twenty-seven, fresh out of the University of Chicago business school. He was soon heading a group at Salomon that invested the firm's own capital in arbitrage trades—not the kind of arbitrage that Bob Rubin did at Goldman, which involved merger stocks, but a form of investing even more rooted in precise calculations of mathematical probabilities. He hired Ph.D.s and assistant professors who built computer models showing how different types of securities— bonds, in particular—had maintained highly predictable relationships with each other over time, meaning that money could be made when those relationships diverged from their historical patterns. Meriwether and his team were particularly fond of exploiting the profit opportunities that presented themselves when the spreads on relatively risky, high-yielding bonds widened to unusual levels beyond the yields on safer, lower-yielding bonds. The yield on corporate bonds with a single-A rating, for example, tended to be about 1.25 to 1.5 percentage points above Treasuries. If that spread widened to an abnormal extent, the computer model would signal to Meriwether's group that corporate bonds were a bargain—specifically, a bargain relative to Treasuries. So the group would buy tens of millions of dollars worth of corporate bonds, while selling short an equal amount of Treasury bonds, anticipating that when the yields converged toward a more normal level, the profits they made on one side of their trade would exceed their losses on the other. The strategy worked so beautifully that the arbitrage group accounted for the bulk of Salomon's profits in the late 1980s, earning about $500 million a year.

Meriwether hatched plans to create his own arbitrage firm after resigning from Salomon in 1991 because of a bond-trading scandal in which he was tangentially involved. Thanks to his Midas reputation, he was able to raise $1.25 billion from a host of investors, including foreign banks, U.S. university endowment funds, Wall Street executives, and business big shots such as Hollywood agent Michael Ovitz and Nike chief executive Phil Knight—each of whom had to pony up a minimum of $10 million. In February 1994, Long-Term set up shop in a Greenwich office complex, with a trading floor overlooking Long Island Sound.

If you were to try to duplicate Long-Term's strategy at home using the funds in your bank account, you wouldn't get very far (unless your net worth approximates Bill Gates's), because an integral part of the formula the firm used was its size and its capacity to use enormous amounts of borrowed money to leverage its bets on tiny anomalies in the markets. For example, one of the firm's first trades was based on the observation that the thirty-year Treasuries issued in August 1993 (the on-the-run bond at the time) was yielding 7.24 percent, while the off-the-run thirty-year bond issued the previous February was yielding 7.36 percent—a spread greater than normal. The two bonds, each with a face value of $1,000, differed only about $16 in price. By buying the bond issued in February and shorting the one issued in August, Long-Term was certain it could pocket a couple of dollars profit on each pair of bonds. But the only way to make such a bet worthwhile was to buy and sell in enormous volume—to be exact, a $1 billion "long position" and a $1 billion "short position." To make the gamble pay off handsomely, Long-

Term used borrowed funds to finance the transaction, fattening its own bottom line by employing money provided by others.

Although this trade differed in some important respects from the thousands of others Long-Term executed, it illustrates the basic approach the firm took as it arbitraged Italian bonds against German bonds, ten-year German bonds against five-year German bonds, and a variety of other trades involving such exotica as Danish mortgages and options on the Tokyo stock index. Meriwether and the professors knew their strategy was not totally foolproof, that sometimes their trades would lose money. When that happened, the firm would have to forfeit cash instantly; it collected on its winners, and paid up on its losers, on a daily basis. But the models showed that with the passage of enough time, historical relationships would reassert themselves, so that all the firm had to do was hold on, maintain a comfortable cushion of capital, and play the law of averages. The results seemed to leave little doubt about Long-Term's basis for faith in its models. In 1994, Long-Term earned 28 percent on its investors' money (of which the investors got 20 percent after deducting the hefty fees Meriwether and his partners took for themselves). In 1995, it earned 59 percent (43 percent after deduction for fees), and in 1996 it earned 57 percent (41 percent after fees).

Wall Street firms and commercial banks, awed by Meriwether's seeming invincibility and the professors' braininess, lined up to lend money to the firm on extremely easy terms. As a result, by the end of 1995, Long-Term had accumulated over $102 billion in assets, all but $3.6 billion of which was derived from borrowing, and it continued to operate with debt twenty to thirty times the size of its capital. Creditors received quarterly statements showing Long-Term's assets and liabilities, but they knew almost nothing about the details of its trades—and neither did the firm's investors, for Meriwether and his team were fiercely determined to prevent rivals from stealing the secrets of their success. In fact, to throw an even thicker smoke screen around its activities, Long-Term typically avoided relying on a single lender to finance both "legs" of a trade; it might rely on Goldman, Sachs to lend the money for the purchase of some bonds and on Merrill Lynch to finance the offsetting short position. Lenders could take comfort from the knowledge that they held collateral—that is, the securities involved in the individual trades they financed. The danger inherent in this arrangement—that nearly all of Long-Term's bets would go sour at the same time, and the creditors might have to dispose of all that collateral in a hurry—was given little thought; it seemed only a theoretical possibility as long as the firm continued to rack up double-digit returns.

But the theoretical started moving closer to reality five days after Russia's default; on August 21, 1998, markets began moving in ways that Long-Term's battery of Ph.D.s had figured almost impossibly remote. That day, much of the top brass was away from the firm's new headquarters, which included an expanded trading floor and a 3,000-square-foot gym. Meriwether was in Beijing, and one of his chief lieutenants, Eric Rosenfeld, was just starting a family vacation in Sun Valley, Idaho. They were soon jetting back to Greenwich after getting frantic reports from colleagues about the figures appearing on the screens of their Sun workstations. The flight for safety was in full wing. All over the world, investors were piling into Treasury bonds, German government bonds, anything that carried the least amount of risk possible, and bailing out of bonds with lower ratings. That, of course, meant that bonds Long-Term had bought were falling in price, while those it had sold short were rising. Spreads between low-risk and high-risk bonds were not only widening but widening at speeds nobody in the markets had ever seen before. Long-Term was losing tens of millions of dollars an hour on its sup-posedly well-hedged bets on pairs of bonds, because it held such huge positions and had borrowed so much to do so. For good meas-ure, the firm also took big hits on speculative plays it had uncharac-teristically made in Russian bonds and merger stocks. By day's end, the firm's losses totaled more than a half billion dollars.

In a meeting that began at 7 A.M. on Sunday, August 23, Long-Term's partners gathered to concoct a turnaround strategy based on

the new and shocking reality that more days like August 21 might be
in store. Although the firm still had its own capital of nearly $3 bil-
lion, its position was perilous nonetheless, because with over $100
billion in assets purchased with borrowed money, further losses in its
positions of even a few percentage points would wipe out the capital. Unlike a gambler in a casino who decides to quit while ahead,
Long-Term didn't have the option of cashing in its chips. Its holdings
were so enormous that modest sales would send prices plummeting
and reduce the value of other securities that it still held. Their best
hope, the partners agreed, was to persuade a deep-pocketed out-
sider, or several deep-pocketed outsiders, with the following pitch:
All we need is a couple of billion dollars in capital to help us ride out
this storm, because sooner or later, markets will return to normal,
and our trades will turn profitable again.

Meriwether and his partners tried tapping George Soros. They
called Warren Buffett, the billionaire "sage of Omaha" who ran one
of the world's most successful investment companies, Berkshire
Hathaway Inc. They sought help from Salomon Smith Barney, Merrill Lynch, Goldman, Sachs, and other investment banks, offering
partnership deals in exchange for capital. Nobody was seriously
interested. Instead of gaining the capital it needed, Long-Term continued to lose tens of millions or hundreds of millions a day in the
markets. At the beginning of September, with the firm's capital
down to $2.28 billion, Meriwether was forced to inform his
investors that the firm's net worth had shrunk 44 percent in the
month of August. "Losses of this magnitude are a shock to us as they
surely are to you, especially in light of the historical volatility of the
fund," he wrote.

Although Long-Term's partners were convinced that the markets
had to right themselves soon, spreads widened relentlessly in September as the chain of events in the bond markets described by
Salomon's Purcell took hold. By the middle of the month, further
losses had eroded the firm's capital to the $1.5 billion level. Long-
Term continued to implore its Wall Street creditors for help in find-

ing capital, but this was proving a double-edged sword. Goldman, Sachs was finally enlisted to seek potential investors and arrange a possible takeover of the firm. But the chances of finding willing investors were far from certain, and in the meantime, rumors on the Street about Long-Term's desperation were leading traders to intensify the selling of securities that they suspected the firm might be forced to liquidate. Naturally, that only aggravated the spiral.

What Wall Street needed at that moment was someone to fill the role J. P. Morgan had performed in 1907 when the Knickerbocker Trust Co. failed, triggering hysteria that threatened to drag down other financial houses and throw the economy into recession. The formidable Morgan, whose bank was by far the largest and most powerful in the land, ordered the stock market to remain open, delivered a public warning that short-sellers would be "properly attended to," and summoned leading bankers to his Manhattan library to craft a plan for dealing with Knickerbocker's debts. They obeyed, and Morgan's efforts would go down in history for bringing the panic of 1907 to a swift and relatively painless halt.

But in 1998, no single financier had the clout to duplicate Morgan's feat. The task of rounding up market players and exhorting them to act in their collective self-interest could be performed only by someone vested with the moral authority of government.

As in the Korean crisis, the New York Fed—the "eyes and ears" of the U.S. central bank on Wall Street—stepped into the breach. This time, however, the political sensitivities were explosive. It is one thing to use official influence to help prevent a country from going under. It is quite another to do the same for a hedge fund.

Friday, September 18 was a particularly rough day in the markets, as investors were just getting over their dashed hopes for a coordinated interest rate cut by the G-7. The New York Fed's McDonough was aware of Long-Term's travails, since Meriwether had called him a couple of times earlier in the month to inform him of the firm's efforts to raise fresh money. Now, with Long-Term apparently unlikely to survive the next week on its current trajectory, the firm had invited McDonough to visit Greenwich for a briefing on the firm's portfolio. McDonough called a number of Wall Street CEOs, and as he later told a congressional panel, their opinion was unanimous: Long-Term's demise could have a "serious effect" on world markets. Following conversations with Greenspan and Rubin, agreement was reached that the New York Fed would take the lead in assessing the situation and determining what the market impact might be. McDonough himself would not go to Greenwich; he was scheduled to deliver a speech in London on Tuesday, and he told Greenspan and Rubin that he feared canceling the trip would only roil the markets even more. Instead, Peter Fisher would go to Greenwich.

The next morning, a Saturday, Gary Gensler, the Treasury's assistant secretary for financial markets, was bouncing his two-year-old daughter on his knee at his Chevy Chase, Maryland, home when a call came from Rubin. Gensler, a balding forty-year-old former partner of Rubin's at Goldman, had joined the Treasury in fall 1997 and, because of his experience in markets, often took part in meetings in Rubin's office about how to handle the crises in Asia. Now he was going to become more directly involved in crisis containment. "Shhh!—Isabel, please!" he admonished his daughter as Rubin started to speak.

The Treasury, like the Fed, had been watching U.S. financial markets keenly for any sign of an imminent failure by a major financial institution that might present "systemic risk"—the term economists use to describe the problem of one firm's bankruptcy threatening to cause a much broader-based collapse. Only in cases posing systemic risk is the government supposed to get involved in saving a financial institution from going belly-up. Mostly, the department's officials were keeping an eye on the dozen or so biggest money-center banks and the four or five biggest broker-dealers on Wall Street, since a failure by one of those to fulfill a financial obligation could cause such widespread interruptions in payments as to bring down many other institutions. Among the banks, Bankers Trust was reportedly in some distress, as was Lehman Brothers among the broker-dealers. Since hedge funds presumably posed no systemic dangers, the Treasury hadn't been paying much attention to them, but Long-Term looked well out of the ordinary. Although the New York Fed was playing the lead role, Rubin asked Gensler to accompany Fisher to Greenwich the next day, because the Treasury chief wanted as much information as possible about the potential impact of a default by Long-Term. "They have $1.3 trillion in derivatives," Rubin said. "Gary, is that a lot?"

The quip was characteristically Rubinesque humor, of course, but behind the joke was a serious question about whether Wall Street had changed so much since Rubin's day that it was no longer unusual for firms to have positions measured in the trillions. "Bob, I left Goldman, Sachs a year ago," Gensler replied, "but that is a number that is as significant as [the size of the derivative position held by] any money-center commercial bank and maybe a handful of investment banks."

Rubin was asking about a type of trade that allowed Long-Term to place a bet on trends in stock prices, bond prices, interest rates, and other financial phenomena without actually buying or selling stocks or bonds. "Derivatives," as the name implies, derive their value from movements in underlying securities. Options on stocks are one of the best-known forms of derivatives; for a couple of hundred dollars an investor can obtain the option (the right) to buy or sell thousands of dollars worth of a company's shares at a certain price in the future. Whereas options trade on organized exchanges, other forms of derivatives are so specialized that they involve custom-tailored contracts that change hands in private transactions. One example is an interest-rate swap, in which, say, Bank X agrees to pay Bank Y the interest that would be earned on $500 million if it were invested at a floating rate over the next five years, and Bank Y agrees to pay Bank X the interest that would be earned on $500 million if invested at a fixed rate. The $500 million is called the "notional value," because neither bank owes the other $500 million, and neither can be sure how much it will owe or receive until it sees what happens to interest rates.

This sort of financial engineering, which started in the 1980s and burgeoned in the 1990s, may seem to have no purpose other than rank speculation, and that is true in some cases. But many of Long-Term's derivative activities provided genuine service to the smooth functioning of capital markets—though obviously, the firm was not motivated by altruism. Consider, for instance, a particularly arcane trade that Long-Term engaged in called "shorting equity volatility." This involved bets that the U.S. stock market would maintain its historical pattern of rising and falling no more than about 15 percent a year, and that the magnitude of foreign stock market fluctuations would likewise stay within historical trends. It isn't necessary to know the precise mechanics of how Long-Term made its wager; suffice to say that Long-Term sold option contracts on the Standard & Poor's 500 stock index and on foreign stock indexes. In effect, Long-Term was selling insurance, or hedges, to investors who wanted protection against unusually violent downward swings (and in some cases upward swings) in the prices of the stocks they held. Just like an insurance company that believes it can make a profit by selling high-priced flood insurance to anxious homeowners living along major rivers, Long-Term thought it could make a profit by looking at the historical odds of a catastrophic series of events in the stock market and selling high-priced stock insurance to anxious investors. The odds, unfortunately, had proved a bad basis for such a decision, since stock market volatility was exceptionally high in 1998.

On the morning of Sunday, September 20, Gensler met Fisher and two other Fed staffers at Long-Term's Greenwich headquarters, which was empty except for a handful of top Long-Term partners, including Meriwether, and a team from Goldman examining the firm's files. Long-Term had once been a notoriously arrogant firm, demanding the highest of fees from its investors, maintaining the tightest of secrecy about its strategies, and generally acting as if it were the greatest repository of financial brains in the world. Now its style was changing. When Gensler asked to be shown to the men's room, Meriwether politely ushered him to his personal, wood-paneled bathroom—a gesture that Gensler couldn't help thinking symbolized the firm's comeuppance. Gensler also got a more substantive sense of how desperate the partners were when he questioned one of them, Eric Rosenfeld, about their personal finances. Surely, Gensler asked, their personal holdings would be reasonably safe even if Long-Term went down? An ashen-faced Rosenfeld explained that on the contrary, many of the partners were facing probable personal bankruptcy because of loans they had taken out on their investments in the firm.

In a large conference room, Fisher and Gensler sat through several presentations in which Long-Term's partners showed them page after page of computer printouts, with notations like "USD_Z+D-shift," and explained what the data meant. Both men had heard a fair amount about Long-Term before going to Greenwich, but much of what they saw that day left them shaken. For one thing, a number of Long-Term's individual positions were much larger than they had anticipated, so large that the firm held a huge share of the total market in certain financial instruments—examples being Danish mortgage-backed bonds and futures contracts on British ten-year government bonds. Gensler was particularly struck by the size of Long-Term's position in equity volatility; he told Rubin and Summers that it was at least ten times greater than he had ever seen at Goldman, Sachs, one of the Street's richest firms.

One key question was how many days remained before Long-Term would be thrown into default. A conversation Fisher and Gensler had with a representative from the Wall Street firm of Bear Stearns suggested that Long-Term probably had only two or three days left. Bear Stearns was Long-Term's "prime broker," meaning that it cleared the firm's trades and handled the daily flow of cash as money from winning positions came in and money on losing positions went out. Once the amount of cash Long-Term held on call at Bear Stearns dipped below $500 million, Bear was planning to stop clearing for Long-Term, which would effectively pull the plug. And Long-Term was already having difficulty meeting that requirement.

Readers who have a passing familiarity with bankruptcy proce-dures might find it puzzling that all this should matter so much. For most companies, a bankruptcy filing is designed to stop the rush by creditors to seize assets, and to give the debtor some breathing space to work out a new business plan or dispose of its assets in an orderly fashion. But Long-Term was not like a department store or a steel company that, upon going bust, would liquidate its inventory over a few weeks and parcel out the proceeds to creditors standing in line. Under the financing arrangements Long-Term used, most of its assets were already in the hands of creditors in the form of collateral that the creditors were legally entitled to sell as soon as Long-Term was declared in default by any single one of them.

Fisher and Gensler envisioned the nightmare that would unfold once Long-Term failed to pay a sum owed to one of its creditors or to Bear Stearns or to one of the counterparties to its thousands of trades. Since Long-Term was subject to a web of cross-default clauses in which default to one constitutes default to all, the fax machines at the firm's Greenwich headquarters would begin spitting out notices from the counterparties declaring their intention to sell the collateral they held. Then would come the coup de grâce—the fire-sale liqui-dation of bonds, stocks, and other securities worth tens of billions of dollars, all at the same time. The derivatives posed the most signifi-cant problem of all: how the counterparties would react once Long-Term was no longer able to fulfill its obligations under its derivative contracts. If the "insurance company" providing insurance to investors could no longer pay off its "policyholders," investors would suddenly realize how they and many others were exposed to the same risk, and they would join in the selling spree.

What would such a fire sale mean? A lot of red ink on Wall Street, definitely; probably nothing more than that—but no one could be sure. Long-Term had estimated the losses its seventeen largest counterparties would suffer at $2.8 billion, not by any means an impossibly big sum for the Street to swallow. But that was just the "first-order loss," as Gensler put it later; the estimate didn't account for the fact that markets were in an overwrought state already, thanks to the Russian default, the flight to quality, the drying up of liquidity, rumors about troubles at other firms, and worries that a new crisis was brewing in Brazil. So although a failure of Long-Term might simply depress prices a great deal, the question weighing on Fisher and Gensler's minds was whether it might cause something much worse, a malfunctioning in the market mechanism that would impede the funneling of credit to American businesses. The magnitude of the potential problem, Gensler told his Treasury superiors, looked every bit as great as previous bankruptcies of financial houses—such as the collapse of Drexel Burnam Lambert and Barings Securities—in which government authorities had felt obliged to intervene in trying to limit the damage; and Long-Term had a uniquely worrisome facet, the size of its derivatives portfolio, which made the impact all the more uncertain.

In conversations with McDonough, Fisher estimated that the odds were perhaps one in ten that Long-Term's collapse would disrupt the U.S. government bond market—that is, effectively shut it down for some period of time. Although obviously imprecise, this estimate nevertheless suggested that the risks to the overall financial system were plenty high.

A shutdown in the Treasury bond markets would be different from a trading halt on an organized exchange like the New York Stock Exchange. Buying and selling continues on a twenty-four-hour basis in the Treasury bond market, with scores of broker-dealer firms around the world making bids and offers on U.S. government securities, so nobody can turn the lights off. But if those dealers were to stop making bids and offers for a day or two, nobody could be sure whether it would take a week, or a month, for them to feel confident enough to start again, given the staggering losses they might incur

by making a faulty guess on price levels. Since investors use Treasuries to hedge their risks on corporate bonds, a prolonged hiatus in
Treasury-bond trading would likely destroy price-setting in the corporate bond market as well, rendering it impossible for pension
funds, mutual funds, and other institutions to buy corporate bonds.

For Fisher, a seminal event was seeing the evidence at 5 A.M. on
Monday, September 21, and later that day as well, that a fire sale
was already under way in U.S. and overseas markets among traders
who were merely anticipating a Long-Term default. Long-Term
dropped another half billion dollars that day, reducing its capital
below $1 billion. There was no more time to lose if the Fed was
going to help prevent default from occurring.

A major step toward a Fed-organized rescue came on the afternoon
of September 21. After extensive conversations with executives of
firms that ranked among Long-Term's top counterparties, Fisher
agreed to meet several of them for breakfast at the New York Fed's
headquarters the next morning. They included Jon Corzine, chief
executive of Goldman, Sachs, and Goldman's chief financial officer,
John Thain; David Komansky and Herbert Allison, Merrill Lynch's
chairman and president respectively; and Roberto Mendoza, vice
chairman of J. P. Morgan & Co. Fisher got approval for his actions
from McDonough, and Greenspan was being kept informed in
Washington.

The Fed's first choice, naturally, was a rescue in which well-
heeled private investors, acting entirely on their own, took over
Long-Term's assets or provided the firm with the capital injection it
needed to survive. But the chances for an outside rescuer materializing looked unpromising, so during the September 22 breakfast,
Fisher and the Goldman, Merrill, and Morgan executives discussed
other possible avenues that would avert the dreaded "disorderly
closeout." Hopes were not high; the executives figured the odds
were thirty to one against avoiding it.

Fisher told them that if they produced a plan that looked fruitful, and if all four stood behind it, he would invite other major firms to the New York Fed to listen to a presentation. By late afternoon, after being joined by a fourth large counterparty, the Swiss bank UBS, they coalesced around the simplest approach, a proposal advanced by Merrill Lynch for the Street's sixteen largest firms to form a consortium that would provide Long-Term with a $4 billion cushion— $250 million per firm. An emergency meeting to consider the consortium plan was called for eight o'clock that evening.

Shortly after the appointed hour, an extraordinary cavalcade of about twenty-five financial executives trooped into the New York Fed's stately boardroom and seated themselves at a conference table surrounded by ornately framed paintings of the reserve bank's past presidents. In addition to the executives who had been at breakfast, the group included Deryck Maughan, co–chief executive of Salomon Smith Barney; Philip Purcell, chairman of Morgan Stanley Dean Witter; James Cayne, chief executive of Bear Stearns; Thomas Labrecque, president of Chase Manhattan; and Allen Wheat, chief executive of Credit Suisse First Boston. Meanwhile, McDonough was racing back from delivering his speech in London. The New York Fed chief landed in New York around eleven that evening and spent much of the night briefing central bankers in Europe about developments.

Fisher opened the meeting, saying as little as possible and choosing his words with care. He told the group that he had convened the session because four of them—Merrill, Goldman, Morgan, and UBS—had a proposal to put forward aimed at preventing a default by Long-Term; it was their proposal, he stressed, not the Fed's, but the Fed thought the other firms should listen to what the four had to say. The Fed, he said, had an interest in seeing a private-sector solution that avoided a disorderly liquidation. He didn't have to tell the group he was concerned about systemic risk; the mere fact the meeting was taking place showed the Fed saw Long-Term's woes as a systemic issue.

"No Federal Reserve official pressured anyone, and no promises were made," McDonough emphasized in his congressional testimony a few days later. "Not one penny of public money was spent or committed." Yet even by furnishing the meeting room, the Fed was crossing an important threshold. The Fed had the power to make life difficult for any of the firms represented at the meeting—by turning down a bank seeking regulatory approval for a merger, to take a particularly obvious example. Subtle and tacit though the pressure may have been, it was not entirely absent.

The meeting soon dissolved into disputes over particulars. Why should all firms in the consortium put up $250 million each when their exposures to Long-Term differed? If Long-Term were to be saved, how much of a stake should its partners be allowed to keep, if any, to provide them with an incentive to continue operating it? The meeting adjourned around 11 P.M., with plans to reconvene the following morning, though it wasn't certain that Long-Term would survive until then. Gensler, briefed by Fisher on the state of play, told Summers late that night that the chances of success were slim. Too many players were involved, with too many different interests and too many legal hassles to get agreement in the time remaining, Gensler thought. But McDonough and Fisher, who were keeping top Treasury and Fed officials in Washington apprised of developments, took the view "that if you can just keep these guys in a room talking, you had a shot, and they would see it as being in their self-interest to work something out," Gensler recalled.

A larger group of executives representing seventeen firms arrived at the New York Fed when the meeting resumed at 10 A.M. on Wednesday, September 23, to make one last stab at keeping Long-Term from going under. After about only a half hour, the meeting took an unexpected turn when McDonough appeared in the boardroom and said he was suspending the proceedings. A bid for Long-Term's portfolio was coming by fax from Warren Buffett, in conjunction with Goldman and the insurance giant AIG as minority participants. To McDonough, the Buffett deal was manna from heaven, since it wouldn't embroil the Fed. But the bid came with extremely tough conditions: The Long-Term partners would be fired, and since they had borrowed against their share of the firm's capital, they would be destroyed financially. Moreover, the offer would be withdrawn at 12:30 P.M.—less than two hours after it was received at Long-Term's headquarters. Meriwether turned it down, telling McDonough he was legally unable to accept such an offer under the terms of the firm's partnership agreement.

Talks resumed in the early afternoon on the original proposal for each firm to pony up $250 million toward a $4 billion bailout. Although most of the executives present were willing to go along, Bear Stearns's Cayne refused, asserting that his firm was already exposed because of its role in clearing Long-Term's trades. Two French banks said they would ante up no more than $125 million, and Lehman Brothers said it could manage only $100 million. Much bickering ensued, including a "What the fuck are you doing?" bellowed by Merrill Lynch's Komansky at Cayne of Bear Stearns.

Finally, with time running short, Merrill Lynch's Allison said the other eleven firms would have to put in $300 million each for the deal to work—and they grudgingly agreed. That brought the total to $3.65 billion, which together with Long-Term's remaining capital was enough to top the $4 billion goal. The deal would take another five days to finalize—and it would nearly blow up again amid wrangling over details—but on September 23, the immediate crisis was averted.

The next morning, with newspaper front pages blazing the story of how the meeting at the New York Fed had kept Long-Term afloat, Gensler came in for some ribbing at the Treasury's senior staff meeting from department colleagues who had been principally responsible for overseeing the rescues in Asia and Russia. "So, you had to do a bailout too, huh?" Tim Geithner joked. Retorted Gensler: "Well, you guys were getting too much attention."

It was no laughing matter, however, that the United States was now seen by some observers as having behaved essentially the same

as those Asian countries that Washington so often scolded for propping up insolvent financial institutions. At the Treasury staff meeting
that morning, the discussion quickly turned serious about how to
rebut the criticism that was already starting to pour in from abroad
and at home. The key point, the meeting participants agreed, was
that the Fed's actions couldn't be called a bailout, since no taxpayer
money was being used, just the central bank's good offices. Moreover, Long-Term's partners were losing 90 percent of their equity in
the firm, so although they were in better shape than they would have
been under a default scenario, they were not being made whole.

Those arguments did not allay the moral-hazard concerns of
experts like Burton Malkiel, an economics professor at Princeton,
and J. P. Mei, a business professor at New York University, whose
analysis in *The Wall Street Journal* on September 29, 1998, was particularly trenchant:

> If unsuccessful hedge funds are not allowed to fail, if brokerage
> firms believe they will somehow be protected from the effects of
> far too liberal margin requirements, if banks believe help will be
> forthcoming should loans go sour during unsettled market condi-
> tions, how will we discipline future decisions of investors and
> lenders? Will such intervention make our financial system even
> more fragile later?
>
> . . . To be sure, the current intervention resembles a bank-
> ruptcy reorganization more than a true bailout. What distin-
> guishes this rescue, however, is the active role played by an
> agency of the U.S. government. Anything that weakens the effect
> of market discipline and that lessens the punishment the market
> affords speculators when they have made incorrect decisions is
> likely in the long run to lead to more instability.

Greenspan and McDonough faced unusually caustic questioning
at a four-and-a-half-hour congressional hearing on October 1. "We
hear a lot of speeches about free enterprise and the marketplace,"

complained Rep. Bruce Vento, a Minnesota Democrat. "There seem to be two rules, a double standard: one for Main Street and another for Wall Street." In a like vein, Rep. Spencer Bachus III, an Alabama Republican, said that since Washington had told welfare mothers and small business executives to fend for themselves, the same message "ought to also apply to rich Greenwich, Connecticut, investors who are multimillionaires."

But Greenspan, who held perhaps the greatest concerns among top U.S. officials about moral hazard, did not believe such criticism outweighed the justification for intervening. He later told associates that he might have preferred if the meeting of the bank and brokerage firm executives had been held at one of the firms' offices instead of the New York Fed. But since the Fed had done nothing more than help people draw conclusions about their own self-interest, he saw no great harm done and possibly much good. "Financial market participants were already unsettled by recent global events," he said in his congressional testimony. "Had the failure of [Long-Term] triggered the seizing up of markets, substantial damage could have been inflicted on many market participants, including some not directly involved in the firm, and could have potentially impaired the economies of many nations, including our own."

Nobody can say whether that damage would have been as great as Fisher, McDonough, Greenspan, and the other policymakers feared. But they certainly perceived grave risks, and although their success in addressing those risks deserves credit, it is hardly comforting that those risks came so close to materializing.

Alan Greenspan was never explicit in public about what the Federal Reserve intended to do about interest rates. But when he appeared before the Senate Budget Committee on September 23, 1998, the seventy-two-year-old Fed chairman was as plainspoken as he ever got in hinting that a rate cut was coming. "I think we know where we have to go," he said. "I do not think we underestimate the severity of the problems with which we are dealing." As markets cheered—the Dow closed up 257 points that day—Greenspan cited a litany of factors impelling the Fed toward an easier credit policy. "The more recent, more virulent phase of the crisis has infected our markets," he said. "Flows of funds through financial markets have been disrupted, at least temporarily. . . . Issuance of equity, and of bonds by lower-rated corporations, has come virtually to a halt. Even investment-grade companies have cut back substantially on their borrowing in capital markets." And although some corporations shut out of the bond markets were tapping banks for their cash needs, Greenspan was concerned about surveys of bankers showing that this source of funding might soon dry up as well. "Banks also are reportedly becoming more cautious and more expensive lenders to many companies," he said. Accordingly, financial market stability must be restored "reasonably shortly to prevent the contagion from spilling over and creating difficulties for all of us."

Still, Greenspan's remarks left a major question for the markets to puzzle over: How much would the Fed cut rates? For a year and a half, the central bank had kept the federal funds rate—the key overnight lending rate for banks—at a steady 5.5 percent. Now speculation was mounting about what would happen to that rate at the following week's meeting of the Federal Open Market Committee (FOMC) on September 29. Would the Fed lower the rate by 25 basis points (a quarter of a percentage point)? Fifty basis points? More? A lot was riding on the outcome. If the Fed cut rates only 0.25 percent, markets might draw the disheartening conclusion that Greenspan and his colleagues didn't comprehend the extent to which the financial system was teetering. On the other hand, a bigger move might generate concerns that the Fed was aware of even worse problems in the system than were already known.

At the New York Fed, Peter Fisher was contacting Wall Street bond traders and analysts to gauge the likely market reaction to each option. This sort of intelligence-gathering is an art form at which Fisher was well-practiced, and which he performed with the utmost care, because the traders were naturally cocking their ears for the slightest hint about which way the central bank was leaning. So as was his custom, Fisher asked his questions often and in a neutral way so as to avoid providing any information. Is the market now "pricing in" a Fed easing? (That is, have traders already factored the assumption of a lower federal funds rate into the price of securities?) If so, how much of a Fed easing has been priced in? Is the trading activity in various government securities—say, the one-year and two-year Treasury notes—reflecting the anticipation of a Fed move, or is some other factor involved?

The dominant voice in the market was that the Fed had to do something—but it wasn't clear whether that something ought to be a 25-basis-point rate cut or a larger one, just so long as it was something.

The group charged with making the final call, the FOMC, is one of Washington's most peculiar decisionmaking bodies, deliberately designed to be insulated from short-term political pressure without being totally insensitive to the demands of the American people and their elected representatives. Among its twelve voting members are the seven governors of the Washington-based Reserve Board, who are appointed to fourteen-year terms by the president and confirmed by the Senate. (The chairman's and vice chairman's terms are four years, though they are legally entitled to serve their full terms as board members if they wish.) Another vote belongs to the president of the New York Fed, and the other four votes are apportioned on an annually rotating basis among the remaining eleven reserve-bank presidents (the heads of the Kansas City Fed, the San Francisco Fed, the Chicago Fed, and so forth).

FOMC members—many of whom are economists, though others are bankers or banking experts—arrive at the eight meetings each year well briefed on business and financial conditions. Seated around a massive oval table, they spend hours in decorous debate, seeking to agree on a "directive" summarizing goals for money growth and the federal funds rate over the period before the next meeting. The directive, an abstruse document, guides the trading desk at the New York Fed as it buys and sells Treasury bills in an effort to achieve the panel's targets.

The chairman's power within the FOMC is considerable. He controls the agenda and directs the Washington staff, which prepares the so-called blue book containing policy options for each meeting. But much of the chairman's power flows from the loyalty that FOMC members, some of whom are former Fed staffers themselves, show their institution and its chief. Members who frequently dissent or repeat dogmatic arguments tend to become isolated and lose influence.

Greenspan, whose Fed chairmanship began in August 1987, derived much of his clout from his expertise as an economic forecaster. Except for a two-year stint as chairman of the Council of Economic Advisers under President Ford, his career prior to the Fed was spent running an economic consulting firm, where he earned a national reputation and a lucrative client list based on meticulous scrutiny of statistics concerning manufacturing, labor markets, credit conditions, and other indicators suggesting when and how the economy was likely to grow, slow, or contract. Greenspan treated his Fed colleagues with deference, using his wry sense of humor to soften disagreements. But those who challenged him had a high burden of proof, for Greenspan steeped himself in the economy's minutiae, constantly mining the central bank's unrivaled data-gathering capabilities and probing its staff of over 200 economists for insights on linkages, trends, and statistical quirks. (An example: What are the implications, he once queried a group of staffers, of the Mortgage Bankers Association's mortgage-refinancing index in weeks with a holiday?)

Scrutinizing the data, in Greenspan's view, was essential because monetary policy works with a lag; that is, a change in interest rates usually takes nine months or even more before it produces an impact on output, jobs, and pricing decisions. Accordingly, as Greenspan once put it, "We need to be forward-looking. . . . There is no alternative to basing actions on forecasts." His prognostications sometimes missed the mark, notably in 1991 when he overestimated the strength of the economy and kept interest rates high, contributing to a brief recession. But his 1991 mistake faded into memory as the Fed kept the economy humming with stable prices well into the second half of the 1990s. By mid-1998, his image as a peerless economic helmsman had reached an all-time high thanks to his apparent success in orchestrating a "Goldilocks economy"—not too hot, not too cold, but just right.

But the FOMC meeting on September 29, 1998, was concerned with something different from the usual questions about how a rate change might affect homebuying and business capital spending and other aspects of the "real" economy. The concern was the much more immediate and intangible problem of how to restore confidence in the financial markets. The staff presented a forecast showing a considerable slowing in the economy in months ahead, even though almost no data had emerged showing that consumers or businesses were reducing spending; the forecast was based mainly on expectations about how the market upheaval would affect consumer and business behavior.

Debate at the meeting revolved around this issue: Since the Fed had kept the funds rate unchanged for so long, was it sufficient for the central bank to move in the direction the markets were so desperate to see, even if only by a quarter of a point? Or did the Fed have to move further, to send a clearer signal of its intentions to take whatever steps were required to alleviate the markets' stress? The preponderance of views, including Greenspan's, favored the 25-basis-point option. The panel's hawks argued that although the risk of rising inflation may be receding, it was not eliminated, so a larger easing would be unwise. Others warned that a half-point rate cut might spook the markets by conveying an exaggerated sense of the Fed's worries. Greenspan himself felt the Fed ought to keep as much of its powder dry as possible; the central bank would likely have to cut rates again soon, depending on what happened in the markets, so it should move incrementally at first.

Following Greenspan's lead, the committee unanimously approved the 25-basis-point cut. Rivlin favored a 50-basis-point move but didn't argue particularly strongly for it; as she admitted later, "It was a close question." One reassuring consideration was that the Fed could change the rate again, if it chose, before the next FOMC meeting, although it had not taken such action between meetings since 1994. Indeed, the committee, despite misgivings among some of the hawks, adopted an "asymmetric directive," implying a bias in favor of another easing move. In classic Fedspeak, the directive stated: "A slightly higher federal funds rate might or a somewhat lower federal funds rate would be acceptable in the inter-meeting period." (The tipoff: "would" is a stronger word than "might.")

In the early afternoon of September 29, the Fed announced the committee's decision to cut the funds rate by 25 basis points, citing "recent changes in the global economy and adjustments in U.S. financial markets," but it said nothing about the bias in favor of ease. The markets first yawned with disappointment—then all hell broke loose.

The Dow fell 28 points the day of the announcement, then 237 points the next day, and 210 the next. More distressing, from Fed officials' points of view, was the continued dash for safety in the bond markets. On September 30, the yield on the thirty-year Treasury bond fell below 5 percent for the first time since the administration of Lyndon Johnson, and the following day the yield fell to 4.88 percent—down nearly a quarter of a percentage point in two days, an astonishingly rapid move for such a supposedly stable government security. Although the decline in Treasury yields might sound like good news, it meant that the market's faith was continuing to erode in any bond lacking Uncle Sam's imprimatur. Foreign stock markets also took a drubbing on September 30, with Brazil down 9.6 percent, Frankfurt off 7.6 percent, and Paris shedding 5 percent. "The message [of the 25-basis-point cut in the funds rate] was supposed to be, 'We're on the case, and if the situation demands, we'll do more,'" said Fed Governor Laurence Meyer. "That latter part of the message didn't get across."

The Fed's image as a crisis-fighter suffered as well, even among the general public. A few days after the meeting, Edward Boehne, president of the Philadelphia Fed, checked into a hotel in a small Pennsylvania town, where the clerk looked at his title and declared: "You didn't do enough."

Before the era of antiglobalization protests, the annual meetings of the IMF and World Bank were renowned for glittery social gatherings, and the conclave held the first week of October 1998 was no different, notwithstanding the dismal state of global economic affairs. Limousines clogged Washington's downtown streets as they always had during these meetings, which attracted several thousand financiers from all over the world eager to rub elbows with top economic policymakers and potential business partners. Guests feasted on pea pancakes topped with caviar, oysters on the half shell, bowls of shrimp, and platters of lamb at a reception hosted by the National Commercial Bank of Saudi Arabia at the National Air and Space Museum. Merrill Lynch held a party at a Georgetown estate once owned by descendants of Martha Washington's family, where attendants wearing colonial costumes played musical instruments and announced guests as they arrived. At the Turkish Bankers Association's reception, plates of sumptuous Turkish specialties were piled high. The Phillips Gallery, with its famous collection of Impressionist paintings, was the site of J. P. Morgan & Co.'s soiree, and Goldman, Sachs chose the Corcoran Gallery as its party locale.

Yet as the liquor flowed, the tuxedo-clad waiters hovered, and the string quartets serenaded, the mood among the partygoers was bleak, sometimes shockingly so. Vernon Jordan, the high-powered attorney and Clinton golfing buddy, held a dinner party at his north-west Washington home, and asked five or six of his most prominent guests, including Larry Summers and Jim Wolfensohn, to say something after dinner about where the global economy was going. Their assessments "all had the same world-is-coming-to-an-end theme," recalled James Harmon, then president of the U.S. Export-Import Bank, whose wife remarked to him as they were leaving the party: "My God, we're all going to be buying canned goods!"

The pessimism was not uniform. Europeans came to the meetings far less alarmed than the Americans, and they were taken aback by the dire tone of their U.S.-based counterparts, in both the public and private sectors. The Europeans had seen little if any evidence in their markets of banks and bondholders refusing to extend credit, so "it was striking to see these American financial figures panicking," said one British official. At a breakfast organized by a major New York-based commercial bank, top European central bankers listened agape as the bank's CEO warned them to brace themselves for the fallout that would soon ensue when his bank withdrew its credit lines from every hedge fund it had ever financed.

Partly as a result of these differences in perception, sharp clashes marred the weeklong meetings. To U.S. and IMF officials, the Europeans were hopelessly inward-looking, obsessed with the forthcoming launch of the euro and clueless regarding the likely impact of the crisis on their countries' economies. As far as the Europeans were concerned, American officials were overreacting to the Long-Term problem and seemed excessively eager to take bold action—perhaps, the Europeans suspected, because of Clinton's desire to look presidential and bury the Monica Lewinsky scandal.

Fueling the antagonism was Clinton's announcement on October 2, just as the meetings were getting under way, of a proposal for a change in the IMF's strategy that was aimed at enabling the Fund to act earlier in heading off crises before they started. The president unveiled the proposal during remarks on the South Lawn of the White House only hours before the House Judiciary Committee was scheduled to release voluminous grand jury testimony and other documents concerning the Lewinsky case—no coincidence, as far as the Europeans were concerned. "We have got a vested interest in averting a global financial slowdown by taking initiatives and doing it now," Clinton declared. "We know we are going into an unprecedented time. This country has got to lead."

The hoopla surrounding the proposal aroused European suspicion that one of its main motivating factors was to show the president taking command, and that suspicion was correct. The proposal was originally something the Treasury had been working on, based on an idea that had been bruited about for a while at the IMF, and White House aides had seized on it as an opportunity for Clinton to exercise U.S. leadership even though some Treasury officials harbored misgivings.

The proposal aimed to create a new type of IMF loan package, called a "Contingent Credit Line" (CCL). Its purpose, Clinton explained, was to "help countries ward off financial contagion" rather than wait until they were undergoing full-blown attacks on their currencies. Under the CCL, a country could "prequalify" for a loan from the IMF by running sound economic policies, so if a crisis erupted elsewhere, speculators would be deterred from attacking the country's currency because of their knowledge that its government had access to a sizable line of credit.

Similar ideas had been rejected by the IMF in the past as likely to create more problems than they would solve. One main disadvantage is that if a country that has prequalified starts running bad economic policies, the IMF would be compelled to announce that the country no longer has access to the credit line—thus risking the very crisis the whole arrangement was supposed to prevent. Another drawback is that simply by signing up for a CCL, a country would risk sending a signal to the markets that it fears a speculative attack.

Despite such problems, Gene Sperling, the top White House aide on economic issues, decided the proposal was tailor-made for Clinton when he first heard about it from Treasury officials. He knew the president wanted to duplicate the success of his Council on Foreign Relations speech on September 14, which garnered much glowing feedback from fellow world leaders. Under pressure from the White House, the Treasury acquiesced to plans for Clinton to present the CCL as an American proposal. Although some in the department were unenthusiastic, "We felt it was a further useful tool for the IMF—not a cosmic redesign of the institution, but on balance, the right thing to do," Summers said.

A bitter debate arose over the plan during the meeting of G-7 finance ministers and central bank governors on Saturday, October 3, 1998, at Blair House, across Lafayette Park from the White House. As might be expected, the Germans were the principal antagonists of the United States, because they saw the CCL as yet another Fund facility that risked creating moral hazard. Klaus Regling, Germany's G-7 deputy, attacked the idea at some length, voicing skepticism whether any well-run country would want to make use of such a financing arrangement. Rubin acknowledged that he had heard a similar objection from Camdessus. But the U.S. Treasury chief would not be denied, suggesting that the meeting would continue all evening until the issue was resolved. ("He said something about bringing in dinner if we have to, or maybe it was sleeping bags," one participant recalled.) In the end, the G-7 agreed to state that it would "explore" the CCL.

The divisions healed to some extent when Greenspan delivered an extraordinarily downbeat appraisal of the economic outlook. The Fed chief told the G-7 that in almost fifty years of watching the U.S. economy, he had never witnessed anything like the drying up of markets in the previous few days and weeks. He would use similar words in public several days later, but at the time, they sobered his elite audience. The Europeans, though convinced that the overall U.S. approach was influenced by politics, respected and trusted Greenspan without reservation. "He usually doesn't talk a lot in the G-7, but he was worried, and we were impressed," said Jean

Lemierre, who was the French G-7 deputy. Regling, too, said: "I had never heard Greenspan so alarmist like that."

U.S.-European tensions surfaced again, however, in a meeting on Monday, October 5 of a new group called the G-22, which brought together finance ministers and central bankers from a number of industrialized countries and emerging markets to consider ways of averting and containing future crises. The first problem was that Clinton decided to chair the group's meeting personally—and then failed to show up on time. After enduring security checks to enter the hotel, the senior economic policymakers of about two dozen countries—including Britain, Germany, Japan, France, South Korea, Mexico, Argentina, and Singapore—cooled their heels for an hour and a half waiting for the president's arrival. An announcement of Clinton's appearance finally came—in the form of a request asking the attendees to stand, as a military band blared "Hail to the Chief." With eyes rolling, the ministers and central bankers shuffled to their feet, wondering why they were being subjected to such ceremonial fanfare at what was supposed to be a working meeting.

Much of the meeting went smoothly, from the U.S. perspective, with ministers from several emerging-market nations asserting that the crisis had proved the importance of exercising prudent policies such as avoiding excessive short-term borrowing. Clinton, despite his tardiness, wowed the group with his focus and mastery of the subject; even the Europeans had to admit he showed no signs of being under political siege.

But then Hans Tietmeyer took the floor. The Bundesbank president objected to Clinton's characterization of how serious the crisis was. Sure, Tietmeyer said, the turmoil in the markets had created difficulties in some parts of the world, such as Russia, Asia, and Latin America, but the world as a whole was not in the same situation. Europe, a very large part of the global economy, was relatively quiet, the central banker observed, and it was enjoying solid economic growth as it moved into the euro era. Talk of global recession should not be exaggerated, because it would send the wrong signal to the markets and only exacerbate financial strains, he said. Responding to Tietmeyer, Clinton said he hoped the group could at least agree that the crisis was serious.

This and other conflicts at the IMF–World Bank meeting were symptomatic of a mounting frustration within the High Command, especially among the Europeans, over the heaping quantities of official money that had been deployed in international rescues and the extent to which that money had flowed out of the very countries it was supposed to help. Already, battle lines were forming over plans for one more megabailout.

STUMBLING OUT

On this much, there was consensus: Contagion *had* to be stopped at Brazil.

For months, the High Command had watched Latin America uneasily for signs of the same symptoms that first surfaced in Asia, and now the country that accounted for nearly 45 percent of the region's output was undoubtedly contracting a case of what economist Paul Krugman had dubbed "bahtulism." Despite Brazil's many differences with Russia—Brazilian banks were reasonably healthy, the country's industries were vibrant, its government was capable of collecting taxes—the similarities were too striking for the Electronic Herd to ignore. Brazil's $65 billion budget deficit was equal to about 8 percent of its GDP, and the government had issued a large amount of short-term bonds to cover the shortfall between revenue and expenses. Furthermore, like the ruble had been, the Brazilian real was subject to a "crawling peg," in which the central bank of Brazil allowed the currency's value to slide only modestly each year against the U.S. dollar. The system obliged the central bank to dole out dollars when people demanded them in exchange for reais—and in the weeks following the Russian default, demand for dollars was shooting through the roof.

During August and September 1998, the country's reserves of hard currency had dropped from $75 billion to about $45 billion as financial institutions and other investors cashed in their reais for dollars; prominent among these nervous Nellies were a number of foreign banks that were paring their interbank lines in a manner that resonated of the Korean episode. The São Paulo stock exchange, a favorite of emerging-market investors in 1997, was taking stomach-churning dips of up to 16 percent a day during September 1998.

Having seen what the Russian collapse had wrought, the High Command was petrified of a similar outcome in Brazil, the world's eighth-largest economy with a GDP of $800 billion. Much of the press commentary at the time suggested that the main worry was the potentially adverse effect on U.S. bank loans and corporate foreign investment in Brazil. But what really kept policymakers like Bob Rubin and Stan Fischer awake nights was a scenario in which a Brazilian bust engendered a multiple-ricochet effect around the globe, ultimately bringing down the biggest industrial economies.

Under this scenario, the most direct impact would fall on Argentina, which depended on the Brazilian market for about one-third of its exports, and a slump in Argentina would force the government in Buenos Aires to expand the money supply and abandon its currency board. That in turn would prompt speculators to test the world's other prominent currency board, Hong Kong's, and once the Hong Kong dollar fell victim, Asia would undergo a whole new cycle of devaluations just as it was starting to climb out of its hole. With the world's most promising export markets flattened, and Western financial institutions debilitated by losses, recession would set in virtually everywhere. "The discussions about Brazil were based on the idea that it was probably the last case before the collapse of the system," said Jean Lemierre, France's G-7 deputy at the time. "Strong military words were used—'last line of defense,' that kind of thing. The feeling was that if we and the IMF are unable to save Brazil, it's the end of the story."

But how to save Brazil? On that question, the High Command

was all over the map. The outcome would show more starkly than ever the extent of U.S. dominance over the G-7.

Around 11 P.M. on October 5, 1998—the same night as the meeting at which Tietmeyer tangled with Clinton—another contentious gathering of high-level officials got under way at a hotel a few blocks away. The Europeans were on the warpath, the target of their ire being the IMF and the U.S. Treasury, which they perceived as working hand-in-glove on an ill-conceived bailout for Brazil. Much of the heat was aimed at Teresa Ter-Minassian, deputy director of the Western Hemisphere Department of the IMF, who did most of the talking at the meeting in her capacity as the Fund economist with principal responsibility for Brazil and Argentina. An Italian, born and raised in Rome (the Armenian surname is her husband's), with a Ph.D. in economics from Harvard, Ter-Minassian was one of the highest-ranking women on the IMF staff. Her career at the Fund, which spanned more than twenty-five years, included the distinction of having led the team that negotiated the last program for a Western industrial country, Portugal, in 1983 and 1984.

Ter-Minassian made the case that an international loan package in the tens of billions of dollars could give Brazil a "breathing space" and a "safety net" that would enable the government to achieve one of its most critical goals—maintaining the fixed exchange rate for the real, which helped keep inflation in check. The government, led by President Fernando Henrique Cardoso, was determined at all costs to avoid a devaluation, and Ter-Minassian outlined a plan for the IMF to support the government's strategy, a key component of which was a strong and sustained effort to shrink the budget deficit. Cardoso, who had just won reelection, was showing every sign of getting tough on the deficit, Ter-Minassian noted. The president had made a nationally televised speech during his campaign warning the electorate in unusually blunt terms of his intention to take painful fiscal measures if he was reelected. Now that the election was over, Cardoso would have to persuade the nation's notoriously balky Congress to raise taxes and cut government benefits. But for Brazil to survive its battering in the markets, investors also needed to see that the international community had faith in the government's policies and that the country had plenty of hard currency to meet its obligations, Ter-Minassian contended.

European officials, including Germany's Klaus Regling and Jürgen Stark and the Bank of England's deputy governor, Mervyn King, voiced deep skepticism that Brazil could avoid devaluing the real, even with a sizable loan package. At the exchange rate of 1.2 reais to the dollar, the real was seriously overvalued, they believed; it was making Brazilian goods uncompetitive on world markets, the result being that the country's exports were falling well short of its imports, with the current account deficit ballooning to over $30 billion, or 4 percent of GDP. The Europeans cited articles by Rudiger Dornbusch, an MIT economist credited with predicting the Mexican peso crisis in 1994, who had been arguing for months that the real was overvalued by roughly 25–35 percent. Canadian and Japanese policymakers supported the European view.

Ter-Minassian's European tormentors weren't swayed by her arguments that by certain measures, Brazilian competitiveness was improving. And they were indignant over the attitude of the IMF and the U.S. Treasury that the Brazilians should get a Fund-led rescue even without accepting the need for a devaluation. As far as the Europeans were concerned, it looked as if the IMF's money—and the European taxpayers' money that would be included in a rescue—would simply provide the means for members of the Herd to pull their money out of the country before the real crashed. "We left that meeting deeply dissatisfied," one European official recalled.

Behind this dispute lay a series of events involving some bad advice the Fund had offered Brazil a few years earlier—which the Brazilians had rejected.

The old saw about Brazil, a country of 165 million people richly endowed with natural resources, is that it's "the country of the

future . . . and always will be." One reason the country's vast potential has proved so evanescent is its propensity for hyperinflation, a
problem so ingrained that for years the government had indexed
wages in an effort to adjust them to prices—the result, of course,
being worse inflation.

In early 1994, the Brazilian economy was undergoing the latest
in a series of hyperinflationary outbreaks, with prices rising at close
to 30 percent a month, or 2,700 percent a year. So rapid were the
changes that, under the indexation system, many products were
priced in terms of "UVRs" (real units of value); if you went into a
hardware store, for example, you might see a hammer being sold for
30 UVRs, and the amount of money you paid for it was some multiple of the 30 UVRs times a conversion figure that reflected the
increase in inflation over the past couple of days.

The government had tried a variety of highly touted anti-inflation initiatives over the years to attack the problem, but nothing had
worked in restoring a semblance of economic stability for more than
a few months at a time. Cardoso, who was then finance minister,
and the central bank governor, Pedro Malan, were determined to
put an end to the scourge. They conceived the *Plano Real,* which
would replace the old currency with the real and make it equal to
the UVR. Inflation ultimately results from too much money chasing
too few goods, so shortly after the plan's introduction, Cardoso and
Malan also imposed a special form of discipline over money creation.
The discipline involved using the exchange rate as an "anchor"; that
is, the central bank would be required to keep the real's market
value closely linked to the dollar, thereby limiting its ability to
increase the amount of reais circulating in the economy.

In private discussions with the Brazilians, the IMF pooh-poohed
the *Plano Real* as too impractical and gimmicky. The Fund's advice
was analogous to that of a diet doctor telling an obese patient, "Forget about wiring your jaws shut. Just stick to eating carrot sticks and
cabbage soup." IMF staffers would later recall the episode with cha-
grin, for the plan, which Cardoso and Malan launched anyway in

March 1994, worked better than its architects had dared to dream. Monthly inflation dropped to the single digits by the end of the year; by 1996, the annual rate was 9.6 percent. Cardoso, a sociologist who had moved from the left wing to the political center, won the presidency in 1994 based in part on his anti-inflation credentials, and he named Malan his finance minister. As Brazil at long last seemed to be conquering its demons of instability, the country's fortunes glowed with promise. Foreign money poured in, not just short-term but long-term as well, including European and American multinationals eager to set up factories and stake their claims. In a sign of the country's burgeoning middle-class market, McDonald's announced in autumn 1996 that it would invest $500 million to increase its Brazilian outlets from 200 to 530. Most gratifying, living standards of the poorest Brazilians improved as workers' paychecks finally started keeping up with prices in a meaningful way. The number of households with color televisions and freezers soared.

No one championed the *Plano Real* more ardently than Malan, a pipe-smoking former professor with sternly handsome features and swept-back hair. Born in 1943 near Rio de Janeiro, the son of a general, Malan earned a Ph.D. in economics from the University of California at Berkeley, writing a thesis attacking the protectionism that favored well-connected Brazilian industrialists. He taught at the Catholic University of Rio de Janeiro and returned to the United States in the mid-1980s as his country's representative on the World Bank's board and also as its chief debt negotiator with commercial banks. But he gave up the cushy life of a World Bank executive director to return to Brasília at Cardoso's behest, and as finance minister he gained a reputation as a serious, dogged practitioner of the orthodox economic principles in which he was schooled. When Brazilian markets came under speculative pressure during the Mexican peso crisis of 1994–1995, he fought off government colleagues who favored lowering interest rates and allowing the real to fall, arguing that to do so would ensure the return of inflation. He got

Cardoso's backing, and Brazil stayed the course—the result being even further declines in inflation, to a mere 3 percent in 1998.

But the longer the *Plano Real* remained operative, the stronger and more overvalued the Brazilian currency became. By mid-1998, the only question in most analysts' minds was whether the real was 30 percent overvalued, as Dornbusch, Sachs, and others estimated, or maybe only half that much, as senior IMF economists including Stan Fischer believed.

There is no magic point where an overvalued currency crashes back to earth. Sometimes traders will persist in driving it upward long after the overvaluation has become apparent. If the markets had held enough faith in Brazil to let it keep charging imports on its national credit card (that is, run up its current account deficit), the country might have continued on its merry way for quite some time. But in autumn 1998, investors in their infinite wisdom had suddenly concluded that the credit cards of all the world's emerging markets were maxed out.

The upshot was that Brazil was being sucked into one of those vicious cycles similar to those that swallowed Thailand, Indonesia, South Korea, and Russia. To induce the Herd to keep money in reais, Brazil's central bank had to raise interest rates to around 40 per-cent—an excruciatingly high level in a country with low single-digit inflation. Painful as this was for Brazilian companies, the even more urgent problem it posed was the impact on the government's ability to meet its obligations on its $265 billion in debt. The government's deficit of 8 percent of GDP went almost entirely to pay interest on borrowings, and when interest rates were high, the deficit rose in tandem, adding to the debt. The arithmetic was depressingly familiar to people who had observed Russia's struggles with exploding debt dynamics. The bonds issued by the government to cover the deficit had an average maturity of less than seven months, and more than half of them paid interest that was indexed to the overnight lending rate. So high interest rates translated into a larger interest bill for the government, which translated into a wider deficit, which translated into more borrowing. Analysts who crunched the numbers in autumn 1998 estimated that on its current trajectory, Brazil's deficit would nearly double in a year just because of the higher interest costs. As market participants grew increasingly convinced that Brazil couldn't afford to keep interest rates so ruinously high, the greater their inclination to dump reais, and the further rates had to rise— and so on, and so on, and so on.

Malan girded for battle like a Stonewall Jackson of the currency markets when the real came under renewed pressure following the Russian default. Brazil was no Thailand, he told IMF officials; nor was it Russia, nor was it Mexico, whose policymakers had lost a test of wills over the peso by letting slip that they might bend their fixed-rate system a bit. He shunned even the slightest hint of willingness to consider devaluing for fear it would become a self-fulfilling prophecy. Surrendering to the Herd's hysteria and giving up on the *Plano Real*, in Malan's view, would be a tragic mistake. Without the real as an anchor, he warned, Brazil would soon revert to its hyper-inflationary ways.

At an emergency meeting of Latin American finance ministers in Washington in early September 1998, Malan joked darkly to his colleagues that the opening line of Tolstoy's *Anna Karenina*—"Happy families are all alike; every unhappy family is unhappy in its own way"—had been turned on its head by recent events. His point was that the Herd was acting as if all emerging markets were like Russia, instead of drawing distinctions among them. Once investors recognized Brazil's fundamental strengths and the government's willingness to tackle its fiscal imbalance, he believed, the country could put itself on a virtuous cycle in which interest rates and the deficit would fall instead of rising; in the meantime, Brazil had to stand firm to preserve its hard-won stability. He was interested in support from the IMF, provided it came in such a way as to reflect the differences between Brazil and the other more desperate countries that had turned to the Fund for help.

Malan's argument found a sympathetic audience at the IMF, whose top officials issued numerous statements during September and October pledging their readiness to marshal a package of loans for Brazil and endorsing the government's exchange-rate policy. To some degree, the Fund's position stemmed from the fact that "we felt guilty" about having earlier scorned the *Plano Real*, according to one senior Fund official, who added ruefully: "I would have to say that because we had not given them the benefit of the doubt a few years earlier, we gave them much more, and maybe too much benefit of the doubt this time."

The IMF, with Fischer in the lead, joined with the top ranks of the U.S. Treasury in coalescing around a guiding principle: Since the Brazilian government was refusing to consider a devaluation of the real, the international community could not insist on one as the price of a loan package. Malan and his handpicked team of technocrats at the Finance Ministry were the most competent economic policymakers Brazil had had in recent memory, and if they feared a devaluation would destroy the country's victory over inflation, then how could outsiders overrule them? "The Brazilians were absolutely committed to maintaining the exchange rate," said the Treasury's Tim Geithner. "And the question we faced was whether we could have sufficient confidence in our judgment to force them to renounce that commitment as a condition for getting the money, particularly given how vulnerable the world seemed at that time. I argued that we should be hesitant to force them to blink."

Still, senior policymakers in Washington did not lack misgivings over the Brazilian strategy. They could not overlook the cruel arithmetic that made it so daunting for Brazil to win market confidence. Fischer, among others, believed the real was sufficiently overvalued to justify accelerating the 7.5 percent "rate of crawl" at which the Brazilian currency was allowed to decline against the dollar each year, and he and Ter-Minassian privately exhorted the Brazilians to speed up the crawl rate to around 12 to 15 percent.

The Brazilians adamantly refused. Malan and his aides feared such a move would only convey weakness that would lead to an uncontrollable run on the real, and they wondered whether the IMF genuinely understood the psychology of currency traders. Amaury Bier, the secretary for economic policy at the Finance Ministry, who was the former chief economist for Citibank in São Paulo, told IMF officials: "You never worked in the trading room of a bank. I have. If they see you even breathe a little stronger, you will transmit anxiety and doubts."

Likewise, Larry Summers got a polite but firm brush-off when he pressed the Brazilians to devise a fallback position should it become impossible to sustain the value of the real. In meetings at his Bethesda home during autumn 1998, Summers urged Bier and other Brazilian officials to "hope for the best and plan for the worst," and he repeatedly asked, "What's your Plan B?" The Brazilians, who feared that discussing such matters would risk leaks, retorted: There is no Plan B.

Once again, the IMF was going to lay its tattered credibility on the line. Four times, Fund-led rescues had been followed by collapsing currencies. Yet now, despite their qualms, Fund officials, together with their main backers at the Treasury, pressed ahead with plans to provide a megabailout for Brazil shortly after the country held state runoff elections in late October. To the Europeans, it looked as if the IMF was being set up for another fall—and a ripoff by the Herd to boot.

The only way international support for Brazil made sense, the Europeans insisted, was if it were accompanied by a concerted effort to "involve the private sector," as the international community had done in the Korean case by pressuring Seoul's bank creditors to stop pulling their money out of the country. Without a similar arrangement in Brazil, a rescue would turn into another "foreign investor exit facility," because it would prop up an overvalued real and thus encourage people to unload the Brazilian currency—or so Tietmeyer and others argued at the IMF–World Bank meeting in early October 1998 and in meetings and conference calls over the following weeks.

The Bank of England's Mervyn King, and top officials of the U.K. Treasury, were particularly militant. Some sort of coercion was probably necessary to keep short-term money from fleeing Brazil, they argued, and they even raised the shocking suggestion that perhaps exchange controls were warranted. They demanded to know—and felt they weren't getting useful answers—about the assumptions the IMF was making regarding how much money was likely to leave the country after the Brazilians received an international loan. Would the foreign banks stay in? Would domestic Brazilian residents ship their capital abroad? If the chief problem was locals engaging in capital flight, then controls might be in order, the Brits said.

But the Brazilians rejected proposals to "bail in" the banks, just as they did with proposals for devaluing the real. Their reaction may seem odd: What country, after all, wouldn't like its creditors to be obliged to keep extending loans? But Malan and his technocrats were convinced that if the banks felt coerced, Brazil would suffer a blow to its long-term creditworthiness. The country had declared a moratorium on its debts in the 1980s, and banks were still demanding slightly higher interest rates on their loans as a result. Furthermore, the markets were still in an uproar over the way Russia had ended up forcing its GKO creditors to take losses, and the Brazilians wanted to distance themselves as much as possible from the appearance of bullying their bankers, for fear of reducing their access to foreign credit.

Malan agreed to go on a "road show" to financial capitals in the United States, Europe, and Asia, asking banks to maintain their credit lines on a voluntary basis. But he wouldn't go further, taking the stance that he wanted to avoid any precipitous action that might have adverse consequences for the next ten or fifteen years on Brazil's relations with the financial community.

The U.S. Treasury supported the Brazilian position on this issue as well. In arguments with their European counterparts, Summers, Geithner, and Truman questioned whether Brazil's bank creditors would agree to a bail-in, and they raised concerns that such a move would backfire by sparking a panic—a reprise of the Korean debate. Brazil's case did not lend itself nearly so easily to a bail-in as Korea's did, Treasury officials contended. In the first place, much of its foreign debt was owed to bondholders who couldn't be organized into collective action. Furthermore, Brazil wasn't on the brink of default as Korea was, so scaring the banks into a bail-in with dire admonitions about a global cataclysm wouldn't work. Even *talking* about a Korean-style standstill was counterproductive, the Treasury team added, because it was prompting some banks to pull their money out of Brazil in advance of one.

So the Brazilians got their way, and the Europeans weren't the only ones rankled. "This is a double standard!" Japan's Sakakibara complained to his fellow G-7 deputies. The IMF and the Clinton administration had crammed reforms down the throats of Asian governments seeking international assistance. So why, Sakakibara asked, should Brazil be given so much discretion over important aspects of its IMF program, such as maintaining the value of the real? It was desirable, to be sure, for countries to "own" their programs; countries that are force-fed IMF remedies often go off track for lack of proper implementation. "Ownership" was a buzzword, much mouthed by both IMF and World Bank officials, to emphasize their belief that the most successful loans they make go to nations that cook up their own reform agendas. But having shown little concern about ownership in Asia, Sakakibara griped, the Fund and the Treasury were suddenly acting as if it were crucial in Brazil's case. European policymakers sympathized; some of them fumed that Brazil was getting special treatment because of its proximity to the United States.

Still, the Europeans and Japanese found themselves hog-tied. They couldn't be sure that a loan package for Brazil would fail. And they feared that if they blocked one, they would be blamed for the resulting chaos in global markets.

Within the G-7, the American position "was a pretty lone voice but a pretty determined one," recalled one G-7 deputy. "At the end of the day, it was made quite clear to everybody that we were not going to supplant our political judgment in the place of the judgment the Brazilians had brought to the table, even though it was a judgment one could easily disagree with. Nobody was willing to tell Pedro Malan, 'Tough luck. You're not getting the money.'"

Giving speeches off-the-cuff was not Alan Greenspan's style, especially when he knew that TV cameras would be rolling and markets could be hanging on his every word. The Federal Reserve chairman preferred to draft his public remarks carefully, and he usually stuck religiously to his prepared text. But on Wednesday, October 7, 1998, the next-to-last day of the IMF–World Bank meetings, Greenspan had no time to write the speech he was scheduled to deliver that morning to the National Association for Business Economics. He had spent long hours the previous few days going to one appointment, meeting, and social function after another, and that had deprived him of the opportunity to prepare anything more than a sketchy outline. He had originally planned to speak to the economists about statistical issues, but he knew he couldn't get away with droning on about such an irrelevant subject at a time when market confidence was disintegrating. So he winged it, and in one of the most important speeches of his chairmanship, he laid the foundations for more interest rate cuts. "I have been looking at the American economy on a day-by-day basis for almost a half century, but I have never seen anything like this," Greenspan said, using some of the same language that had impressed European officials during the G-7 meeting. "The Russian experience has created a major shift toward risk aversion pretty much throughout the world."

It wasn't only the flight from risky securities that disturbed him, he continued; it was also the mad scramble among investors to protect themselves by holding only the most liquid, easily salable assets. The market participants who were unloading off-the-run Treasuries to buy the more liquid on-the-run issues, according to Greenspan, "are basically saying, 'I want out. I don't want to know anything about whether a particular investment is risky or not. I just want to disengage.'" Financial markets "cannot effectively function in an efficient manner in that environment," the Fed chairman said, and he concluded: "To date, the economy has remained in reasonable shape, with good growth and low if not declining inflation.... But we are clearly facing a set of forces that should be dampening demand going forward to an unknown extent.... We do not know how far it will go or how much it will affect consumer and business spending here at home. This is a time for monetary policy to be especially alert."

Recession forecasts for the U.S. economy were beginning to surface; on the same day as Greenspan's speech, economists at J. P. Morgan Securities Inc. predicted a downturn in 1999, citing the strains in financial markets. Much of what Greenspan and his Fed colleagues were hearing privately pointed to a similar conclusion. Shortly after Greenspan's speech, for example, the seven-member Fed board met with a group of academic and private-sector consultants. Among the attendees was Jeffrey Shafer, a former Treasury undersecretary and Fed economist, now an executive at Salomon Smith Barney—where he had been told by the firm's traders that no new corporate bond issues were likely for the remainder of the year. In corporate boardrooms across America, Shafer said, business executives were undoubtedly looking at the prospect of the bond market being closed for some time, and adjusting their capital spending plans accordingly—the likely upshot, in the absence of preventive measures, being a recession.

At the Fed, few disagreed with the need for another rate cut. The question was when. Within the FOMC, two of the most influential members, McDonough and Rivlin, were quietly lobbying for a dramatic step—an "intermeeting" cut, in which Greenspan would use the authority he had to ease rates downward before the committee's next scheduled meeting on November 17. During a visit to Washington on October 12, McDonough joined Rivlin in the chairman's office, where they suggested that an intermeeting move would be just the right sort of signal to send the markets, because it would convey the Fed's willingness to do whatever it took to restore confidence. In fact, Greenspan changed rates often between meetings during the late 1980s and early 1990s; the FOMC frequently approved directives that gave the chairman the right to ease or tighten as he saw fit. But the practice had not been employed since 1994, in part because it delegated so much power to the chairman, so taking the step now would make a big splash. Although Greenspan had the right, under the directive of September 29, to order a rate cut, he was noncommittal about the idea when he met with McDonough and Rivlin.

Very shortly thereafter, however, Greenspan passed the word that he would convene a conference call of the FOMC, as was the custom before taking intermeeting moves, and in the early afternoon of October 15, the board members gathered in the boardroom with the reserve bank presidents piped in on speaker phones.

Greenspan let it be known that he was considering another 25-basis-point reduction in the federal funds rate, but before doing so he wanted to know the committee members' sentiments. Some members fretted that taking action so soon after the late September rate cut would unsettle the markets, but the general reaction was positive. Even Laurence Meyer, one of the most resolute anti-inflation hawks, supported the cut. Meyer disliked intermeeting rate changes; like a number of other FOMC members, he generally saw no advantage, given the long lagged effect of monetary policy, in moving a few weeks earlier or later than a scheduled committee meeting. But when the rate cut was primarily for psychological purposes, that was another matter—and Meyer, the former head of a St. Louis-based economic forecasting firm, could easily see the need to change market psychology. "I had gotten a call from a former client of mine [in the bond markets]," he recalled, "who said, 'I've never called you before, and I wouldn't do it, but I owe it to you to let you know, it's never been like this before out here.'"

Greenspan didn't take a vote in the FOMC—he wasn't required to—but immediately after the conference call, the board voted unanimously to cut the benchmark discount rate as well by 25 basis points. A few minutes after 3 P.M., the wires transmitted the Fed's announcement of a reduction in both the federal funds rate and the discount rate.

This time, the markets got the right message. The Dow staged a 330-point rally, its third-largest point gain in history. Within three weeks, the index was up another 8 percent, to nearly 9,000. The bond market gradually began to return to normal, in part because the lower federal funds rate made it cheaper for portfolio managers to borrow the money they needed to buy bonds. Yields on the riskiest issues moved back toward their historical relationships with Treasuries.

Like soldiers emerging from foxholes after artillery shells have stopped pounding their positions, analysts began to venture predictions in late October that the worst of the crisis appeared to be over. "We are potentially turning the corner," declared David Hale, global chief economist at the Zurich Group in Chicago.

The Fed's intermeeting rate cut, which was followed by another quarter-point reduction in the federal funds rate at the FOMC meeting on November 17, justifiably added to Greenspan's aura as an economic virtuoso. It surely helped that U.S. inflation was quiescent; had the crisis come at a time when markets were hypersensitive to worries about a wage-price surge, perhaps the Fed would have been more reluctant to issue such a potent signal of monetary ease, and perhaps the outcome would have been less favorable. But in any event, the rate cut did the trick, and though it was the most important factor changing the market's mood for the better, it was by no means the only one.

Japan's ruling and opposition parties reached an agreement on October 12 that would provide several hundred billion dollars in government funds to shore up the financial condition of solvent but shaky banks. At the same time, the nation's parliament approved landmark banking legislation that would allow the government to nationalize banks that were failing.

The moves came three days after the Nikkei index plummeted to 12,879, the lowest level since December 1985, and they appeared to mark a significant change in Tokyo's attitude about the need to confront its banking problems. Japanese banks clearly required vast sums of money to boost their capital before they could resume lending, so the promise of a large amount of government funds (for which the government would receive shares of the banks' stock) came as a welcome relief to the markets. So too did word that Japan appeared ready to deal with insolvent banks more aggressively. Under the legislation passed by the parliament, the government would nationalize such banks or liquidate them, and establish a public institution to resell the good assets and deal with the bad ones, a process similar (on the surface, at least) to the U.S. strategy during the savings and loan crisis.

The Nikkei responded with a rally that lifted it more than 10 percent in two weeks, and other Asian markets also roared back to life, as Hong Kong's Hang Seng Index gained 24 percent from October 8 to 23 in tandem with similar upward moves in Thai and Korean stocks. Helping to improve sentiment in Asia was a sharp rise in the yen, which appreciated 17 percent against the dollar from October 5 to October 19, easing competitive pressure on the currencies of Japan's neighbors.

Meanwhile, on October 15—the same day as the Fed's rate cut—the Clinton administration reached agreement with Congress on a compromise IMF funding bill, adding to the general sense of relief in the markets. The deal cleared the way for Washington to make its contribution toward a $90 billion increase in Fund quotas, as well as its contribution toward an expanded credit line for the Fund. To obtain majority support in the House, the Treasury agreed to secure a number of reforms at the IMF, including a rise in the Fund's lending rates to make it less attractive for governments to seek its aid.

Market-buoying news came from Europe as well, where policymakers who had once assumed their region was insulated from the crisis began waking up to the need for stimulative action. Central banks in five European capitals cut interest rates in early November, followed by an eleven-nation coordinated rate cut on December 3, with even Tietmeyer acknowledging that developments overseas posed a greater danger to the continent's economy than he had expected.

Finally, on November 13, the IMF and the world's major industrial countries unveiled a $41.5 billion package of loans for Brazil. Unlike the emergency rescues provided to Thailand, Korea, Indonesia, and Russia, this program came at a time of relative calm for the country and was billed as a prophylactic against any further outbreaks of turbulence.

The program contained several features hailed by the High Command as innovative responses to the dangers of contagion. The main idea was that if Brazil came under speculative attack, the government wouldn't have to wait to have the bailout money doled out in dribs and drabs as is customary in IMF programs. The Brazilians could draw the first tranche of about $9 billion immediately if they wanted, and if it became necessary, they could draw a second $9 billion too—dubbed a "floating tranche"—without waiting for an arbitrary deadline. Within twelve months, they could have up to $37 billion, provided they abided by the conditions of the program. Moreover, the "headline" figure of $41.5 billion was much less questionable than in other packages, such as Korea's and Indonesia's, in which the contribution by the United States and other industrial countries came in the form of second lines of defense. In Brazil's case, the $14 billion bilateral portion of the package was provided up-front, alongside IMF money, through loans granted by the Bank for International Settlements and guaranteed by individual governments. The Europeans, despite feeling buffaloed into backing a bailout they didn't like, kicked in their share and declared their support.

Fischer struck a confident air at a press conference when he and Camdessus unveiled the program. He emphasized that "the most important element in making a financing package succeed is the actions that the Brazilian government is taking," which included ambitious commitments by the Cardoso administration to cut spending and raise taxes by about 3 percent of GDP. In describing the package, Fischer presented the $41.5 billion in loans as a formidable manifestation of overwhelming force: "The international community is providing a very large, sufficiently front-loaded package to give confidence that Brazil has the resources to deal with any possible drawings on reserves that might become necessary in the next few months or during the course of the program. . . . You want to provide assurance to the markets that you're not sort of slicing it very, very thin. You want the markets to know there's a sufficient amount available comfortably."

The global financial system gained a much healthier pallor in the final two months of 1998, thanks to the rate cuts in the United States and Europe, the Japanese bank reforms, the passage of the IMF bill, and the Fund's package of loans for Brazil. But the crisis was not over. European skepticism about the IMF's Brazil program would soon be vindicated.

The Brazilian economy initially emitted positive signals following the announcement of the country's IMF program. The amount of money leaving the country dropped to $1.9 billion in November 1998, about one-tenth the rate it had been two months earlier. The government made steady progress, albeit with occasional setbacks, toward winning congressional approval of the Cardoso administration's deficit-cutting program.

But even within the IMF, there were worries that maintaining Brazil's fixed exchange rate was akin to an act of levitation. At a meeting with still-dubious European officials in Paris in early December, Mussa privately put the chances of the program's success at fifty-fifty. That month, the capital outflow began to pick up again, totaling $5.2 billion. Fund staffers blamed interest rate cuts by the central bank, which trimmed the benchmark overnight lending rate from 42 percent on November 10 to 29 percent in late December. In phone calls, Fischer protested to central bank officials that their policy was undermining the program and reducing the incentive for people to keep their money invested in reais. But he was told that rates were still plenty high and inflicting much more damage on the economy than he seemed to understand. A recession appeared almost certain, with most indicators of production having fallen, and unemployment having risen by two percentage points, to 8 percent, since the beginning of the year.

Whatever the underlying reason Brazil's rescue plan went up in flames, there is no dispute about the proximate cause—the moment at which, figuratively speaking, the cow kicked over the lantern in Mrs. O'Leary's barn. The cow was Itamar Franco, the newly elected governor of Brazil's second-largest state, Minas Gerais, and a bitter rival of Cardoso's. He kicked over the lantern on January 6, 1999, with the announcement that his state would suspend payments on its $15.4 billion debt owed to the federal government. A few other governors followed Franco's lead in demanding relief on the debts they owed the federal government, and although the Cardoso administration vowed to beat Franco in court, the specter of debt moratoriums was enough to send investors bolting.

From January 6 to 12, the country lost another $2 billion in reserves. This meant that most of the $9 billion that Brazil had drawn from the first tranche of its international loan package was gone—into the pockets of banks, investors, and speculators who had changed reais into dollars at the high exchange rate, just as the Europeans had predicted.

Ter-Minassian knew something nasty was brewing on Tuesday, January 12, a particularly tumultuous day in Brazilian markets, because she couldn't reach any of the country's economic policy-makers on the phone. Figuring that Fischer could get his calls returned, she asked him to try—but before he could get around to it, a call came for him around 6 P.M. from Pedro Malan.

President Cardoso had appointed a new governor of the central bank, Malan informed Fischer. The new governor, whose nomination would be submitted to the Brazilian Senate for confirmation, was Francisco Lopes, the central bank's director of monetary policy and son of a former finance minister, who went by the nickname "Chico." In his first major move as acting governor, Lopes was changing the country's exchange-rate policy, and he would call shortly to explain the new approach, Malan said.

On a speakerphone in his office, together with Ter-Minassian, Fischer listened with dismay as Lopes told him that the next morning, Brazil would drop the ironclad defense of its currency, in the hopes that a less-overvalued exchange rate would make it possible for Brazil to move quickly toward lower interest rates. The move, though, would not be a clean break from the *Plano Real;* the currency would be devalued by about 8 percent, and new, modestly lower target ranges would be set for it. Specifically, the central bank would change the trading range for the real, from a band that was adjusted slightly every few days—it stood at 1.12 to 1.21 reais per dollar on January 12—to a broader range of 1.20 to 1.32 reais per dollar.

Fischer and his colleagues were concerned about the devaluation, even though it had been anticipated for some time. But they were at least as worried about the way the new exchange-rate arrangement would work. They were certain that the markets would blast the new currency system to smithereens; the Brazilian stance resembled that of a boy with a bloody nose who, having been shoved backward a few steps, draws a line in the sand and dares his tormentors to step across it. The IMF deputy managing director, who recalled this moment as one of the most frightening of the entire crisis, could not imagine what would come next. "I thought, this is it," he said. "We're going to lose Latin America, and then it will go back to Asia."

The "last line of defense" had been breached. The military metaphors invoked by the High Command about halting the crisis at Brazil now sounded like so much bravado. This was a mortifying setback for the IMF, especially after all the fanfare surrounding the announcement of its Brazil program on November 13.

What you're proposing won't work, Fischer told Lopes. "Controlled" devaluations like these had been tried amid crises in countries as diverse as Mexico and Russia, and the markets had quickly concluded—correctly—that the authorities wouldn't be able to hold the line at just one devaluation. The real will be blown through its bands, Fischer argued.

Lopes replied that he was aware the new policy might prove unsustainable, but its chances of success would be greater if the IMF endorsed it. If it didn't work, Brazil could always abandon its defense of the real altogether and let the currency float. But the IMF thought Lopes's approach risked causing the markets to lose so much faith in the real that the currency would go into free fall.

IMF officials weren't sure what was going on. They found it inconceivable that Malan, the upholder of the *Plano Real,* was in accord with this move. It was well known that the finance minister's rivals had been trying to persuade President Cardoso to take a step like this with the aim of jump-starting the economy by depreciating the currency and lowering interest rates quickly. Fischer called Malan and implored him to persuade the president to change his mind. But Malan was playing the role of the loyal minister and wouldn't reveal his reservations about the policy change.

This much the IMF hierarchy knew: Lopes, a fifty-three-year-old former economics professor, did not hold the Fund in high esteem. He had spoken disparagingly about the IMF in autumn 1998 when Malan was in Washington negotiating Brazil's program. "The bureaucrats in Washington are all excited by the idea of creating a rescue package for Brazil so they can cover the tracks of their recent mistakes in Asia and Russia," Lopes told *O Estado de São Paulo,* a leading Brazilian daily.

Fischer spent much of the night of January 12 on the phone, first at his office, and later at his home, with both Malan and Lopes. The next morning, at seven o'clock, the phone rang at Ter-Minassian's home.

"Teresa, I failed," Fischer said. "I wasn't able to convince them."

"What do we do now?" Ter-Minassian asked.

"Well, they'll have to bear the consequences," Fischer replied.

That day, as Fischer and his colleagues had feared, the new currency regime fared abysmally in its debut, despite Lopes's assurances that it represented "an improvement in policy" rather than a departure from the past. Brazilian stocks fell more than 10 percent in the first few minutes of trading before recovering somewhat to end the day down 5 percent. The real popped through the bottom part of the new range, prompting the central bank to sell a significant amount of dollars to brake the currency's descent. Markets went into paroxysms the world over, with the Dow plummeting as much as 261 points, Germany's main stock index down 4 percent, and Argentina's down 10 percent.

The markets showed every sign of bleeding the central bank's reserves dry—the obvious assumption being that there might never be a better time to obtain dollars for reais. During January 13 and 14, the central bank's reserves fell by another $4.8 billion.

A deluge of phone calls from top officials in Washington conveyed the message to Brasília: Stop this policy now, or you're cut off from international support. Fischer told Malan that the international community would never countenance providing additional IMF loans to Brazil if the country's reserves were going to be frittered away on an indefensible exchange-rate policy. The Brazilians agreed that on Friday, January 15, they would stop using reserves to defend the new band—allowing the real to float, at least for the day—and Malan and Lopes flew to Washington for a weekend of talks, with the stated intention of announcing a new currency plan on Monday. "When they came here, they had no clue what to do," a senior IMF economist recalled. "We ourselves were somewhat, shall we say, unclear."

Sandwiches, fruit, and soft drinks were provided for the top Brazilian officials and IMF staffers who gathered in Camdessus's office on the twelfth floor of the IMF building on Saturday, January 16. But the atmosphere in the talks was often as frigid as the blustery weather outside. Fischer, who had gone far out on a limb for the Brazilian program, made it clear he was furious with the short notice the Fund had received of the change in exchange-rate policy. Malan, a friend of Fischer's from his days on the World Bank board, was apologetic; Lopes, though civil, made little effort to disguise his disdain for Fund staffers whose grasp of economics he considered inferior to his own. He agreed to speak by phone with Fischer, whom he respected, on a daily basis—but decreed that other IMF personnel, including Ter-Minassian, would have to deal with his subordinates at the central bank.

The substantive discussions started off with an aggressive proposal by Camdessus: Brazil, he said, ought to adopt a currency board, with the real rigidly linked to the dollar at a somewhat lower level than the then-current 1.47 reais per dollar. "Why not?" the managing director demanded. A currency board, after all, would be even stronger anti-inflation medicine than the *Plano Real* had been, since the central bank would have no discretionary power whatsoever to increase the supply of reais. Moreover, Brazil was better equipped than Indonesia to establish a currency board, because it had a well-functioning banking system.

Malan, Lopes, and their aides wouldn't hear of it. A currency board, they felt, might ideally suit the IMF's purposes—namely, preventing a round of devaluations in Latin America. But they didn't think it suited Brazil's self-interest to handcuff the central bank so completely and irrevocably, and they offered compelling technical objections as well. (Brazil's short-term government bonds were so liquid—so much like ordinary money—that establishing a credible currency board was impossible, they contended.)

Once convinced that a currency board wouldn't fly, Camdessus said that Brazil would have to go to the opposite extreme—a free float of the real, with no bands or targets to defend. The Brazilians agreed; the markets had reacted enthusiastically on Friday when the real was floated for a day, since the danger had receded that the central bank would squander all its reserves propping up the currency's value.

But the discussion turned fractious when the two sides got down to particulars. Camdessus argued that under a free float, Brazil would have to boost interest rates sharply—he mentioned levels of 60 percent and 70 percent—because with the death of the *Plano Real,* inflation fears would be rampant and investors would be leaving the country in droves unless given sufficient incentives to keep their money there. Once confidence was restored, rates could come down, Camdessus said, but the first thing the central bank should do is show its resolve on Monday morning by raising the overnight rate from 30 percent to 34 percent.

Lopes scorned this approach as an exercise in macho central banking. Borrowing costs were already very high, he said, and if rate hikes proved necessary, it would make more sense to do them gradually. President Cardoso had supported rate increases in the past, he added, but the central bank needed to be able to explain the reasons to the president rather than tighten credit arbitrarily. In any case, Lopes continued, he couldn't simply order a rate increase on Monday morning; such a step required a meeting and formal approval of the central bank's monetary policy board. Okay, Camdessus countered, then how about calling the members of the committee on the phone immediately to obtain their assent? Lopes refused.

Lopes departed in a rush to catch his plane back to Brasília on Sunday, January 17, leaving behind an unhappy group of IMF officials. Since Brazil was dropping its band-changing scheme for the real and replacing it with a float, the Fund was no longer threatening to cut off the country. But Lopes's unwillingness to tighten money dramatically, the Fund believed, meant that the real would surely depreciate even further—and that, IMF economists feared, would decimate other Latin American currencies as well.

A nightmarish two weeks ensued, during which the real followed a path similar to that blazed almost exactly one year earlier by the Indonesian rupiah.

When the new floating policy was announced on Monday, January 19, the real dropped to 1.59 per dollar, 31 percent below its level before the devaluation, and it continued falling vertiginously, dipping below two reais per dollar by the end of January. Most disturbing, the dumping of reais continued apace even on days when Brazil's Congress was approving politically controversial deficit-reduction measures, and even on days when Lopes's central bank board raised interest rates, which it did in a series of steps that brought the overnight level to 39 percent by the beginning of February. To the IMF's way of thinking, of course, the problem was that Lopes was tightening credit too slowly and timidly. Whether this explains the market's behavior or not remains a matter of dispute. But one fact was glaringly evident: With every downtick in the real, and every uptick in interest rates, Brazil's predicament was becoming more insurmountable. A lower value for the real increased the government's burden of servicing its debt, because the principal and interest payments on some of its bonds were linked to the dollar. And higher interest rates caused the debt-repayment cost to swell as well, by more than $1 billion a year for each extra 1 percent in rates.

Rumors flew that the government was considering imposing exchange controls or a moratorium on debt payments—and capital continued to exit the country at about a half billion dollars a day. "Cardoso is under massive political pressure from his party, from already rebellious governors and from the public to switch policies quickly if this last gasp at conventional policy fails," Medley Global Advisors, a New York firm providing information and advice to institutional investors, told its clients in its daily newsletter on January 24. "That would mean moving to Plan C—a new cabinet, perhaps capital controls and lower interest rates, perhaps a return to inflationary times." On January 29, ordinary citizens became swept up in the panic as word spread that Cardoso would freeze bank accounts, as one of his predecessors had done a decade before. Queues of anxious depositors formed at banks. Brazil was at the precipice.

The moon was full, imparting luminosity to the snow coating the Alps as Stan Fischer left Davos, Switzerland, at 3 A.M. on February 1, 1999. A long day lay ahead for the IMF deputy managing director, who was on his way to Brazil after attending the Global Economic Forum, an annual gathering of policymakers, tycoons, and assorted movers and shakers. Davos lies about 3 hours by car from Zurich's airport; from there Fischer would fly to London, and from there to São Paulo, and from there to Brasília, where he would land late in the evening. He was going at the request of the Brazilian government but also at the urging of Ter-Minassian, who wanted to be sure the government would be convinced to take the steps necessary to pull the country out of its financial nosedive. "You should come," she had told him, "to deliver the message at the highest level."

Electrifying news came shortly after Fischer's arrival in Brasília: Lopes was going to lose his job running the central bank after only nineteen days in the post, and President Cardoso was replacing him with Arminio Fraga, a top executive with George Soros's hedge-fund firm. The decision was the result of a high-stakes maneuver by Malan, who had submitted a letter to President Cardoso suggesting that both he and Lopes should resign. The move forced Cardoso into deciding whether he was truly prepared to jettison economic orthodoxy, and his answer was no. Instead of replacing both men, the president fired Lopes and asked Malan to stay on as finance minister.

Fischer holed up at his hotel on February 2, the morning after his arrival, waiting for the public announcement of the switch at the central bank. Going to the Finance Ministry before that, as he had originally planned, would give the impression that the Fund had orchestrated or demanded the personnel changes. Although suspicion naturally arose that the IMF was indeed behind Lopes's sacking, Fund officials have always insisted they would never interfere so brazenly in a member country's affairs. But they had made it clear in their conversations with the Brazilians that they didn't like the central bank's policies under Lopes, so they were naturally relieved to see him go, and they regarded Fraga's nomination as a courageous masterstroke by Cardoso. The forty-two-year-old Fraga, a Princeton economics Ph.D. and former director of international affairs at the central bank, had worked for Soros Fund Management since 1993 as manager of its $1.4 billion emerging-markets fund. His appointment created an easy target for opposition politicians, who accused the administration of handing the country's fortunes over to the very speculators responsible for the country's woes. But the IMF viewed Fraga's qualifications as almost ideal, since his Soros experience provided him with considerable insight into how to instill confidence in markets. After his nomination was unveiled on February 2, the real jumped more than 8 percent.

Once the Fraga announcement was out of the way, Fischer met with Malan and Fraga at the Finance Ministry around noon and the following day with Cardoso and Malan at the presidential residence. Brazil's IMF program was in need of a major overhaul—or "strengthening," in Fund parlance—for the depreciation of the real had made a hash of the first one. Strengthening the program had worked in Korea, where the accord struck on Christmas Eve 1997 saved the country from default. But the Indonesian case had shown that program strengthenings sometimes produce quite the opposite sorts of results.

To induce the Brazilians to act, the Fund could dangle the $9 billion second tranche that was pending under its $41.5 billion international loan package. At the rate the country was losing dollars, that injection of hard currency would provide a most welcome boost. But Brazil would have to reciprocate. "You've only got one chance," Fischer exhorted Cardoso. "There has got to be a stronger program."

The government would have to cut the budget deficit even more deeply than previously planned, Fischer said. The country's debt dynamics were out of control, with bigger deficits and higher interest rates mutually exacerbating each other, creating an ever-rising debt with ever-rising servicing costs. One way to try changing the dynamic, of course, was for the central bank to cut interest rates and print the money to pay off the debt. But in the IMF's view—and Malan's and Fraga's as well—that route led back to Brazil's bad old hyperinflationary ways. Instead, Fischer said, the government would have to cut spending and raise taxes sufficiently to convince the markets of its resolve to contain the problem. Brazil had already committed to generate a budget surplus (not including interest payments) equal to 2.6 percent of GDP in 1999 and more in 2000 and 2001; Fischer wanted those targets to be raised substantially. If the government acted convincingly enough, he said, the debt dynamic might turn virtuous very quickly, because interest rates on much of its borrowing were tied to the overnight interest rate. But making the dynamic virtuous would require another bite on the bullet.

The economy's weakness was not conducive to such austerity. Joblessness in São Paulo had soared to around 20 percent, and nearly all forecasters anticipated a recession of somewhere between −2 percent growth and −5 percent growth for the year. But if the government didn't move decisively, Fischer warned, all the stabilization that Cardoso had accomplished since 1994 would be in danger.

Belt-tightening wasn't the only thing Fischer had on his mind for Brazil. Another crucial component of a strengthened program, he told Cardoso, was that the private sector had to become "involved"—to wit, Brazil's foreign bank creditors would have to reach some sort of arrangement to keep their money in the country, as Korea's had done, and as the Europeans had been demanding.

Foreign banks had cut nearly one-third of the $60 billion in short-term interbank and trade lines that they had extended to Brazil as of August 1998, and although that move didn't constitute a run as devastating as the one that had triggered the Korean crisis, it had the potential to develop into one. So the Brazilians could no longer resist bailing in their banks as they had in autumn 1998. The G-7, including the United States, would not agree to pour more IMF money into the country without some assurances against the funds going to pay off foreign bankers, Fischer told his Brazilian interlocutors.

More than a month passed before all the negotiations were finished and the loose ends tied up. But once things started coming together for Brazil, they came together quickly—and this time, the IMF was taken by surprise because of how positive the outcome was, instead of the reverse.

Thursday, March 4 was Fraga's first day as president of the central bank after being confirmed by the Senate, and he promptly drove short-term interest rates up from 39 percent to 45 percent in a display of determination to contain inflation and lure investors into reais. The Brazilian currency had fallen to an all-time low of 2.22 per dollar on March 2, but following Fraga's move, the real appreciated to 2.06 per dollar, and it continued strengthening over the next several weeks, hitting 1.66 reais per dollar on April 13. For the IMF, this episode was sweet vindication of its faith in using high interest rates to stabilize a currency.

On March 5, a Fund mission in Brasília completed negotiations on the terms under which the government would receive the next $9 billion from its international loan package. The Brazilians agreed to additional budget measures, as Fischer had urged, with the goal of increasing the government's budget surplus targets by about 0.5 percent of GDP. They also pledged to keep monetary policy tight, the aim being to tamp down quickly the inflationary impact of the devaluation.

One final element remained to be completed—bailing in the foreign banks. On March 8, Camdessus and Rubin suggested in separate statements that providing additional official funds to Brazil depended on a satisfactory arrangement in which the banks would undertake to maintain their credit lines. "The Brazilian authorities intend to seek, starting this week, voluntary commitments by their creditor banks. . . . This effort . . . will be a key factor in the consideration of the program by the Executive Board of the IMF in late March or early April," Camdessus stated.

The New York Fed hosted a breakfast meeting of nine American banks and two Canadian banks on March 11. After considerable internal debate, U.S. officials had decided to take a relatively light touch in concerting Brazil's creditor banks. Some within the High Command had wanted a Korea-style operation, with officials in each country prodding bank executives into signing individual commitments to keep their money in Brazil; these included the Germans, IMF officials, and one or two policymakers at the U.S. Treasury. But others, including New York Fed officials, argued that browbeating the banks might prove counterproductive and wasn't necessary anyway. The banks regarded Brazil as a market with vast potential; inducing them to maintain their credit lines might require only a little encouragement and the tacit assurance that they were joining in a collective effort.

Terry Checki, executive vice president of the New York Fed, chaired the meeting, and Bill Rhodes of Citibank, who had served as coordinator for the banks during the Korean bail-in, was tapped to do the same for Brazil. As in the case of Long-Term Capital, New York Fed officials applied no explicit pressure on the banks—indeed, Malan, who was the featured speaker, emphasized that Brazil was asking for their voluntary cooperation—but the location of the meeting carried its own unspoken message. The light touch worked; the banks agreed to a joint statement that "signaled their intention to maintain" their credit lines to Brazil, at least until August 31, 1999. In Washington, Fischer insisted that the statement be made public, so he could show the evidence of the bail-in to the IMF Executive Board before approval of the next loan tranche. Following similar meetings of bankers over the next couple of weeks at central banks in London, Paris, and other financial capitals, the Fund's board issued its approval on March 30.

With that new lease on life, the Brazilian economy proceeded to make fools of those in the economic forecasting profession. The consensus among economists in early 1999 had been that the collapse of the real would cause Brazil to undergo not only a deep recession but a bout of inflation of between 40 percent and 80 percent. Instead, the economy eked out growth of about 1 percent in 1999, and prices rose at less than 9 percent. (The IMF's Mussa, who had made so many right calls during the crisis, was among those whose pessimism about Brazil proved way off the mark.)

The IMF deserves considerable credit for helping Brazil recover in spring 1999 from the collapse of the real. The Fund's prescriptions were apt, and its support—combined with the bank bail-in—produced the desired effect on confidence. A particular source of pride for Fund officials was the speed with which Brazil was able to lower interest rates following the initial upward spike in early March that stabilized the currency. In a textbook example of IMF economics working according to plan, the Fraga-run central bank cut the overnight borrowing rate to 34 percent in mid-April, 11 points below the March peak, and to 23.5 percent on May 19.

But the Fund's credibility suffered a grievous blow when its first Brazil program failed to achieve its declared aim of sustaining the country's currency peg. Later in 1999, IMF and Treasury officials publicly declared that the international community should be chary of bailing out countries with fixed or crawling exchange-rate systems like the one Brazil had. Though they left open the possibility of exceptions, they said that rescues should be confined generally to countries with pure floats or rock-solid pegs like a currency board.

This does not mean that Fischer, Summers, and their colleagues acknowledge having erred by approving the late-1998 program for Brazil. On the contrary, they believe it may have helped save the global economy. Their reasoning is that since the devaluation of the real was averted until January 1999, global markets were spared the trauma in autumn 1998, when the impact might have been too great to withstand. "You didn't want a devaluation then [in the autumn]," said Fischer. "The world was highly unstable. You didn't want to throw another firecracker into the mix."

Sensible though this justification may be in hindsight, the IMF and the Treasury can take little credit for concocting a masterfully timed strategy. No one recalls hearing the architects of the Brazilian rescue suggesting in autumn 1998 that the point was to defer devaluation for a few months. Perhaps the best way of summarizing the outcome is that the Treasury and the IMF stumbled on the right solution.

Stan Fischer could tell by his personal schedule that a change for the better was afoot in April 1999. Weekend strategy meetings at the IMF had suddenly become a thing of the past. He was able to finish his taxes more than two weeks before the April 15 deadline; the previous year, he had barely filed on time because of the crisis in Indonesia. His optional reading material at home was finally getting some attention.

Practically every day, the world's most economically troubled countries were exhibiting new signs of health. Hong Kong's stock market hit an eighteen-month high on April 16, and earlier that week, South Korea announced it would make early repayments on its IMF loans, as the Korean stock market soared above its precrisis level. Brazil joined a host of nations, including Colombia, Hungary, and Argentina, in announcing plans to raise billions of dollars on the international bond market.

The Brazilian crisis had not produced the worldwide contagion that Fischer and others in the High Command had feared. (It would later be blamed for contributing to Argentina's 2001–2002 crisis, but that is another story.) Nobody could be certain why the contagion was so limited. The most logical explanation was that hedge funds and other international money managers had been forced, at least temporarily, to stop borrowing to the hilt as they had done formerly, which meant that losses in one market no longer required them to sell their holdings in others.

In the same unpredictable manner with which it first materialized and spread, the global financial crisis was ending, leaving perplexing questions about how to stop the next one.

· 13 ·

COOLING OFF

The table in the Treasury secretary's private dining room was set with a breakfast of fresh fruit and toasted bagels as a small group of reporters and editors from *The Washington Post* filed in to interview Paul O'Neill, the new secretary, in early February 2001, a couple of weeks after the inauguration of President George W. Bush. Eager to get a close-up look at the feisty O'Neill, who had previously headed Alcoa Inc., the journalists opened by asking him how he might handle international financial crises differently from his Clinton administration predecessors. With the tart tongue for which he would become renowned, O'Neill conveyed his conviction that the crises of the late 1990s could have been anticipated and managed much better than they were. Deriding the 1998 Russian rescue as particularly ill-advised, he said: "What happened in Russia was foretold. It was not a surprise. You ever try to do business in Russia? You ever try to write an enforceable contract? It doesn't take a genius to figure out it's not a great place to put capital." When the Indonesian crisis was mentioned, he demanded, "Was that a surprise?" In response to the assertion that Indonesia's collapse had indeed come as a terrible shock, at least to the IMF and World Bank, he shot back: "To the *world*? They didn't have internal structural problems?"

In the months that followed, O'Neill's disdain for the IMF and its shortcomings during the Clinton years became the barbed edge of the Bush administration's new rhetorical stance concerning financial crises. The media dubbed the administration's approach "tough love" because it appeared aimed at putting a stop to big bailouts, based on the theory that countries and financial markets, like wayward children, sometimes need harsh discipline rather than rescue. For all of O'Neill's bluster and lack of regard for the diplomatic harm his thunderbolts might inflict, the Treasury chief made some incisive points on the issue. The IMF had been "too often associated with failure," he noted; and its loans—which ultimately came from "plumbers and carpenters" and other taxpayers—frequently helped investors and lenders avoid losses on their risky bets in far-off lands. "We could teach some very valuable lessons by letting so-called hot money take a bath," he told a House committee in May 2001. He added, referring to investors who had earned high yields on their emerging-market plays: "The nasty part of what we have done in bailing out some of these countries is we have . . . let people get away without paying the risk premium that was implied in the rate of return that they were able to get. And we need to figure out a way that when somebody, in effect, bets the farm on a 25 percent interest-rate environment, if the circumstances suggest they should lose it all, they should lose it all."

The desire of the Bush administration to distance itself from the international policies of Bob Rubin and Larry Summers struck some observers as odd. After all, the world economy had escaped with only a mild slowdown in 1998–1999, and the U.S. economy had emerged virtually unscathed, despite Korea's near-default in late 1997 and the seize-up in U.S. markets during autumn 1998. For this achievement, the small band of top officials who were then running the Treasury, the Fed, and the IMF could take justifiable pride.

But the Bush team inherited something of a mess. The IMF's credibility as a crisis fighter had taken a beating in every one of the countries whose crises have been recounted in this book, because its giant loan packages so often proved ineffective at restoring investor confidence. As a result, the impact of future IMF rescues would be diminished by the memories of 1997–1999. At the same time, the enormity of these packages had created expectations in the minds of the global public, and global markets, about what would be forthcoming in future cases. If any good-sized emerging market were to become financially strapped, a refusal to provide it with large-scale emergency loans would risk creating the impression that the High Command cared little about what might happen to the nation in question.

Thus, O'Neill and his colleagues were understandably concerned that they were confronting the worst of both worlds—as was Horst Köhler, the IMF's new managing director, who made it clear when he took office in spring 2000 that he wanted to limit the amount of assistance the Fund could give to individual countries. It was bad enough that the large sums of money involved in international rescues often failed to achieve the desired aims of calming nerves, halting the withdrawal of capital, and helping countries regain their footing when crises erupted. To make matters worse, the fact that megabailouts had become such an accepted part of the global financial landscape engendered moral hazard, because some members of the Electronic Herd—figuring they stood a good chance of getting their money back regardless of what happened to the countries in question—would be tempted to invest and lend recklessly, setting the stage for future crises.

But despite the scorn heaped by O'Neill on previous IMF bailouts, and all the tough-love talk, the policies adopted by the High Command under Köhler and Team Bush have differed very little from the policies of Camdessus and Team Clinton. For the real-life crises that have arisen in the first few years of the twenty-first century, large bailouts have materialized pretty much as they did in the late 1990s.

Under the new regime, several countries including Turkey,

Uruguay, and Brazil have received loans from the IMF—and in some cases, new loans on top of existing loans—that substantially exceeded the Fund's normal limits considering the size of those countries' quotas. Tiny Uruguay, for example, is normally entitled under IMF rules to borrow a cumulative total of $1.2 billion from the Fund at any one time. But because its problems were deemed to be "exceptional circumstances"—the crises in large neighboring countries have hammered confidence in the country's financial system—Uruguay received IMF commitments totaling $2.8 billion in 2002. As for Turkey, its borrowing ceiling is supposed to be $3.8 billion, but in 2002 it owed the IMF about five times that much; the Bush White House signed off on a $10 billion "augmentation" to Turkey's Fund program in spring 2001. Brazil, meanwhile, reaped the biggest pledge of direct IMF loans ever given to a single country—a $30 billion program, approved in summer 2002.

One tough-love display came in December 2001, when the IMF refused further loans to Argentina, forcing the Argentine government to default on its debts and drop the currency board arrangement that had pegged the peso to the dollar at a one-to-one ratio. But that came only after Argentina had received an $8 billion increase the previous August in its already sizable aid package. With that exception (which closely resembled the Clinton team's decision to give Russia an additional loan and then cut the country off when the rescue failed to work), the IMF and its overseers in the Bush administration have bowed to arguments that every effort must be made to avoid meltdowns. Explaining the discrepancy between the administration's rhetoric and actions, John Taylor, the undersecretary of the Treasury for international affairs, said in August 2002: "There's always a matter of degree in how fast you move to change a system. It shouldn't be done rapidly. It should be done as gradually as possible."

As lame as that rationalization might sound, the current rules of the global financial system offer no attractive alternatives to the options the Bush team has chosen. Today's crisis fighters face a grim, essentially binary dilemma: They can hold their noses and approve large conventional IMF bailouts, with all the attendant disadvantages of moral hazard and high probability of failure; or they can throw countries to the wolves by consigning them to default. The appalling dangers of the latter choice were vividly illustrated in Argentina, where deadly riots at the end of 2001 toppled two presidents, and in ensuing months the economy sank so low that children died of malnutrition in a country known as one of the world's great food producers.

Therein lies a fundamental challenge for the designers of what has become known as the "new international financial architecture." Ever since the Mexican peso crisis, in finance ministries, think tanks, and universities around the world, and at the IMF too, some of the world's foremost economic minds have been sifting and crafting proposals for changing the rules and practices of the global financial system, with the goal of minimizing the risks of future crises and improving the international community's response when they do occur.

These efforts have borne some fruit, albeit slowly and in piecemeal fashion. The IMF is strongly encouraging countries to disclose key information about their financial situation and hard-currency reserves on a timely basis, to minimize the chances of unsettling markets with shocking revelations. More than fifty countries have met a special standard the Fund has established on data dissemination. Separately, to help countries strengthen their banking systems, the Fund joined with the World Bank in a program that intensively surveys banks and regulatory systems in about two dozen countries a year and provides advice about how to reduce risks and vulnerabilities. Furthermore, Köhler created a new Capital Markets Department in the IMF as part of an initiative to spot early warning signs of crises. An additional innovation is the establishment of the IMF's Contingent Credit Line (CCL), available to countries with certifiably sound policies, ensuring that they can obtain emergency loans quickly if a speculative attack should occur.

But nobody pretends that these steps amount to anything very sweeping. (In the first three and a half years of the CCL's existence, not a single country signed up for the insurance it supposedly provided.) The IMF has floated one radical proposal (more on that shortly), but in the meantime the system's basic vulnerabilities remain, and the smart money is betting that the only changes likely to be implemented soon will be cosmetic—an interior decorating job instead of new architecture, to cite a favorite metaphor of the skeptics. Now that O'Neill has been discharged, the responsibility for proving the skeptics wrong will weigh heavily on his successor, John Snow, and his administration colleagues as they exercise Washington's traditional leadership role in the international community.

Among the bailouts that failed in the late 1990s, two shining exceptions stand out, and they provide a beacon to guide the architects of the new system. One is the second rescue of South Korea on Christmas Eve 1997, and the other is the second rescue of Brazil in March 1999. Those two—call them Korea II and Brazil II—worked brilliantly at bringing the countries in question back from the brink.

One explanation for these positive outcomes, favored by some of the folks from the Rubin-era Treasury Department and the IMF, is that it was mainly a function of the countries implementing the conditions pledged in their Fund programs. Korea, under its newly elected President Kim Dae Jung, showed a determination to reform the country's economic system; and Brazil, under its new central banker Arminio Fraga, showed a determination to maintain a disciplined monetary policy. Accordingly, once the markets perceived a change in the countries' policies, confidence rapidly returned—or so the theory goes—especially by comparison with what happened in Indonesia and Russia, where reforms were resisted. Thailand's turnaround in early 1998 following the accession of a new, more reform-minded government is offered as further proof of this theory.

This argument should not be dismissed lightly; a crisis-stricken country that shows little sign of changing its economic policies, or of living up to its promises, isn't going to instill confidence in investors or lenders, no matter how great the support it gets from the international community. The old cliché about how "you can't help someone who isn't willing to help himself" applies to countries as well as people.

Yet a fair reading of the evidence does not support the view that IMF programs have worked when they were faithfully implemented by the countries' authorities but have failed when they weren't. The rescues of Thailand and Indonesia began souring even before the authorities had the chance to demonstrate a lack of fidelity to Fund conditions. And the first rescues of Korea and Brazil went sour mainly for reasons unrelated to the authorities' adherence to the terms of their programs. Likewise, the flop of the IMF's Russian program, though no doubt due in part to the clear inability of the country's reformers to deliver, was also attributable to problems associated with the Goldman, Sachs exchange offer.

So what made Korea II and Brazil II successful where the others failed? The most crucial common factor was surely the bailing-in of the countries' private creditors. In both crises, the High Command finally intervened—more heavy-handedly in the Korean case, less so in the Brazilian episode—to confront the Electronic Herd and constrain its members from acting in a manner destructive of the countries' well-being and that of the global financial system (not to mention the Herd's collective self-interest). It is no coincidence that private-sector involvement was a major element in the rescues that ended triumphantly, whereas it was absent (or instituted too late or half-heartedly) in the rescues that fizzled. Bail-ins were thus beneficial from the standpoint of justice, in the sense that taxpayer funds were kept from flowing into the pockets of the undeserving rich; and also from the standpoint of welfare, in the sense that financial stampedes were halted.

That lesson, among all that should be learned from the crises of the 1990s, ranks near the top in importance. Global capital markets have gotten so huge, so unruly, and so panic-prone that the High Command can be easily overwhelmed when crises arise, and this is especially true if the High Command's response is confined to large loan packages and demands for economic reforms in the country involved.

Two prescriptions naturally follow from this diagnosis. First, actions should be taken to cull the short-termers among the Electronic Herd, to reduce the sheer volume of their inflows and outflows in developing countries and thereby reduce the likelihood and intensity of crises. The most sensible measure in this regard is for developing countries to tax foreign capital that flows in for relatively brief periods, as Chile has done during times when such capital is abundant. Second, when the short-termers are bolting, the High Command should be bolder in corralling them. That means aggressively formulating bail-in schemes that induce investors and lenders to stop panicky withdrawals of money, and require them to bear a fair share of the burden for ending crises.

The first of these proposals is relatively straightforward, but the second is far easier said than done, because global capital markets are not only much larger than they used to be; they're also more complex. The Korea II and Brazil II rescues were possible because both countries (Korea in particular) had such a large proportion of their foreign debt in the form of bank loans, and the High Command was able to round up the bankers and pressure them to keep their money in those countries. But in recent years, many emerging-market countries have obtained substantial amounts of capital from overseas in the form of bonds or other securities, whose owners—as noted in the case of Russian GKOs—number in the thousands and are not amenable to being ordered around. Indeed, their securities are often subject to U.S. laws that give them the right to file lawsuits and block changes in repayment terms.

The bad news is, there's no simple way to corral the Electronic Herd in these instances. This is the thorniest, most contentious issue in the debate over the new architecture. According to one line of argument, it is best not even to try resolving it systematically, because that approach involves risks to the smooth functioning of global finance. The fear is that if the High Command becomes too assertive in restricting outflows of capital or forcing members of the Herd to accept slower or lower paybacks, the Herd will shrink from supplying funds to emerging markets, and it will flee countries at the first sign of trouble.

In his book *The Lexus and the Olive Tree,* Tom Friedman presents the case against allowing the High Command to use a stronger hand in taming the Herd's excesses. The Herd not only provides capital that helps countries to grow, Friedman argues; it also disciplines them into adopting good policies because governments have learned that sticking with their old ways—cronyism and poorly supervised banking systems, for example—may subject them to the Herd's bru-tal treatment. Although the Herd often "overreacts and overshoots" by first swamping countries with capital and then abandoning them in a flash, it always returns in the end to countries with sound fun-damentals, Friedman contends, so "globalization did us all a favor" by melting down the economies of Asia, Russia, and Brazil, "because it laid bare a lot of rotten practices and institutions." He also argues against putting a little "sand in the gears" to slow the global move-ment of hot money: "I don't think it is ever very wise to put sand in the gears of a machine when you barely know where the gears are. If you put sand in the gears of such a fast, lubricated, stainless-steel machine, it might not slow down. It could come to a screeching, metal-bending halt."

One doesn't have to be anticapitalism, or antiglobalization, to find this sort of faith in markets to be inordinate. The "longhorns" within the Herd—the Nikes, the Hewlett-Packards, and other multi-nationals that build factories abroad—may indeed confer the bless-ings of resources and technology, but the fact remains that when the "shorthorns," or financial investors and lenders, become too ebul-lient about a country, the excessive amounts of capital they inject may lull the political leadership into ignoring festering problems rather than addressing them. A government basking in the glow of market optimism over its nation's prospects is unlikely to bother fixing underlying weaknesses in the economy. This was clearly a major part of what went wrong in Thailand and Russia in particular.

As for what happens when the shorthorns' sentiment suddenly turns negative, the human cost of the recent slew of crises is reason enough to question whether the result "did us all a favor." Even if the Thais, Koreans, and others ultimately gained by having their countries' rotten practices and institutions exposed, the phenomenon of contagion offers yet another compelling reason for doubting the wisdom of leaving global capital markets unfettered. Consider the fact that, thanks to the Herd's whims, Hong Kong suffered a sharp recession in 1999 as a result of the global financial crisis. Hong Kong wasn't a bastion of rottenness; its financial system enjoyed a reputation as one of the cleanest and best-run on earth, but its authorities were obliged to keep interest rates painfully high because currency speculators were betting that the Hong Kong dollar would follow the Thai baht, the Indonesian rupiah, and other neighboring countries' currencies down the drain. Or consider the fact that the United States came so close to falling prey to the contagion of 1998. Doesn't that suggest that, at the very least, we should be searching hard for some appropriate places in the gears of the global financial system to sprinkle some sand?

Some ideas for fixing the international financial architecture involve much more than sand-sprinkling. The most noteworthy of these include the following:

1. *Abolish the IMF.* This may sound like the mantra of antiglobalization protesters, but it is also a prescription put forward by a number of prominent conservatives, including former Secretary of State and Treasury George Shultz. For anyone who yearns to see the Electronic Herd get its just deserts, the idea of a no-IMF world has its charms. Without an IMF, if a country runs out of hard currency, its

foreign creditors would be forced to accept whatever they could get in negotiations or lawsuits. If the foreign creditors weren't satisfied, they could refuse to extend additional hard currency. In theory, everyone would take extra care to avoid a crisis, knowing how disastrous the consequences would be. Government officials would run more prudent economic policies, and the Herd would be more vigilant about where its money goes.

But is the world truly prepared to stand by while countries go bust—especially important ones? For Byeon Yang Ho and Lee Kyung Shik, the Korean officials who explained that default was an unacceptable option because of the long-lasting damage it would inflict on their country's ability to obtain credit for essential imports, a no-IMF world would have no charms at all. Without the IMF, a country in Korea's position in late 1997 would be out of luck.

And is the world truly prepared to stand by while the dogs of financial contagion run wild? After Russia went under, turmoil spread quickly in part because of the conclusions of investors like David Tepper that the world's safety net had been shredded. If Russia could be allowed to default, so might Mexico, Brazil, and other countries. The mere existence of a strong, active IMF can limit the transmission of crisis conditions from one country to another—maybe not wholly effectively but at least to some extent.

The events of autumn 1998, moreover, showed that the entire global economy may be at risk when contagion flares. That the world survived does not mean that the systemic risk some policymakers perceived was merely a figment of their imaginations. Even if they overestimated it—and they may well have done so—the episode suggests that we ignore such risks at our peril.

In response to those who would terminate the IMF for all its mistakes and helplessness in the face of crises, Alan Greenspan has an illuminating way of looking at this issue: He has likened the IMF to a Model T—a "Tin Lizzie"—and observed that given the choice between a Tin Lizzie and no vehicular conveyance at all, the Tin Lizzie is worth keeping. A sleek new sports car would obviously be preferable, but if we're stuck with the Tin Lizzie, a garage with some good auto mechanics might be a better place to take her than the junkyard.

2. *Since abolition is impractical, truncate the IMF severely.* This option was proposed by the majority on a congressionally appointed panel headed by conservative economist Allan Meltzer. The panel's plan, advanced in March 2000, has gained many adherents among Republicans on Capitol Hill and holds appeal for some Bush administration officials as well. The Meltzer Commission would drastically change the nature of IMF programs in two ways. First, loans would go only to countries that prequalified for an IMF seal of approval—those that had met various criteria of sound economic policy, including adherence to prudential banking standards that ensure that banks are maintaining sufficient capital. Second, the Fund wouldn't impose policy conditions when it made loans, since it would have determined in advance whether a country qualified. One advantage of such an approach is that the IMF would generate less overall moral hazard; the Electronic Herd would presumably think long and hard before lending or investing in a country that didn't have the seal of approval. Countries would also have a strong incentive to improve their policies so that they could qualify for the Fund's endorsement. Furthermore, the IMF could stop worrying about scrambling to determine the best economic policies for crisis-stricken countries to follow.

But here's the downside. Suppose the IMF had to drop a country from the list of prequalifiers; imagine how fast a crisis would erupt in that country in response to the Fund's signal that the country's authorities were adopting irresponsible policies. In addition, there are good reasons to doubt that the international community could restrain itself from lending to countries that had failed to prequalify. South Korea and Brazil presumably wouldn't have prequalified, yet the pressure to lend to them was overwhelming, and it would be a sure bet that if such important countries suffered crises, the international community would find a way to mobilize rescues and circumvent the Meltzer rules, undermining their credibility.

3. *Return to Bretton Woods.* Still other reformers favor moving toward a system in which currencies are fixed the way they used to be, or are stabilized much more than they are now, or are reduced in number. Indeed, the world is awash in proposals for steadying currencies, linking them, or merging them. Some Asian officials, for example, have suggested the creation of an Asian currency unit that would rival the euro. Many Latin American economic policymakers have seriously weighed adopting the U.S. dollar as an official currency of their countries. (Ecuador, El Salvador, and Guatemala recently went through with it.) French and Japanese officials, meanwhile, have touted plans for a pact among the G-7 that would eliminate "excessive volatility" among the dollar, the euro, and the yen. The impulse behind these proposals is a perfectly understandable unease about the impact of currency swings on the world's economic health and the crises that sometimes ensue.

Carefully calibrated exchange rates aren't worth the cost for most countries, however, because they often require governments to take actions that make no sense domestically. A classic illustration is the case of a country (like the United States in 1995 or Japan in 1998) where the currency is weakening at the same time as the economy is softening; to attract investors and keep the currency within bounds, the central bank would have to raise interest rates—precisely the opposite of what should be done to fight recessionary forces. This helps explain why Bob Rubin, for one, sees no viable alternative to the world's present currency regime. "To paraphrase Winston Churchill's famous statement about democracy," Rubin said in a speech in 1999, "the floating exchange-rate system is the worst possible system, except for all others."

As for currency unions such as Europe's, there are ample grounds for skepticism that they would work in Asia or the Western Hemisphere. Creating a currency union means that a supranational central bank decides when to print money, when to lower interest rates to combat recessions, and when to raise them to curb inflation. The

Euroland countries have agreed to such an arrangement as the crowning step in their effort to bind themselves together and avert the strife that has afflicted their continent for centuries. But to reach that point, they have spent the better part of fifty years making their economic structures and policies as similar as possible; the deal won't hold together if, say, recession-bound Spaniards are screaming for easy money while inflation-wary Germans want to keep money tight. The economies of Asia and the Western Hemisphere are far more disparate and less integrated.

The bull—or rather, the Electronic Herd—must be taken by the horns if the global financial system is to undergo change that is meaningful, effective, and sensible. That is, the High Command must have the means to involve the private sector in a more systematic way when crises arise. Top economic policymakers and the IMF's official governing bodies have issued much rhetoric about their determination to bail in private creditors; as long ago as 1996, the finance ministers of wealthy countries, including Rubin, warned in a joint report that neither bankers nor bondholders should expect official money to save them from incurring losses on their overseas loans. To give force to those words, something more daring is in order.

Anne Krueger is not the sort of person who would seem likely to spearhead a plan calling for greater government intervention in markets. At sixty-seven, Krueger, a short-haired woman quite capable of stating her views bluntly, was the Bush administration's choice to succeed Stan Fischer as the IMF's first deputy managing director in September 2001. Her conservative credentials were impeccable: As a professor at Stanford, she was a senior fellow at the Hoover Institution, a think tank teeming with former Reagan administration officials and leading intellects of free-market economics. During a stint as chief economist of the World Bank from 1982 to 1986, Krueger had played a key role in shifting the institution's ideology sharply to the right, toward a much greater emphasis than before on open trade, privatization, and deregulation.

Thus, many of her fellow economists were dumbstruck when Krueger in a late November 2001 speech proposed that the IMF should move toward adopting a new approach to financial crises by creating a sort of international bankruptcy procedure. The plan would fill what Krueger called a "gaping hole" in the international financial system by giving crisis-stricken, overly indebted countries a means to block panicky investors and lenders from withdrawing their money and to provide an orderly process for working out debts. For the Fund, which had historically frowned on measures restricting the flow of capital across international borders, the proposal was a radical departure.

"Our model is one of a domestic bankruptcy court," Krueger said in her speech, although "it could not operate exactly like that." This was music to the ears of many experts—most notably Jeff Sachs, who had been arguing for years that nations sometimes need protection from their creditors just as companies and people do. After all, a bankruptcy court can grant multiple protective measures to a financially troubled company whose bankers and bondholders are snatching every dollar available and refusing new credit. Filing for protection with the court brings the "grab race" to a halt, thereby giving the firm breathing space while it negotiates new and more realistic terms for repaying its debts; and a court decree can enable the firm to obtain the cash it needs to continue operating, by guaranteeing that new loans will be repaid ahead of old loans. However, no such court exists at the international level to aid countries on the brink of default. Countries that unilaterally default risk becoming embroiled in destructive wrangles with the Herd, whose members may refuse to extend new credit for a long time and seek legal redress by seizing the country's overseas assets.

Under Krueger's plan, called the Sovereign Debt Restructuring Mechanism (SDRM), the IMF could call a halt to a run on a country whose government had become so burdened with debt as to cause the markets to stampede. In effect, the Fund would be sanctioning the country's decision to suspend payments to foreigners and impose controls on outflows of capital. The country would have to ask the Fund first, of course, and show that it was prepared to correct problems with its economic fundamentals and negotiate in good faith with its creditors.

Just as in Korea's second rescue, the creditors would be roped into a standstill temporarily abrogating their right to collect interest and principal. This cooling-off period would allow creditors to gather their wits, the country's authorities to devise a sensible plan of action, and all parties to begin an orderly process for deciding how claims will be repaid. The procedure could also induce new financing for the country by providing assurance that any loans made after the commencement of the standstill would be treated as senior to all preexisting private claims. Once an agreement was struck for debt repayment—which might well involve reduction of principal and lower interest than the creditors were initially entitled to—all creditors would be bound to honor the terms negotiated, provided they agreed by supermajority vote representing, say, three-quarters of the principal amount of the debt.

Krueger's SDRM had a number of other complex wrinkles, which needn't be spelled out here, but one point is essential to understand: To make the whole scheme work, the world's nations would have to agree collectively to make legal changes that would run roughshod over the claims of some creditors. That is because many bondholders have the right to insist on full repayment of their individual claims, especially when their bonds are issued under U.S. law. Typically, such bonds require the unanimous consent of all bondholders to changes in payment terms, which means that "rogue creditors" can hold out for full repayment regardless of what the others are willing to accept.

The rogue-creditor scenario is not merely hypothetical. As Krueger pointed out in her speech, when the Peruvian government was negotiating a debt restructuring plan with its creditors during the late 1990s, a New York "vulture fund" named Elliott Associates that had bought Peruvian bonds at distressed prices filed suit demanding full payment and won a court judgment in 2000 giving it the right to attach certain Peruvian assets deposited abroad. Krueger's proposal was designed to overcome that loophole while still preserving basic creditor rights; a supermajority vote would bind all creditors to a restructuring of the debt. (Likewise, in corporate bankruptcy law, judges typically have the power to force all creditors to comply with the new terms accepted by the majority.)

Though loaded with technical jargon, Krueger's speech ended on what passes for a rousing note by an IMF official:

> Some approach along these lines would serve the causes of better crisis prevention and better crisis management simultaneously, to the benefit of debtors, creditors and the international community. The political imponderable is whether our members are prepared to constrain the ability of their citizens to pursue foreign governments through their national courts as an investment in a more stable—and therefore more prosperous—world economy.

With few exceptions, the Herd's reaction to the proposed SDRM ranged from strongly negative to highly outraged. That was unsurprising: Bankers, fund managers, and other financial executives recoil at the threat of having their rights impaired. In speeches, seminars, and letters to the IMF and G-7, members of the financial community denounced Krueger's plan as certain to increase the chances that countries would renege on their obligations—and thus certain to cause a serious reduction in the amount of capital flowing to emerging markets. Upon hearing that borrowing from the Herd would likely become more difficult and costly, many government officials in emerging markets also declared their opposition to the plan, even though it was supposed to benefit their people.

These objections were based on legitimate concerns. Abrogating contracts—the covenants that govern borrowers' obligations to pay interest and principal on loans and bonds—is no trifling matter, and if creditors' rights are weakened too much, credit will cease to flow or become prohibitively expensive. To cite a simple example, home-buyers would not benefit if the law were changed to prevent banks from foreclosing on people defaulting on their mortgages; banks merely would stop lending on homes.

But SDRM proponents offered compelling answers to these objections. Under the plan, countries could not cavalierly renounce their debts; as Krueger put it in her speech: "It would be ridiculous to argue that our approach would make restructuring an easy option. I would not support it if it did—countries, like anyone else, should pay their debts as long as they are able to do so." Signing on to the SDRM would be unpleasant and thus presumably rare. A country using it would incur damage to its creditworthiness (though in theory not as much as if it unilaterally defaulted), and it would have to submit to the rigors of an IMF program.

As for the concern about a drying-up of money flowing to emerging markets, consider what happened to Malaysia after it shocked the global establishment by imposing capital controls in September 1998. Despite the dire predictions of officials in the U.S. Treasury and the IMF, who thought Malaysia would pay grievously for its transgression, the country subsequently performed well economically; indeed, less than a year after instituting controls, the Malaysian government was able to tap international markets for a major bond issue. Global financiers, in other words, often would be willing to overlook infringements on the sanctity of property and provide funds when they spotted profitable opportunities. And even if the SDRM put a damper on their eagerness to invest in emerging markets, it would be no tragedy if they provided less capital, or charged more for it, than they did during the mid-1990s.

The Herd wields formidable political clout, probably enough to kill legislation in Congress that would effectuate the legal changes envisioned under Krueger's proposal. Partly to soften the bankers' opposition, Krueger agreed to dilute her plan somewhat, with some of the main concessions coming in the standstill provision, which was a particularly contentious element. First she proposed that standstills could be extended past three months only if approved by a supermajority of creditors. Later an IMF staff paper spelled out plans for an SDRM that entirely abandoned the idea of a formal stay on creditor litigation. Dropping that element, Krueger and her colleagues concluded, wouldn't substantially weaken the plan, thanks to other protections from creditors that the SDRM affords. Rogue creditors would be unlikely to pursue costly and time-consuming litigation for full repayment of their claims, Fund officials reasoned, because the reward for filing a lawsuit might well be zero if a debt restructuring plan won supermajority approval, binding rogue creditors to the same terms as everybody else.

The Herd has remained implacable, notwithstanding these concessions and counterarguments. In a joint statement issued in December 2002, major associations representing international banks, securities firms, and fund managers declared: "No changes in any specific aspects of the SDRM would alter [our] serious concerns about the proposal."

John Taylor is not the sort of person who would seem likely to cross swords with Anne Krueger. The mild-mannered Taylor was a colleague of Krueger's at Stanford and the Hoover Institution, and as Treasury undersecretary for international affairs, he played a role in her selection as the IMF's second in command. But in a speech delivered at the Institute for International Economics in April 2002, Taylor gave the strong impression that he was bringing the full weight of the U.S. government to bear against Krueger's plan, when he advanced a different, less potent bankruptcy proposal that has won support, albeit grudging, from the Herd. The episode sparked ill will between the Treasury and the IMF, which was quickly papered over with public statements that both ideas could move forward on "separate tracks."

Taylor's plan involved no centralized official action to override creditors' rights. Instead, international lenders and the countries they financed would voluntarily agree to insert provisions called "collective action clauses" (CACs) into the contracts of bonds issued by national governments. The CACs would specify procedures for what would happen in the event of a crisis, allowing a supermajority of bondholders, rather than 100 percent, to approve a standstill or debt restructuring if such actions proved necessary. This "decentralized approach," Taylor contended, "makes much more sense and is much more workable" than Krueger's plan.

CACs seemed such an excellent idea in principle that the finance ministers of wealthy countries first urged the governments of developing nations in 1996 to incorporate them into their bond contracts. But nobody followed up, because in practice CACs have some drawbacks. First, emerging-market officials have shied from issuing bonds with CACs, fearing that Wall Street would demand higher interest rates to compensate for the reduction in individual bondholder rights. Second, and more important, the clauses wouldn't provide much immediate benefit because of what might be called the "overhang" issue: Many old-style bonds—that is, those with clauses requiring unanimous approval for changes in payment terms—remain outstanding and won't mature for a number of years. Thus, even if all newly issued bonds contained CACs, using them to provide the option of orderly debt restructuring for countries would still be a distant dream.

In sum, words like "thorny" and "contentious" (which were used previously to describe the issue of how to corral an Electronic Herd that includes bondholders) may understate the difficulties involved. Clearly, agreeing on the principle that the private sector ought to be bailed in when crises occur, and that an alternative to big bailouts and default is needed, is much easier than devising a method for accomplishing those goals.

In fact, another huge drawback afflicts both the SDRM and CAC proposals. Since they apply only to debt issued by national governments, they don't address the sorts of crises that struck Thailand, Indonesia, and Korea, where the problematic debt was issued by private companies and banks.

Tempting as it may be for policymakers to throw up their hands in the face of these complexities, such a response would be shameful. Too many years have already passed with no major alteration in the international financial architecture. If the international community is serious about limiting the damage from the sorts of crises that so cruelly reverse the progress of countries striving to reach advanced stages of development, and if the U.S. government in particular is serious about repudiating the endless cycle of IMF bailouts, then an international bankruptcy regime is essential, however imperfect it may be. Implementing both the SDRM and CAC proposals, or something very much like them, would represent a major step in that direction. But both plans need strengthening and broader scope.

Professor Peter Kenen of Princeton University has proposed an ingenious variant of CACs, which he calls "a comprehensive contractual approach." All new standardized debt contracts—private-sector as well as those of sovereign governments—would have to include CACs. Furthermore, in the event of a crisis, the clauses would automatically provide for three-month standstills if the government of the country in question declared a financial emergency and the IMF certified that judgment. Nations of the world would obviously have to enact laws requiring such clauses, and to spur them to do so, Kenen proposed in an article published in 2002 that countries failing to adopt the necessary legislation "after, say, a five-year period" would be penalized by suffering a cut in their access to IMF loans.

Kenen's plan represents solid architecture, not interior decoration. But given the urgency of the problem, as demonstrated by Latin America's travails, why give countries five years to change their laws? Why not require a time frame of one or two years? And why not deal with the overhang problem of CACs by mandating new laws that would declare null and void the existing bond provisions requiring unanimous approval for changes in payment terms?

The Herd, and many emerging-market governments as well, can be expected to fight such measures tooth and nail. The finance ministers of emerging markets want to borrow plenty of money cheaply to fund their governments' current activities; the Herd wants to supply that money; and they won't look kindly on legal changes that might spoil their game. Only vigorous and determined U.S. leadership could possibly overcome the opposition. So far, the Bush administration has shown scant signs of being inclined to take up the cudgels.

In other words, far-reaching change in the international financial architecture is a long shot. By the time this book is published, the SDRM may be dead politically; the IMF's policy-setting committee is scheduled to consider a formal proposal at the spring 2003 IMF–World Bank meetings, and earlier in the year bankers were voicing confidence that support for the SDRM was fading fast. But perhaps the powers in Washington will yet come around, for the radical options must be evaluated on a "compared-with-what" basis, against the alternatives of more large bailouts or unilateral defaults—neither of which should appeal to policymakers concerned about both shunning moral hazard and sustaining economic growth.

There can be no excuse for ignoring the implications of what happened during the late 1990s. The current institutions and mechanisms safeguarding the global system are dangerously weak, and boldness is warranted in shoring up the system's defenses before catastrophe strikes anew. Deservedly chastened by those events, the High Command must now choose the lessons it will draw. The health of the world economy depends, in substantial measure, on how that chastening is translated into action.

NOTES

Except where noted here, the information in this book was derived from interviews. Some of the people interviewed were willing to be quoted by name, whereas others felt comfortable speaking candidly only if assured a cloak of anonymity—indeed, many were promised, in accord with "deep background" rules, that they would not be quoted even anonymously unless they granted me permission to do so.

A list of interviewees follows. People interviewed on deep background were asked permission to be included on the list. The list does not include a number of people who wished to remain entirely anonymous. Titles are those held during the crisis of the 1990s or during the period covered by the interview.

INTERNATIONAL MONETARY FUND

Stanley Fischer, First Deputy Managing Director

Executive Board

Karin Lissakers, United States
Yukio Yoshimura, Japan
Bernd Esdar, Germany
Gus O'Donnell, United Kingdom
Onno Wijnholds, Netherlands (and 11 other countries)
Aleksei Mozhin, Russia
Greg Taylor, Australia (and 13 other countries)

Policy Development and Review Department

Jack Boorman, Director
Matthew Fisher, Division Chief, Capital Account Issues Division
David Burton, Senior Adviser
Robert Kahn, Senior Economist

Research Department

Michael Mussa, Director (and Economic Counsellor)

IMF Institute

Mohsin Khan, Director

Asia and Pacific Department

Hubert Neiss, Director
Bijan Aghevli, Deputy Director
Anoop Singh, Deputy Director
Wanda Tseng, Deputy Director
Charles Adams, Assistant Director
David Robinson, Division Chief for Thailand
John Dodsworth, Senior Resident Representative for India
Kadhim Al-Eyd, Senior Resident Representative for Indonesia
Sharmini Coorey, Assistant to the Director
Mahmood Pradhan, Senior Desk Economist, Indonesia

European II Department

John Odling-Smee, Director
Yusuke Horiguchi, Deputy Director
Daniel Citrin, Division Chief for Russia
Martin Gilman, Senior Resident Representative for Russia
Thomas Richardson, Resident Representative for Russia

Western Hemisphere Department

Claudio Loser, Director
Teresa Ter-Minassian, Deputy Director

Monetary and Exchange Affairs Department

Peter Hayward, Financial Sector Adviser
Peter Dattels, Deputy Division Chief, Financial Institutions and Markets
   Division

External Relations Department

Thomas Dawson, Director
Roberto Brauning
Vasuki Shastry

UNITED STATES GOVERNMENT

Treasury Department

Robert Rubin, Secretary
Lawrence Summers, Deputy Secretary (G-7 Deputy)
David Lipton, Undersecretary for International Affairs
Timothy Geithner, Assistant Secretary/Undersecretary for International Affairs
Daniel Zelikow, Deputy Assistant Secretary for Asia, the Americas and Africa
Caroline Atkinson, Senior Deputy Assistant Secretary for International
    Monetary and Financial Policy
Gary Gensler, Assistant Secretary for Financial Markets
Michael Froman, Chief of Staff
Robert Boorstin, Senior Adviser to the Secretary
Howard Schloss, Assistant Secretary for Public Affairs

Federal Reserve Board

Alice Rivlin, Vice Chairman
Laurence Meyer, Governor
Edwin Truman, Director, Division of International Finance (also Assistant
    Secretary of the Treasury for International Affairs)
Charles Siegman, Senior Associate Director, Division of International Finance
Larry Promisel, Senior Adviser, Division of International Finance

Federal Reserve Bank of New York

William McDonough, President
Peter Fisher, Executive Vice President
Terrence Checki, Executive Vice President

White House

James Steinberg, Deputy National Security Adviser
Sandra Kristoff, Senior Director for Asian Affairs, National Security Council
Gene Sperling, Director, National Economic Council
Daniel Tarullo, Assistant to the President for International Economic Policy
Lael Brainard, Deputy Assistant to the President for International Economics
W. Bowman Cutter, Deputy Assistant to the President for Economic Policy
Alan Blinder, Member, Council of Economic Advisers (also Vice Chairman,
    Federal Reserve Board)

State Department

Stuart Eizenstat, Undersecretary for Economic, Business and Agricultural
    Affairs
Stapleton Roy, Ambassador to Indonesia
Michael Owens, Minister-Counselor, U.S. Embassy, Jakarta

Walter Mondale, special presidential envoy to Indonesia
Thomas Graham, Chief Political Analyst, U.S. Embassy, Moscow

Commerce Department

David Rothkopf, Deputy Undersecretary for International Trade

Export-Import Bank

James Harmon, President

WORLD BANK

Mark Malloch Brown, Vice President, External Affairs
Joseph Stiglitz, Vice President and Chief Economist
Dennis de Tray, Resident Representative for Indonesia
James Hanson, Lead Economist, East Asia Dept. IV, based in Indonesia
Stijn Claessens, Lead Economist, Financial Strategy and Policy Group
Brian Pinto, Lead Economist, Poverty Reduction and Economic Management
     Department, Europe and Central Asia Region
Lloyd Kenward, Senior Economist, Indonesian Resident Mission
John Nellis, Private Sector Specialist
David Ellerman, Economic Adviser to the Chief Economist

GROUP OF SEVEN GOVERNMENTS

Great Britain

Mervyn King, Deputy Governor, Bank of England
David Peretz, G7 Financial Sous-Sherpa
Ed Balls, Economic Adviser to the Chancellor of the Exchequer

France

Jean-Claude Trichet, Governor, Bank of France
Dominique Strauss-Kahn, Minister of Economy, Finance and Industry
Jean Lemierre, Director of the Treasury (G-7 Deputy)

Germany

Jürgen Stark, State Secretary, Finance Ministry (G-7 Deputy)
Klaus Regling, State Secretary, Finance Ministry (G-7 Deputy)
Heiner Flassbeck, State Secretary, Finance Ministry (G-7 Deputy)

Japan

Eisuke Sakakibara, Vice Minister of Finance for International Affairs (G-7
     Deputy)
Haruhiko Kuroda, Director-General, International Finance Bureau, Ministry of
     Finance

Canada

Paul Martin, Minister of Finance
Ian Bennett, Associate Deputy Minister (G-7 Deputy)

CRISIS COUNTRY GOVERNMENTS

Thailand

Kleo-Thong Hetrakul, Director, Economic Research Department, Bank of Thailand

Indonesia

Sudradjad Djiwandono, Governor, Bank Indonesia
Saleh Afiff, Coordinating Minister for Economic Affairs

South Korea

Kang Kyung Shik, Minister of Finance and Economy
Byeon Yang Ho, Director for Policy Coordination, Ministry of Finance and Economy
Oh Jong Nam, Director, International Economic Policy Division, Ministry of Finance and Economy
Lee Kyung Shik, Governor, Bank of Korea
Cho Sung Jong, Deputy Director, International Department, Bank of Korea
Shin Hyun Chul, Director, International Relations Office, Bank of Korea
Kim Ki Hwan, Ambassador at Large for Economic Affairs

Russia

Mikhail Zadornov, Minister of Finance
Oleg Vyugin, Deputy Minister of Finance
Sergei Vasiliev, Chief of Staff
Sergei Dubinin, Chairman, Central Bank of Russia
Sergei Alexashenko, Deputy Chairman, Central Bank of Russia

Brazil

Fernando Henrique Cardoso, President
Pedro Malan, Minister of Finance
Arminio Fraga, President, Central Bank of Brazil
Amaury Bier, Secretary for Economic Policy, Ministry of Finance

PRIVATE SECTOR

Charles Blitzer, Donaldson, Lufkin, & Jenrette
Peter Boone, Brunswick Warburg (Moscow)
Al Breach, Goldman Sachs (Moscow)
David Folkerts-Landau, Deutsche Bank

Quentin Marshall, UBS Warburg
Roland Nash, MFK Renaissance (Moscow)
Heather Neale, Salomon Smith Barney
John Purcell, Salomon Smith Barney
William Rhodes, Citicorp
Jeffrey Shafer, Salomon Smith Barney
George Soros, Soros Fund Management
Ernest Stern, J.P. Morgan
David Tepper, Appaloosa Management

ACADEMICS, OTHER EXPERTS

Anders Aslund, Carnegie Endowment for International Peace
Choi Inbom, Institute for International Economics
Michael Dooley, University of California-Santa Cruz
Barry Eichengreen, University of California-Berkeley
Greg Fager, Institute of International Finance
Clifford Gaddy, Brookings Institution
Morris Goldstein, Institute for International Economics
Steve Hanke, The Johns Hopkins University (adviser to Indonesian
    government)
Gary Hufbauer, Institute for International Economics
Peter Kenen, Princeton University
Catherine Mann, Institute for International Economics
Pendarell ("Pen") Kent, former Executive Director, Bank of England (adviser to
    Indonesian government)
Steven Radelet, Harvard University
Carmen Reinhart, University of Maryland
Jeffrey Sachs, Harvard University
Makoto Utsumi, Keio University
Paul Volcker, former Federal Reserve Board chairman (adviser to Indonesian
    government)
John Williamson, Institute for International Economics

CHAPTER ONE: THE COMMITTEE TO SAVE THE WORLD

Many of the facts and conclusions in this chapter are drawn from material cited in later chapters, particularly Chapters 5 and 7 where I explore the Korean crisis in greater detail.

Page 1: Details concerning Hubert Neiss's career and education come from IMF news release, "IMF Sets Organization and Senior Staff Changes," December 6, 1996, published on the IMF website, www.imf.org.

Page 7: Details on Korea's program come from documents published on the IMF website, including "IMF Approves SDR 15.5 Billion Stand-by Credit for Korea," news release, December 4, 1997.

The $55 billion "headline" figure of the program rose in the days immediately following the announcement to as much as $60 billion as additional wealthy countries pledged contributions.

Camdessus's quotes are contained in IMF news brief, "Camdessus Welcomes Conclusion of Talks with Korea on IMF Program," December 3, 1997, available on the IMF website; and in David Holley, "South Korea, IMF Finalize $55-billion Bailout Plan," *Los Angeles Times*, December 4, 1997.

Page 10: I thank David Rothkopf for the analogy between the IMF's rescues and well-trained orthopedic surgeons trying to cure a ward of patients suffering emotional breakdowns.

Page 11: The *Time* story "The Committee to Save the World" was published February 15, 1999.

Page 15: I am grateful to Thomas Dawson, director of the IMF's External Relations Department, for permitting me to cite him as the source of the anecdote about the IMF report on Vietnam, which he recalled from his days as U.S. executive director to the Fund.

Pages 16–17: Figures on cross-border transactions in securities come from the annual report of the Bank for International Settlements, June 8, 1998, available on the BIS website, www.bis.org. Figures on private flows to emerging markets come from data supplied by the IMF's Research Department. Figures on the IMF's war chest are based on the Fund's "usable resources," consisting of hard currencies contributed by member countries, including resources that have been committed in IMF programs, but excluding the IMF's gold. The figures are on the IMF's website.

CHAPTER 2: OPENING THE SPIGOT

Pages 19–20: The information about the number of economists who join the IMF each year was supplied by Mohsin Khan of the IMF Institute. The figures on the numbers of staff, staff nationalities, and salaries come from the IMF's 2002 Annual Report.

The salaries of U.S. citizens on the IMF staff are subject to tax the same as those of other Americans; however, the Fund provides them with substantial supplements to their salaries so that their after-tax earnings are comparable to those of staffers from other nations.

Page 28: Laura Papi has returned to the IMF. Her quotes come from an interview she gave me for a newspaper article in *The Washington Post* during the time she was employed at a banking firm in London.

Pages 32–33: Information about Camdessus comes from his official biography published on the IMF website; and from Paul Lewis, "The New Man at the IMF," *The New York Times*, December 18, 1986; and George Graham, "Latin America Propels Camdessus to Top of IMF," *Financial Times*, December 19, 1986. The quote by Fischer about Camdessus irritating "every bloc of the Fund's membership," but "never all at once," is from Dow Jones News Service, "IMF Staff Bids Adieu to 'Master Politician' Camdessus," February 10, 2000. Camdessus's quote about being a "French socialist . . . [and] an ultra neoliberal Anglo-Saxon" is from his press conference September 30, 1999, as cited in a transcript compiled by Federal News Service.

Page 34: Figures on the voting shares of IMF member countries come from the IMF website.

Pages 36–38: Information about Harry Dexter White and the history of the IMF comes from David Rees, *Harry Dexter White: A Study in Paradox* (Coward, McCann, and Geoghegan, New York, 1973); Margaret Garritsen de Vries, *The IMF in a Changing World 1945–85* (International Monetary Fund, Washington, D.C., 1986); Lawrence J. McQuillan and Peter C. Montgomery, *The International Monetary Fund: Financial Medic to the World?* (Hoover Institution Press, Stanford, Calif., 1999); and James M. Boughton, "Harry Dexter White and the International Monetary Fund," *Finance and Development* (IMF, September 1998).

Pages 39–40: Information about Mark Mobius comes from his books *Passport to Profits* (Warner Books, New York, 1999) and *The Investor's Guide to Emerging Markets* (Pitman Publishing, London, 1996); and articles about him in the *Los Angeles Times*, May 13, 1997; *Sunday Telegraph*, June 8, 1997; *Toronto Star*, November 24, 1996; *Tampa Tribune*, December 25, 1996; and *Financial Post*, March 16, 1996. Information about the shareholder meeting at Roy Thompson Hall was reported by Kathryn Haines, "Templeton Growth Fund Meeting Attracts 8,000 Shareholders," Dow Jones News Service, July 18, 1996.

Page 40: The figures on the rapidly growing involvement of mutual funds in emerging markets come from "Private Market Financing for Developing Countries" (IMF, 1995), cited in Miles Kahler (ed.), *Capital Flows and Financial Crises* (Cornell University Press, Ithaca, N.Y., 1998), p. 165.

Pages 41–42: The figures on capital flows from rich countries to developed countries come from "Capital Flows to Emerging Market Economies," published by the Institute of International Finance, Washington, D.C.

Pages 42–43: Figures on the carry trade come from the IMF's "International Capital Markets Report," 1998, available on the IMF website.

Page 43: Information about Antoine Van Agtmael and the origin of the term "emerging markets" comes from Leslie P. Norton, "Emerging Again? The Father of Emerging-Markets Investing Has Been Through a Rough Patch," *Barron's*, September 16, 1996.

An extensive account of the craze of the 1820s in South American bonds and gold mining shares is contained in Edward Chancellor, *Devil Take the Hindmost: A History of Financial Speculation* (Farrar, Straus and Giroux, New York, 1999).

Pages 43–44: An account of the development of "emerging markets" in the nineteenth and twentieth centuries is contained in Barry Eichengreen and

Albert Fishlow, "Contending with Capital Flows: What Is Different About the 1990s?" in Kahler (ed.), *Capital Flows and Financial Crises*.

Pages 45–47: Biographical information on Larry Summers comes from Paul Blustein, "Something About Larry; Treasury's Famously Prickly Deputy Wears the Mantle of Heir Apparent—and a Smile," *The Washington Post*, March 14, 1999; also David Warsh, "Why Bush Named Dukakis' Economist to a Bully Pulpit," *The Boston Globe*, October 28, 1990; Rich Miller, "'This Is About Winning': Playing the Economics Game Treasury's No. 2 Leads the Charge When Battling Global Crises," *USA Today*, January 18, 1999; and John Cassidy, "The Triumphalist," *The New Yorker*, July 6, 1998.

Pages 49–50: Statement of the Interim Committee, Hong Kong, China, September 21, 1997; Address by the Managing Director to the Board of Governors of the IMF, September 23, 1997; both available on the IMF website.

CHAPTER 3: WINNIE THE POOH AND THE BIG SECRET

Background about Asia's economies and the origins of its crisis comes from the following sources, among others: Paul Krugman, *The Return of Depression Economics* (W. W. Norton & Co., New York, 1999); Stephan Haggard, *The Political Economy of the Asian Financial Crisis* (Institute for International Economics, Washington, D.C., 2000); Mark L. Clifford and Pete Engardio, *Meltdown* (Prentice-Hall, Englewood Cliffs, N.J., 2000); Morris Goldstein, *The Asian Financial Crisis: Causes, Cures, and Systemic Implications* (Institute for International Economics, Washington, D.C., 1998); William C. Hunter, George G. Kaufman, and Thomas H. Krueger (eds.), *The Asian Financial Crisis: Origins, Implications, and Solutions* (Kluwer Academic Publishers, Boston, 1999); Philippe F. Delhaise, *Asia in Crisis: The Implosion of the Banking and Finance Systems* (John Wiley & Sons [Asia] Ltd., 1998); Collum Henderson, *Asia Falling: Making Sense of the Asian Crisis and Its Aftermath* (BusinessWeek Books, 1998); Giancarlo Corsetti, Paolo Pesenti, and Nouriel Roubini, "What Caused the Asian Currency and Financial Crisis?" (published on Roubini's homepage concerning the crisis, http://www.stern.nyu.edu/~nroubini/asia/Asia-Homepage.html); Nicholas D. Kristof and Sheryl WuDunn, *Thunder from the East: Portrait of a Rising Asia* (Alfred A. Knopf, New York, 2000); and Kahler (ed.), *Capital Flows and Financial Crises*.

Also extremely helpful are several IMF publications: Carl-Johan Lindgren et al., "Financial-Sector Crisis and Restructuring: Lessons from Asia," IMF Occasional Paper, 1999; Timothy Lane et al., "IMF-Supported Programs in Indonesia, Korea, and Thailand: A Preliminary Assessment," IMF Occasional Paper, 1999; and Jack Boorman et al., "Managing Financial Crises: The Experience in East Asia," IMF Working Paper, 2000.

Background about Thailand's economy and the origins of its crisis comes from Pasuk Phongpaichit and Chris Baker, *Thailand's Boom and Bust* (Silkworm Books, Chiang Mai, 1998); also invaluable was the so-called Nukul Commission

Report, based on an investigation by a government-appointed panel. The panel's formal name is The Commission Tasked with Making Recommendations to Improve the Efficiency and Management of Thailand's Financial System, and its report was translated into English and published in 1998 by Nation Multimedia Group, Bangkok.

Page 54: Information about how Thailand's fixed exchange-rate system worked comes from the Nukul Commission Report and from Vatchara Charoonsantikul and Thanong Khantong, "Paiboon's Role in Baht Defense," *The Nation* (Bangkok), April 3, 1998.

Page 56: Information about Finance One comes from Raphael Pura, "One Finance Tale: How Optimism Built—and Doomed—a Thai Empire," *The Asian Wall Street Journal*, March 31, 1997; and Henny Sender, "Mirror Man: Finance One Head's Fall Reflects Sector's Woes," *Far Eastern Economic Review*, March 27, 1997.

Page 57: Information about overall credit to private borrowers comes from Bank of Thailand statistics furnished to me by the Institute for International Finance, Washington, D.C.

Figures about the margin loans held by finance companies in 1996 come from Gordon Fairclough, "Tick, Tick, Tick," *Far Eastern Economic Review*, October 3, 1996. Figures about the overbuilding of Bangkok come from Michael Vatikiotis and Gary Silverman, "State of Denial," *Far Eastern Economic Review*, March 6, 1997. Information about Muang Thong Thani Estate comes from Kristof and WuDunn, *Thunder from the East*, and Clifford and Engardio, *Meltdown*.

The figure on nonperforming loans comes from Carl-Johan Lindgren et al., "Financial-Sector Crisis and Restructuring: Lessons from Asia," IMF, 1999.

Pages 57–58: Information about the Bangkok Bank of Commerce scandal comes from the Nukul Commission Report and from Phongpaichit and Baker, *Thailand's Boom and Bust*.

Pages 59–61: The IMF Article IV mission report was, and remains, a confidential document.

Page 59: The Bank of Thailand plan and letter concerning the idea for turning Bangkok into a financial center are quoted in the Nukul Commission Report.

Pages 59–60: Information about the Bangkok International Banking Facilities, including the figure showing their growth from 1994 to 1997, comes from the Bank of Thailand's "Economic Focus," vol. 2, no. 2, April–June 1998, p. 4.

Page 60: The purchase by Mobius's emerging-market fund of stock in the parent company of Muang Thong Thani was reported by Nicholas D. Kristof and David E. Sanger in "How U.S. Wooed Asia to Let Cash Flow In," *The New York Times*, February 16, 1999.

Concerning the recommendation in the IMF's Article IV report for Thailand: Paradoxical as it may seem today, the idea was that by unfixing the baht, the Thai currency would rise somewhat, in response to the simple laws of supply and demand as dollars poured into the country. The result would be a decrease in the inflow of dollars, because the riskiness of, say, purchasing a Thai certificate of deposit would increase once the baht began fluctuating more in value against the dollar.

Pages 61–62: Information on hedge funds and their chiefs comes from "The Risk Business," *The Economist,* October 17, 1998; Joshua Chaffin, William Lewis, and Gary Silverman, "Sinking Fortunes," *Financial Times,* May 5, 2000; Randall Smith, "Louis Bacon Aims to Win at All Costs . . . and Does," *The Wall Street Journal,* September 23, 1993; and Roger Lowenstein, *When Genius Failed: The Rise and Fall of Long-Term Capital Management* (Random House, New York, 2000).

Pages 62–63: The quote is from George Soros, *The Crisis of Global Capitalism: Open Society Endangered* (PublicAffairs, New York, 1998), p. 142.

Pages 63–64: The letters from Camdessus and Fischer to Amnuay, and the information about the IMF Article IV mission and Camdessus's pleading with Rerngchai, are reported in the Nukul Commission Report.

Pages 65–66: Information about Chaiyawat, in addition to interview material, comes from a profile in the *Bangkok Post,* March 8, 1997.

Chaiyawat sought to downplay his role in formulating the Bank of Thailand's foreign exchange policy in the period leading up to the floating of the baht. He was quoted in the Nukul Commission Report as saying that he "was surprised to hear that the Governor [Rerngchai] viewed him as a key person in important policy decisions." He also pointed out that he "was not in charge of the BOT's Banking Department which was tasked with the daily foreign exchange market's daily supervision and intervention," and he said he didn't even have "access to operational information in the departments not under my supervision." However, the report concluded that Chaiyawat's role was much greater than he had acknowledged. As the Bank of Thailand's "major technocrat," who was its "most capable BOT finance and foreign exchange official," his "foreign exchange views carried important weight with BOT officials, including Rerngchai," the report said, adding: "Both Rerngchai and Amnuay didn't take any actions which contradicted Chaiyawat's point of view. Ultimately, though, Rerngchai still should be held responsible for any policy decisions."

Pages 66–67: The episode on May 22 in which Fischer and other IMF officials urged Thailand to widen the currency band is cited in the Nukul Commission Report.

Page 69: Attackers of the baht are listed in Michael R. Sesit and Laura Jereski, "Traders Burnt in Thailand's Battle of Baht," *The Wall Street Journal,* May 22, 1997.

Pages 69–71: A detailed explanation of the Bank of Thailand's strategy and thinking, including the quote "The market is not afraid," is contained in the Nukul Commission Report.

Pages 71–72: Information about the May 15 counterattack by the Bank of Thailand, including the estimated losses inflicted on foreign financial institutions, comes from Deborah Orr, "Banks Get Burnt by Baht," *South China Morning Post*, May 24, 1997; and AP–Dow Jones, "Thai Central Bank Earns up to $250M from May Baht Crisis," May 28, 1997. Chaiyawat's quote is from AP–Dow Jones, "Speculators Must 'Pay the Price,'" May 16, 1997; and Druckenmiller's quote is from "Druckenmiller Applauds Thai Central Bank's Play Against Them," Bloomberg News, July 2, 1997.

Among the market speculators who concluded that the Bank of Thailand had triumphed was Daniel Lian, head of Natwest Markets' Asian bonds and currency research, who was quoted in AP–Dow Jones, "Thai Central Bank Earns up to $250M from May Baht Crisis," May 28, 1997. "I don't think the offshore speculators have the muscle to come back and launch another massive [attack] again," he said.

Page 72: Information about Chavalit's promise of a victory party, and the June 21 meeting at the Bank of Thailand, comes from the Nukul Commission Report.

Pages 72–73: Details of the Bank of Thailand's July 2 announcement about the baht, and Rerngchai's quote, come from "Floating the Baht," *Bangkok Post*, July 3, 1997.

Page 75: Information about the conditions of the IMF's program for Thailand comes from an IMF press release, "IMF Approves Stand-by Credit for Thailand," August 20, 1997, on the IMF website.

Page 77: The $20 billion figure for the amount of loans extended to financial institutions comes from the Bank of Thailand's "Economic Focus," vol. 2, no. 2, April–June 1998.

Pages 77–78: Before the August 5 announcement that the operations would be suspended for a total of fifty-eight finance companies, sixteen had already been suspended, including Finance One; now forty-two more were being added to the list, with the understanding that they would be taken over by the government if they couldn't shore up their financial conditions.

The plan to provide a guarantee to all depositors and creditors in banks and finance companies was built on earlier announcements by the Thai government. It did not apply to some creditors in the sixteen finance companies for which operations had already been suspended. The guarantee was funded by the imposition of a new fee on financial institutions.

Pages 78–79: The quotes by Geithner and Thanong to Sakakibara come from Sakakibara's article, "Thai Crisis Played Part in IMF Idea," *Daily Yomiuri*, November 26, 1999.

Details of the IMF's program and the amounts contributed by the various donors come from the IMF press release, "IMF Approves Stand-by Credit for Thailand," August 20, 1997, on the IMF website.

Pages 79–80: Camdessus's quote comes from "IMF's Camdessus Says Worst of Thai Crisis Is Past," *Bloomberg News*, August 21, 1997.

Page 80: The markets' reaction to the IMF's Thailand program is derived from G. Pierre Goad, "Investors Lack Faith in Thailand's Bailout," *The Asian Wall Street Journal*, August 25, 1997; and Dow Jones News Service, "Baht Ends at Record Low on Fears over Reserves," August 22, 1997. Hanna's quote is from Paul M. Sherer and G. Pierre Goad, "Rescue Package Isn't a Panacea for Thailand," *The Asian Wall Street Journal*, August 22, 1997.

Pages 80–81: Taylor's quote was first reported in Thanong Khanthong and Vatchara Charoonsantikul, "Lack of Data Made Thai Woes Worse," *The Nation* (Bangkok), February 25, 1999.

Pages 81–82: The report in which IMF staff members express criticism about the disclosure concerning Thailand's reserves, and about fiscal policy in the Thai program, is titled "IMF-Supported Programs in Indonesia, Korea, and Thailand: A Preliminary Assessment," IMF, Washington, D.C., 1999.

Page 83: The independent panel report faulting the IMF staff on the issue of capital account liberalization is titled "External Evaluation of IMF Surveillance: Report by a Group of Independent Experts," IMF, 1999.

CHAPTER 4: MALIGNANCY

Among the particularly useful sources on the Indonesian crisis is a study written by a former World Bank staff member, Lloyd R. Kenward, "From the Trenches: The First Year of Indonesia's Crisis of 1997/98 as Seen from the World Bank Offices in Jakarta." Also helpful is John Bresnan, "The United States, the IMF, and the Indonesian Financial Crisis," in Adam Schwartz and Jonathan Paris, eds., *The Politics of Post-Suharto Indonesia* (Council on Foreign Relations, New York, 1999).

Page 86: The quote from the senior IMF official comes from Paul Blustein, "IMF Readies Credit Line at Indonesia's Request," *The Washington Post*, October 9, 1997.

Page 87: The figures on the impact of the crisis on Indonesian workers and their wages come from Frankenberg et al., "The Real Costs of Indonesia's Economic Crisis: Preliminary Findings from the Indonesia Family Life Surveys," 1999, cited in a consultation draft of a World Bank report.

Pages 88–89: Information on Widjojo comes from Raphael Pura, "Indonesia Hands Economy to Veteran Trouble-Shooter," *The Asian Wall Street Journal*, October 12, 1997.

Page 89: The quote from the World Bank report comes from Paul Blustein, "Indonesia a Good Provider for All, Including Leader's Children, Cronies," *The Washington Post*, November 14, 1994.

Page 90: Figures on Indonesia's development come from the World Bank, Operations Evaluation Department, "Indonesia Country Assistance Note," February 4, 1999.

Pages 91–92: Information on the KKN-related holdings of Suharto kin and cronies comes from John McBeth, "Dept. of Connections," *Far Eastern Economic Review*, October 16, 1997; John McBeth and Jay Solomon, "First Friend," *Far Eastern Economic Review*, February 20, 1997; Jay Solomon, "Cars—The Timor Gap," *Far Eastern Economic Review*, February 27, 1997; Philip Shenon, "The Suharto Billions," *The New York Times*, January 16, 1998; and Paul Blustein, "Indonesia a Good Provider to All, Including Leader's Children, Cronies," *The Washington Post*, November 14, 1994.

Page 91: The percentage of Indonesia's wealth controlled by ethnic Chinese was put at 40 percent in a U.S. Treasury memorandum, and at 70 percent in a number of articles published in *Far Eastern Economic Review*.

Page 92: The passage from Wolfensohn's speech comes from Louise Williams, "Private Sector Gets the Nod," *Sydney Morning Herald*, May 14, 1996.

Page 94: The figures on the increase in the number of Indonesian banks come from Steven Radelet, "Indonesia's Implosion," *Harvard Asia Pacific Review*, September 1998.

Pages 94–96: In addition to interviews, information about the Chu mission's findings and results comes from the World Bank, Operations Evaluation Department, "Indonesia Country Assistance Note," February 4, 1999. This is the report that castigated the World Bank's management for having downplayed the evidence the mission unearthed.

Page 96: The optimistic staff report submitted to the World Bank Board is titled "Memorandum of the President of the International Bank for Reconstruction and Development and the International Finance Corporation to the Executive Directors on a Country Assistance Strategy for the Republic of Indonesia," June 13, 1997.

Ironically, de Tray's office in Jakarta had prepared a less optimistic report about Indonesia almost at the same time, titled "Indonesia: Sustaining High Growth with Equity," May 30, 1997. This report, prepared by a team led by Lloyd Kenward, James Hanson, and Lloyd McKay, included this passage: "Looking ahead, the current account is likely to worsen further next year, and problems in other East Asian economies could spill over into Indonesia. These factors, *inter alia*, risk a reversal of capital inflows, a risk that is magnified by Indonesia's large external debt and the increasing sensitivity of global capital flows to changes in indicators."

Page 98: Figures on the cost of foreign versus rupiah loans come from Darren McDermott and Richard Borsuk, "Freeing of Rupiah Deals Double Blow to Debt-Burdened Indonesian Firms," *The Asian Wall Street Journal*, August 15, 1997.

The figure on capital flows into Indonesia comes from Steven Radelet, "Indonesia: Long Road to Recovery," Harvard Institute for International Development, March 1999, www2.cid.harvard.edu/hiidpapers/indonesia. pdf.

Pages 99–100: The report by SBC Warburg Dillon Read is "Indonesia Equity Review: A Whole New Ball Game," November 1997.

Page 102: Sakakibara's recollections of his "heated discussion" with Aghevli come from an article he authored, "IMF's Indonesia Reforms Too Severe," *Daily Yomiuri*, December 10, 1999.

Pages 106–107: Key features of the IMF's program for Indonesia, as well as details about the runs on Indonesian banks, are contained in Kenward, "From the Trenches." Other details about the panic among depositors come from Cesar Bacani, "Now the Hard Part," *AsiaWeek*, November 14, 1997; and John McBeth, "Big Is Best," *Far Eastern Economic Review*, November 13, 1997.

Page 109: The IMF staff report calling the Fund's approach concerning deposit guarantees "ill-advised" is "IMF-Supported Programs in Indonesia, Korea, and Thailand: A Preliminary Assessment."

Pages 109–110: The statements by presidential son Bambang concerning his takeover of Bank Alfa come from Louise Williams, "Soeharto Son Gets New Bank," *Sydney Morning Herald*, November 22, 1997.

Page 111: Paradoxically, the Monetary and Exchange Affairs Department was the department of Carl-John Lindgren, the Finnish economist who had successfully made the case for a blanket deposit guarantee in Thailand. The Thai program had rankled many at the Fund as being too lax on this score, and that may help explain why the Fund took a harder line in Indonesia.

Pages 112–113: Information about the issuance of plastic souvenir 50,000 rupiah banknotes comes from Kenward, "From the Trenches."

Page 114: Data concerning the amount of liquidity that was pumped into Indonesian banks come from Kenward, "From the Trenches"; and from the World Bank, "Indonesia Country Assistance Note."

Information about the improper provision of central bank loans to politically connected companies and banks comes from Joe Leahy, "Fears Grow over Indonesia Central Bank Losses," *Financial Times*, January 10, 2000; and Tom McCawley, "Indonesia Attorney General's Office Questions Ex–Central Bank Governor on Fate of Ten Billion Pounds in Emergency Loans," *Financial Times*, January 5, 2001.

Page 115: The U.S. Treasury memo was obtained under a Freedom of Information Act request.

CHAPTER 5: SLEEPLESS IN SEOUL

A particularly useful background source on the Korean economy and the origins of its crisis is Marcus Noland, *Avoiding the Apocalypse: The Future of the Two*

Koreas (Institute for International Economics, Washington, June 2000), which I was fortunate to read in draft form. Another is Donald Kirk, *Korean Crisis: Unraveling of the Miracle in the IMF Era* (St. Martin's Press, New York, 1999).

Page 117: President Kim's words in his address to the nation come from numerous dispatches, including Sang-Hun Choe, "South Koreans Accept IMF Bailout—with Humiliation and Anger," Associated Press, November 22, 1997.

Pages 117–118: The October 15, 1997, Article IV report on Korea was, and remains, a confidential document.

Page 119: Joan Robinson's prediction is cited in Noland, *Avoiding the Apocalypse.*

Pages 119–121: Many of the figures concerning Korea's development, including the data on policy loans and the rise in spending on new plant and equipment, come from Noland, *Avoiding the Apocalypse.*

Pages 121–122: Information concerning the Ssang Yong Group's M. P. Kim comes from Steven Mufson, "Rebuilding South Korea's House of Cards," *The Washington Post,* December 22, 1997. Information concerning the Halla Group's shipyard comes from Kirk, *Korean Crisis.* To the best of my knowledge, a connection has never been proved between the location of Samsung's plant and presidential approval for its entry into the auto industry; however, the coincidence has been widely noted in the Korean media, and informed Koreans believe a connection exists.

Page 122: In a separate aide-mémoire about the Korean banking system, the IMF's Article IV mission fretted that the capital held by the banks as cushions against loan losses had been so eroded that if proper accounting methods were used, the average ratio of capital to total assets would be as low as 4 percent to 6 percent, well below the 8 percent international standard that the banks claimed to have surpassed.

Pages 124–125: The study by Carmen Reinhart, coauthored by Graciela L. Kaminsky, is "Bank Lending and Contagion: Evidence from the Asian Crisis," and is on the web at www.puaf.umd.edu/papers/reinhart.htm.

Page 126: The data on Korea's liabilities to foreigners come from Bank for International Settlements figures cited in Noland, *Avoiding the Apocalypse,* p. 196.

Page 131: Lim's comment that "it is in [the] interests [of Japan and the United States] to help" comes from Michael Schuman and Namju Cho, "South Korea to Seek Help from U.S. in Bid to Stem Currency Crisis," Dow Jones News Service, November 20, 1997.

Page 132: The headlines from Korean papers come from Sang-Hun Choe, "South Koreans Accept IMF Bailout—with Humiliation and Anger," Associated Press, November 22, 1997.

Pages 132–133: In a letter to me, Lee Keun Yung acknowledged that in his November 26 visit to Siegman, he said "that the Bank of Korea's reserves were decreasing fast and that we might run out in a fairly short period of time." But he said that at the breakfast earlier in the week attended by Greenspan, Siegman, Bank of Korea Governor Lee, and himself, "the seriousness of the reserve problem was fully understood among the participants." It is entirely possible that Bank of Korea officials thought they were adequately conveying the seriousness of the reserve problem at the breakfast, but it also seems clear that the Fed did not feel the situation was nearly so dire until the meeting on November 26.

Pages 134–136: Information about Rubin's background comes mainly from Clay Chandler, "Treasury's High-Stakes Player," *The Washington Post*, June 18, 1998; Jacob Weisberg, "Keeping the Boom from Busting," *The New York Times Magazine*, July 19, 1998; and Bob Woodward, *The Agenda: Inside the Clinton White House* (Simon & Schuster, New York, 1994).

Pages 136–137: Information about Geithner's background comes from his biography published on the Treasury's website, www.ustreas.gov; and Dean Foust et al., "The Swat Team from Washington," *Business Week*, March 2, 1998.

Page 146: Lim's assertion that "the talks are virtually completed" was reported by Dow Jones News Service, December 2, 1997.

Pages 148–149: Details of the Korean program come from "Korea—Memorandum on the Economic Program," December 3, 1997, available on the IMF website.

Page 149: The suspension of the nine insolvent merchant banks was announced the day before Camdessus's visit and was not negotiated by him.

The contrast between the visages of Camdessus and Lim comes from Kirk, *Korean Crisis*. The quotes from Lim at the press conference and the Treasury official at the Washington briefing come from Paul Blustein and Sandra Sugawara, "Seoul Accepts $55 Billion Bailout Terms," *The Washington Post*, December 4, 1997.

CHAPTER 6: THE NAYSAYERS

Page 152: The passage from Sachs's op-ed comes from his article "Power unto Itself," *Financial Times*, December 12, 1997.

Page 153: The reference to Sachs's lack of shyness comes from Leslie Wayne, "A Doctor for Struggling Economies," *The New York Times*, October 1, 1989.

Pages 153–154: Information about Sachs's background and career and his exploits in Bolivia and Poland comes from Peter Passell, "Dr. Jeffrey Sachs, Shock Therapist," *The New York Times*, June 27, 1993; Steven Pearlstein, "Tiff in the Economists' Temple," *The Washington Post*, April 5, 1998; Leslie Wayne, "A Doctor for Struggling Economies," *The New York Times*, October 1, 1998; Mac Margolis, "Bolivia Shifts from Hyperinflation to Stability," *The Washington Post*, May 17, 1988; William R. Long, "Thousands Fast to Protest Economic Austerity in Bolivia," *Los Angeles Times*, May 7, 1988; and Daniel

Yergin and Joseph Stanislaw, *The Commanding Heights* (Touchstone, New York, 1998).

Page 155: The quote "The crisis is mainly the result of a self-fulfilling panic" is from Steven Radelet and Jeffrey Sachs, "What Have We Learned, So Far, from the Asian Financial Crisis?" Discussion Paper, Consulting Assistance on Economic Reform Project, Harvard Institute for International Development, March 1999, www.hiid.harvard.edu/caer2/htm/content/papers/paper37/paper37.htm.

Page 158: Stiglitz's Chicago speech is available on the World Bank website, www.worldbank.org.

Page 159: The figure on the increase in World Bank structural adjustment loans is compiled from data in its annual report released in September 1998, cited in Paul Blustein, "World Bank's Role Evolves with Crisis," *The Washington Post*, September 25, 1998.

Pages 159–161: Information on Stiglitz comes from Owen Ullman, "Mad Dog," *The International Economy*, March/April 1999; Peter Passell, "From the Ivory Tower, a Tough Economist for the World Bank," *The New York Times*, December 12, 1996; Sylvia Nasar, "Stiglitz, Idea Man Among the Economic Advisers," *The New York Times*, February 9, 1994; Louis Uchitelle, "The Economics of Intervention," *The New York Times*, May 31, 1998; and David Moberg, "Capital Crusader," Salon.com, September 25, 1999. Stiglitz's book is *Globalization and Its Discontents* (W. W. Norton & Co., New York, 2002).

Page 162: Summers's quote "I thought you were my friend" comes from Sakakibara's article, "Thai Crisis Played Part in IMF Idea," *Daily Yomiuri*, November 26, 1999.

Pages 162–163: Information about Sakakibara's background, career, and views comes from Sachiko Sakamaki, "Mr. Yen Moves Up," *Far Eastern Economic Review*, July 17, 1997; Peter Landers, "Outspoken Crusader for Yen Policy, Sakakibara, Is Planning to Step Down," *The Wall Street Journal*, June 29, 1999; Peter Hartcher and Andrew Cornell, "Mr. Yen Regrets," *Australian Financial Review*, June 25, 1999; and Edmund L. Andrews, "Blunt-Spoken Economist Is Japan's Mr. Yen," *The New York Times*, September 16, 1995.

Page 164: Sakakibara's quote "Personally, I like the Japanese system" comes from Paul Blustein, "Japan's Corporate Connections Create Challenge for U.S. Businesses," *The Washington Post*, October 6, 1991.

Sakakibara's quote "not an Asian crisis but a crisis of global capitalism" comes from Michael Hirsh, "The Way It Looks to Mr. Yen," *Newsweek*, February 2, 1998.

Page 165: Sakakibara's quotes about "the unity of Asian countries," "it was all too hasty," and "the AMF might act independently of the IMF" come from his article in the *Daily Yomiuri*, November 26, 1999.

Pages 167–168: The September 17 Rubin-Greenspan letter, and the September

30 memo from Geithner to administration colleagues, were provided to me by the U.S. Treasury in response to a Freedom of Information Act request.

Page 168: Sakakibara's quote about having been "taught a valuable lesson" comes from his *Daily Yomiuri* article of November 26, 1997.

Pages 170–171: Information about Tietmeyer's background, career, and views comes from "Hans Tietmeyer, the D-mark's Dogged Defender," *The Economist*, March 21, 1998; Brendan Glacken, "A Banker of Steely Austerity Bows Out," *The Irish Times*, September 2, 1999; John Eisenhammer, "The Mark's New Minder," *The Independent*, October 3, 1993; and Bill Javetski et al., "The Bundesbank—Under Hans Tietmeyer, the Mark Comes First," *Business Week*, October 4, 1993.

Page 172: A thorough account of the Mexican episode can be found in George Graham, Peter Norman, Stephen Fidler, and Ted Bardacke, "Mexican Rescue," *Financial Times*, February 16, 1995.

Although the German and British representatives on the IMF board sought to register abstentions after the meeting approving the Mexican loan had ended, they were told that it was too late.

Page 173: Tietmeyer's quote about the "generous involvement in Mexico" comes from a brief story on the AFX wire service on April 26, 1995. Mussa's quote about the *Titanic* was delivered at an IMF conference I attended in 1999.

Page 174: Concerning the German view that the Powell doctrine was a fraud, a particularly trenchant comment can be found in Helmut Schieber, "Moral Hazard and the Role of International Rescue Operations," in Hunter, Kaufman, and Krueger (eds.), *The Asian Financial Crisis*: "I do not share the view that extraordinarily large financial packages have automatically calming effects on financial markets," wrote Schieber, a member of the Bundesbank board. "Neither in Asia nor in Russia did the announcement of large packages stop the capital outflows, either immediately, or later, because . . . everyone could see that even these large packages were by far not large enough to finance all possible capital outflows."

CHAPTER 7: THE BOSUN'S MATE

Page 178: Details concerning the Korean package come from an IMF press release, "Camdessus Welcomes Conclusion of Talks with Korea on IMF Program," available on the IMF website.

Page 180: The IMF staff report was available for a time on the website of the Korean newspaper *Chosun Ilbo* (www.chosun.com).

A transcript of Fischer's press conference is available on the IMF website.

Page 181: The quote "It was one of a series of dubious decisions" comes from David E. Sanger, "Talk of Tougher Medicine for Korea's Ills," *The New York Times*, December 12, 1997. Rubin's statement about Korea having a "strong program" comes from Virginie Montet, "U.S. Investors Still Jittery over South Korea's Financial Crisis," Agence France Presse, December 11, 1997.

Pages 182–183: Lejoindre's quote "The calculation is simple" comes from Philippe Ries, "South Korea Crisis Threatens World Payments System," Agence France Presse, December 12, 1997. The action by Thompson Financial Services was reported in Timothy L. O'Brien with Andrew Pollack, "Korea Situation Deteriorates, Raising Specter of a Default," *The New York Times*, December 12, 1997.

Part of the problem contributing to the rundown in the Bank of Korea's reserves was that the central bank, in its desperation to keep the banking system from collapse, was lending reserves on excessively generous terms— charging commercial banks only about 1 percentage point above the London Interbank Offered Rate (LIBOR), the market rate banks customarily charge each other for short-term loans. Around the time of the December 3 program, the Fund demanded that the Bank of Korea charge a much higher rate in the hope that banks, instead of asking for loans of reserves, would negotiate with their foreign creditors for rollovers. Grudgingly, the central bank complied by charging 4 percentage points above LIBOR, and when that proved to be insufficient, it raised the rate to LIBOR plus 6 points and eventually to LIBOR plus 10 points.

Page 184: The quote by the unidentified senior Fund official, "We had during the last few days," comes from my notes of the briefing.

Page 187: Information about Truman's background and career comes from John M. Berry, "At the Fed, a Power Struggle over Information," *The Washington Post*, July 8, 1996; and Owen Ullman, "Ted Truman Unchained," *The International Economy*, September/October 1999.

Page 188: A thorough account of the arm-twisting that went on during the debt crisis of the 1980s can be found in Steven Solomon, *The Confidence Game: How Unelected Central Bankers Are Governing the Changed World Economy* (Simon & Schuster, New York, 1995).

Page 194: Information about McDonough's background and career comes from John M. Berry, "Fighting Inflation for Just Plain Folks: New York Fed Chief William McDonough Puts Bank's Mission in Populist Terms," *The Washington Post*, December 29, 1993; and Sylvia Nasar, "Deputy Chosen as Head of New York Fed," *The New York Times*, July 17, 1993.

Pages 197–198: Some of the details about Lipton's meeting with Kim Dae Jung, including the banner on the building and Kim's reply that his "first priority is the competitiveness of the Korean economy," come from a memo based on reporting by my *Washington Post* colleague Clay Chandler, who was in Seoul at the time.

Page 199: The statement on the new rescue plan, "Korea Strengthens Economic Program: IMF to Activate Additional Financial Support," December 24, 1997, is available on the IMF website.

Page 202: An extensive account of the negotiations between the banks and the Korean government can be found in Peter Lee, "Korea Stares into the Abyss," *Euromoney,* March 1998.

Pages 202–203: Hong Kwan Pyo's story comes from Mary Jordan, "Middle Class Plunging Back into Poverty," *The Washington Post,* September 6, 1998.

Page 203: The passage from Rubin's speech comes from Floyd Norris, "Giving Credit Where Blame Might Be Due," *The New York Times,* January 25, 1998.

Page 204: A particularly cogent argument against the IMF's overuse of structural conditions in its Korea program is presented in Martin Feldstein, "Refocusing the IMF," *Foreign Affairs,* March/April 1998.

CHAPTER 8: DOWN THE TUBES

Pages 207–208: Information about the chaotic situation in Indonesia in early January comes from S. N. Vasuki, "Jakarta Residents Start Hoarding Basic Commodities," *Business Times* (Singapore), January 9, 1998; and Susan Sim, "Indonesians Go on Panic Buying of Food Items," *Straits Times* (Singapore), January 9, 1998.

Pages 208–209: Details of the conversation between Presidents Clinton and Suharto were provided by a source with access to the transcript.

Page 210: The comment "It's not that he tried the program and the program has failed" comes from my notes of an interview I held at the time.

Page 211: Details of the second Indonesia program are available on the IMF website; also in Kenward, "In the Trenches."

Page 214: Camdessus's remarks at his January 15, 1998, press conference, which I attended, are available on the IMF website.

Aghevli's comments about the celebratory lunch on January 15 come from Paul Blustein, "At the IMF, a Struggle Shrouded in Secrecy," *The Washington Post,* March 30, 1998.

Pages 214–215: My impressions of the situation in Indonesia in late January are reported in detail in Paul Blustein, "Indonesia Braces for Worst As Its Currency Collapses," *The Washington Post,* January 24, 1998.

Page 215: Aghevli's comments about his surprise over the program's failure come from Paul Blustein, "Indonesian Currency Still Falling: Officials Surprised Reform Plan Hasn't Steadied Rupiah," *The Washington Post,* January 17, 1998.

Page 216: Other financial analysts who took a line similar to Singh's included the following:

Daragh Maher of ING Barings told clients in his "Indonesia Morning Agenda" of January 16, 1998: "Certainly many of Indonesia's technocrats and possibly the International Monetary Fund will be wringing their hands with glee following President Suharto's commitment to a wide range of structural reforms. However, although this package will remove concerns that the government is unwilling to commit to structural reforms, it will do little to ease many of the pressures facing Indonesia's economy, notably with regard to servicing external debt obligations."

Irene Cheung of Merrill Lynch wrote in a bulletin to clients on January 15 after listing the reform measures to which Suharto had agreed: "These measures, if implemented, should largely meet the demand of the investment community ... however, our immediate concern is that the measures offer little relief to the problems faced by corporates and the population at large, at this point in time."

SBC Warburg Dillon Read, in its assessment of the IMF package, told clients: "In our view, the proposed reforms are broadly positive in all respects and should enhance Indonesia's medium- to long-term economic prospects. ... However, what was noticeably absent in the Letter of Intent was how the private sector external-debt problem will be dealt with."

Page 219: The comprehensive deposit guarantee was combined with the establishment of the Indonesian Bank Restructuring Agency (IBRA), which was designed to take over and rehabilitate weak banks and manage the nonperforming assets of other troubled banks.

Page 220: The IMF staff report lamenting the delay in addressing the corporate debt problem is Lane et al., "IMF-Supported Programs in Indonesia, Korea and Thailand: A Preliminary Assessment."

Kohler's statement that "I will not have another Indonesia" comes from Joseph Kahn, "International Lenders' New Image: A Human Face," *The New York Times*, September 26, 2000.

Page 222: Suharto's statement that "we must quickly fix the currency at a certain rate" comes from Darren McDermott, Jay Solomon, and Raphael Pura, "Suharto Considers Pegging Rupiah to Dollar," *The Wall Street Journal*, February 10, 1998.

Page 223: Hanke's quote that "I know what causes currencies to blow out" comes from Paul Blustein, "The Professor Who Is Testing U.S. Patience," *The Washington Post*, February 12, 1998.

Page 225: Camdessus's letter to Suharto was reported in Paul Blustein, "Currency Dispute Threatens Indonesia's Bailout," *The Washington Post*, February 14, 1998.

Page 226: Information about the deferral of the currency-board proposal comes from Bob Davis and Jay Solomon, "Suharto's Dukun," *The Wall Street Journal*, February 23, 1998. Suharto's statement that "whatever measure we shall take, we need the support of the IMF" comes from Richard Borsuk, "Suharto Says New Path Needs IMF Blessing," *The Asian Wall Street Journal*, March 2, 1998.

Pages 232–233: Details about the third IMF program for Indonesia, and the events of April and May 1998 leading to the resignation of Suharto, come from Kenward, "From the Trenches."

CHAPTER 9: GETTING TO NYET

An excellent and entertaining history of Russia during the Yeltsin years is Chrystia Freeland, *Sale of the Century* (Random House, New York, 2000). Also very helpful are Anders Aslund, "Why Has Russia's Economic Transformation Been So Arduous?" paper prepared for the World Bank Conference on Development Economics, April 28–30, 1999; General Accounting Office (GAO), "International Efforts to Aid Russia's Transition Have Had Mixed Results," GAO, Washington, D.C., November 2000; and Homi Kharas, Brian Pinto, and Sergei Ulatov, "An Analysis of Russia's 1998 Meltdown: Fundamentals and Market Signals," Spring 2001 Brookings Panel, Meeting Draft, March 2001.

Pages 240–241: Information about the privatization campaign, and the disappointments associated with reform in the early years, comes from Freeland, *Sale of the Century*; Aslund, "Why Has Russia's Economic Transformation Been So Arduous?"; Maxim Boycko, Andrei Shleifer, and Robert Vishny, *Privatizing Russia* (MIT Press, Cambridge, Mass., 1995); Yegor Gaidar, *Days of Defeat and Victory*, translated by Jane Ann Miller (University of Washington Press, Seattle, 1999); Joseph Stiglitz, "Quis Custodiet Ipsos Custodes? (Who is to guard the guards themselves?): Corporate Governance Failures in the Transition," keynote address at the Annual Bank Conference on Development Economics—Europe; and John Nellis, "Time to Rethink Privatization in Transition Economies?" *Finance and Development*, June 1999.

Pages 241–242: Information about the 1995 and 1996 programs, and the disappointments associated with them including the rigged auctions of state property, comes from Freeland, *Sale of the Century*; Aslund, "Why Has Russia's Economic Transformation Been So Arduous?"; and the GAO report, "International Efforts to Aid Russia's Transition Have Had Mixed Results." Among other sources is Ira Lieberman and Rogi Veimetra, "The Rush for State Shares in the 'Klondyke' of Wild East Capitalism: Loans-for-Shares Transactions in Russia," a paper presented to the Second Annual Institute on Current Issues in World Trade, March 28–29, 1996.

The IMF staff report that credited the Russians for "fully complying with the quantitative targets of the program" is available from the Fund archivist, as it is more than five years old. The title is "Staff Report on the Discussions for the Eighth Monthly Review Under the Stand-By Arrangement," December 20, 1995.

Fischer's quote "The realistic view on Russia" comes from Michael Dobbs and Paul Blustein, "Lost Illusions About Russia," *The Washington Post*, September 12, 1999.

Page 243: Figures for Russia's budget deficit as a percentage of GDP vary by a few tenths of a percentage point depending upon the source and basis used. My figures come from Aslund, "Why Has Russia's Transformation Been So Arduous?"

Pages 244–245: Sources on the barter and nonpayments problem in Russia include Clifford G. Gaddy and Barry W. Ickes, *Russia's Virtual Economy* (Brookings Institution Press, Washington, D.C., forthcoming); and Brian Pinto, Vladimir Drebentsov, and Alexander Morozov, "Dismantling Russia's Nonpayments System: Creating Conditions for Growth," World Bank Technical Paper, 2000.

Anecdotes about workers being paid in brassieres and shot glasses come from David Hoffman, "Goods Replace Rubles in Russia's Vast Web of Trade," *The Washington Post*, January 31, 1997.

Information about the IMF's efforts to dismantle the virtual economy comes from the IMF's "Russian Federation: Recent Economic Developments," September 1999, p. 59.

Page 245: The figure on portfolio investment in Russia comes from the website of the Central Bank of Russia, www.cbr.ru.

Page 246: Information about investment firms piling into Moscow comes from Betsy McKay, "Rushing into Russia," *The Wall Street Journal Europe*, March 30, 1998; and Christopher Rhoads and Betsy McKay, "Playing with Pain," *The Wall Street Journal Europe*, June 23, 1998.

Pages 246–247: Lipton spoke of being alarmed about the phrase "the latest moral-hazard play" at a 1999 IMF conference I attended.

Page 248: The $20 billion figure for foreign investment in GKOs comes from a number of sources, including William F. Browder, "Russia's Crisis of Confidence," op-ed article, *The Wall Street Journal Europe*, May 28, 1998.

Yield figures on GKOs come from the Central Bank of Russia website, www.cbr.ru.

The figure on the deterioration in Russia's trade balance comes from the September 1998 edition of *Russian Economic Trends*, an invaluable source of information and statistics, www.recep.ru.

Pages 249–250: Data on the Russian government's interest expense come from *Russian Economic Trends*, June 1998; and Interfax Russian News, "T-Bill Market Suffers Biggest Crisis in Its History," July 29, 1998.

Page 252: The op-ed to which Gilman referred was Browder, "Russia's Crisis of Confidence."

Page 254: The White House statement is cited in Paul Blustein, "Clinton Supports New International Bailout for Russia," *The Washington Post*, June 1, 1998.

Pages 254–256: Details of the Clinton-Yeltsin phone call were provided by a source with access to the transcript.

Data on developments in the GKO market in the period immediately prior to the Clinton-Yeltsin call come from Interfax Russian News, "T-Bill Market Suffers Biggest Crisis in Its History," July 29, 1998.

Page 256: Information about Odling-Smee's background and career comes from the IMF's press release, "International Monetary Fund Appoints Director of New Department," January 9, 1992.

Page 257: Details of the July 1998 program for Russia are spelled out in Kharas, Pinto, and Ulatov, "An Analysis of Russia's 1998 Meltdown: Fundamentals and Market Signals."

Page 259: The quote from Chubais, "Now we are safe," comes from David Hoffman, "Russia's Devaluation Drama," *The Washington Post*, August 23, 1998.

Page 260: The scene at the Goldman, Sachs reception, including former President George Bush's comments, comes from Christopher Rhoads and Betsy McKay, "Playing with Pain," *The Wall Street Journal*, June 23, 1998.

Information about the competition among investment banks for bond deals in 1997 and 1998, especially Goldman's activities with Menatep and other clients, comes from Joseph Kahn and Timothy L. O'Brien, "Easy Money: For Russia and Its U.S. Bankers, Match Wasn't Made in Heaven," *The New York Times*, October 18, 1998.

Pages 261–262: The projection that the Russian government faced a $32 billion debt-service outlay in the second half of 1998 comes from Kharas, Pinto, and Ulatov, "An Analysis of Russia's 1998 Meltdown," as does the information about the amounts of GKOs tendered by investors in the Goldman exchange.

Page 263: At the time I interviewed Al Breach, he was employed by Goldman.

The statement "With the threat of a ruble devaluation now waning" could mean trading a 'bronco for a mule'" comes from Matthew Brzezinski and Andrew Higgins, "Ruble Rebounds, Stocks Surge 17%, Bond Yields Drop," *The Wall Street Journal Europe*, July 15, 1998.

Page 264: The figures on the increase in Russia's Eurobonds outstanding, the resulting price decline, and the fees Goldman earned come from Kahn and O'Brien, "Easy Money."

Page 265: Figures documenting the dissipation of the $4.8 billion the Fund had disbursed are contained in Kharas, Pinto, and Ulatov, "An Analysis of Russia's 1998 Meltdown," p. 8.

Page 266: Information about rubles being exchanged into dollars at eight rubles per dollar comes from *Russian Economic Trends*, August 1998.

Page 270: Details about the meeting among Yeltsin, Kiriyenko, and Chubais comes from Freeland, *Sale of the Century*.

Page 272: Kiriyenko's statement, "The measures are tough ones," comes from David Hoffman, "Russia Devalues the Ruble to Prop up Banking System," *The Washington Post*, August 18, 1998.

Camdessus's statement of August 17 is available on the IMF website.

Pages 273–276: A transcript of this conference call comes from a Deutsche Bank web page, to which I was graciously given a password with the consent of David Folkerts-Landau.

Page 274: Information about Deutsche Bank's exposure to the GKO market comes from Charles Piggott, "Bankers Shore up Their Assets," *The European,* August 31, 1998. Information about the bank's loss of its triple-A rating comes from John Schmid, "Deutsche Bank Slips from Top of Ratings," *International Herald Tribune,* August 27, 1998.

Page 277: Soros's quote comes from his op-ed article "The Crisis of Global Capitalism," *The Wall Street Journal,* September 15, 1998.

CHAPTER 10: THE BALANCE OF RISKS

Pages 281–283: Information concerning the Fed's thinking in 1998 comes from John M. Berry, "A Quiet End to the Fed's Wild Year," *The Washington Post,* December 22, 1998; and David Wessel, "Credit Record: How the Fed Fumbled, and Then Recovered, in Making Policy," *The Wall Street Journal,* November 17, 1998. The quote from Thomas Hoenig, "Our finger was poised to push," comes from Berry's article.

Page 283: Greenspan's statement that "it is just not credible that the United States can remain an oasis of prosperity" is cited in John M. Berry, "Fed Chief Hints at Possible Rate Cut," *The Washington Post,* September 5, 1998.

Page 285: The quote from the senior Treasury official about Malaysia providing "a good negative example to everybody" comes from Paul Blustein, "Financial Crises Could Stall Capitalism's Global March," *The Washington Post,* September 4, 1998.

Krugman's *Fortune* article appeared in the September 7, 1998, issue.

Sakakibara's recollection of Summers's remark "Eisuke, the world is going to hell" comes from his article "To Brink of Global Depression and Back," *Daily Yomiuri,* August 4, 1999.

Page 288: Clinton's statement that "the balance of risks has now shifted" and the other quotations about the need to focus on growth come from a transcript of the speech he delivered at the Council on Foreign Relations on September 14, 1998.

Pages 289–290: Information about how the BIS meetings work comes from John M. Berry, "Banking's Key Players," *The Washington Post,* June 28, 1998. Since the establishment of the European Central Bank in 1999, a senior representative of the ECB has joined the gatherings.

Page 292: Speculation about coordinated interest-rate cuts based on the G-7 communiqué appeared in a number of press articles, including David E. Sanger, "Clinton Presents Strategy to Quell Economic Threat," *The New York Times,* September 15, 1998; Paul Blustein, "Clinton and G–7: We're on the Case," *The Washington Post,* September 15, 1998; and Stephen Fidler, "G-7 Statement Response to Turmoil," *Financial Times,* September 15, 1998.

Information concerning how the air went out of the coordinated-rate-cut balloon comes from David E. Sanger, "What Happened to Those Global Rate Cuts?" *The New York Times,* September 18, 1998.

Page 294: A lucid explanation of the IMF's reasoning concerning its finances is provided in "A Peek Inside the IMF's Vaults," *The Economist,* July 18, 1998.

Page 295: Saxton's statement that "the bottom line is that the IMF is not destitute" comes from Michael M. Phillips, "IMF and Critics Debate Accounting Principles," *The Wall Street Journal,* September 28, 1998.

Page 297: The estimate that 70 to 80 percent of all corporate and mortgage lending now goes through the capital markets comes from Jacob M. Schlesinger and Paul Beckett, "Investors' Fear of Risk Translates into a Curb on Credit for Business," *The Wall Street Journal,* October 7, 1998.

Pages 298–299: The IMF description of September–October 1998 as "a period of turmoil in mature markets that is virtually without precedent" comes from the Fund's International Capital Markets report, 1999.

Page 301: The figures on junk-bond spreads come from Gretchen Morgenson, "The Bear Is Rampant in the Markets for Riskier Bonds," *The New York Times,* September 17, 1998. Figures on emerging-market spreads come from Kerry Capell, Mike McNamee, et al., "The Fed Steps In: Will It Work?" *Business Week,* October 12, 1998; and the IMF's 1999 International Capital Markets report, which cited the doubling in spreads for Mexico and South Korea.

Page 303: The figure on the peak spread between on-the-run and off-the-run Treasury bonds comes from the IMF's 1999 International Capital Markets report, as does the figure about the decline in the amount of high-yield corporate bonds issued in U.S. markets in October 1998.

CHAPTER 11: PLUMBING THE DEPTHS

Although my own reporting forms the basis for much of the material in this chapter concerning the activities of Fed and Treasury policymakers during the Long-Term Capital episode, a source from which I drew repeatedly is Lowenstein, *When Genius Failed,* a fascinating and exhaustively reported book by an estimable former *Wall Street Journal* colleague.

Other sources that helped inform this chapter are Carol J. Loomis, "A House Built on Sand," *Fortune,* October 26, 1998; Diana B. Henriques, "Billions upon Billions," *The New York Times,* September 27, 1998; Michael Siconolfi, Anita Raghavan, and Mitchell Pacelle, "How the Salesmanship and Brainpower Failed at Long-Term Capital," *The Wall Street Journal,* November 16, 1998; Timothy L. O'Brien and Laura M. Holson, "A Hedge Fund's Stars Didn't Tell, and Savvy Financiers Didn't Ask," *The New York Times,* October 23, 1998; and Diana B. Henriques and Joseph Kahn, "The Fear That Made the Fed Step In," *The New York Times,* December 6, 1998.

Page 305: Information about Peter Fisher's background, career, and the procedure he instituted at the New York Fed's trading desk comes from John M. Berry, "The New York Fed Opens Up: To Bank Official, Benefits of Change Are No Secret," *The Washington Post,* May 13, 1998; and Jacob M. Schlesinger,

"Long-Term Capital Bailout Spotlights a Fed 'Radical,'" *The Wall Street Journal*, November 2, 1998.

Pages 307–311: The figures concerning Long-Term's payroll peaking at 190, and its 1996 profits exceeding those of McDonald's and other major corporations, and its $7 billion in capital exceeding that of Salomon Smith Barney, come from Lowenstein, *When Genius Failed*. So also does much of the information about Meriwether's background, as well as the information about Long-Term's first trade in August 1993 and the returns the firm earned for its investors and its financial position.

Page 313: Information about J. P. Morgan's role in the panic of 1907 comes from John Steele Gordon, "History Repeats in Finance Company Bailouts," *The Wall Street Journal*, October 7, 1998.

Page 314: McDonough's statement that Long-Term's demise could have a "serious effect" on world markets comes from his testimony before the House Committee on Banking and Financial Services, October 1, 1998.

Pages 316–317: I am indebted to Roger Lowenstein for the lucid explanation of shorting equity volatility in his *When Genius Failed*. Information about the document with the notation "USD_Z+D-shift" also comes from Lowenstein's book.

Page 319: The estimate that Long-Term's counterparties would suffer a $2.8 billion loss was also reported in Lowenstein, *When Genius Failed*.

Page 322: McDonough's statement that "No Federal Reserve official pressured anyone" comes from his testimony before the House Banking and Financial Services Committee, October 1, 1998.

Page 323: The quote "What the fuck are you doing?" comes from Lowenstein, *When Genius Failed*.

Pages 324–325: The comments by Reps. Vento and Bachus and Chairman Greenspan come from the October 1, 1998, hearing of the House Banking and Financial Services Committee.

Page 328: Information about Greenspan querying the staff about economic minutiae, and his quote "We need to be forward looking," come from David Wessel, "In Setting Fed's Policy, Chairman Bets Heavily on His Own Judgment," *The Wall Street Journal*, January 27, 1997.

Page 330: The Fed's directive of September 29, 1998, and the announcement of the FOMC decision to cut the funds rate by 25 basis points, are available on the Fed's website, www.federalreserve.gov.

Page 331: The story about Philadelphia Fed President Edward Boehne and the clerk at the Pennsylvania hotel comes from David Wessel, "Credit Record: How the Fed Fumbled, and Then Recovered, in Making Policy," *The Wall Street Journal*, November 17, 1998.

Details about the investment firm parties at the IMF–World Bank meetings come from Steven Mufson, "Bankers Meet Under Dark Cloud with Silver-Service Lining," *The Washington Post*, October 8, 1998; and Leslie

Wayne, "A Champagne Evening Awash in Gloom," *The New York Times*, October 9, 1998.

Page 333: Clinton's statements about the Contingent Credit Line, including "We have got a vested interest," come from Paul Blustein, "U.S. Offers Plan to Aid Global Economy," *The Washington Post*, October 3, 1998; and David E. Sanger, "Clinton Proposes IMF Act Earlier to Prevent Crises," *The New York Times*, October 3, 1998.

CHAPTER 12: STUMBLING OUT

Page 338: Figures showing the outflow of hard currency come from Brazil's central bank and are cited in "History of Brazil Dollar Outflows," Reuters, January 14, 1999.

Page 342: Information about Brazil's glowing promise and burgeoning middle class in the mid–1990s comes from Diana Jean Schemo, "Brazil's Economic Samba," *The New York Times*, September 7, 1996.

 Information about Malan's background and career comes from Luis Emerson, "Mr. Real," The Ethnic NewsWatch, News from Brazil, January 31, 1995; and Elliot Blair Smith, "Digging Brazil Out of Trouble," *USA Today*, November 16, 1998.

Pages 343–344: An analysis of Brazil's exploding debt burden is contained in ING Barings's "Emerging Markets Weekly Report," October 9, 1998. Information on the seven-month average maturity for government bonds, and the extent to which interest payments on those bonds were linked to the overnight lending rate, comes from an October 14, 1998, research report by Salomon Smith Barney's emerging-markets analyst Desmond Lachman, titled "Brazil and the IMF: The Road Chosen."

Page 348: Despite Japan's objections to the U.S.–IMF position on Brazil, Tokyo nonetheless fell in behind the effort to design a program for the country. Sakakibara attributes this in part to an "understanding" he says he reached with Summers. The episode is worth a brief examination for the light it sheds on the peculiar combination of mutual suspicion and mutual dependence that pervaded relations between the world's two largest economies during the crisis.

 According to Sakakibara's recollections published in the *Daily Yomiuri* in late 1999, Tokyo's concern over the Brazilian rescue was subsumed by its interest in advancing an initiative, the New Miyazawa Plan, that provided $30 billion in financial aid to Asian economies. Although the plan involved Japanese money only rather than a pool of resources from the region, it looked to some extent like an attempt to resurrect the Asian Monetary Fund. Sakakibara gave this accounting:

 Japan supported the European stance [criticizing the Brazilian rescue], but during several bilateral meetings held in September, Summers and I developed an understanding that Japan would argue for the European position, but would not ultimately oppose the U.S. plan. In return, the U.S. would not oppose Japan's rescue package for Malaysia and other Asian countries. The Asian rescue package was announced in the form of the $30 billion New Miyazawa Plan during a meeting October 3.

Malaysia had been the target of international criticism after it announced on Sept. 2 unilateral restrictions on the outflow of capital that inflicted huge losses on many U.S. and European financial institutions. Malaysia, however, was important to Japan, and Tokyo was not necessarily opposed to the control on capital outflows to avert a crisis. It was, therefore, unthinkable to exclude Malaysia from the list of recipients of the New Miyazawa Plan.

Summers and I were well aware that we had to compromise as we were representing different national interests.

Summers hotly disputes the suggestion that he and Sakakibara struck such an agreement. Unlike the Asian Monetary Fund, the Miyazawa initiative was a unilateral action by a sovereign nation, and the United States wasn't in a position to approve or disapprove it. When I pressed Sakakibara about this, he conceded that his accord with Summers "wasn't an explicit deal. We developed a vague understanding."

A memo written to Rubin and Summers by Assistant Treasury Secretary Tim Geithner on September 25, 1998(which I obtained pursuant to a Freedom of Information Act request), shows that U.S. officials were indeed convinced of their powerlessness to prevent Tokyo from proceeding with the Miyazawa initiative. But it also indicates that they were unhappy to see the initiative materialize, and hoped to use whatever leverage Washington had to extract Japanese concessions in other areas, possibly including the issue of Brazil. The memo stated:

We continue to believe that the most important thing Japan could do to help overcome the crisis would be to restore robust growth and a sound financial system in Japan, but the Miyazawa Plan will happen regardless and now is our opportunity to shape it.

Our ability to block this plan from proceeding is extremely limited at this point and would probably be inadvisable in any case given how this would be viewed by other Asian governments.

We may nonetheless be able to encourage the Japanese to move in a productive direction with their plan and possibly provide assistance to Latin America in exchange for at least our neutrality and perhaps public support for their efforts.

Elsewhere in the memo, under a list of proposed changes "that would allow us to express support for the initiative," Geithner included "Japanese provision of financial assistance to Brazil."

Pages 349–350: An edited transcript of Greenspan's speech, "Risk, Liquidity, and the Economic Outlook," is contained in a January 1999 publication of the National Association for Business Economics that was furnished to me by NABE.

Page 350: Information about J. P. Morgan Securities' recession forecast comes from John M. Berry, "A Time of Uncertainty," *The Washington Post*, October 8, 1998.

Pages 350–351: Information about the meeting among Greenspan, McDonough, and Rivlin, and the attitude of Fed Governor Meyer concerning the intermeeting rate cut, was first reported in Bob Woodward, *Maestro* (Simon & Schuster, New York, 2000).

Page 352: David Hale's quote, "We are potentially turning the corner," comes from Paul Blustein, "Is Worst of Global Crisis Over?" *The Washington Post*, October 23, 1998.

Pages 354–355: Information about the November 13 IMF program for Brazil, and Fischer's comments at the news conference, come from an IMF transcript of the news conference, available on the IMF website.

Page 355: Figures on the amounts of hard currency leaving Brazil come from Brazil's central bank, reported in Reuters, "History of Brazil Dollar Outflows," January 14, 1999.

Page 358: Lopes's quote from *O Estado de São Paulo*, "The bureaucrats in Washington are all excited," is cited in Peter Fritsch, "Brazil Central Bank Drama Strengthens Malan's Hand," *The Wall Street Journal*, February 5, 1999.

Pages 362–363: Information about the panic that swept Brazil in the final days of January comes from Diana Jean Schemo, "Jitters Anew in Brazil as Currency Plunges Again," *The New York Times*, January 29, 1999.

Page 364: Information on Fraga's background and career comes from Geoff Dyer and Richard Waters, "Brazil Picks Hedge-Fund Poacher as Economic Gamekeeper," *Financial Times*, February 3, 1999.

Page 365: Information about Brazil's grim outlook, including the consensus among forecasters that the economy was heading into recession in 1999, comes from "Tempest-Tossed but Floating," *The Economist*, January 23, 1999.

Page 366: Information about the IMF program agreed to on March 5, and Camdessus's statement of March 8, come from the IMF press release "Camdessus Recommends Approval of Brazil's Revised Program," March 8, 1999, available on the IMF website.

Page 368: Information on the Treasury's postcrisis position concerning bailouts of countries with fixed or crawling exchange rates comes from Paul Blustein, "Rubin: Fix Global System in Small Steps," *The Washington Post*, April 22, 1999.

Page 369: Information about the changes in Stan Fischer's personal schedule in April 1999 comes from Michael M. Phillips, "Apocalypse? No: Around the Globe, Signs Point to Final Days of the Financial Crisis," *The Wall Street Journal*, April 14, 1999. Other information about the easing of the crisis during this period comes from Paul Blustein, "World Economy Passes from Crisis to Caution," *The Washington Post*, April 17, 1999.

CHAPTER 13: COOLING OFF

Countless reports have been published in recent years on the international financial architecture, but one that I found particularly helpful was the report of a Council on Foreign Relations task force, "Safeguarding Prosperity in a Global Financial System," 1999. The task force was chaired by Carla A. Hills and Peter G. Peterson, and the project director was Morris Goldstein.

Also helpful is a survey of the main proposals for changing the architecture, in John Williamson, "The Role of the IMF: A Guide to the Reports," May 2000, a policy brief of the Institute for International Economics, Washington, D.C. On private-sector involvement, international bankruptcy regimes, and standstills, other highly informative sources include Barry Eichengreen, "Can the Moral Hazard Caused by IMF Bailouts Be Reduced?" International Center for Monetary and Banking Studies, Geneva, 2000; "Involving the Private Sector in the Resolution of Financial Crises: Restructuring International Sovereign Bonds," by the IMF's Policy Development and Review and Legal Departments, 2001, available on the IMF website; and Jack Boorman, "Sovereign Debt Restructuring: Where Stands the Debate?" speech delivered to a conference cosponsored by the Cato Institute and *The Economist*, New York, October 17, 2002, also available on the IMF website.

Page 372: O'Neill's quotes in May 2001 come from a transcript of a hearing of the House Financial Services Committee on the state of the international monetary and financial system on May 22, 2001.

Pages 373–374: The figures on the IMF loans to Turkey, Uruguay, and Brazil, and the normal limits for lending, come from data on the IMF website showing quotas and outstanding borrowings for individual countries. The normal limit for a country's cumulative borrowing is 300 percent of its quota.

Page 374: Taylor's quote comes from Paul Blustein, "Tough Talk Aside, the Aid Flows," *The Washington Post*, August 6, 2002.

Page 375: A list of actions the IMF and other institutions have taken to strengthen the international financial architecture is available on the IMF website.

Page 379: Friedman's book is *The Lexus and the Olive Tree: Understanding Globalization* (Farrar, Straus and Giroux, New York, 1999).

Page 380: Shultz's advocacy of IMF elimination was made in an op-ed article he coauthored with William E. Simon and Walter B. Wriston, titled "Who Needs the IMF?" *The Wall Street Journal*, February 3, 1998.

Page 382: The Meltzer Commission recommendations are formally presented in a document titled "Report of the International Financial Institution Advisory Commission," available on the website of the congressional Joint Economic Committee, www.house.gov/jec/imf/imfpage.htm.

Pages 382–383: The Meltzer Commission recommendations do allow for loans to be made in exceptional cases where crises pose a danger to the global financial system, but it is questionable whether such exceptions are sufficiently broad as to be realistic. Turkey's crisis, for example, didn't pose much of a financial problem for the rest of the world, but Turkey is a U.S. ally of immense strategic importance in the Middle East, with air bases that are used to patrol "no-fly zones" in Iraq. When Turkey requested additional IMF loans in April 2001, the Bush administration went along, having apparently concluded that it would be unwise to get overly dogmatic about financial principles when no-fly zones are at stake.

Page 383: Rubin's quote "To paraphrase Winston Churchill's famous statement" is cited in Paul Blustein, "Currencies in Crisis," *The Washington Post,* February 7, 1999.

Pages 383–384: The joint report by the finance ministers of wealthy countries—the so-called Group of Ten—is commonly known as the Rey Report, after the group's then-chairman, Jean-Jacques Rey of Belgium. The formal title of the report, which was issued in April 1996, is "The Resolution of Sovereign Liquidity Crises: A Report to the Ministers and Governors."

Page 385: Krueger's speech, titled "A New Approach to Sovereign Debt Restructuring," delivered November 26, 2001, is available on the IMF website, as are modifications she subsequently proposed.

Information about the initial speech and reaction to it is reported in Alan Beattie, "IMF in Support of Bankruptcy Plan," *The Financial Times,* November 28, 2001; and Paul Blustein, "IMF Mulls New Protection for Debt-Stricken Countries," *The Washington Post,* November 28, 2001.

Page 389: Information about the views of bankers, securities firms, and other financial institutions, including the December 2002 joint statement of major associations representing financial firms, is available on the website of the Institute of International Finance, www.iif.com.

Page 389: Information about Taylor's speech and its aftermath is reported in Alan Beattie, "U.S. Call for Limited Reforms Will Deal Blow to IMF Plan," *The Financial Times,* April 3, 2002; Alan Beattie and Raymond Collitt, "U.S. Scorns IMF Plan for Bankrupt Governments," *The Financial Times,* April 6, 2002; Paul Blustein, "IMF Crisis Plan Torpedoed," *The Washington Post,* April 3, 2002; and Paul Blustein, "IMF Reform Plan Makes Comeback," *The Washington Post,* April 9, 2002.

Page 390: The 1996 recommendation to include CACs in sovereign bond contracts was made in the Rey Report.

Page 391: Kenen's proposal is spelled out in his article "The International Financial Architecture: Old Issues and New Initiatives," *International Finance,* Spring 2002.

INDEX

PublicAffairs is a publishing house founded in 1997. It is a tribute to the standards, values, and flair of three persons who have served as mentors to countless reporters, writers, editors, and book people of all kinds, including me.

I. F. STONE, proprietor of *I. F. Stone's Weekly*, combined a commitment to the First Amendment with entrepreneurial zeal and reporting skill and became one of the great independent journalists in American history. At the age of eighty, Izzy published *The Trial of Socrates*, which was a national bestseller. He wrote the book after he taught himself ancient Greek.

BENJAMIN C. BRADLEE was for nearly thirty years the charismatic editorial leader of *The Washington Post*. It was Ben who gave the *Post* the range and courage to pursue such historic issues as Watergate. He supported his reporters with a tenacity that made them fearless and it is no accident that so many became authors of influential, best-selling books.

ROBERT L. BERNSTEIN, the chief executive of Random House for more than a quarter century, guided one of the nation's premier publishing houses. Bob was personally responsible for many books of political dissent and argument that challenged tyranny around the globe. He is also the founder and longtime chair of Human Rights Watch, one of the most respected human rights organizations in the world.

For fifty years, the banner of Public Affairs Press was carried by its owner, Morris B. Schnapper, who published Gandhi, Nasser, Toynbee, Truman, and about 1,500 other authors. In 1983, Schnapper was described by *The Washington Post* as "a redoubtable gadfly." His legacy will endure in the books to come.

Peter Osnos, *Publisher*

Made in the USA
Lexington, KY
20 January 2010